Reconnecting Education and Foundations

The Carnegie Foundation for the Advancement of Teaching

Founded by Andrew Carnegie in 1905 and chartered in 1906 by an Act of Congress, The Carnegie Foundation for the Advancement of Teaching is an independent policy and research center whose charge is "to do and perform all things necessary to encourage, uphold, and dignify the profession of the teacher and the cause of higher education."

The Foundation is a major national and international center for research and policy studies about teaching. Its mission is to address the hardest problems faced in teaching in public schools, colleges, and universities—that is, how to succeed in the classroom, how best to achieve lasting student learning, and how to asses the impact of teaching on students.

JB JOSSEY-BASS

RECONNECTING EDUCATION AND FOUNDATIONS

Turning Good Intentions into Educational Capital

Ray Bacchetti and Thomas Ehrlich, Editors

o

Foreword by Lee S. Shulman

CARNEGIE CENTENNIAL

John Wiley & Sons, Inc.

Published by Jossey-Bass
A Wiley Imprint
989 Market Street, San Francisco, CA 94103-1741   www.josseybass.com

Jossey-Bass books and products are available through most bookstores. To contact Jossey-Bass directly call our Customer Care Department within the U.S. at 800-956-7739, outside the U.S. at 317-572-3986, or fax 317-572-4002.

Jossey-Bass also publishes its books in a variety of electronic formats. Some content that appears in print may not be available in electronic books.

Library of Congress Cataloging-in-Publication Data

Reconnecting education and foundations : turning good intentions into educational capital / Ray Bacchetti and Thomas Ehrlich, editors.
       p. cm.
    Includes bibliographical references and index.
    ISBN-13: 978-0-7879-8818-0 (cloth)
    ISBN-10: 0-7879-8818-9 (cloth)
    1. Education—United States—Endowments.   2. Endowments—United States—History—20th century.   3. Educational fund raising—United States.   I. Bacchetti, Ray. II. Ehrlich, Thomas, 1934-
    LC243.A1R43   2006
    371.2'06—dc22   2006023721

Printed in the United States of America
FIRST EDITION
HB Printing   10 9 8 7 6 5 4 3 2 1

CONTENTS

LIST OF TABLES AND FIGURES

FOREWORD

Lee S. Shulman

As I finished the first draft of this Foreword, the front page of most of the nation's newspapers and the top item on most of the news Web pages told the same story. The second richest man in the world, seventy-five-year-old Warren Buffet, announced that he was going to give away all his money—with most of it going to the richest couple in the world, Bill and Melinda Gates! The purpose of this generosity was to have that couple, through their philanthropic foundation, systematically distribute Buffet's wealth along with their own. When asked whether he found it ironic that he was giving his money to the world's richest people, he replied that he wasn't giving it *to* Bill and Melinda; he was giving it *through* them. As I read the news stories, I imagined the eternal soul of Andrew Carnegie witnessing this transaction and laughing out loud: "They get it! They really get it."

In his *Gospel of Wealth,* written in 1889, Carnegie expressed his theory of philanthropy: "that the best means of benefiting the community is to place within its reach the ladders upon which the aspiring can rise—free libraries, parks, and means of recreation, by which men are helped in body and mind; works of art, certain to give pleasure and improve the public taste; and public institutions of various kinds, which will improve the general condition of the people; in this manner returning their surplus wealth to the mass of their fellows in the forms best calculated to do them lasting good" (2001, p. 25).

Carnegie's *Gospel of Wealth,* was predicated on a deep belief that money and knowledge, when accumulated by individuals, should not be hoarded and should not be viewed as an entitlement to be acquired and held indefinitely. Instead, wealth should trigger the responsibility to give back in ways that invest in the potential of others to become richer themselves. "This, then, is held to be the duty of the man of wealth: first, to set an example of modest unostentatious living, shunning display or extravagance; to provide moderately for the legitimate wants of those dependent upon him; and, after doing so, to consider all surplus revenues which come to him simply as trust funds, which he is . . . strictly bound as a matter of duty to administer in the manner which, in his judgment, is best calculated to produce the most beneficial results for the community" (2001, p. 23).

Carnegie and John D. Rockefeller, like Gates and Buffet today, were not giving their money directly to the needy, the promising, or the worthy. They created a special type of institution called a "foundation" whose sole purpose was to manage the donated wealth for the benefit of others. Moreover, those institutions rarely "gave back" the wealth to individuals (prizes and fellowships notwithstanding). More often, they contributed the resources to other institutions whose responsibility was, in turn, to invest the money in worthwhile activities and entities. Thus, the transactions between the rich and their beneficiaries were twice-buffered, by the philanthropic institutions that represented the donors' general wishes and by the intermediary institutions—schools, colleges, research centers, museums, orchestras—that used the contributed assets to improve the quality of life of those in the society.

In this sense, the impulse to philanthropy, and hence the work of foundations, is essentially moral. The moral imperative may grow out of religious convictions as it did for Rockefeller or out of a more secular source, as was the case for Carnegie. The moral argument for philanthropy as a fundamental human responsibility unites thinkers as remote as Maimonides, the Jewish philosopher and religious leader of the twelfth century, and twentieth century libertarians such as F. A. Harper. It is no accident that there are both liberal and conservative foundations.

This book grew out of discussions about the best ways to celebrate the centennial of The Carnegie Foundation for the Advancement of Teaching. The foundation's efforts for a century have been devoted to improving the quality of education at all levels. Mr. Carnegie dedicated his foundation "to do and perform all things necessary to uphold, encourage, and dignify the profession of the teacher and the cause of higher education." Yet, at the beginning of the foundation's second century, there were indications that several of the major foundations in the United States were pulling back from their traditional commitment to education. Indeed, the centennial occurs at a time when both kinds of institution—foundations on the one hand and schools, colleges, and universities on the other—and have been asked to subject their work to much higher levels of public scrutiny and evaluation. Examples include No Child Left Behind, the Secretary's Commission on Higher Education, and Congressional calls for more accountability from foundations. How might institutions of philanthropy and of education respond to new sets of public expectations even as they review their long-term relations with one another? And how can the relations between foundations and education, that ideal pairing of private wealth with the public interest, be repaired and strengthened?

This volume, edited by Ray Bacchetti and Tom Ehrlich, is filled with valuable responses to these questions. At the heart of their recommendations, Bacchetti and Ehrlich propose that foundations dedicate themselves to initiatives that will promote the development of "educational capital." This strategy would discourage direct assistance to operational support or physical improvements—benefits with no payoff beyond the school-yard fence or the campus boundary—in favor of programs whose outcomes will be new knowledge, tools, or institutional arrangements that strengthen the capacities of educational organizations to do their work more effectively in the future

Among the very important ideas to emerge from the deliberations of those who gathered for the conference that helped to inform this volume was the need for foundations, like the institutions they fund, to become relentless learning institutions. That idea is inherent in the concept of educational capital and is threaded throughout the volume. Foundations must not only learn from the careful evaluation and investigation of their own efforts, but their activities must also be sufficiently transparent and well-documented that the other foundations in the "community of philanthropy" can learn from the lessons they have learned. This kind of "scholarship of philanthropy" should be as important to the philanthropic community as the scholarship of teaching and learning should be to educational organizations.

Indeed, a scholarship of philanthropy for foundations might well be based on the same principles as the scholarship of teaching and learning for schools and colleges. At the Carnegie Foundation, we have built our work around three principles for the scholarship of teaching and learning: 1) becoming more public, visible, and transparent about one's work, 2) subjecting the work to critical review and discussion, and 3) engaging in actions across the community to build upon the lessons learned by one's own and other institutions to guide future practice. These are, I would propose, equally legitimate and desirable features of the work of foundations.

To put the matter gently, educational institutions have a long way to go to realize the objective of truly being places where teaching and learning are community property. And foundations are also some distance from the key goals proposed by Bacchetti and Ehrlich. But in a future world in which foundations and educational institutions both function as learning communities, the sudden shifts of policy and practice that currently so often shape both arenas are less likely to occur. In saying this, I do not call for a simple "rational" model of change. Neither education nor philan-thropy has a single "bottom line" against which goals and missions can be evaluated. There will remain a need for well-grounded human judgments in both worlds. Nevertheless, with the development of educational capital and greater transparency, critique, and exchange of data, the vision of foundations as institutions directly parallel to the ideal of those that edu-cate could become a reality. This image of a community of foundations, characterized by contrasting and even competing missions, values, and pri-orities, yet knitted together in learning communities animated by a "schol-arship of philanthropy," emerges directly from the essays in this fine volume.

One of a series of proposals by Bacchetti and Ehrlich, related to their core notion of "educational capital," is that foundations become much more transparent in their decision making, grant making, and follow-up. Educational institutions at every level should also become more open in their work. Citing Andrew Carnegie as a powerful exemplar of that prin-ciple, the South African scholar of Scottish lineage, Renfrew Christie, asserted to the American Historical Association (2002):

> For I speak today, as a minor Scot born in Johannesburg, on behalf of the Great Scot, Andrew Carnegie. If the greatest American capitalist ever, Andrew Carnegie, were in this room today, he would be shiver-ing. Nay, not from the cold would he shiver. He would shiver with righteous Protestant rage! He would be apoplectic with fury, that ye who have benefited by his great public libraries, ye who have gained by his giving his entire fortune to free scholarship, would hide your writing from the greatest free public library of all time, the Internet! Shame be upon ye! (http://www.uwc.ac.za/research/talks/HnetComment.htm)

Christie argues, and I agree, that wealth in the form of knowledge and understanding is as much in need of free and generous distribution as the more traditional sources of material and financial resources. The current movement toward "open source" access to knowledge and tools via the Internet is a powerful expression of those ideals.

The scholar and the philanthropist occupy parallel roles in any society. A scholar acquires knowledge because of the efforts, indeed the labor, of others. Scholars stand on the shoulders of the scholars that preceded them. They are subsidized by the institutions (and their donors, including tuition-paying students) who support them. Their work is enabled by the contemporary community of scholars in the discipline or profession in which they are interactively embedded. If scholars could not cite, draw from, and build upon the work of fellow investigators, their own work would be impossible. The knowledge they accrue is therefore much like the wealth acquired by the rich. Having been blessed by the receipt and invention of knowledge, they must now play their stewardly role and pass it on to others for the benefit of all. A scholar does not own her knowledge; she holds it, as Carnegie said of wealth, in trust for the benefit of humanity. Yet the scholar also has one huge advantage over the owner of material capital. The scholar can give her knowledge away and still remain as rich as she was before her generosity began. Indeed, somewhat paradoxically, the scholar's largesse often leads to the growth of her intellectual riches rather than their reduction.

We could not have asked for two more experienced and gifted thinkers about foundations and education than Ray Bacchetti and Tom Ehrlich. This volume thoughtfully explores the growing divide between the interests and perspectives of foundations and of educational institutions, which both understand at a deep level, having played prominent roles in both kinds of institutions. It is difficult to imagine a distribution of experience and insight better suited than theirs to the challenges of this book.

The moral imperatives that animated Andrew Carnegie remain as legitimate and necessary today as they were one hundred years ago. The editors and authors who contributed to this volume disagree about many things, but not about the central values of both education and philanthropy, and the belief that, properly undertaken, the two communities share a common commitment.

I know I am joined by the readers of this volume in thanking Ray Bacchetti, Tom Ehrlich, and their fellow writers for their contributions to this volume. We promise to learn from it, to examine its contents critically, and most important, to pass it on.

REFERENCES

Carnegie, A. *The Gospel of Wealth*. New York: The Carnegie Corporation of New York, 2001.

Christie, R. Invited comment on the paper "Alternatives to Pay for View: The Case for Open Access to Historical Research and Scholarship" at the Annual Meeting of the American Historical Association (2002), http://www.uwc.ac.za/research/talks/HnetComment.htm, last accessed July 7, 2006.

To our wives—

Carol Bacchetti
Ellen Ehrlich

—whose support and love
make so many things possible.

ACKNOWLEDGMENTS

WE OWE THANKS to many people who made this work possible. We express particular gratitude to Lee Shulman and Pat Hutchings, leaders of The Carnegie Foundation for the Advancement of Teaching, to our other colleagues at the Carnegie Foundation, and to its board members for their support and wise counsel. Throughout the project that has led to this book, we have been ably aided by our colleagues Gay Clyburn, Kristen Garabedian, Megan Gutelius, and Ruby Kerawalla.

Our colleagues Steve Guisti, Denise Livengood, and Charlene Moran were extremely helpful with our organization of the Carnegie Foundation Centennial Conference on Foundations and Education. Lenny Lind and his company, CoVision, enabled conference participants to interact with each other throughout the conference. And Ellen Wert gave splendid editorial help for this volume.

We thank also our board of advisers, who helped us at numerous points along the way from idea to implementation:

Roger Benjamin, president, Council for Aid to Education

Alison R. Bernstein, vice president, Knowledge, Creativity and Freedom, Ford Foundation

Alden Dunham, director of education programs, emeritus, Carnegie Corporation of New York

Russell Edgerton, director, Pew Forum on Undergraduate Learning

Ann Lieberman, senior scholar, The Carnegie Foundation for the Advancement of Teaching

Thomas Payzant, superintendent, Boston Public Schools

Diane Ravitch, senior fellow, Brookings Institution, and research professor at New York University

Carol Schneider, president, Association of American Colleges and Universities

Robert B. Schwartz, director, Administration, Planning, and Social Policy Program, Harvard Graduate School of Education

Kim Smith, cofounder and former CEO, New Schools
Venture Fund

Donald M. Stewart, president, emeritus, Chicago
Community Trust

Deborah Stipek, dean, Graduate School of Education, Stanford
University

In addition, we give special thanks to the foundations that supported our work: the Carnegie Corporation of New York, the Bill & Melinda Gates Foundation, Lumina Foundation for Education, the Andrew W. Mellon Foundation, the Spencer Foundation, and the TIAA-CREF Institute.

The opinions expressed in this book are those of the authors and do not necessarily represent the view of these institutions or their employers.

ABOUT THE AUTHORS

Ray Bacchetti is a scholar in residence at The Carnegie Foundation for the Advancement of Teaching. He has been education program officer of The William and Flora Hewlett Foundation, vice president for planning and management at Stanford University, and an elementary school teacher. He has served as a Board of Education member, a community college district trustee, and a board member for a number of education, arts, and civic groups; he has given workshops on higher education in the United States and abroad.

Edgar F. Beckham, who died in May of 2006, spent much of his professional life working to promote diversity in American higher education. At his death, he was a senior fellow at the Association of American Colleges and Universities and dean of the college, emeritus, of Wesleyan University. In 1990 he joined the Ford Foundation, where he coordinated the foundation's Campus Diversity Initiative until 1998. A Connecticut native, Beckham was chairman of the Connecticut State Board of Education from 1992 to 1995 and had chaired the boards of the Connecticut Humanities Council, the Connecticut Housing Investment Fund, Middlesex Hospital, the Rockfall Foundation, and the Donna Wood Foundation.

Barbara Cervone is cofounder and president of What Kids Can Do, Inc., and Next Generation Press. She previously served as the national coordinator for the Annenberg Challenge at Brown University and, before that, as the associate director of the Rhode Island Community Foundation. She has been a consultant in program evaluation and an investigator for several national education research projects. She has written extensively about school reform. Early in her career, she worked in the alternative school movement, first as a researcher and later as the coordinator of a network of thirty alternative high schools in ten states.

Charles T. Clotfelter is Z. Smith Reynolds Professor of Public Policy Studies and professor of economics and law at Duke University. He is also director of the Center for the Study of Philanthropy and Voluntarism at Duke and is a research associate with the National Bureau of Economic Research. During the 2005–06 academic year he was a visiting scholar at the Russell Sage Foundation. His research has covered the economics of education, public finance, gambling and state lotteries, tax policy, and charitable behavior, as well as policies related to the nonprofit sector. His most recent book is *After Brown: The Rise and Retreat of School Desegregation* (Princeton University Press, 2004).

Jennifer de Forest is an assistant professor at the University of Virginia, where she teaches educational history. Her research includes the history of foundations' role in school reform efforts and the promotion of conservative college student movements. She was previously cochair of the editorial board of the *Harvard Educational Review* and has published articles in *Women's History Review, Teachers College Record,* and *Change* magazine.

Thomas Ehrlich is a senior scholar at The Carnegie Foundation for the Advancement of Teaching. He previously was president of Indiana University, provost of the University of Pennsylvania, and dean of the Stanford Law School; he has held several positions in the federal government. Before coming to the Carnegie Foundation he was Distinguished University Scholar at California State University and taught regularly at San Francisco State University. He is the author, coauthor, or editor of ten other books.

Thomas Hatch is an associate professor of education at Teachers College, Columbia University, where he is also a codirector of the National Center for Restructuring Education, Schools, and Teaching (NCREST). His research focuses on issues of large-scale school reform and teacher learning. He is also involved in a variety of efforts to use multimedia and the Internet to document teaching and share teachers' expertise. He previously served as a senior scholar at The Carnegie Foundation for the Advancement of Teaching, where he codirected the K–12 program of the Carnegie Academy for the Scholarship of Teaching and Learning (CASTL) and the Knowledge Media Laboratory.

Nancy Hoffman is vice president of Youth Transitions and director of the Early College Initiative at Jobs for the Future, in Boston. She has been a professor and academic administrator at public metropolitan universities, as well as at Brown, Harvard, and MIT. Hoffman holds a Ph.D. in comparative literature from the UC-Berkeley. Publications include *Women's True Profession: Voices from the History of Teaching* (McGraw-Hill, 1981), and *Double the Numbers: Increasing Postsecondary Credentials for Underrepresented Youth,* coedited with Richard Kazis and Joel Vargas (Harvard Education Press, 2004).

Pat Hutchings is vice president of The Carnegie Foundation for the Advancement of Teaching. She has written and spoken widely about building a culture in which the scholarly work of teaching and learning is documented, evaluated, and rewarded. Before coming to the foundation in 1998, she was a senior staff member at the American Association for Higher Education (AAHE) and a faculty member in English on several campuses.

Ellen Condliffe Lagemann is the Charles Warren Professor of the History of American Education at Harvard University. The author or editor of nine books and many articles, she has also served as dean of the Harvard Graduate School of Education and as president of the Spencer Foundation. Lagemann has been a member of many boards and national committees and is a past president of the National Academy of Education and the History of Education Society.

Leslie Lenkowsky is professor of public affairs and philanthropic studies at Indiana University and director of graduate programs for the Center on Philanthropy at the university. He rejoined the university faculty after serving as chief executive officer of the Corporation for National and Community Service. From 1976 through 1983, he was director of research at the Smith Richardson Foundation.

Ann Lieberman is a senior scholar at The Carnegie Foundation for the Advancement of Teaching. She is an emeritus professor from Teachers College, Columbia University. She has consulted all over the world in areas of teacher development and leadership, networks, and school-university partnerships and educational change. She is author, coauthor, or editor of fifteen books.

Theodore Lobman is a consultant to foundations and nonprofits. He helped develop the priorities and operation for the Stuart Foundation when it was created and served as president for thirteen years. As its first program officer, he helped develop the Hewlett Foundation's education and public policy programs. His career has been devoted to improvements in education, youth, and social services, including helping launch several major initiatives and organizations and serving on a variety of nonprofit boards.

Robert Orrill is the executive director of the National Council on Education and the Disciplines and senior adviser at the Woodrow Wilson National Fellowship Foundation. Among other academic and teaching positions, he was executive director, Office of Academic Affairs, at the College Board. He has organized and edited numerous publications on American education, including *The Future of Education: Perspectives on National Standards in America* (College Entrance Examination Board, 1994), *The Condition of American Liberal Education: Pragmatism and a Changing Tradition* (College Entrance Examination Board, 1995), and *Education and Democracy: Re-imagining Liberal Learning in America* (College Entrance Examination Board, 1997).

James Piereson is currently president of the William E. Simon Foundation and a senior fellow at The Manhattan Institute. For twenty years, from 1985 to 2005, he was executive director of The John M. Olin Foundation.

Robert Schwartz is professor of practice at the Harvard Graduate School of Education, where he cochairs the Education Policy and Management Program. Previously, he has been a high school teacher and principal, education adviser to the mayor of Boston and the governor of Massachusetts, education program director at The Pew Charitable Trusts, and president of Achieve. He currently serves as a trustee of The Noyce Foundation and senior adviser to the Aspen Institute Education Program.

Robert Weisbuch assumed the presidency of Drew University in 2005. Prior to that, he was president of the Woodrow Wilson National Fellowship Foundation for eight years. He joined the foundation after twenty-five years at the University of Michigan, where he was a professor of English, department chair, and academic officer in research, faculty programs, and graduate studies. At Woodrow Wilson, he was engaged in initiatives from high school to the Ph.D. He is the author of books on Emily Dickinson and the stormy relations between British and American authors in the nineteenth century.

RECONNECTING EDUCATION AND FOUNDATIONS

PART ONE

INTRODUCTION — RECOMMENDATIONS — HISTORY

FOUNDATIONS AND EDUCATION: INTRODUCTION

Ray Bacchetti and Thomas Ehrlich

IN THE LATE 1950S, C. P. Snow wrote a little book based on a lecture he had given at Harvard. In *The Two Cultures and the Scientific Revolution*, Snow argues that the culture of scientists and the culture of humanists were orbiting away from each other to the detriment of each culture, particularly to the detriment of society. Perhaps because Snow was much involved in British science during World War II and also wrote a series of best-selling novels, his idea caught the public imagination. "Two cultures" became popular buzz words and were also used as shorthand for perceived disconnects among other segments of society.

Two Cultures Drifting Apart?

When we began to reflect on how The Carnegie Foundation for the Advancement of Teaching might celebrate its centennial in ways that would further both education and philanthropy—twin goals of Andrew Carnegie—we wondered whether the two cultures of education and foundations were, as they seemed in our experience to be, spinning away from each other, much as Snow had suggested in another time and context.

The culture of foundations in America began early in the twentieth century with the generosity of Andrew Carnegie and a small band of other philanthropists. They chose foundations as a means to organize their philanthropy. These philanthropists saw education—in both K–12 schools and in colleges and universities—as worthy of their support, in large measure

3

because education gave individuals opportunities to be successful if they were willing to work hard. They believed in the "teach-a-man-to-fish" strategy of charitable giving, and educational institutions were the prime vehicles.

In the early years of the twenty-first century, however, a number of foundations appeared to grow weary of support for education and more hesitant about the assumption that educational institutions can deliver on their promise of leveraging philanthropic funding into individual and societal progress. At the same time, we sensed that the two cultures had, indeed, grown apart. We have both spent some time working in each culture, and we recognize that indulging in nostalgia for an earlier era is almost always fruitless. But we were concerned that relations between foundations and educational institutions often appeared frayed—or worse. This volume grew out of these concerns.

We recognize, of course, that there is no single culture of education or of foundations, any more than there was a single culture of science or of the humanities in the time of C. P. Snow. But Snow was focusing on how leaders in those two realms were prepared and on the attitudes of mind that shaped their judgments. In that same sense, we found ourselves considering the culture of foundations and the culture of education, and perceiving that these cultures were not mutually interactive and supportive to the extent that they could be and should be.

Our concerns were brought to center stage by the shift away from support for education by a number of major foundations such as The Pew Charitable Trusts and The Atlantic Philanthropies. We were not at all sure about the reasons for this shift, but it served to focus our attention on foundations and educational institutions and how they view each other.

The partnerships between foundations and those institutions have been a distinctive strength of American society and culture, particularly during the last half-century. As we reviewed the history of education in the last century, we were struck by how important major foundations have been, particularly since the end of World War II. In recent decades, the major reform movements that have shaped K–12 have been fueled by foundations, as discussed by Nancy Hoffman and Robert Schwartz in Chapter Five of this volume. These include the emphasis on standards and testing, the move for school choice, and what Hoffman and Schwartz term "the network-based reform" movement, such as the Coalition of Essential Schools (CES). Similarly, in higher education, as Charles Clotfelter summarizes at the outset of Chapter Nine, foundations have provided the margin of difference that enabled new and innovative programs and projects in a wide array of arenas. The reform of medical education and the promotion of new interdisciplinary fields such as urban studies and women's studies are examples of significant shifts in higher education that were substantially shaped and fostered by large foundations.

As we stress elsewhere in this volume, we have been regularly struck, as we examined the evidence, by how much constructive strengthening of education at every level has been promoted by foundations, even though the share of their support, compared to the totals spent on education in any given year, is modest. Foundations have been powerful engines in promoting and supporting excellence in education from kindergarten through graduate education and in research across many fields.

Over the course of our own careers, we have developed a strong commitment to enhancing the partnerships between foundations and education. Each of us has served in various roles in universities, in foundations, and in educational organizations that depend on foundations for financial support. In those roles, we have worked to promote collaborative relations between foundations and institutions of education. We were especially troubled, therefore, by our perception that the two cultures have drifted apart.

At the same time, the president of The Carnegie Foundation for the Advancement of Teaching, Lee Shulman, and the board of the foundation were beginning to think about how best to recognize the centennial of the foundation in ways that would be consistent with both the vision of Andrew Carnegie and the foundation's current work. We decided to design a project that would probe the relations between the larger and better-known foundations and two main collections of beneficiaries—K–12 education and higher education—with a volume on the key issues involved in those relations as its centerpiece.

Our aim, we concluded, would be not merely celebratory, though one hundred years of energetic work on education by the Carnegie Foundation is certainly worthy of celebration. Rather, we wanted to provide critical and constructive commentary on two questions: (1) How can relations between and among institutions of education and foundations be more powerful, focused, and consequential in the years ahead? and (2) What lessons can be learned from the past and applied to the future?

We wanted a set of recommendations to result, along with persuasive evidence on which those recommendations could be based, that would speak to qualities to be preserved, as well as to be modified, replaced, or introduced. Most important, we wanted to generate ideas, as well as provide information, thus provoking and promoting constructive dialogue in which the Carnegie Foundation, as well as others, would play continuing roles.

Initially, we wondered if the palette for our inquiry should be the full spectrum of philanthropy's relations with education, given that Andrew Carnegie's interests covered that spectrum. We soon decided, however, that we needed to focus on issues involving major foundations because of their influence. (We define *major* to include the largest one hundred foundations that provide grants to education.) Even those foundations have widely varying relations with educational institutions.

A number of friendly critics also urged that we narrow our attention to either higher education or K–12 education. They pointed out that the differences between the two realms are enormous. In addition, most of the support from large foundations for K–12 education has been directed around major policy issues such as school reform, whereas support for higher education has been predominantly provided to individual campuses. In the end, we decided that we should include both realms, for three reasons. The first is our belief that there should be lessons to be learned in one realm that can be applied usefully in the other, in spite of their disparities. Second, we have increasingly come to the judgment that a primary focus of attention from foundations and leaders in education should be on bridges between K–12 and higher education. Finally, we want to recognize that Andrew Carnegie was involved in both K–12 and higher education and that the Carnegie Foundation today sponsors programs designed to improve teaching and learning in both.

In our preliminary conception, therefore, the volume was influenced by our sense of two cultures drifting apart; their leaders were often irritated at each other, not listening to each other, and not collaborating with each other. The next section of this chapter describes the basis for that framing. We then solicited essays for this volume and talked and corresponded extensively with their authors and with others. Based on the insights we gained from these essays, our own experiences, and counsel from a wide range of knowledgeable advisers, we drafted a preliminary set of recommendations on how relations between foundations and institutions of education might be strengthened.

When the volume and our preliminary recommendations were in draft form, we circulated them to a group of fifty wise and thoughtful leaders in education and foundations whom we had invited to the Carnegie Foundation for a Carnegie Foundation Centennial Conference. Over the course of the conference, we hoped that our recommendations could be reshaped and strengthened and that the essays in the volume could be related to those recommendations in ways that would both give the book coherence and give its readers the clearest possible understanding of our considered judgments.

Fortunately from our perspective, just that process occurred. Chapter Two introduces the concept of *educational capital* and uses the challenge of bridging K–12 and higher education as an illustration. That chapter also outlines a series of related recommendations that we think will strengthen relations between foundations and educational institutions, as well as help build educational capital. Chapter Four develops the idea of educational capital in some detail, as applied to foundation support for K–12 education. We return to the approach in Chapter Ten in reference to higher education.

We report in the second section of this chapter—What We Heard from Foundation and Education Leaders—what we heard initially from leaders in foundations and education about their shared sense of disaffection and why we became increasingly concerned about the issues this volume is designed to address.

The third section—Foundation Support for Education: A Quantitative Overview—gives an overview of foundation support for education. Over and over in our conversations with leaders in both fields, we were surprised by the assumptions that were made concerning the amounts of that support—assumptions that proved incorrect when we examined the facts. The section is designed to summarize the basic facts. (Appendix B to this volume provides a much more detailed look at foundation support for education over the last fifteen years so that readers can gain a more in-depth sense of what, in financial terms, is at stake.)

Finally, the last section—What to Expect from This Volume—gives a brief capsule of what lies ahead for the reader. To strengthen the cohesion of the volume, we also include a short introduction before each chapter that relates it to our recommendations.

The participants in the Centennial Conference helped us understand that sea changes had occurred in the political, social, and economic environments that undergird foundations on the one hand and institutions of education on the other. Expectations for both sectors have changed radically just since the end of World War II; in the full century since Andrew Carnegie established The Carnegie Foundation for the Advancement of Teaching, the changes in expectations have been breathtaking. It is no wonder, then, the participants stressed, that relations between foundations and education have frayed. Each sector and its leaders want to behave as though the other has been stable, while the ground has been shifting under them.

We will not try to capture those sea changes in any detail. But it is worth remembering that when Andrew Carnegie set up the Carnegie Foundation, less than half of adult Americans had eight years or more of schooling.

That threshold was passed in 1910. In 1968, adult U.S. citizens averaged, for the first time, more than twelve years of schooling. Since then, the average has risen steadily. Increasing levels of education are required in a new economy dominated by information, technology, and professional services rather than manufacturing and agriculture. No less significant is the fact that the civic, social, and political environments in which the new economy operates are escalating in complexity. Educational institutions at every level have struggled—and sometimes failed—to keep pace with the multiple expectations for graduates. They must be agile and effective in the new economy, capable and principled in meeting their civic and social responsibility, literate in a wide range of realms, and able on a continuing basis to absorb new ideas and learn new skills. It should be no surprise that foundations interested in education have been scrambling—sometimes floundering—in an effort to support innovation in such rapidly changing educational environments.[1]

We hope it is enough to emphasize that what K–12 schools and institutions of higher education are called on to do these days is more complex and difficult than was true in earlier eras—more difficult in ways that extend beyond differences in degree.

The same is true, though in quite different ways, for foundations, for those who provide support for foundations, and for those who serve on their boards. The scope of their interests and approaches has changed radically. Ellen Lagemann and Jennifer de Forest remind us in Chapter Three that there are some constants and that we had best try to learn from the past. But much has shifted in the underlying economic, social, and political settings in which foundations operate. The Centennial Conference participants emphasized to us that these shifts present opportunities for rethinking how best to work together—a key goal of this effort.

What We Heard from Foundation and Education Leaders

A key initial step in the project that led to this book was to listen more widely and systematically to what some influential leaders in K–12, higher education, and major foundations were saying, particularly about relations with each other. We wanted to test our sense of growing disconnects between foundations and education. To that end, we interviewed about three dozen individuals who had worked with or for foundations and educational institutions, or both. Some were involved primarily in K–12 education or in higher education, some in foundation administration, and some in both spheres. We also convened a group of our Carnegie Foundation colleagues to review what we had heard, and we listened as well to the thoughts of the foundation's board of trustees. These steps have helped to guide us in organizing this book and the continuing conversations that we hope it will promote.

We did not hear any single answer to why foundation interest in education has diminished. Indeed, one of those we interviewed challenged that conclusion.[2] When we tried to examine the existing data to determine whether that challenge or our initial impression was correct, we found it difficult to look with confidence to any single source of data. Foundation grants to promote health care through university hospitals and medical schools, for example, were sometimes classified under "health care" and sometimes under "higher education." These experiences reinforced the views of several commentators who told us that it would be useful to have a common database to measure support for education (both K–12 and higher education) from large foundations over the past decade because this would provide a baseline for future analysis. Appendix B to this volume is designed to that end, and the next section of this chapter summarizes the relevant data.

When we questioned our initial advisers, many gave credit to foundations as a "first cause" in some important educational advances and as significant boosters for many more. Examples frequently cited in higher education include

○ The Ford Foundation's instrumental role in establishing the social sciences as a quantitative set of disciplines and in starting many area studies programs

○ The James Irvine Foundation's help of private colleges and universities in developing their fundraising capacities

○ The Alfred P. Sloan Foundation in boosting microbiology and cognitive sciences

Among the illustrations cited in K–12 education were the Carnegie Corporation's and Edna McConnell Clark Foundation's work in middle schools and the work on equity in school finance of The Pew Charitable Trusts and The Ford Foundation.

At the same time, we were struck by the level of discontent from leaders in foundations about educational institutions, both K–12 and higher education. We were no less struck by the unhappiness expressed about foundations by those in the institutions with whom we talked. Leaders in each realm were more than grumpy about the ways those in the other realm operated and about their perceptions that the needs and interests of their own sphere were not adequately considered by those in the other sphere. These criticisms—sometimes harsh, sometimes muted—from both sides seemed widely shared.

In talking about higher education, for example, a number of foundation leaders said they found colleges and universities to be self-contained institutions with little concern about the social issues around them. Higher education, they thought, was chasing funds and seeing foundations as just another source of support and has abdicated the role it played in an earlier time—as a shaper of society.

Several also said they find that higher education looks and acts unaccountable. Foundations cannot tell who is in charge in higher education, and institutions do not seem able to tell them. As one commentator put it, "It's hard to get traction in higher education." Those in colleges and universities, several foundation officials told us, see their campuses as ends in themselves, not means to social ends. It would come as news to most in higher education, one adviser said, that foundations have agendas and look for colleges and universities to help carry out those agendas. To the contrary, he suggested that most campuses want to set their own agendas and then expect foundations to support them.

Some foundation leaders complained that helping individual campuses rarely led to change across broad clusters of campuses. They see the elite schools as feeling little need to change and the other campuses modeling themselves as pale shadows of those schools. One leader commented that as he looked at grants to higher education from large foundations, only a few stood out as promoting real change beyond the boundaries of a single campus. There are some 3,550 colleges and universities in the country,[3] and the leverage from a grant to one of them simply was too small.

Several advisers asked a question we have certainly heard before: Why is there so little real shift in the primary mode of educating undergraduates—lecturing—in spite of advances in learning about learning? Several also mentioned how little schools of education are honored on many campuses; some added that they thought this was with good reason.

The comments about higher education from foundation leaders were by no means uniform. Most of them, at least at some level, celebrated the great diversity of colleges and universities and saw the freedom of action they have as sources of great energy and creativity. The system may waste money, but they realize this is a price of that diversity. They know that even with the waste, the U.S. system of higher education is a source of envy throughout the world, though worldwide competition for the best faculty and students has intensified. But they also saw troubling trends in higher education, such as a growing commercialization, and asked whether they should join the struggle against these trends or simply fold their financial tents and turn to other, more pressing, matters until those in higher education got their institutional acts together.

The picture of K–12 education that we heard from foundation leaders was not any more encouraging. As in higher education, it was not clear exactly why a number of large foundations such as the Edna McConnell Clark Foundation and The Annenberg Foundation had turned away from policy issues involving K–12 schools. We heard a repeated sense that foundations have invested a lot in K–12 schools without much return, and they are souring on continuing that investment. The policy issues such as school reform and testing, several said, have become both more difficult and messier. Even when there were successes, the challenges of "scaling up"—moving from success in a single school or district to impact on many—seemed intractable.

Some foundations have turned away, we were told, because they became discouraged with the system of K–12 education as a whole and the difficulties of systemic change. The issues are so large that no one foundation, even the Bill & Melinda Gates Foundation, can do much alone. Foundations need to partner with other foundations to have real impact, but they rarely do that well, as a number of foundation leaders admitted. Several said that K–12 schools have become so insular that they are not interested in foundation support for systemic change. A number of commentators suggested that some large foundations no longer feel they have to pay much attention to K–12 schools because school change is on everyone's agenda.

As was true about higher education, those in foundations with whom we talked underscored the importance of K–12 schools, along with their discouragement about the current state of public funding. They recognized that investments in education can sometimes lead to transformative results and that experimentation is needed for a system as diverse as America's. But a number were pessimistic about the extent to which foundations could make a significant difference in the quality of K–12 education.

When we turned to advisers in both higher education and K–12 education, we heard some unhappy commentaries about foundations and their leaders. Foundations "make lousy lovers," one said, because they abandon things. He was pointing to a common view among foundations that their role is to provide seed capital, and once an effort is under way, sustainability should be someone else's responsibility. Foundations often chase fads, some commentators complained. Campuses and schools, however, generally want a revenue stream that will continue to support programs and projects into the future.

Most foundations, several said, talk a lot about collaborations but rarely do much of it, or even have sustained conversations with each other.

Campuses and schools have to bring the foundations together around educational programs and projects, if the foundations are going to get together at all.

A frequent concern voiced about foundations was that they are overly focused on measurable outcomes in particular and on business models in general. They also say they want to support new ideas and innovations. But they often do not have the expertise to identify those ideas; when they do, they are not prepared to undertake the risk that they might fail. Further, they think things can happen in education faster than is usually possible. They are so action-oriented that they frequently lurch after solutions without comprehending the problem, let alone its causes.

Another complaint raised by educational leaders is that many in foundations have little or no experience with organizational strategy in educational institutions and have few training programs available to them. The foundations' front-line people—the program officers—are rarely chosen because they are strategically adept in the use of grantmaking to influence new ways of thinking and acting in education. In addition, foundations seldom have much internal expertise in education, so they are heavily dependent on proposals to learn what is going on in K–12 schools or higher education. They often do not understand the culture and organizational characteristics of the educational institutions they seek to influence. One consequence is that they reinvent the wheel nearly every time. If education travels on reinvented wheels, we should not be surprised if it rarely goes in new directions.

The lack of accountability of foundations was frequently mentioned by educational leaders as a serious weakness. Their decision-making processes are often opaque. Foundation program officers have no obligations except to their boards and so have no checks and balances on their decisions to make or reject grants or to continue in or shift away from an area of interest. The flexibility that results can be a strength, of course, but it can also present difficulties for educational institutions that may wait for months for a decision, and when it comes they may have little sense of how the decision was made. If it is negative, the institutions do not know why. If it is positive, they do not know what the foundation's long-term commitment will be to the initiative.

Leaders on both sides observed that it is difficult to be honest in foundation-education relations. There exists an unspoken collusion—"a mating dance"—when colleges and universities seek foundation support and when foundations turn to campuses to carry out the ambitious agendas they develop. Both sides want to look good. Institutions of higher education and their leaders promise far more than they can deliver. Foundations recognize the hyperbole, but they go along, even though they know that promises are being made that cannot be fulfilled. As one former foundation president sardonically put it, "All our geese are swans." Both sides, at some level, understand this charade, but they play along because it seems in their parochial interests, though not necessarily the public interest, to do so. In the business of doing good, the chief occupational hazard involves foundations overexpecting, grantseekers overpromising, and, in the end, both sides overclaiming.

Many of the concerns, complaints, and observations registered by colleagues about foundations suggest that the source lay deeper than issues of who is in charge and what a foundation's individual style might be. Working relationships that should work better were often artificial and uneven. The awkwardness wasn't about intention or purpose or aspiration. At least one promising place to look seemed to us to be in design, in form. When the architect Louis Sullivan declared at the end of the nineteenth century that form follows function, he influenced thinking beyond his field. And, indeed, the early form of foundations did follow their function. But what has proved more difficult to change is an established organizational form lagging behind a changing function.

When foundations began, their form and function were established by the creators of the early fortunes of the industrial revolution in the United States. Briefly put, the function was to disburse funds for public benefit to targeted objectives and entities. The customary form of the philanthropic foundations set up to accomplish this function was that of hierarchical organizations that implemented donor-set priorities, then later, board-set priorities. The organizations thus established tended to function in secret and in a highly individual and independent manner. That form essentially continues today. Its persistence makes it difficult for foundations to respond effectively to other functions required to achieve philanthropic purposes in the immensely more complicated world one hundred years after the original form was set.

Of course, the present form is suitable for accomplishing many things. It enables the disbursement of funds substantially unrestrained by regulations or, indeed, by any constraint, except minimal legal ones, not of the foundation's own choosing. It leaves foundations largely unaccountable to anyone beyond their own boards. It is not, however, a form that comfortably facilitates other approaches that might be more suitable to solving complex problems. Many of the issues confronting education require, as we have noted, more expertise than is likely to be found within a single foundation, a level of investment that exceeds what one foundation may be able or willing to commit, and follow-through that would strain the program-management capacity of a solitary grantmaker.

If, for example, a foundation wanted to become adept at interfoundation collaboration, it would need to resolve a variety of tensions inherent in its form. It would need to take steps that would be highly unusual in the field as it exists today. Examples would be to

- o Build collaborations with prospective partners
- o Establish the protocols for membership, for mutual learning, and for decision making within the collaborative, along with means for renegotiation as a project proceeds
- o Set collaborative goals, objectives, and work plans
- o Specify and commit to the human and financial resources that will be needed overall to carry through
- o Estimate a time frame adequate to reach a satisfactory level of accomplishment
- o Develop a governance and project-management agreement suitable to the partners and to that time frame
- o Capture what is learned in a form useable by others[4]

These are not undertakings that can be successfully taken on by most foundations. Staff expertise and time are seldom in adequate supply, and these would be minimal conditions of success. However, the sufficient conditions—the mind-set of most foundations, either as initiating or responding partner—would likely be resisted. As one of our conference participants put it, foundations are better at one-night stands than longer-term relationships. Their form predisposes such behavior.

These and other ideas flowed from the multiple aspects of this project. Following through on the several themes from the conference and acting on the recommendations in Chapter Two presents a set of intellectual and organizational challenges that, we believe, deserve a kind of critical dialogue to achieve a better balance between the improvement of education and the independence of foundations. The superior status of the latter comes at the expense of the former. More to the point, independence limits accountability, leaving education with little leverage to complain or influence the organizational habits and operating styles that foundations put forward. The important but limited sums available for educational change, then, are discounted to the extent that well-designed, multifoundation responses to complex issues don't happen.

At the same time, along with the frustration that we heard, we found a real longing for efforts that would bridge the gaps between foundations and institutions of education without losing the qualities that are prized in either sector. We found eagerness to consider avenues that would build on successes and learn from them, with both recognizing the differing resources and conditions in which different educational institutions operate and without requiring lock-step approaches.

We developed our proposal that foundations, with their partners in education, focus on producing what we term "educational capital," in part as a response to these reactions from leaders in both realms. It is crafted for those who want foundation support to be structured in ways that promote learning from the results of the support: learning that is widely disseminated, discussed, and debated publicly so that the learning can be built upon by others. Too often, as we discuss in Chapter Two, the results of foundation grants in education are secrets from those in the foundations involved—sometimes even from senior administrators in the schools and colleges receiving the grants. We advocate an approach of building educational capital because it features the accumulation of both learning and interdependence, while providing flexibility to meet unique circumstances.

The design of educational capital that we offer recognizes that there is a serious gap between foundations and institutions of education and that their cultures are drifting apart. But we also realize that this divergence is a symptom of fundamental changes in the functions that educational institutions, on the one hand, and foundations, on the other, are expected to realize in our society. Both realms must operate in environments that are radically different from those in earlier times. Building educational capital is an approach that not only can help bridge the two cultures but can also help in the decades ahead to strengthen both education and the foundations that support education.

Before we turn to that approach, here is a quantitative look at the landscape for the last decade and a half.

Foundation Support for Education: A Quantitative Overview

In sketching some statistical background as context for what is to follow, we relied on data collected annually since 1990 by the Foundation Center. (In Appendix B are most of the data we used for this summary and a good deal more.) The center has developed definitions and data-collection techniques that go a long way toward organizing inherently messy information from foundations that have no particular stake in keeping their books in a common format to facilitate comparative analyses. For data about educational expenditures, we rely on the National Center for Education Statistics (NCES). Within individual chapters, data sources different from these are identified.

K–12 Education

There are roughly 68,000 grantmaking foundations in the United States, and the Foundation Center estimates that around 80 percent of them contribute to K–12 education. The one hundred largest K–12 grantmaking foundations accounted for approximately 31 percent of the total foundation giving to K–12 in 2004—a number that has declined from 36 percent in 1990 and 33 percent in 1997.

At the broadest level, when total expenditures are related to total foundation grants, the numbers look like those in Table 1.1.

Although K–12 expenditures stood in 2004 at 207 percent of their 1990 total, foundation support for K–12 was at 671 percent of 1990 numbers—a degree of growth roughly 3.2 times as great.

Though foundation support has grown over the fifteen years surveyed here, it nevertheless stands today at barely more than 0.50 percent of the total spending level of K–12 nationally. It is, however, the growth of foundation support from 0.16 percent to 0.53 percent of total K–12 expenditures rather than the absolute level that strikes us as the more important figure.

In higher education, 50 percent of the colleges and universities are private (though they account for less than 20 percent of the students), and virtually all the public institutions have fundraising programs, some of them (mainly universities) highly significant in dollar terms. By contrast, K–12 has only recently come to seek private philanthropy, especially from

---

Table 1.1. K–12 Education.

Year	A: Total Foundation Grants	B: Total K–12 Expenditures	A ÷ B
1990	$ 407	$249,000	0.16%
1997	1,151	361,000	0.32
2004	2,729	514,000	0.53

Note: *Numbers in millions.*

foundations. As a largely public and tax-supported undertaking, K–12 education used to be able to count on that support to meet its needs. Faced with public resistance to new taxes, growing demands, and increased competition for the public resources that are available, schools—sometimes with great reluctance—have moved into the fundraising business.

Many foundation grants, however, go not to schools and districts but to intermediary organizations. In the 1990s and on into the new century, for example, considerable foundation resources went to the following: New American Schools; the several Annenberg-established citywide or regional agencies created by the Annenberg Challenge; the National Board of Professional Teaching Standards; many reform movements related to teaching, leadership, and school improvement; and a great many other local and regional intermediaries. A look at the top one hundred recipients of foundation support reveals that only about nine of those recipients are public school districts or foundations of such districts. Of the remainder, private and parochial schools, universities, and special-purpose agencies largely populate the other ninety-one positions on the list.

Higher Education

Of the 68,000 grantmaking foundations in the United States, the one hundred largest that give to higher education accounted for approximately 29 percent of the total foundation giving to higher education in 2004—a number that has declined from 41 percent in the 1990s and 37 percent in 1997.

The figures comparable to Table 1.1 look like those in Table 1.2.

While higher education expenditures in 2004 had grown roughly in parallel to K–12 (standing at 213 percent of the 1990 total, compared to 207 percent for K–12), foundation support grew only half as much (standing at 328 percent, compared to K–12's 671 percent). The higher education foundation grant total, however, was more than 2.6 times higher than

Table 1.2. Higher Education.

Year	A: Total Foundation Grants	B: Total Higher Education Expenditures	A ÷ B
1990	$2,173	$164,000	1.33%
1997	4,293	233,000	1.84
2004	7,138	351,000	2.03

Note: *Numbers in millions.*

the K–12 number and represented a much larger proportion of total expenditures (2.03 percent, compared to 0.53 percent in K–12).

Colleges and universities (though mostly the latter) are sometimes recipients of particularly large gifts. From 1973 to 2004, there were eighty-two grants by foundations of $35 million or more. Thirty-eight of these went to higher education, with the Gates, Woodruff, Annenberg, Danforth, and Lilly foundations granting twenty-seven of them. Another difference between higher education and K–12 is that the preponderance of the gifts and grants go to the institutions directly rather than to intermediaries, as is true in K–12 education. Gifts and grants are also concentrated in a limited number of recipients. The one hundred colleges and universities with the best record of fundraising received 70 percent of the funds from the one hundred foundations most generous to higher education. The other 3,450 institutions received 30 percent of those one hundred foundations' grants to higher educations. Those one hundred campuses took in 27 percent of the total of *all* foundation grants to higher education in 2004.

Raw or semi-raw numbers do not tell us very much beyond these few cornerstone numbers and ratios. More telling is the leverage that particular grants or sets of grants can have on change, or if they do not, why not. That issue occupies much of this book.

What to Expect from This Volume

Here is a brief review of what is ahead. Chapter Two, as already mentioned, proposes the concept of educational capital and our other recommendations for enhancing relations between foundations and educational institutions. Chapter Three is a historical overview that provides a set of chronological frames for thinking about philanthropy and education over the last century since the time of Andrew Carnegie. In the two main sections of the volume that follow, the first focuses on K–12 schools and foundations, the second on higher education and foundations. Each of these two sections includes five chapters: the initial chapter concerns the impact of foundation giving on educational institutions; the second chapter examines the cultures of those institutions and the extent to which those cultures clash or conform with those of foundations, and three case-study chapters explore foundation support in action. In the context of concrete circumstances, the case studies reveal important lessons about how to do grantmaking wisely in education. Following these two sections are two final chapters, one on the growth and impact on education of foundations with a conservative ideology and one on operating foundations and the contributions they make in the overall picture of foundations and education.

Our aim in this book is to raise useful questions. Even the recommendations in the second chapter are proffered more as provocations than as firm conclusions. Part of the reason to favor well-stated issues and challenges over tactical suggestions and strategic principles is the nature of philanthropy and education and of the people drawn to those fields. Independent institutions and independent thinkers nourish a genuine and vigorous democracy—one that values curiosity as well as confidence, experiments as much as customs. We offer our recommendations in that spirit.

We also realize that foundations, schools, colleges, and universities are—and ought to be—moving targets. (We wish more people would recognize that fact by dropping the term "best practices" and its implication of finality in favor of "better practices.") Their leaders, of course, are not indifferent about direction. They are moving their institutions in order to improve in a world that daily announces that its resources are limited. Foundation support for education is less than 1.2 percent of the combined expenditures of K–12 and higher education. That is not much, especially when we consider that much of it goes for capital needs, equipment, and specialized research. As a result, foundations currently exert little force—too little, we think—on core issues of teaching and learning, the organization of knowledge, character development, and civic responsibility. We hope that the size of foundation resources devoted to education will grow as newly created fortunes are transferred to philanthropy. Even if they were to double, however, we realize that the levers they represent would still be short and the proper fulcrums still difficult to identify—all the more reason, then, to focus on improving the effectiveness of relations between foundations and education. That is our purpose.

NOTES

1. We are indebted to Daniel Fallon of the Carnegie Corporation for forcefully making many of the points in this paragraph during the Centennial Conference on Foundations and Education. They are detailed in "Who Pays for Higher Education in a Globalized World? Lessons from an American Perspective" (Fallon, 2003).

2. For example, see "Is Philanthropy Abandoning Higher Education?" (Bernstein, 2003).

3. National Center for Educational Statistics. *Postsecondary Institutions in the United States: Fall 2004*, Table 1 (Knapp and others, 2005, p. 4). This

number is the total of U.S., public and private not-for-profit, 2-year and 4-year, degree-granting institutions eligible to participate in federal Title IV financial aid programs.

4. Based on Heather Creech's "Form Follows Function: Management and Governance of a Formal Knowledge Network" (Creech, 2001, p. 1).

REFERENCES

Bernstein, A. "Is Philanthropy Abandoning Higher Education?" *The Presidency,* Fall 2003, 34–37.

Creech, H. "Form Follows Function: Management and Governance of a Formal Knowledge Network." Version 1.0. Winnipeg, Canada: International Institute for Sustainable Development, 2001. http://www.iisd.org/pdf/2001/networks_structure.pdf.

Fallon, D. "Who Pays for Higher Education in a Globalized World? Lessons from an American Perspective." In G. Bach, S. Broeck, and U. Schulenberg, "Americanization-Globalization-Education." Conference paper presented at Universitatsverlag, Heidelberg, Germany, Winter 2003.

Knapp, L. G., and others. *Postsecondary Institutions in the United States: Fall 2004 and Degrees and Other Awards Conferred: 2003–04* (NCES 2005–182). U.S. Department of Education. Washington, D.C.: National Center for Education Statistics, 2005.

2

RECOMMENDATIONS

BUILDING EDUCATIONAL CAPITAL

Ray Bacchetti and Thomas Ehrlich

ON SOME DAYS, K–12 and higher education seem like second cousins twice removed. The one's educational operations are highly regulated, the other's scarcely at all (but for occasional well-intentioned forays by accrediting agencies); schools are under much greater pressure to reform than their higher education counterparts; teachers get a year or two of training to teach, professors get none but what they seek out voluntarily. And K–12 and higher education treat time differently: professors at elite institutions control their time and have a good deal of it, while school teachers' schedules leave little to spare, and administrators or unions limit their discretion over it. As interesting as these and many other differences are, it is the family resemblances and similarities that we find even more interesting and, in terms of foundation philanthropy, far more significant.

Both domains have enormous influence on the eventual economic self-determination, civic competence, and character of their students, as well as on the social coherence of the society in which they will live. Both are full of individual actors (persons *and* institutions) loosely but meaning-fully linked in a grand design that continuously confirms educational attainment as a necessary condition of personal success and national strength. Each depends on the other in legion ways, most obviously K–12 on higher education for the basic and professional education of future teachers and higher education on K–12 for prepared and curious students.

Both have a love-hate relationship with new ideas about how teaching and learning are conceived and practiced, especially when those ideas come from outside. Higher education's fierce independence and the norms that accompany it, among other reasons, account for disinterest in using ideas proffered by others. In K–12 the personal nature—indeed the intimacy—of teacher-student interaction, the distinctiveness of teaching and learning contexts, and the fact (though sometimes only the echo) of local control, impede the spread of ideas across the educational terrain. Schools and colleges are not fertile ground for Johnny Appleseed.

For their part, most foundations combine a strong desire to make a difference with an indisposition toward the investments that difference making requires. The larger their grants budget, the more they want that significance to be broad in scope and lasting in benefits. For the most part, however, they have small staffs; they assume that people hired for their experience in education are also competent in organizational change. And they invest lightly, if at all, in building on existing knowledge and in managing newly created knowledge as an asset for themselves, their grantees, and the field.

Many foundation grants simply don't meet their makers' aspirations. The reasons include choosing marginally important or inadequately analyzed problems, insufficient grounding in relevant research and prior work, overly specific framing, uneven implementation, too-short time frames, the absence or weakness of assessment, and a lack of articulation with organizational factors required to nourish and sustain change. To act with greater consequence on K–12 and higher education in regard to teaching and learning, foundations need to respond more effectively not just to what schools, colleges, and universities propose to do but to their problematic organizational characteristics that can thwart genuine improvement.

What may look like a chicken-and-egg dilemma (who changes first and with what effects on the other) need not be. Just as a chicken is an egg's way of making another egg (or vice versa), knowing where to begin is not as critical as breaking into the circle with new thinking about old problems.

The recommendations that follow are designed with that aim in mind. Besides breaking into organizational habits, they overlap and interconnect: taking any one seriously invites careful consideration of the others. By examining these recommendations first, readers can reflect on them, read the remaining chapters, and then reflect again to see what reactions the chapters stir and what modifications or additions in the recommendations seem warranted. This book is intended to inform and reinforce a continuing conversation about the role of foundations in education, and these recommendations are meant to promote that goal. The more effective use of foundation dollars in education is our purpose. The test of these recommendations is whether they move in that direction.

Recommendation One: Building Educational Capital

Many people, including the two of us and this book's other authors, have puzzled over the question of foundation effectiveness. How can what foundations and their grantees have learned and are learning be put to widespread and strategic use? How can so scarce a resource as foundation dollars work harder and smarter? These questions sit in the center of our concerns. Joining them there is the question of the form taken by proposals, foundation grants, and funded projects.

In our experience, the prevalent form comes with twin faults. The first fault of flawed proposals is their poor (no pun intended) foundation. Taking account of related work, building on that work, and thereby advancing that work are not normally characteristics of the proposals foundations receive (and often fund). Instead, a grantseeker, relying primarily on locally available information and ideas, develops a project design with significant potential for a local payoff. A foundation funds it; the project's results approximate its aims—for example, teachers in a school may take a fresh (to them) approach to, say, service learning, or a college may fashion a new (to it) orientation program for its first-year students. Neither party will know if it has created something new or repeated what others have done before.

The second fault results when elements are missing from what a robust, exportable design requires. When the focus is local, elements essential to application elsewhere often are missing. A grantee may, for example, take for granted some critical piece of institutional prehistory or indigenous talent, leaving implicit what another institution would have to understand explicitly.

The upshot of such flaws is that the grantee institutions may work better, but others are not likely to know that they do so or why. Foundations, then, often contribute to a norm of scattered and sporadic rather than steady and broad improvement, even though they set out to make significant, sustainable, and widely useable differences in education.

Into this search for greater potency in the foundation-education relationship, especially in teaching and learning, we introduce as our main recommendation the proposal that foundations should use grants to create educational capital—the progressive accumulation, in forms useable by educators, of validated experience and knowledge about successful educational ideas and strategies. Educational capital is about the design of foundation-funded projects so that they add important material to the stock of available knowledge on which comparable schools, colleges, and universities can draw. The five additional recommendations in this chapter support and reinforce the concept, while advancing other ways to strengthen foundation performance.

The first step in building educational capital involves identification of a significant problem or challenge faced by educators in the grantseeking institution and, of equal importance, in other, similar institutions. The potential funder is likely to see the principle of broad benefit more clearly than the grantseeker. Building educational capital often begins, therefore, in an asymmetric tension between a grantmaker who wants to introduce performance-improving ideas to a field and a grantseeker who wants to tackle a local problem or challenge. At that stage, the grantseeker is untroubled by the likelihood that a successful project will disappear into the ether of its institution and nothing will remain visible. And the foundation confronts the fact that there are no norms in the field on whether a project's animating ideas and results should have a postpartum life and what the nature and duration of that life ought to be. With some irony we note that even those who endure the frustration of reinventing a wheel seldom position their results so that others can be spared a similar fate.

When, however, problems important enough to be grantworthy are identified, the solutions to those problems should take the form of capital on which others can draw. Educational capital can be strategic or tactical in character, but above all else it should inform, guide, and perform in the actual challenges of real schools and colleges. The motivation, then, that mobilizes a grantmaker should be to put educators, broadly defined, in a more potent position to reach their goals.

Five Criteria for Building Educational Capital

When a significant problem is identified, the process of creating educational capital can begin. We propose five criteria that should be met to ensure that the process of designing and implementing a project will create educational capital. To illustrate these criteria, we use an example that bridges the worlds of both K–12 schools and institutions of higher education. Faculty at those institutions frequently complain that their students do not come to college with the abilities they need to write a research paper. Those abilities include the knowledge and skills required to conceptualize an issue and examine it in depth. A good research paper requires mastery of a range of tools in libraries, on the Internet, and in the field. It demands the ability to break a problem into component parts, to examine each part, and then to arrive at judgments backed by reasoned analysis and based on evidence. These abilities will be needed in one form or another by students for the rest of their lives in their personal and work environments.

If a consortium of school districts seeks support for a project to promote the research-paper-writing abilities of their students, and a group of foundations is interested in and considers funding the project, what should the project look like and what questions should the foundations be asking? These issues are just part of the larger challenge of bringing schools and higher education together to advance the prospects that youngsters, especially those who have been poorly served by prior schooling, can leave high school with the confidence and momentum to succeed in college.

The research-paper illustration is just one among many examples that could have been developed. Chapter Four uses the example of an elementary school to illustrate the concept of educational capital, solely in the context of K–12 education. Readers may find it useful to run a mind experiment of their own to fit the criteria to challenges and problems they consider significant.

Criterion 1: Ground the Project Design

For a project to increase understanding, it must be grounded in and then must build on relevant research and examined experience. Then the effort can knowingly advance rather than unknowingly repeat prior learning about what works. Equally important, knowledge of prior work allows one to steer clear of what's been shown *not* to work and thus avoids wasted effort and squandered aspirations.

To ground the design of a program to improve the teaching of research-paper writing sends one looking for and building on what has already been learned—studies that analyze, for example, what is known about age-appropriate methods (to enable an effective start early in high school); how best to teach the separate elements (for example, interpretation of evidence, informational writing), and theme-and-variation across disciplines (the better to tease out common elements from discipline-specific ones). Involving college and university faculty in project design deepens the consortium's resources. Such collaboration involves those whose complaints give rise to the project, thereby enlisting them as colleagues in the effort rather than critics of the result.

Grounding the design is about making a solid beginning, not pouring a fixative over a set of first principles. Indeed, an interesting project will seek to add to knowledge about teaching research-paper writing, not simply rearrange what's known into more productive formats. Grounded design is a practical form of insurance that the project will end with the best set of design features possible, having begun with the then-best-available set.

Criterion 2: Identify the Non-Negotiable Core

Successful tools are good at what they do and can be used under a variety of conditions. So too with educational capital. Building educational capital requires making clear what the core elements in the design are and how they can be faithfully applied by all concerned. If a teacher is determined to hew to her familiar ways and selectively incorporate only pieces of a successful strategy, or if she omits aspects with which she is inexpert and uneasy, the logic and power of the new practice are likely to be compromised and perhaps lost entirely. A similar argument applies to higher education. Ken Bain, in his book *What the Best College Teachers Do* (2004), said it this way:

> We cannot take single pieces of the pattern . . . and simply combine them with other, less effective or even destructive habits and expect them to transform someone's teaching any more than adopting Rembrandt's brush stokes would by itself, replicate his genius. (p. 20)

Future users must be enabled to understand the core concepts—the non-negotiables—and to put them into operation with fidelity to the program's design. Fidelity is the price exacted to secure the program's benefits in student learning.

No less important, educational capital should be applicable in diverse circumstances. No single approach can engage all students or be right for all contexts. Different student backgrounds and different connections to subject matter need to be used, even as the teaching is true to the program's design.

A project to promote the research-paper abilities of high school students might include

- Critical use of library and Internet resources (accompanied by respect for academic integrity and an understanding of what constitutes plagiarism)
- Varied teaching methods applied to the full range of students
- Opportunities to learn new skills that deepen student mastery of particular core elements (for example, statistical skills that allow quantitatively based inference)

○ Approaches that reveal different disciplines' ways of knowing

○ Team and interdisciplinary approaches to research and reporting

Criterion 3: Incorporate the Means for Ensuring Staying Power

Education at all levels struggles with change. For an idea to become educational capital, it must take account of the barriers to entry into educators' repertoires. This means providing a road map for its own continuity. At a minimum this will oblige documentation of both the idea and of how it can be put into play, as well as of the resources—intellectual, logistical, administrative, and otherwise—that a supportive setting will need to provide.

Examples of this criterion in action for developing research-paper expertise might include

○ Building core research-paper principles into curricular standards

○ Providing in-service development and ways to train new teachers to ensure continuity of school practice

○ Ensuring that the project has a long-enough period to give the approach a proper test, engaging higher education faculty in both design and testing, and documenting the results in ways that will be useful for others

Criterion 4: Build in Assessment at Every Stage

Assessment is an essential condition for creating educational capital. Different assessments methods, of course, can be useful in different settings and levels. Few foundation-funded education projects, for example, will warrant random assignment studies. A project should use the most appropriate research method suitable to the project's character and use it as rigorously as circumstances allow. As assessment becomes an essential element in the ecology of educational improvement and is increasingly integrated into foundation-education relationships, both foundations and grantees will need to demand more of themselves. The quality of a project's design and the significance of its inputs must connect like a plug and a socket, with a demanding evaluation scheme to confirm the worth of the project. This will oblige most practitioners to become familiar with new technical skills and expand their range of ways to interpret evidence of learning.

Formative assessment (using feedback to make beneficial adjustments along the way) is no less important than any final judgment on the success of a project. When the project directors detect unproductive steps or missing pieces, they should be able to make midcourse corrections. Unfortunately, too many foundations, in our experience, view such corrections as signs of weakness. Steady diagnosis and adjustment beats slavish adherence to original design in educational capital building, as well as elsewhere.

A project to improve research-paper writing offers a bonus: students, individually or in pairs and groups, can learn the process of self-assessment. Self-criticism is a central element in learning how to learn and can add great collateral value to the direct task of writing research papers. In this and other capital-building instances, an assessment approach, guided by expert counsel, is needed to ensure that student self-improvement is actually taking place.

A task as complex as research-paper writing at various grade and college levels and in a variety of subjects obliges a suite of evaluation techniques. Examples are value-added assessment, criterion-referenced paper rating, case studies, and teacher-made tests of specific skills or knowledge. Used in formative ways, they can refine the project's strategy while in process. Used summatively, assessment can support serious postproject peer review, dissemination, and publication.

Criterion 5: Encourage Interconnectedness

Though the denizens of K–12 and higher education are famously independent, they also operate in local contexts and as members of local organizations. Educational capital must be designed and built in ways that fit into these contexts and organizations, even as it generalizes across them. Looking laterally, a project should reinforce other objectives of the school or college, or at least be consistent with them. Looking vertically, it should be supported by the levels of leadership above and below. A foundation that wants to build educational capital must assure itself that a project is consistent with the norms and practices of the institutions for which it is meant and capable of interconnecting with them effectively. An analogy to weaving is apt.

To build educational capital from a proposal for making research papers integral and possibly even signature tools of a school-college continuum, a project might forge the following kinds of interconnections:

○ Engage teachers and professors across vertical and horizontal lines to develop shared understandings of what is required to prepare a first-rate research paper, what are the common student problems in writing a research paper, and what are the most useful teacher responses to those problems.

o Create opportunities for teamwork among both teachers and students to integrate research and writing into each student's educational development.

o Create online exercises for students needing extra help.

o Share some of the best papers by former students with current ones.

o Have school alumni visit while in college to talk with students about the role of research and paper writing in college.

The creation of educational capital starts with a problem of *relevance to educators* and reaches fruition when that educational capital becomes a *dynamic resource* in their work. This approach, particularly the application of the five criteria, requires a more systematic approach to foundation efforts in education than is common. Educational capital is a way of managing knowledge from its creation onward. When it is created with utility for users as a prime goal, educators will be able to work with material of proven value rather than be challenged only to tweak material that is already unruly in respect to coherence, consistency, and completeness.

Educational capital is not a template. As we have defined it, it is a working asset rather than an end product. As an asset, it respects the individuality of both foundations and educational institutions, which seems to us a great strength. We are skeptical that many educational problems will be solved with prepackaged ideas. Given the repeated frustration and limited success of those seeking to scale up, that is, to spread a single idea over multiple institutions, educational capital offers an alternative. It is a means to put proven ideas into circulation in ways that enable end users to compose the mix of know-how that best meets their needs. It also provides those institutions that are already learning organizations more to work with than what they could create from scratch.

Making the creation or enhancement of educational capital a defining characteristic of foundation-education relationships could lead to a number of benefits, among them:

o *Building more effective means to shared ends.* Most foundations involved in educational grantmaking seek to improve some aspect of institutional performance. They approach this shared end from many angles (good) in ways often idiosyncratic to their foundation's style and personnel (confusing). Attention to educational capital creation recognizes a difference between making a grant and moving on, compared to adding to the store of knowledge useable by others. The former is an event or episode; the latter creates a tool, a resource, a means to educational ends. Educational capital as an organizing principle introduces a level of quality control into grant-making practices that now vary widely from foundation to foundation and within a single foundation over time as its interests and personnel change.

o *Encouraging cooperation among foundations, schools, and institutions of higher education.* The meagerness of such cooperation is no secret. Neither is the growing importance of post–high school education and the shrinking supply of resources relative to ensuring that more students will be enabled to move into and successfully through college. Though collaboration between high school and college is one of many possible examples of educational capital, lying behind it is our hope that what is now a sharp division between high school and college may become a ramp. On that ramp teachers and professors, now living only at either end, may begin to mingle and learn from one another, and students may grow steadily in maturity and learning without confronting the steep transition to college that presents such a formidable barrier to many.

o *Enabling a shared definition of success among grantees, program officers, and foundation trustees.* Educational capital could provide a basis for agreement on what a foundation was after and the expected contribution to it from all levels. By getting all the actors on the same page and speaking the same language, misunderstandings can be reduced and alignment enhanced. Moreover, by building up shared understandings about goals and objectives among trustees, executive leadership, program officers, and grantees, the strategic planning and grantmaking process can diminish overpromising results in the beginning and overclaiming them at the end.

A further virtue of building educational capital is that it does not undermine qualities that are themselves of great worth. We have in mind qualities such as the independence of colleges and universities, the diversity of foundations, the local nature of public schools, and the engagement of parents and other citizens with them. Respecting those qualities, educational capital becomes a form of intellectual wealth—a bank of assets that can be drawn upon in response to locally apprehended problems. The size of each educational capital asset will be a product of the generality of the problem to which it responds and the degree of consensus leading to collaboration regarding its priority at any given time and place. This, too, seems to us a strength. Because each student is simultaneously like all other people, like some other people, and like no other person, those who teach them need a repertoire responsive to problems generic to all, distinctive to some, and unique to each. Those who pay the bills also need to know which strategies, techniques, or findings developed elsewhere can readily be applied in their setting without a local investment and which need some tailoring but do not require original work and the costs associated with it. They can also look at their own problems and ask which can justify the investment in solutions that others can use.

When we refer to *creating* or *building* educational capital, we do so for emphasis and not because we are overlooking the educational capital that already exists. One could say that our educational capital recommendation is about putting old, as well as new, wine in new bottles. As with anything claiming to be an asset, educational capital must function as promised and be widely available. Creating new or repackaging old educational capital is a task uniquely suited to foundations. The larger ones—on which we concentrate in this book—have the capacity to ground the concept of educational capital and produce many of its more consequential applications. But medium and smaller foundations can also create educational capital at scales appropriate to them (alone or in collaboration) and make capital developed by others available to the educational institutions in which they are interested.

Recommendation Two: Openness

There are no accidental tourists in the places where educational capital is built. As we hope is clear from the last section, a high degree of intentionality is required in each stage of foundation grantmaking, from the time that grant criteria begin to be developed to the time when results of grants are reviewed. Openness at every stage is a key factor in increasing the likelihood of success in building educational capital. Openness (compared to its opposite—secrecy) makes it more likely that leaders of foundations and educational institutions will understand each other and each other's goals. Openness does not guarantee success, but secrecy greatly increases the odds of failure.

We realize, of course, that the processes we are discussing are neither open nor closed. There are degrees of openness. But the system, as now established, assumes that information flows primarily one way: from grantseeker to grantmaker so that the latter can make a decision. That approach leaves successful grantees validated and others in the dark.

The recommendation that follows is designed to shed as much light as possible throughout the grantmaking cycle. We encourage foundation boards and their staffs to consider the proposal, ideally in open dialogue with their grantees and potential grantees. If the leaders of a foundation decide not to be as open as this proposal suggests, we hope they will be open, at least with each other, about the reasons and then pick points on the open-closed spectrum that are as open as possible.

o We recommend that *major foundations should maintain an Internet Web site for public review on which are available*

All proposals they receive for funding

Written decisions describing the proposals that are funded and the foundation's rationale for doing so

A reasonable sampling of the proposals that are not funded, accompanied by a written explanation characterizing in as specific terms as possible the reasons why those proposals, grouped appropriately, were not funded

Organizations that receive large grants from major foundations should be required (as a condition of the grants) to report on the results of those grants within a stated period of time after the grant period, such as three years, and those reports should also be made publicly available on the same Internet Web site.

This recommendation is about sending information from foundations back to existing and potential grantseekers, giving them a basis for improving the grantworthiness of their projects. In most cases now, foundation staff prepare for their boards a brief written explanation of a funding proposal and the rationale for supporting it, so we do not think it will be particularly burdensome to make these explanations, expanding if context is required. Providing written rationales for proposals not funded will be more time consuming. But the process will give those who are applying for support or considering applying a much clearer understanding of the decision-making process and the qualities of successful proposals than now exists.

By making the flow of information a two-way affair, a genuine dialogue can go on, the field can grow in sophistication, and the quality of proposals and thus the productivity of foundation programs can be improved. Ideally, the quality of the better proposals will increase, and the poorer proposals will begin to disappear, as those seeking grants come to understand why poor proposals are poor and good ones good.

No less important, we urge that those who receive foundation support (beyond some minimum) should be required to report on the results of their projects and programs and that those reports should also be public. These reports will help build educational capital. They will help educational institutions everywhere build on lessons learned by grantees. And they will aid future applicants for foundation support to learn from past efforts.

In response to this call for openness, we heard a barrage of comments, both positive and negative, by the participants in the Carnegie Foundation Centennial Conference. The last part of the proposal, concerning publicizing the results of grants, was added as a result of those comments. Some of those who reacted to our proposal were totally enthusiastic and urged that it was long overdue. But others urged caution, and a number suggested that we soften the proposal. Ultimately, we concluded that it is best to present the recommendation in this form with the hope that it will promote serious inquiry by leaders in foundations on what they could do to promote openness, even if they are not willing to go as far as we suggest. We hope it will prompt the boards of foundations to ask themselves and the foundation staff tough questions about why there is not more openness in what the foundation does.

We do recognize one potential danger in this approach that is worth comment. If foundations are as open as we urge them to be, some would-be grantees may think they should simply imitate successful proposals rather than craft their own. This is not what should happen, and foundations should make clear in their guidelines that they want grantees to help build educational capital, not replicate what has already been built. Once educational capital has been developed in response to a particular problem, foundations should expect educational institutions to use that educational capital without further foundation investment.

Recommendation Three: External Review

External review is the sibling of openness in the building of educational capital. By promoting external review we mean nothing more complicated than consciously infusing a foundation's decision making with steps to ensure that decision makers learn the views of individuals outside the foundation who can bring experience, wisdom, and judgment to the issues involved. Some foundations do good jobs of ensuring that their work is regularly subject to such external review. On the whole, however, our impression is that most foundations do a poor job in this arena, and that judgment was a common theme running through comments we heard both from our initial interviews to determine whether to undertake this project and from the participants at the Centennial Conference on Foundations and Education.

We initially used the term *peer review* to capture the kind of consideration we had in mind. But a number of the participants in the Centennial

Conference convinced us that this term carried too much baggage. It suggested more of a hard-edged or numeric evaluation than we think is required or wise. Rather, in our view, a range of means can be adopted to gain the insights and understanding of knowledgeable outsiders.

The ideal external reviewer depends, of course, on what is to be reviewed. If a foundation is seeking out-of-the-box ideas, then a group of individuals in well-established settings may not be the best approach. But those same individuals may well be able to give sound counsel about the extent to which a radical approach can work within traditional organizations.

○ We recommend that *foundations use external reviewers—individuals with relevant experience working in educational institutions—to review each stage of their work. This review can bring a degree of trust, as well as expertise, to the process. External review can bring objectivity and perspective. External reviewers should supplement, not supplant, the judgment of foundation boards, officers, and staff.*

The external review process should start when a foundation policy is formulated. A group of external reviewers can help ensure that the policy is built on the best available research and comparable experience of other foundations, that its ends are both bold and reasonable and its means sound and practical, that the policy is clearly stated, and that it means to prospective grantees and other readers what the policymakers intend it to mean. The review process should continue as guidelines for grants are formulated, to help ensure that the guidelines are clear and will engage those most likely to do the best work. External reviewers can also help ensure that the strongest potential grantseekers will see their own aims reflected in the guidelines.

External review of programs over time can provide important insights that are lacking in snapshot reviews. Although it is not always possible to keep an external review process open long enough to gain such continuity, it is useful to try whenever possible. Finally, the process should include evaluation of the results of grants, again using external reviewers.

We do not underestimate the difficulty of implementing this recommendation, nor suggest that it should apply to every program or grant. Often evaluation of a field—where it is and where it has been—is more likely to yield useful insights than evaluation of individual projects. This, too, would make a valuable use of external reviewers. They can bring more minds and voices into what are now predominantly closed foundation processes.

Collaborations among foundations and among institutions of education are as important in evaluation as in grantmaking itself, and collaborative use of external reviewers can help in evaluation. External reviews, particularly done collaboratively among foundations, will help build a common base of validated knowledge that the foundations can put into the field and on which future grants can be built, increasing educational capital and reducing the scatter of individual projects unconnected to larger bodies of knowledge.

Recommendation Four: Professional Development

Foundation program officers and presidents are two of a diminishing number of professional positions for which there is no established preparation or identifiable career path. Candidates for these two positions who will be involved in making grants to educational institutions are chosen most often either from one of those institutions—usually an elite university—or from another foundation. The program officer, in particular, is the chief information source to the field about the foundation's interests, strategic objectives, and decision-making criteria. He or she is also the foundation's "intake filter." In these two roles, the program officer wields much of the practical power in relationships with grantseekers.

The usual preparation for foundation work is experience in the field to which grants will be made. The virtues of that approach are matched by formidable deficits. Experience in one or a few educational institutions is a small base. Working on the ground with institutional tools is vastly different from attempting to influence them from a distance with grants, and understanding the work of foundations currently and in the recent past is usually absent from the repertoire of new program officers. Once hired into a foundation, the individual's responsibility for learning how to be effective is thus placed on potential but uncertain resources such as on-the-job training or self-directed learning. To influence educational institutions at any level, from elementary schools to research universities, we believe the preparation of program officers falls far short of adequacy, let alone excellence.

o We recommend that *a consortium of prominent foundations, working with leaders from K–12 and higher education and an organization such as Grantmakers for Education, develop a curriculum for delivery by online methods, classroom-based programs, and internships and similar means for purposes of introductory training and ongoing professional development for foundation staff.*

The primary purposes of these efforts should be to increase the strategic acuity of program staff and leaders, to ground the aspirations of foundations, and to build strong and productive relationships with educational institutions.

Building educational capital knowledge with the support of a foundation requires educating the individuals involved in making foundation grants to educational institutions. Those individuals need to know what has been done in relevant past efforts, what has been learned from those efforts, and how that knowledge might be usefully applied in the future. All the elements that we described in the first section of this chapter are part of the professional development we have in mind. The goal of that professional development is to organize individual experiences into the wisdom of educational practice so that it can be the basis for building more educational capital.

In addition to the content of such a program, we see other benefits, such as the networking begun by the shared experience of enrollment in professional development programs and expanded to the alumni of such programs. Another is the potential for introducing new ideas as a means of encouraging program officers and presidents to be self-critical observers and learners, as well as practitioners within foundations. Encouraging and facilitating the experience of being a member of an especially consequential professional group that shares professional standards, technical and strategic knowledge, and responsibilities to each other and the field, as well as to one's foundation, seems likely to add to the intellectual richness of individuals' careers and to have payoffs to the improvement of educational practice. The benefits of professional development to program officers would also accrue indirectly to foundation presidents as what is learned is brought back to influence foundation processes, style, and operations.

Recommendation Five: Collaboration

Each educational institution has its own identity and needs, but all share common concerns. Building educational capital means focusing collaboratively on those concerns. It means making investments that are deliberately designed both to benefit from past experience and to provide useful wisdom for future investments. Too often, when foundations invest in a single institution of education, the knowledge resulting from that investment benefits only those within the receiving institution.

We have divided the recommendation that follows into three parts. The first focuses on K–12 education, the second on higher education, and the third on K–16 collaborations. The deep division in American education between K–12 schooling and higher education has much to do with how educational institutions developed and little to do with the contemporary educational needs of students or our society. That division is reflected in so many ways, however, that this three-part approach seems, to us, needed. But the third part of our recommendation underscores how important we think it is for foundations to invest in approaches that treat education as a continuum and an integrated process from kindergarten through the bachelor's degree.

K–12 Education

Few public schools or foundations have the time or capacity for sustained attention to complex capital-building initiatives that aim at significant change. This problem is discussed in Lobman and Bacchetti (Chapter Four) and amplified by Hoffman and Schwartz (Chapter Five). Hatch develops the time-and-capacity issue relative to schools in his case (Chapter Seven), as does Lieberman (Chapter Eight). These challenges will not abate any time soon. An increasing response is the use of third parties to amplify and implement defined change strategies. We believe this trend should be encouraged.

○ We recommend that *foundations and K–12 schools should enlist existing intermediary organizations or create new ones (1) to build capacity in grantees to implement and sustain program improvements and (2) to advise foundations on how to make increasingly effective grants. Foundations should encourage and cultivate the establishment of such organizations as a key part of the public education system designed to support the improvement of teaching, raise student performance, and close the achievement gap.*

Hoffman and Schwartz note in Chapter Five that a wide variety of organizations could be grouped as intermediary organizations and that no generally accepted definition exists. They suggest this definition: "Intermediaries mediate and coordinate between organizations for the purposes of promoting innovation, improvement, and changes in practices." For financial and other reasons, this function will not be brought into public schools, nor does it make sense, except in well-defined instances, for foundations to expand to do it themselves. These intermediary organizations need not always be private nonprofits. Depending on the circumstances, they may be public agencies, such as county, regional, or university-affiliated public education intermediary organizations. In addition to their benefits, as stated in the recommendation, their appeal can also be found in their capacity to develop deep expertise in particular areas, to enable that expertise to travel and not to be created anew each time a grant is made, to work with and accumulate experience from many partnerships, and to be a relatively impartial voice in educational reform.

Intermediary organizations in the field of education are still a young and amorphous collectivity, though they serve functions that increasingly need to be served. Otherwise, ideas often will not travel, and educational capital will not be built. But many intermediary organizations are plagued by financial uncertainties, and some are not of high quality. These are problems worth confronting. In a domain that obliges public schools to focus virtually all their time on instruction and leaves little for exploration and innovation (and in which foundation norms favor small staffs), there is a gap where the engine of change and continuous improvement should be. Incapacity to change leads to declining performance which, in turn, can invoke heavy regulation and prescription. High-quality intermediary organizations spread across the key domains of schooling present a better way.

Higher Education

The individual campus has long been the primary recipient of foundation support. Much of that foundation support has been for ideas, issues, and projects that could benefit other colleges and universities as well. But successful initiatives often stay stuck on the grantee's campus and seldom inform changes in other institutions or increase the pool of common knowledge that others can tap. Foundations that make no effort to work across higher education institutions on common issues, as well as colleges and universities operating under the assumption that purely local payoffs are enough, both act to discount deeply the potency of foundation dollars. A much-needed and long overdue response to this need for leverage lies in more collaboration among foundations and institutions and increased initiative by and reliance on purposeful consortia and regional and national associations.

○ We recommend that *foundations should operate with a presumption that their funding for higher education will be allocated to multicampus collaboratives and to regional and national associations. That presumption could be overcome in specific instances, but the burden of proof should be on the individual campus applicant for funding to show that it is not feasible or practical to collaborate with other campuses directly or through multicampus groups.*

The most common concern that we heard about the increased use of collaboration was from those in higher education who stress that it is hard enough to promote collaboration within their own campuses. Collaboration across campuses, they contend, is even harder. And we agree that it is often difficult. But the case studies by Beckham and Hutchings (Chapters Eleven and Twelve) and the essay by Weisbuch (Chapter Fifteen), all provide, in somewhat different ways, illustrations that it can be done. In both case studies, intermediary organizations assisted in promoting the collaboration. We also point to the National Survey of Student Engagement as a prime example of a foundation-supported collaborative effort that has already benefited teaching and learning on many campuses.

Collaborative efforts also make the development of educational capital from foundation grants more likely than when a single campus is involved. Almost inevitably, if multiple campuses are engaged in a project, they will share lessons learned with each other. If a national or regional organization is assisting, that also facilitates building high-quality educational capital because of the wider range of intellectual resources, experience, and perspectives that can be brought to bear.

K–16 Collaborations

K–12 and higher education need each other. From the perspective of teaching and learning, they are a continuum, not self-contained stages. Higher education, moreover, is the gateway to economic self-determination and a vital factor in civic competence and social cohesion. Evidence includes the work described by Weisbuch in Chapter Fifteen and Hoffman and Schwartz in Chapter Five, as well as the nationwide efforts to qualify a more diverse student body for college success. Foundations are distinctively positioned to accelerate and broaden K–16 collaborations.

○ We recommend that *foundations should work with K–12 and higher education to seed collaborations, particularly, (1) to improve the high school and lower-division college performance in teaching and student learning and (2) to support student progress from high school, at least to a bachelor's degree.*

We consider the following developments, among others, as indications that K–12 and higher education are ready for this recommendation. First, initiatives among foundations, community colleges, and four-year colleges and universities are linking college-going preparations and aspirations.

The Gates Foundation's Early College High School Initiative (touched on in Chapters Five and Fifteen) is a case in point. Some colleges and universities are concentrating on enabling student success from an early stage rather than sorting students in the equivalent of an elimination contest. There are movements growing in charter schools and district schools to strengthen K–12 from its earliest grades so that college-going is an option, whether or not high school graduates take it.

Without more deliberate and focused collaboration among elementary, secondary, and higher education, it is difficult to foresee how educational quality, access to colleges and universities for all who merit it, the improvement of teaching at all levels, and focusing on K–12 teaching as an intellectually demanding and personally enriching career will happen. With such collaborations, toward which foundations can be a powerful stimulus, much can be learned on which to base significant and beneficial change.

Recommendation Six: Putting Educational Capital to Work

When you've got educational capital, how does it get put to work wisely, well, and over a broad sphere? Questions about the dissemination and use of good ideas in education have cycled up and down the reform priority list for a long time. Answers as good as the best of the practice-improving ideas, however, have been hard to find. Many of those answers have dealt with scaling up—or some version of it. Their lack of success can be ascribed to the short attention spans in the field and in foundations, local differences that scrambled the logic of the imported reforms, approach-avoidance and passive-aggressive responses from potential users, and similar behaviors. These and other actions have kept many promising theories and tested practices on the bench and put too few in the game.

Wary of the risk that hope will be blind to experience when framing recommendations, we begin this recommendation with two cautionary observations. First, the fields of education and foundations exemplify social life at the cellular level. Foundations and educational institutions stand largely independent and alone (often proudly so). Where systems or networks exist, they are partial and often possess their own insularities. Second, without credible and user-oriented means for moving ideas into practice across broad swaths of those fields, the individual entities are dependent on the knowledge and networking of their faculties and staffs. This is a considerable resource, but it is a widely varying one where efficacy is concerned. Insularity limits it, and the motivation and rewards for seeking out new ideas are low. A serious effort to make educational capital available in ways that intelligently tackle the relative immobility of ideas for improving teaching and learning is long overdue.

Looking to educators to become change agents in their own or their near-colleagues' practices is not a strategy capable of carrying more than a modest share of the freight in communicating, disseminating, and providing incentives for the use of educational capital. As investors in educational capital, foundations need to invest also in the circulation and use of that capital. Otherwise, they are wasting much of their money.

◌ We recommend that *foundations, acting individually and in concert, take increasing responsibility for moving educational capital into educational practice through the use of information technology, collaborations, and intermediaries.*

In this vital business of circulating educational capital, happily none of the parties begins from a standing start. Organizations, agencies, journals, and convenings are germinating to fill the need for diffusion of convincing ideas, validated tools, and professional expertise applied to the improvement of teaching and learning. But more, much more, needs to be done. These are some instances of what could follow from our recommendation and the associated efforts that are under way.

Using Information Technology

When thinking of next steps, information technology exerts a magnetic pull on the imagination. Building databases out of existing and newly successful research-and-development projects in key focus areas, mobilizing foundations themselves to do this for their own grantees, developing capacious cross-indexed systems of findings and search engines to go with them—these and similar instruments can hasten the day when useful information on educational challenges can function like databases in law, medicine, and libraries, or even in the commercial sector.

In recent years, our colleagues at The Carnegie Foundation for the Advancement of Teaching, through its Knowledge Media Lab, have been developing a range of useful technology-enabled resources and tools for teachers in both K–12 schools and higher education (http://www.carnegie foundation.org/KML). We are still a long way from a Google or an Amazon that offers up information in response to a few keystrokes and a mouse click. But we have already seen how helpful technology can be in strengthening teaching and learning.

The work of Lumina Foundation for Education in supporting commu- nity colleges is a prime example of the kind of foundation efforts we encourage. In its Achieving the Dream Program, the foundation has joined forces with intermediaries and other foundations to promote access and achievement in community colleges. It supports a program to encourage good practices, including Internet links with participating institutions. (See www.luminafoundation.org for details.) In addition, it has an educational knowledge manager whose job is to promote educational capital. She is one of what should be a growing group of professionals who specialize in gathering and making available validated knowledge to improve educa- tional practice. Knowledge managers are needed because ideas in edu- cation are not self-actualizing; they tend, absent special efforts, to stay put where they originate. Fortunately, a national organization—Grant Makers for Effective Organizations—now works to support knowledge managers in this important work (see www.geofunders.org for details).

Information technology for large, complex, and chronically underfunded uses is still more like patent than prescription medicine. Developing its potential, nevertheless, holds great promise. An electronic system of selec- tive retrieval of needed information is more likely to repay investments in its development than any other we can think of. Not, of course, all by itself.

Mobilizing information technology and knowledge management are significant preconditions for the effective diffusion of educational capital. In addition to foundations themselves, there are other means and locales for exploration, which we discuss next.

Acting in Concert

Some two hundred foundations sponsor Grantmakers for Education (GFE)—an organization devoted to helping foundations "learn about both effective educational strategies and effective grantmaking strategies." GFE recently began a Web-based Knowledge Center that enables posting and accessing information, connecting with others to work on shared prob- lems, and using an online library. Although GFE operates across the field, other foundations with narrowly shared interests could assemble a com- parable resource devoted to those interests. The potential of developing inventories and search engines that enable educators or program officers to learn what is known about particular topics would open new territory. Such information could include effective practices, where they are in oper- ation, and how to find out more. If the creation of educational capital obliges building on research and documented experience (Criterion 1), resources such as these are essential.

Acting Through Intermediaries

Education at all levels is rich in intermediaries. Some have a broad scope, for example, the Association of Curriculum and Instruction in K–12 or the Association of American Colleges and University in higher education. Most are specialized, for example, a charter management organization or a center on the teaching of reading in K–12; a disciplinary association in history, mathematics, or physics in higher education. Some span the educational spectrum, as does Jobs for the Future in its work on early college high schools.

There are other areas where gaps exist, and intermediaries may be the ideal solution for filling them. Given their interests, these intermediary organizations could offer the stability, expert depth, and fieldwide reach to make assembling and circulating elements of educational capital a signal contribution to their constituents. An intermediary in K–12, for example, might use what is known about small schools and how to use smallness to enable more effective teaching and learning and work with districts as technical assistance provider, coach, and formative evaluator. An intermediary in higher education could work with a campus center for teaching and learning on the use of technology for enhanced instruction, effective remedial programs, or inter-institutional use of technology to amplify the intellectual resources of a group of collaborating institutions.

Supporting Specialized Organizations

Though overlapping with the categories we've discussed, specialized organizations can offer educational capital to educators that others cannot. The American Memory Project of the Library of Congress is an example, on a national scale, of an unparalleled resource to teachers. Linked with other collections, it demonstrates that narrower specializations can connect with better-known ones to simplify access. The project captures teachers' work and makes available millions of digitized materials from the library's collection. The step to model lessons and thus to educational capital is not a long one. Regional hands-on science organizations, such as San Francisco's Exploratorium or the UC-Berkeley's Lawrence Hall of Science can also be fertile creators and conduits of educational capital.

Many of these strategies (though certainly not all) will depend in some measure on information technology. How to use technology so that it links and adds coherence to the wealth of materials that are now and will come to be available is an associated challenge. Though a multiplication of Web-based means of access to educational capital would represent progress, multiplication can too easily shade off into fragmentation and, ultimately, ignorance by great numbers of educators that a resource even exists. Not being utopians, we don't expect any time soon to see large databases of educational capital driven by search engines that, at the click of a mouse, put into educators' hands a better idea, strategy, or practice for use tomorrow, next week, or next year. Nevertheless, we think this is an important direction in which foundations should head.

At the same time, we underscore that educators need incentives for using educational capital, even when it is widely available and readily understood. The dominant incentive on the individual level, of course, is the desire to improve, but that is not always sufficient, even on that level; on the institutional or system level, more tangible incentives are often essential. Fortunately, relatively modest funds can often bring major gains in spreading educational capital. Primarily, those funds must come from schools, colleges, and universities. But foundations have an important role as well, both in insisting that dissemination be included in educational project proposals and in encouraging educational institutions to adopt incentives for their faculty.

--------------------- o ---------------------

We began this project by asking a group of leaders to evaluate the foundation-education relationship. Many of the responses were negative. It takes a particular kind of criticism, however, to stimulate and inform progress. Conversations need to be inclusive and based in a shared perception of the problem and common use of key terms. Concerned participants need to be pushing each other intellectually and developing and deepening the ideas that will carry the conversation forward.

This book is a down payment in the process of building that kind of vocabulary and having those kinds of conversations. In the idea of educational capital and its criteria, we intend to stimulate a means of looking across different grants to find common elements that can contribute to their success. By challenging the close-to-the-vest character of grantmaking with openness, we hope to encourage new ideas and careful attention to developing the words to convey them. Intermediaries—old in fact but new in concept—require more and better support if their potential is to be realized. When we recommended inviting external review, we struggled for the words to convey our intention. "Peer review" carried unwanted freight, and "outsider" suggested ceding authority. In the company of openness, external review can, we believe, import new ideas and behavior into the foundation-education relationship.

In some ways, "professional development" bites off a big piece of what we are advocating. For it to succeed, professional development must build up the elements of a profession. Professionalism in foundation work traces now mainly to the qualities of intelligence and integrity most program officers should possess and practice. Without an enlarged functional sense of the direction in which excellence lies, intelligence and integrity alone have less to work with than they need. Our recommendation on collaboration connects to an expanded view of professionalism as well. Without it, each collaboration would be ad hoc from start to finish and likely, therefore, to be too costly in time and effort to let momentum build and protocols be perfected.

Our final recommendation on moving educational capital into educational practice depends, of course, on progress in implementing the preceding proposals. This is not to say that good ideas in education won't continue to spread, much as they do now. It is, rather, to insist that today's relatively haphazard proliferation of ideas, findings, and programs has not served well the cause of improving education in more systemic ways. The opportunity for foundations to move diffusion to a new level deserves some genuine risk taking on their part.

We hope these recommendations and the essays that follow encourage a new look at how foundations work in education. The stakes are high, and progress is likely to be slow, which makes it all the more important that we start now.

REFERENCE

Bain, K. *What the Best College Teachers Do*. Cambridge, Mass.: Harvard University Press, 2004.

Chapter Three Overview

What can we learn from the history of efforts by major foundations to promote and strengthen education? At the invitation of the editors, Ellen Condliffe Lagemann and Jennifer de Forest take a look back over the last hundred years, with emphasis on the post–World War II period, and highlight the ways in which foundations have helped shape education, both K–12 and higher education. They consider what history can teach about effective philanthropy and the uncertainties of attempting to spend foundation money purposefully.

Professor Lagemann, who is the Charles Warren Professor of the History of American Education at Harvard University, is the country's leading scholar on foundations and their impact on American education. Professor de Forest teaches at the University of Virginia School of Education and specializes in scholarship on philanthropy and education. Lagemann and de Forest recall in their chapter the era when Andrew Carnegie started The Carnegie Foundation for the Advancement of Teaching and the shifts that have occurred in the century since then. They divide the last century into four periods: (1) "scientific philanthropy" from 1890 to the 1920s, (2) "philanthropic scatteration" from the 1930s to 1945, (3) "strategic philanthropy" from 1945 through the 1960s, and (4) "movement philanthropy" from 1970 to the present. The last section briefly discusses the recent role of conservative foundations in education—a role that is examined more fully in Chapter Fourteen.

The authors reach no simple conclusions, and they encourage "more humility than seems to be in vogue at the current moment among new philanthropists." Their insights give support, we think, for our conclusions about the importance of building educational capital and the need to take the long view when doing so.

3

WHAT MIGHT ANDREW CARNEGIE WANT TO TELL BILL GATES?

REFLECTIONS ON THE HUNDREDTH ANNIVERSARY OF THE CARNEGIE FOUNDATION FOR THE ADVANCEMENT OF TEACHING

Ellen Condliffe Lagemann and Jennifer de Forest

WE LIKE TO IMAGINE THAT if Andrew Carnegie were alive today, he would smile with pleasure on the earnestness of the efforts of philanthropists like Bill Gates, who seem devotedly intent on identifying the root causes of human problems and then attacking them. When he was fifty years old and just beginning to give away what was then the largest fortune in the world, Carnegie had aspirations no less ambitious than those of Gates today.

Gates seems quite modest in his public pronouncement, but we have heard some among those dubbed "venture philanthropists" argue that what they are doing is new and different, precisely because it is designed to have an impact. We have heard venture philanthropists say that, unlike traditional philanthropists, they will not simply fund ideas that are put before them but will instead take the initiative to analyze problems and develop strategies for ameliorating them. Venture philanthropists maintain that, unlike their predecessors, they are not in the business of merely giving away money but rather of creating partnerships with people and organizations with whom they intend to stay in continuing conversation.

Then there are what Ralph Smith of the Annie E. Casey Foundation has termed "muscular philanthropists." In July 2002, three Pittsburgh foundations—the Grable Foundation, the Heinz Endowments, and the Pittsburgh Foundation—flexed their collective muscle when they withdrew their support for the Pittsburgh public schools. "As investors," the foundations stated, "we can no longer be confident that any funds we put into the district will be used wisely and to the maximum benefit of students. Therefore, it would be irresponsible for us to continue support for the district at this time."

In the wake of this announcement, the mayor put together a blue-ribbon commission to investigate their concerns. The commission released a report with recommendations, and things may now be looking up in the Pittsburgh schools. According to Smith, the foundations' blunt talk and their hardball brokering, which produced results, was the result of unprecedented foundation collaboration. No less than venture philanthropy, muscular philanthropy is thought by many to be an innovation and a major departure from "traditional foundation practices" (Smith 2004, p. 26). Once again, we like to imagine knowing smiles on the faces of earlier generations of philanthropists.

At the risk of sounding like old fuddy-duddy historians who have seen it all before, we are here to tell you that, of course, there are differences one hundred years later, but, in fact, the intentions and even the methods of earlier philanthropists were more like those of current philanthropists than meets the eye. Some current claims of innovation are exaggerated. Consider three not-so-out-of-the-ordinary examples from nearly a century ago that have all the marks of the venture and the muscular philanthropists of today.

In many ways the philanthropy of eBay founder Pierre Omidyar echoes the philanthropy of Andrew Carnegie. Carnegie self-consciously and consistently refused to practice traditional charity. He would not give alms to the poor. That was ineffective, he insisted. He was intent, instead, on building institutions through which the poor could improve themselves and, in the future, avoid the need for alms. This was the rationale for the public libraries he built, as well as for all the trusts he created, including The Carnegie Foundation for the Advancement of Teaching. From Carnegie's perspective, the foundation was intended to dignify the noble profession of college teaching and, by making professors "heroes," encourage others to emulate their noble work for the good of others. Carnegie was correcting the wasteful ineffectiveness of the generations that had preceded him, no less than Pierre Omidyar and his wife, Pamela, are organizing their philanthropy to be more effective than traditional foundations. According to Lorna Lathram, their adviser, while the previous generation of foundations has "a tremendous product—money," they lacked "any decent delivery mechanism" (Lathram, 2004, p. 1).

The early years of Carnegie philanthropy were hardly less "muscular" than the actions of the three Pittsburgh foundations. While Andrew Carnegie was trying to improve on his predecessors' approaches to giving, the first president of the foundation, Henry Smith Pritchett, was, in turn, trying to improve on "the old man's" idea (Lagemann, 1983, p. 49). Carnegie was interested in providing professors with pensions, which was at the time an unusual benefit. Pritchett, for his part, wanted to create a pyramid-like "system" of higher education from the country's then highly diverse colleges and universities. Enlisting his close friend Frank A. Vanderlip, then vice president of City Bank, Pritchett convinced Carnegie to appoint other college presidents as trustees of the foundation and to give them discretion as to how to apportion funds. This allowed Pritchett to organize the pension plan through institutions, which had to modify their operations to meet the fund's requirements if their professors were to be eligible for the benefit. Too late, Carnegie realized what Pritchett had done and, rather than leave the remainder of his funds to the foundation, as Pritchett had hoped he would do, instead created a much larger grantmaking foundation—the Carnegie Corporation of New York. Admitting that there are differences of detail, we would again venture that the melodrama so central to the early years of Carnegie philanthropy was no less muscular than the actions of some modern foundations.

One last example, again with some differences, displays similarities between the methods of contemporary philanthropists and those of their predecessors. In 1916, the Cleveland Foundation invited Leonard Ayres, the chief statistician of the Russell Sage Foundation—a larger, national foundation—to come to Cleveland to survey the schools. Ayres agreed to partner with the Cleveland Foundation and put together a group of education experts from Harvard, the University of Chicago, and Teachers College, Columbia University. After two years, Ayres's team had counted and measured everything about the Cleveland schools and had a twenty-five-volume report ready to release to the citizens of Cleveland and the press. The report created a sensation that forced the mayor, over the objections of the school board president, to fire the incumbent superintendent of schools, who was replaced, not coincidentally, with a close ally of Ayres and the other members of the survey team (Lagemann, 1990, pp. 83–87).

The details are unimportant. The pattern is the point. Just as in Pittsburgh, a collaboration among foundations to improve the operation of the Cleveland schools resulted in public reports and eventually a change in school leadership. Eighty-plus years later, a similar set of players engaged in a similar approach to change. *Plus ça change, plus c'ést la même chose.*

Those who do not know history are condemned to repeat it. Whether this old cliché is, in fact, correct, we believe that a general lack of knowledge about the history of foundations is a significant problem for both scholarship and philanthropic practice. It is a problem for the discipline of history, where writing about the history of U.S. culture, science, and education is foreshortened, owing to a failure to take account of the actions of foundations. It is also a problem, we believe, for those involved in philanthropy.

Rather than learn from the past, people involved in philanthropy are all-too-inclined to reinvent the wheel. In consequence, our capacity to use charitable funds to improve education or health—or whatever—has not significantly increased over the last century. The logical response to this situation, of course, would be to encourage historians to do more critical historical writing. But the logical response may not be the right one. At least since 1957, when Merle Curti led a "needs and opportunities" study in the history of philanthropy, there have been repeated calls for more foundation history; these seem to have fallen on deaf ears. In part, this may reflect a reluctance among foundations to open their files to outside scrutiny. In part, it may also be the perverse consequence of a lack of good writing—good literature being likely to spawn more good literature. However, for whatever reasons, admonitions concerning the importance of foundation history—even admonitions accompanied by foundation funds—do not seem to have helped fill what is a serious knowledge gap.

In light of that, foundations might be wise to invest more in program evaluation and in the improvement of tools for such evaluations. As an alternative to full critical histories, encouraging more program evaluation may be a sensible move. Program evaluation became popular in the 1980s, when a good number of foundations refused to make grants without proposals that included evaluation plans. Whether that was a fad or a continuing effort to learn when goals and outcomes matched up well and what accounted for the linkage, program evaluation resembles history in that it traces the evolution of intentional efforts over time. Moreover, the only way methods of evaluation will improve and become more nuanced is if they are called upon and, facing a new challenge, improved upon. This is not the place to recite the history of measurement. Suffice it to say, that were we to review that history (say, developments between the pioneering work in individual measurement of Edward Thorndike and the much later program measurement work of, say, Steven Raudenbusch and Tony Bryk, inventors of hierarchical linear modeling), we believe it would prove our point. Methods develop best in interactions between practice and the more theoretical concerns of the Academy.

Whatever the means, one implication of the argument we will make is that philanthropy is not exempt from the maxim that history matters. We believe that both historians and practitioners need to find ways to be sure that history is neither lost nor its lessons overlooked.

From Scientific to Movement Philanthropy

What, then, can history teach us that may be relevant to practitioners today? History reminds us that foundations exist in an inextricable relationship with the society that sustains them. On the one hand, foundations seek to change the society around them and, on the other, they are composed of staff members and trustees who live and, in various ways, participate in that society's leading ideas, values, and styles. To clarify the ways this relationship has played out over time, we have identified shifts in patterns of giving and delineated periods of twentieth-century grantmaking.

The landscape of U.S. foundations has grown increasingly complex and vast over the course of the century. The community of American foundations did not top 1,000 until the 1940s, but by the 1970s there were 6,906 foundations. By 1980 foundations numbered 11,238, and by 1990 there were over 16,000 (Frumkin, 2002, p. 112).[1] Aside from the period just following the Great Depression, the number of American foundations has steadily increased, and there are no signs that this trend will abate.

Among those scholars and journalists who have written about foundations, it is frequently asked whether foundations lead change or react to it. Do they reinforce the status quo by "cooling out" radical ideas, or do they promote change? As elite organizations, do foundations promote democracy and the marketplace of ideas, or are they a threat to democracy? Although there are valid answers to all these questions on both sides of the aisle, it is our contention that foundations inevitably interact with the contexts they find themselves in.

1890s Through 1920: "Scientific Philanthropy"

The first period of foundation history, which ran from roughly 1890 to 1920, was characterized by a clear and coherent mode of philanthropy and can be styled the era of "scientific philanthropy." This was the period when the earliest trusts founded by John D. Rockefeller and Andrew Carnegie carried the personal philosophies of their founders, as well as the ambitions and values of their initial managers. In both instances, the people who designed these trusts were deeply influenced by changes then remaking the demography of the United States, the density of the landscape, and the organization of industry.

Scientific philanthropy emerged during the early years of the twentieth century, at the same time as economic growth and reorganization, technological advances, population expansion, increasing social diversity, and new ideas derived from and associated with science began to transform a nation of what Wiebe called "island communities" (Wiebe, 1967) into what Graham Wallas first called "The Great Society" (Wallas, 1914). Foundation philanthropy was a response to that transformation. It was rooted in a long tradition of philanthropic efforts to establish the values, shape the beliefs, and define the behaviors that would join people to one another. And yet, it also represented an effort to bring greater deliberateness and a more national orientation to the definition and fulfillment of common needs and interests.

Scientific philanthropy also took form in reaction to nineteenth-century charitable organizations that had generally been associated with Protestant religious denominations: the American Home Missionary Society, the American Bible Society, and the like. When they were not officially denominational or multidenominational, nineteenth-century charitable organizations were still likely to be nondenominational Protestant. That was true, for example, of the public schools. Even though they were "public" schools and nondenominational, texts like the *McGuffey Readers* taught Protestant values and included sections from the Protestant Bible. It was this Protestant, nondenominational, public school culture that had led to the founding of Catholic schools by midcentury.

With the arrival of significant numbers of Jews from Eastern Europe and Catholics from Southern Europe, Protestant cultural hegemony began to wane. In consequence, when foundations like the Rockefeller's General Education Board was founded in 1901, The Carnegie Foundation for the Advancement of Teaching was founded in 1905, and the Russell Sage Foundation was founded in 1907, they were purposefully set up to be free of denominational or interdenominational affiliations. Authoritative knowledge now increasingly needed to be certified by "science." Claiming that knowledge was rooted in the "truth" of religion was no longer sufficient to make it authoritative (Hammack, 1999, pp. 43–68).

The 1925 Scopes trial in Tennessee dramatically symbolized this shift in belief about the nature of knowledge. There modern science in the form of evolution trumped the fundamentalism of William Jennings Bryan, who was made to look ridiculous when he said that he genuinely believed that a whale had swallowed Jonah and that Joshua had made the sun stand still.[2]

Of course, even as science was displacing religion as the source of social authority in the United States, different conceptions of science were very much in contest. Here, too, the early foundations played a significant role in adjudicating whose science would be seen as most legitimate and in which settings science—that is, "real" science—should go on. As was the case with so many choices made in the design and redesign of the ecology of knowledge, matters of gender were centrally involved.

One could see all this rather vividly in a decision made within the Carnegie Corporation of New York—Andrew Carnegie's last and largest philanthropic trust, which was established in 1911. In May of 1921, the corporation's board decided to stop considering applications from social settlements. This seemingly innocuous action, in fact, ruled in university and "think tank" science and ruled out more applied, practical, action-oriented forms of science. Since their inception in Great Britain in the late nineteenth century, settlements had been places where young men and women lived and worked to improve the lives of their "neighbors." The residents conceived of their work as scientific. They gathered "facts" about problems in their neighborhoods that would enable them to lobby city officials or others for the kinds of reforms and improvements that would solve real problems of daily life.

Consider, as an example, the nurses at Lillian Wald's Henry Street Settlement in New York, who discovered that a significant number of children were being sent home from school. Why? Upon investigation, they discovered this was because no one in the school could distinguish between communicable diseases and noncommunicable health problems. Knowing this, they leaned on city authorities to provide schools with nurses who could make this distinction. The absence rate declined.

Though such investigation genuinely met the canons of science early in the twentieth century, by the 1920s, science was moving toward more theoretical, abstract conceptions. Reflecting and accelerating that trend, the Carnegie Corporation decided to discontinue funding for settlements. In so doing, the corporation's trustees privileged university departments, which were largely populated by men, over social settlements, which were predominantly staffed by women (Lagemann, 1989, pp. 66–67). Even for women scientists who found a berth in academia, research grants were hard to come by. For the most part women scientists worked at women's colleges, which did not enjoy foundations' largesse. As a result, women scientists in the early twentieth century were almost wholly forced to turn to private individuals to secure funding for their work (Dzuback, 2005, pp. 120–121).

1930s Through 1945: "Philanthropic Scatteration"

During the years from the Great Depression until the end of World War II, foundations continued to advance formal knowledge through the funding of scientific research. However, doubt spread that scientific research could address social problems as vast as those of economic collapse and continental violence. Moreover, during this period a quarter of American foundations folded, and those that did weather the economic chaos scrambled to meet their previous commitments (Frumkin, 2002, p. 112.). As a result, philanthropy during this era was inevitably marked by rather practical, perhaps opportunistic responses to fundamental challenges. The result was a period called "scatteration" by Frederick P. Keppel, president of the Carnegie Corporation of New York from 1923 to 1941.

In a very real sense the difference between strategic philanthropy and foundation giving during the interwar years was exemplified by, and was a reflection of, the differences between Herbert Hoover and Franklin D. Roosevelt. Hoover was an engineer who believed in finding facts and crafting deliberate strategies. Roosevelt, by contrast, was practical and willing to try pretty much anything to find solutions that would work. The differences between the two men were perhaps less ideological than traditional histories have suggested; they were more differences of temperament. Hoover would not try out a program to provide relief unless he was certain it would work. He needed trusted, convincing evidence before he would act. Roosevelt, by contrast, would listen to an idea from a member of his brain trust and quickly decide to give it a try. The alphabet soup of New Deal programs represented experiments to figure out what would work to alleviate a depression that the federal, state, and local governments were not equipped to combat.

Faced with a national crisis in the 1930s, foundations struggled to avoid a retreat from their efforts to diagnose the root causes of problems back into charity. While social settlements also faced this challenge and tended to succumb, foundations, which were further detached from the actual sufferings of people, were better able to maintain their missions. As the board of the Russell Sage Foundation, which was (and remains) an operating (as opposed to a grantmaking) foundation, put it:

> *Resolved,* that the policy of the Russell Sage Foundation in the present emergency, as always, is in its permanent contribution to the improvement of living and social conditions by its studies and its wide co-

operation with agencies, rather than by contributing directly to relief. Therefore be it resolved that the Russell Sage Foundation make no contribution to the Emergency Relief Committee. (Glenn, Brandt, and Andrews, 1947, p. 489)

Functioning with considerably less money than they had had during the "roaring" 1920s, the foundations began to provide expert personnel to assist government agencies or to support the study of significant public problems. During the 1930s, as power migrated from states and localities to the federal government, federal authorities assumed a role that involved a great deal of mediation among differing factions (Smith, 1991, p. 81). Thus, for example, Russell Sage staff supported the President's Emergency Committee for Employment, and the director of its Department of Statistics was "lent" to the New York Emergency Relief Bureau. As the official history of Russell Sage explains, "it was a period . . . when the longer-range planned programs were constantly being interrupted by emergency demands, first of the great depression, and then of war" (Glenn, Brandt, and Andrews, 1947, p. 494). Having devoted considerable funds during the 1920s to creating independent research institutions, including the National Bureaus of Economic Research and the Brookings Institution, the Rockefeller and Carnegie Foundations spent the 1930s watching as one after another social scientist went off to work in Washington, D.C., for one of the proliferating agencies of the federal government.

In addition to supporting the development of a larger federal role in governance, during the interwar period the foundations focused their attention on the dissemination of culture. This was a logical priority, the belief being that the postschool education of adults via reading and engagement in the arts could foster the values and sensibilities needed to acknowledge the benefits of government by experts. In addition, there was concern that without deliberate intervention and leadership, the market would drive the development of culture. Were the market to drive, it was assumed that low-brow taste would crowd out the high-brow. Jazz would drive out classical music, gothic fiction would drive out classic novels, and reprints would displace a taste for originals. During the 1930s, there was a real fear of cultural decline and chaos. The masses would wrest control of culture from the elite and, if this were to happen, the possibility of having an orderly society governed by scientific knowledge would be lost. Following these beliefs, foundations lent their support to organizations that could safeguard traditional cultural standards.

At the Carnegie Corporation, this resulted in significant funds being spent to support existing organizations like the American Library Association and to create new organizations like the American Adult Education

Association. Ironically, it also resulted in one of the corporation's proudest ventures—the study of "Negro education and Negro problems" that eventually resulted, in 1944, in Gunnar Myrdal's massive two-volume study, *An American Dilemma*. Described as "monumental" by W.E.B. DuBois and cited in *Brown* v. *Board of Education* (1954), *An American Dilemma* argued that the so-called "Negro problem" was a result of discrepancies between what Myrdal called "the American Creed" and the way America actually translated that creed into practice.

Of course, the idea that there is "an American creed" has now become commonplace in the way Americans conceive of their own culture, even though, of late, many would argue for a more diverse perspective concerning different creeds. Despite that, the magisterial Myrdal study was largely ignored within the Carnegie Corporation. As corporation secretary Sara L. Engelhardt stated in 1975, some fifteen years after the corporation had begun to boast of its sponsorship of the Myrdal volume, "the Corporation's failure to follow up on the Myrdal study is perhaps the greatest missed opportunity in its history, one that can be regretted now in hindsight" (quoted in Lagemann, 1989, p. 146).[3] However that may be, having been initially commissioned to resolve questions concerning the capacity of African Americans to learn, *An American Dilemma* instead described a contradiction that was and still is central to American culture. Studying the question of race relations from multiple perspectives, Myrdal was able to capture one of the root causes of inequality in the United States.

Having survived World War II, it is hardly surprising that a new generation of strategic philanthropists—John W. Gardner and McGeorge Bundy—would be dismayed at the large sums of money that had gone to support the fine arts and adult education in the interwar era. In what had been a period of scatteration, it seemed that the foundations had spent a lot of money without having a measurable impact. This helped propel the next generation of grantmakers toward "strategic" grantmaking.

1945 Through 1960s: "Strategic Philanthropy"

If the style of giving we have labeled scientific philanthropy was inspired by a determination to be more intentional and purposive than nineteenth-century charities had been, the style of giving we are labeling strategic philanthropy also took off from implicit, if not explicit, criticisms of prior foundation activities. The era of scientific philanthropy was much like our own era, in that its architects self-consciously and determinedly set out to address major social problems in ways that were different—and, indeed, better—than the ways of earlier philanthropists. That was again true during the period right after the end of World War II. Then, as today, there were self-conscious efforts to make philanthropy more effective. Historians who have studied philanthropy widely agree that this second era, which ran from roughly 1945 until 1969, was one of "strategic philanthropy."[4]

After World War II the Carnegie Corporation, once the nation's giant foundation, was dwarfed by other private foundations and also by newly created public foundations like the National Science Foundation. During this era, the federal government began providing funds directly to universities for research, which, again, challenged the corporation's previous unusual niche. In response, corporation staff members often tried to design programs or policies that other agencies, public or private, might implement or carry out. This was seen as a strategic way in which the corporation could leverage its funds and represented an effort to make its grantmaking even more effective.

Forecasting current venture and muscular philanthropists, at the end of World War II foundation executives and board members spoke with a new sense of urgency about the production and application of knowledge. They were still reeling from the horror of the atom bombs that had been dropped on Hiroshima and Nagasaki, and they were deeply concerned that future wars be avoided at all costs. The evidence that human beings now had a greatly magnified destructive capacity endowed philanthropists' seriousness of purpose with a new seriousness of responsibility. Not surprisingly, this was further heightened as it became clear that, alas, the United States was now again engaged in war—this time a "cold war" with the Soviet Union.

In this atmosphere of urgency in the immediate postwar years, there was also a telling turn of phrase that was to be found widely in public statements. Writing as president of Harvard University, J. B. Conant argued that the scholars working to understand "the behavior of man as a social animal" should be understood as occupying a "strategic post" (quoted in Lagemann, 1989, p. 148). Speaking as one of the nation's leading sociologists, Samuel A. Stouffer of the University of Chicago similarly argued that we needed "a science of society whose engineering applications will help regulate the complex civilization wrought by physical science and technology" (quoted in Lagemann, 1989, p. 148). Stouffer's speech was titled "Sociology and the Strategy of Social Science."

This emphasis on *strategic* thinking and planning was echoed within foundations. So, too, was the belief that investments in the social and behavioral sciences were themselves a strategic investment in social improvement. Resonating with the postwar sense of urgency, these beliefs again illustrate how embedded foundations are in the situations of the societies in which they reside. They had a profound effect on both the style in which grantmaking proceeded and the substance of the grants that were made.

For example, in 1946, John W. Gardner was newly arrived at the Carnegie Corporation. As he surveyed opportunities for the corporation's giving, he wrote that now "when a new project comes up, it will not be sufficient to know that a terribly competent man proposed it, or that it is a socially desirable project, or that it is feasible and well-formulated." Those old criteria would remain necessary but not sufficient, Gardner continued. "We will want to know whether this project is relevant in terms of our basic strategy, whether it is a logical next step (or at least an indispensable step) toward the attainment of one or another of our objectives" (quoted in Lagemann, 1989, p. 148). Already unusual in the eloquence with which he spoke, Gardner was voicing the leitmotif of this new age. Hereafter, the logics for grants at the corporation and other foundations would need to be elaborated as parts of larger strategies.

Deeply influenced by Gardner throughout the postwar era, the grantmaking strategy that was followed within the Carnegie Corporation reflected the strategic importance that Conant and Stouffer had located in the promise of the social and behavioral sciences. During the late 1940s, the corporation concentrated significant funds on the development of the social disciplines, including cross-disciplinary research having to do with different geographical areas and survey research. Carnegie also played an important part in supporting the Department of Social Relations at Harvard University.

By the early 1950s, however, the much larger Ford Foundation had moved into the social sciences. Founded in Michigan in 1936, Ford focused on local initiatives until 1950, when it was reorganized and moved to New York City, where it took up a high-profile national agenda. Ford's aggressive grantmaking contributed to conditions that reshaped the landscape of American foundations in the latter half of the century.

The turbulent events of the 1960s roused America's third sector, especially the giant Ford Foundation. During this period Ford adopted a new strategy, turning sharply away from research as a tool to address social issues and, reflecting the penchant of the era, toward action. Under the leadership of McGeorge Bundy, Ford made grants to projects designed to promote social justice and embraced causes that included environmentalism, the women's movement, and black studies programs (Dowie, 2001, p. 31). In 1967–68, Ford also made grants to former staff members of the recently assassinated Robert F. Kennedy and to Cleveland's Committee on

Racial Equality to spur voter registration in Ohio (Rich, 2004, p. 58; see also footnote 72 on that page).

To many observers, Ford's philanthropic activism overstepped a foundation's role and tipped too directly into national politics. In very real ways, Ford's activities contributed to conditions that led to the passage of the 1969 Tax Reform Act, which limited foundation ownership of any corporation, required minimum annual payouts, and curtailed foundation efforts at influencing legislation. According to Peter Frumkin, these reforms, in turn, led to a "paradigm shift" in which foundation staff became increasingly professionalized and grantmaking was bureaucratized (Frumkin, 1999, p. 70). We would add that the strategic-cum-activist-philanthropy of the 1960s, led by the Ford Foundation, also helped galvanize a conservative countermovement in American philanthropy.

1970s Through the Present: "Movement Philanthropy"

Conservative philanthropists were stirring in the late 1960s in opposition to the philanthropy of foundations like Ford and in response to turbulent events of the era. After Barry Goldwater's resounding defeat, conservative elites began to ponder ways to amplify their political power and public influence. While the activities of the political Left may have been more visible in the sixties, the Right was simultaneously forging a powerful movement that would both support and be supported by conservative philanthropy. Because the grantmaking that emerged from this period was intertwined with the rise of American conservatism and remains so, we have fashioned it "movement philanthropy."

While movement philanthropy had many triggers, it was unusual in that it had what amounted to a founding document. In 1971, two months before Richard Nixon nominated him to the Supreme Court, Lewis F. Powell wrote a memo to the Education Committee of the U.S. Chamber of Commerce. Powell's memo, deemed by some a manifesto, urged conservatives to combat the influence of radicals on college campuses and perceived widespread socialist tendencies in American society. Powell directed concerned American businesses to organize a coalition to oppose attacks on free enterprise from the likes of consumer advocate Ralph Nader and New Left philosopher Herbert Marcuse. Powell also urged businessmen and philanthropists to be vigilant about funding efforts that opposed a free market economy or contradicted individual property rights.

In 1977, Henry Ford II, in a clear expression of the Powell memo, resigned from the board of the Ford Foundation, complaining that the foundation had become anti-capitalist. Ford explained, "I'm just saying that the system that makes the Foundation possible is very probably worth preserving" (Miller, 2001, p. 40). Also in the 1970s, foundations like Olin, Smith-Richardson, Bradley, and Sarah Mellon Scaife became a more visible conservative wing of American foundations. They increased their grants to think tanks like the Hoover Institution and the American Enterprise Institute and helped to create influential new ventures, including the unabashedly ideological Heritage Foundation. As a group these foundations continue to share and promote a vision of the public good that calls for the promotion of free enterprise, individual freedom, and a limited federal government.[5]

What Can History Teach About Effective Philanthropy?

It would be nice if we could assert that efforts to do better at philanthropy have yielded demonstrably better results. Put otherwise, we would like to think that attempts to be more effective, in fact, resulted in more effective activities. Sadly, however, that does not seem to be the case. Deliberate efforts to do things more effectively have not necessarily made a significant systemic difference in improving education, health, or anything else than one might have made without such strenuous effort. Although maverick principals have, for example, created exemplary schools with the help of foundations that claim positions on the Right, Left, and Center, large urban school systems remain plagued by many of the same root social ills that confronted reformers fifty or even a hundred years ago.

Consider, for example, Walter Annenberg's unprecedented $500 million grant to improve public education, which seems also to have left few traces in the sands. Annenberg self-consciously styled his philanthropy on that of Andrew Carnegie and John D. Rockefeller. He left his descendents a one-page statement of his philosophy that echoed what Carnegie and Rockefeller before him had stated: "no scattershot philanthropy" and focus on projects that will have a big impact on "the essentials" (Ogden, 1999, p. 550). When he was asked about his gift to public education, Annenberg explained that he was afraid education was breaking down and with it, "civilization." With that in mind he "wanted to startle our leaders and public and get their attention. I wanted to elevate precollegiate education as a national priority. To do that I felt I had to drop a bomb. It was my responsibility as a citizen" (quoted in Ogden, 1999, p. 539).

Consider also the rather sad example of Andrew Carnegie. Many of the institutions Carnegie founded were intended to promote peace. Even more than helping people to improve themselves, that was the motivating force behind much of his extraordinary giving. Ever an optimist, Carnegie seems for a time to have really been convinced that directly through institutions like the International Court of Justice at The Hague and indirectly through the building of libraries, which would allow the masses to enlighten themselves, the world was moving toward a state of peace.

Then World War I broke out, and Carnegie fell into a deep state of melancholy from which he never recovered. "Men slaying each other like beasts," he wrote in August 1914 (quoted in Lagemann, 1989, pp. 24–25). He died in 1917—the same year the United States declared war on Germany and began requiring its young men to register for the draft. Would Carnegie have judged his philanthropy a success? Even though we cannot know for certain, the evidence suggests that at the end of his life, he did not think he had succeeded.

And what of the faith in the social and behavioral sciences so evident in foundations during the era of "strategic philanthropy"? Certainly, the social and behavioral sciences grew, thanks to foundation largesse. Many more scholars are engaged in these fields; some, notably economists, have developed fieldwide paradigms and standards that have influenced the study of many social activities, including health, education, and the environment. Despite this progress, one would be hard-pressed to maintain that the social and behavioral sciences have helped create the national unity and international peace that the post–World War II philanthropists were so urgently seeking. With the United States starkly divided between "red" and "blue" states and wars raging in Iraq, the Middle East, and Africa, it is easy to believe that post–World War II philanthropy failed.

Finally, that brings us to the efforts of the "movement philanthropists" and what one might suggest they have accomplished. In the field of education, they have propelled voucher experiments, charter schools, and efforts to establish a traditional core curriculum. At the college level, they have funded programs in law and economics, the Federalist Society, and a variety of programs designed to nurture young conservative leaders. Nevertheless, while movement philanthropists may claim some responsibility for the Reagan Revolution, they, too, have found that when it comes to tackling root problems like poverty and illiteracy, silver-bullet solutions remain elusive.

If our analysis is correct, the puzzle for philanthropists is, *What is to be done?* Should we give up on trying to eradicate poverty, ill health, and illiteracy? Certainly not. The conclusion of our argument is not that we should stop trying to use money to do good in the world. What we do suggest is that we try to better understand why some grants have huge impact and others do not and then build on that understanding to develop somewhat less millennial hopes and dreams.

We believe that the success of philanthropy depends on both internal research, thought, and planning—the kind of thinking Gardner described so well as "strategic"—and external circumstances over which one may have absolutely no control. The Myrdal study became a classic for all sorts of reasons that had nothing to do with the original intentions of its sponsors. Matters of timing and fit with the prevailing climate of opinion have at least as much to do with the impact of a grant as careful planning and implementation.

A Nation at Risk achieved its goals and had a huge effect on American perceptions about education. However, it is important to remember that this was largely due to the alarmist tone in which it was written, along with a series of unforeseen events. It just so happened that for a week or so after *A Nation at Risk* appeared, other groups who had been studying education also reported. These reports, now forgotten, created a drumbeat that reinforced the message of *A Nation at Risk*. Then there was the famous Rose Garden press conference at which President Ronald Reagan claimed that *A Nation at Risk* endorsed the closing of the Department of Education and other initiatives he favored. The report, of course, said nothing about closing the Department of Education, which journalists knew because they had copies of the report. The discrepancy piqued their interest, and coverage of *A Nation at Risk* intensified.

Understanding the inevitable uncertainties of attempting to spend money purposefully to improve the world may encourage more humility than seems to be in vogue at the current moment among new philanthropists. And with that may come recognition that effective philanthropy must combine centralized and localized initiatives—the art lying in constantly trying to develop the right mix and balance between the two. The Annenberg Challenge was an example of the combination we urge. It involved both central initiation and the creation of "intermediary" agencies in New York, Chicago, San Francisco, and the other locations involved in the Challenge.

In her chapter in this book, Barbara Cervone analyzes the Challenge, tracing its history from the grant made by Ambassador Annenberg through efforts to evaluate local reforms. We believe the Challenge not only exemplifies the mix we think most effective but also supports our repeated call to continue developing more and better methods of program evaluation. We are further encouraged by some of the social-entrepreneurial grantmaking in education, including the recent $100 million grant to Tufts University by the Omidyars; the program is designed to spur global microfinance, as well as to assist the university.

More humble and realistic expectations for what philanthropy can achieve may also encourage philanthropists to realize that the big problems we face in this country and around the world will not be solved easily or overnight. Take education as an example. The challenges we face in education in the United States are related to the fact that our expectations have changed. Whereas it was once deemed sufficient to offer all children equal educational opportunities, it is now expected that all children will actually achieve at high levels. The burden has shifted from the learner to the teacher. This is a huge shift and is unprecedented in history. It is an appropriate shift for a nation that remains, at least for now, the wealthiest and most powerful in the world. But rather than beat ourselves for failing to achieve our new and higher goals, we would do better to realize that we are going to have to work steadily to improve education over many decades.

The greyhound of our ambitions will probably always exceed our capacity to keep up. That is not to say that we should not work determinedly to ensure that every child in school today is well served. Rather, it is to say that philanthropy that stays the course, that picks a direction and aims at it over a long period of time, is likely to be more effective than philanthropy that targets a goal and expects to achieve it in relatively short order. We hope our recollection of similarities between past and present can contribute to that effort.

NOTES

1. These numbers are based on foundations that either held $1 million in assets or that gave grants of $100,000 or more (Frumkin, 2002, p. 112).

2. A complete transcript of the debate between William Jennings Bryan and Clarence Darrow from the Scopes trial is online at the Center for History and New Media (http://chnm.gmu.edu/courses/hist409/scopes.html).

3. For a full account of the Myrdal study, see Lagemann, 1989, pp. 123–146.

4. See, for example, Dowie and Frumkin. See also de Forest, "The Rise of Conservatism on Campus: The Role of the John M. Olin Foundation," *Change*, 2006, *38*(2), 32–37.

5. Political scientist Andrew Rich found that, in 1996, 45.4 percent of think tanks could be classified as non-ideological, while all others were clearly identifiable as conservative or liberal (Rich, 2004, pp. 20–21).

REFERENCES

Curti, M. "The History of American Philanthropy as a Field of Research." *American Historical Review,* 1957, 62(2), 352–363.

De Forest, J. "The Rise of Conservatism on Campus: The Role of the John M. Olin Foundation." *Change,* 2006, *38*(2), 32–37.

Dowie, M. *American Foundations: An Investigative History.* Cambridge, Mass.: The MIT Press, 2001.

Dzuback, M. A. "Creative Financing in Social Science: Women Scholars and Early Research." In A. Walton (ed.), *Women and Philanthropy in Education.* Bloomington: Indiana University Press, 2005, 105–126.

Frumkin, P. "Private Foundations as Public Institutions." In E. C. Lagemann (ed.), *Philanthropic Foundations: New Scholarship, New Possibilities.* Bloomington: Indiana University Press, 1999, pp. 69–98.

Frumkin, P. *On Being Nonprofit: A Conceptual and Policy Primer.* Cambridge, Mass.: Harvard University Press, 2002.

Glenn, J., Brandt, L., and Andrews, F. E. *Russell Sage Foundation, 1907–1946.* Vol. 2. New York: Russell Sage, 1947.

Hammack, D. C. "Foundation in the American Polity, 1900–1950." In E. C. Lagemann (ed.), *Philanthropic Foundations: New Scholarship, New Possibilities.* Bloomington: Indiana University Press, 1999.

Lagemann, E. C. *Private Power for the Public Good: A History of The Carnegie Foundation for the Advancement of Teaching.* Middletown, Conn.: Wesleyan University Press, 1983.

Lagemann, E. C. *The Politics of Knowledge: The Carnegie Corporation, Philanthropy, and Public Policy.* Middletown, Conn.: Wesleyan University Press, 1989.

Lagemann, E. C. *An Elusive Science: The Troubling History of Education Research.* Chicago: University of Chicago Press, 1990.

Lathram, L. "The Radical Philanthropist" (Forbes.com), Aug. 14, 2004.

Miller, J. "Goodbye, Mr. Olin: When Conservative Funds Dry Up." *National Review,* June 11, 2001.

Ogden, C. *Legacy: A Biography of Moses and Walter Annenberg.* Boston: Little, Brown, 1999.

Rich, A. *Think Tanks, Public Policy, and the Politics of Expertise.* New York: Cambridge University Press, 2004.

Smith, J. A. *The Idea Brokers: Think Tanks and the Rise of the New Policy Elite.* New York: The Free Press, 1991.

Smith, R. "Muscular Philanthropy." *Education Week,* Feb. 11, 2004, 26.

Wallas, G. *The Great Society: A Psychological Analysis.* New York: Macmillan, 1914.

Walton, A. *Women and Philanthropy in Education.* Bloomington: Indiana University Press, 2005.

Wiebe, R. H. *The Search for Order, 1877–1920.* New York: Hill & Wang, 1967.

PART TWO

K–12 AND FOUNDATIONS

Chapter Four Overview

The authors of this chapter examine the reasons for the often below-par effectiveness of foundation grants in K–12 and how those grants might be strengthened. For five decades a substantial group of ambitious foundations has attempted to have an impact in improving public schools, especially those serving low-income students. Because aspirations for a grant and project are usually easy to articulate and justify, they often gather most of the publicity. The results, however, are tangled in the complexities of real schools, attenuated by the competing demands on teachers and administrators, and often obscured by the absence of credible research. Foundation funds, as a consequence, often find themselves in the service of repeating work that had its fifteen minutes of fame and then faded.

Ted Lobman served the Stuart Foundation as president for many years. Ray Bacchetti previously directed the education program of The William and Flora Hewlett Foundation. Both foundations have a strong presence in California, as well as influence beyond that state, and both share the systemic reform goals frequently found in the kinds of foundations that are the subject of this book.

This chapter describes *where* educational capital can be built, as well as *how* it can be built. Citing as examples many foundation-sponsored programs that reflect the characteristics of educational capital, the authors discuss how to improve the prospects for producing educational capital. Their primary emphasis, however, is on future efforts to increase the effectiveness, and therefore the value, of foundation investments so that they produce a stream of payoffs to the field. Following this analysis, they offer recommendations to that end.

4

INCREASING FOUNDATION IMPACT BY BUILDING EDUCATIONAL CAPITAL

Theodore Lobman and Ray Bacchetti

FOR MORE THAN FORTY YEARS, a growing number of foundations have tried to improve public education in fundamental ways and on a large scale. Their principal but not exclusive target has been the performance of low-income students and the effectiveness of the educational and other services they receive. Among thousands of foundations that at least occasionally support public education–related projects, about two hundred are distinguished by the ambition of their goals, as well as the planning, financial, and other efforts that support them.[1] Most foundations and other donors temporarily subsidize helpful services for relatively few students or teachers. The most ambitious donors intend to help *solve* major, widespread, systemic problems. Words like *reform, systems change,* and *strategic* commonly appear in their internal and public documents.

We believe that these foundations would be more likely to obtain such impact if they focused more on the interdependence among their diverse strategies and worked harder to build on past learning and help others build on what their grantees have done. We call this "capital building," partly to convey meaning (creating assets that produce compound returns over time) and partly to distinguish it within the broader concepts of *leverage* and *high impact* that guide the most ambitious foundations today. Capital building requires more than cooperative grantmaking, which usually means making co-investments in the same projects or organizations, often minimally coordinated. To accumulate what counts as capital faster, foundations will have to redefine themselves less as individual agents and more as long-term, strategic partners. Here we make our case for capital building, as well as the easy and difficult strategic and operational shifts required to do it well.

The Effectiveness Challenge

Seeking fundamental and large-scale improvements is a foundation role defined and polished in the late 1960s and 1970s. That is when government seemed to answer almost every call to enter need areas traditionally supported by philanthropy and was expected to respond when philanthropy identified important problems and promising solutions. Then, as now, observers and some prominent foundation executives argued to great effect that grant strategies should be based on foundations' unique advantages: independence, flexibility, and financial security from endowment. They should build specific competence to support innovations and advocate for improvements that government would find politically too difficult and other donors too abstract, complex, or costly. Let public agencies, with their resources and bureaucratic distribution capacity, assume responsibility for policies and practices to serve the general public welfare. Foundations, by contrast, should be "society's venture capitalists" or, more energetically, "society's passing gear."[2]

Foundations' K–12 education budgets are small compared to the difficulty and size of problems they target and institutions they mean to influence. Although some foundations spend millions annually, they rarely support operations in schools or districts where such amounts would be "real money." As their role is to stimulate and to "seed," they do not want to tie up staff or money with ongoing obligations. So they typically fund restricted, time-limited projects in sometimes-renewable grants of five years or fewer. Grantees are mainly large districts or intermediary organizations (associations, technical assistance vendors, and the like) that serve many schools. The most common grant purposes are designing, installing, and testing innovations in policy and practice, along with promoting dissemination when results are judged favorable. The opinion environment is crucial to the fate of innovations in policy and practice, so these foundations also support advocacy and constituency building to change philosophical, as well as political and economic, priorities in schools and systems.

For their goals to seem realistic (to grantees as well as themselves), their strategies must have what they usually call leverage, meaning at least some of their investments must produce the disproportionate returns required of venture capital. Success requires first that proposals are implemented properly, by attracting support from others, as well as the grantee. Next, any improvements must outlast the grant or in some other way be useful to the grantee and its constituents over time; donors often call this result sustainability. Finally, the work must create other benefits over time and across the educational system.

Such ripple effects—tangible if not precisely measurable—are the most satisfying. They are also usually beyond grantees' reach and therefore are the most uncertain. Fundamental changes in priorities, policies, and practices always face heavy competition, if not resistance. Foundations can temporarily change grantee behavior and obtain favorable publicity and nearby policy support. However, once their (or their grantee's) finger lifts, the balloon may begin to resume its original shape.

Sustainability and ripple effects require not just temporary money, champions, programs, and existence proofs; they depend on a high level of understanding, agreement, and informed support by educators, legislators, elites, parents, and public. These groups have widely differing values and needs. Tolerance, let alone commitment to change, requires validation by immediate, practical experience. Rising test scores is one such experience that is obviously meaningful to much of the public; others are that students' eyes light up and stay lit, administrators feel efficacious and appreciated, and budgeteers are confident that costs are covered. The point is that innovations and the sacrifices to get them persist because they work every day at the front line and make sense to those just behind it. Quality implementation, publicity—even student achievement gains—are only interim indicators of progress on systems change. The brass ring is broad consensus that the change is desirable, feasible, and worth the costs, or as business people might say, "ideas with legs."

The ideas that foundations have backed have usually had legs, just not strong ones. Grantmakers must be and are an optimistic group; they usually get applause as they present their new program designs and grants to boards for approval and to the public, once approved. They are typically satisfied with grantees' efforts—their program designs, behavior as promised, and near-term results. For example, foundations have been central in recent movements to increase priority given to teaching and school leadership; increasing parent involvement and school choice; closing race- and class-based achievement gaps; providing social, health, and youth development services, and, arguably the most initially powerful, establishing achievement standards and high-stakes tests to measure them.

One will not find many donors who believe the end is in sight, however. In general, foundations have been better at promoting reform concepts and

sustaining reformers' energy than obtaining durable and broadly implemented, practical improvements that satisfy the demands the public has
made on schools, including expectations they themselves have generated.
Most grantmakers we spoke with privately are frustrated with the progress
on the systemic problems targeted by their strategies. Grantees, researchers,
and others familiar with foundations offer a fairly consistent judgment that
grantmaking effects are very often temporary and confined to a few
schools, districts, and education support organizations rather than rippling,
as expected, beyond them.[3] As one board member said candidly, "The program officers say our grants are great, but the system never gets better.
Why should we keep doing this?"

The goals just described and many others, such as literacy and preparation for success in college, are all far from being met. Even the victories
in promoting equity in school finance that owe heavily to Ford Foundation grants in the 1970s have been undermined by concentration of low-
income families in urban schools and school fundraising in the suburbs.
Doubts about whether urban schools would really improve if given significantly more money have been a drag on taxpayer and legislator willingness to spend more.

Three major education donors—the Edna McConnell Clark Foundation, The Pew Charitable Trusts, and The Atlantic Philanthropies—have
left the K–12 field (although other large foundations such as Gates and
Broad have entered). Many donors now support voucher programs to
reduce, if not remove, government from public education, except as a funder. Others such as the Danforth Foundation and Lilly Endowment have
shrunk from national purposes in favor of responding to more immediate and local needs. Many have shifted strategies, not because they felt
they had succeeded but because the board or new staff wanted to try
something different and, they hoped, more effective.

Much of the disappointment in ambitious grant strategies is a dual failure: (1) failure to build on existing knowledge, skills, and consensus and
(2) failure to attract and enable others to keep building. Foundations
would likely be more effective if they paid more attention to the interdependence of their goals and strategies and if they saw themselves as long-
term strategic partners solving mutually important problems rather than
as independent agents that cooperate inconsistently. Increased cooperation for greater accumulation effects requires revising traditional self-
centered attitudes about impact and how to get it. To explain and justify
such a difficult task, we turn first to the concept of *educational capital*,
which was introduced in Chapter Two of this volume.

Building Educational Capital

Educational capital consists of experience, knowledge, competence, values, attitudes and norms, and other social factors that determine what educators do with children and with what effect. Capital in education stands behind and shapes and guides the work of schools. Capital builds as these factors are validated, that is, proven feasible and beneficial compared to alternatives, among educators and other constituents in the education system. The durability and spread of reform—foundations' ambition— depends on the accumulation of capital, a process that is rarely linear and rarely attributable to single actors.

Five Criteria for Building Educational Capital

Imagine that you are a program officer in a relatively large foundation that wants to improve the writing of elementary school children. You have read news articles, op-ed pieces, and letters to editors expressing (mostly) anger, frustration, and even anguish over a future in which much adult writing from today's students will be clumsy, drab, and wooly. You know that writing is vital and difficult to teach well and that it is particularly important for the academic, social, and economic upward mobility of students. You also know several things about the potential to improve student learning in this area. For example:

○ There is a good deal of well-developed theory, pedagogy, and educational material about elementary school writing.

○ Some of what has been developed appears effective across ethnic, economic, and geographic differences.

○ Writing is assessable, thus improving it can be evidence-driven.

You also know that writing is often assigned rather than taught, that many collateral skills and attitudes affect writing (such as being fluent with ideas, confident enough to experiment, able to imagine and to distinguish clarity from well-intentioned mush), that many teachers are not (and do not consider themselves to be) good writers, and that the main genres (such as informational writing, memoir, poetry, reports, and narrative) require different skills and mind-sets. (In the writing example illustrating the five criteria, the authors have drawn on the exemplary program, Every Child a Reader and Writer, of the Noyce Foundation [www.noycefdn.org].)

The challenge in this example is to design a foundation initiative to build on what is known and to improve upon, organize, and accumulate the knowledge and skills necessary to create a more productive asset—a program for teaching and learning to write in elementary school—that will then be used properly and with predictable, favorable effect in many schools. Our program officer's grantmaking strategy should meet five criteria, in order to provide the best chance of building educational capital (these criteria are also described in Chapter Two). The officer's strategy is examined in the sections to follow.

GROUND THE WORK. Few advances in education are truly unique and independent of others. Rather, they represent accumulations of improvements on available knowledge and experience, adding needed elements (which may be innovative) and arranging the whole in a more potent way. To build capital, then, one needs to (1) critically appraise what is known— in this instance, the well-developed body of knowledge about teaching writing that was developed by Lucy Calkins and her colleagues at Teachers College, Columbia University, and comparably rich programs; (2) look at what has been done by exemplary teachers and examine the challenges to program development and spread—for example, in teacher training, policy priorities, and curricula availability, especially for English learners, then, (3) determine where and what to build, for example, confirming or challenging existing knowledge or bringing new knowledge to an underdeveloped segment of a writing program (Calkins, 1994).

Grounding invites questions: If enough good work has not been done, what is missing? If solid conceptual and strategic work has been done, what is holding back broader application? If research results do not find their way into practice, why not? And if perfectly good alternatives already exist, why not urge school districts to use them instead of encourage districts to seek foundation help to reinvent them?

Then it is time to develop the rationale. How would further work in writing advance teaching and learning in ways that many could use? What kind of program could combine the best of current knowledge with ideas that add pedagogical power to teaching, for example, by integrating in new ways the skills of self-expression, imagination, and grammar, as well as the ability to edit for clarity and revise for impact, understand genres, and read to discern a writer's intentions and techniques and to learn from them?

Skirting the groundwork stage—or treating it as an occasion for citing research rather than drawing shrewdly on it—leads to undemanding and unhelpful grant guidelines that, in turn, unintentionally facilitate superficial proposals. Without groundwork on the part of the foundation, it will not know how to tell which proposals are most likely to produce the most capital. Without groundwork on the part of the applicant, one approach can look as good as another; grounding increases the likelihood that a design will work better. Local donors can help schools use capital, but that seems a lesser use of ambitious foundation resources; there are so many technical weaknesses to be overcome, gaps to be filled, and promising new ideas to be incorporated in existing curricula and other school routines. As the foundation lays out its program and its predicates, the field gets more material to work with. The applicant not only feels the incentive to act but learns of promising directions and how to compete for support to follow them effectively.

IDENTIFY THE NON-NEGOTIABLE CORE. Strategies and skills to improve learning must function faithfully to the concepts from which they come and to each other. For a program or strategy to deserve capital status, it will have identified the core of interdependent elements that produce the intended results. Though a common tendency among teachers is to choose aspects of programs and incorporate them into their existing instructional repertoires, such adaptations often corrupt the program's logic and thus sap its power. One finds evidence of this concern frequently in reports assessing multischool trials of a complex program: they distinguish between the trials that were faithful to the program's design and those that strayed. Findings from the former can then be taken seriously; findings from the latter tend to be confused and inconsistent because implementation has confounded the causal synergy among variables. For change to happen, execution must use the right tools in the right relationship.

When the non-negotiables are in place, their sibling—generalizability—is also present. The hallmark of ambitious, high-leverage foundation philanthropy is the power of effective work to travel over meaningful subdivisions of the school district universe. For grant investments to pay off, they must produce capital that is interesting, credible, and, most important, usable and used by others. Effectiveness and applicability require, therefore, that the core capital elements leave room for teacher judgment and adaptations. One "size" of educational capital does not fit all. "Theme and variations" is more to the point. The goal of teaching and learning writing—ultimately aimed at enabling students to think the way accomplished writers do—is to capitalize on the well-developed and integrated core elements leading to successful writing: shrewd attention to student backgrounds, teachers' imagination and experience, and the potential for writing to enhance students' expressive abilities and writing in various subject matter areas, across the several genres and through time.

Because teachers are more often well read than they are confident writers, many begin writing programs unsure of their own knowledge and skill. Just as one need not be a horse to be a veterinarian, a teacher need not be a writer to teach writing. Indeed, a teacher's own struggle with writing often makes her or him a more empathetic and thus, when supported by proper materials and training, a more capable and credible-to-her-students teacher of writing. One of the capital-creating aspects of a writing program, then, will be ways of teaching teachers to teach writing, such as understanding the overall framework into which the parts (such as the writer's workshop, genres, revisions, the author's chair) fit, grasping the modal learning trajectories that children at certain grade levels follow, merging student imaginative potential with academic standards, and in other ways being faithful to the design of the program while adding the touch of their own experience and familiarity with their students.

ENSURE STAYING POWER. Durability requires that innovations are properly implemented and, if successful, that the grantee provides an adequate level of support after the foundation support ends. Threats to staying power include individual and organizational resistance, teacher and administrator turnover (which is often highest in the neediest schools), and unstable district or state policies that affect time and priorities for professional development and classroom work. Without what students of organizational behavior refer to (positively) as slack—in this case, the time and opportunity to reflect, experiment, and plan—teachers' preparation for change is inadequate, innovations are not implemented well, and cynicism about improvement builds. A foundation program and the hopeful proposals it generates must acknowledge these obstacles and include a strategy for stability and continuity where the forces of slow-motion disintegration might otherwise prevail. The foundation's time frame must also acknowledge the obstacles.

Foundation guidelines for building capital with respect to student writing, for example, should require grantseekers to show how they will preserve continuity when teachers leave (such as through new-teacher orientation and coaching), build in time to use data diagnostically to improve practices, or build a peer community in a school or across a district to provide support in taking risks to adapt and creatively contribute to continuous program improvement. Incentives are crucial as well. Chief among them is the student learning that results. In our experience, nothing enlists teachers in change better than increased student learning and the pleasure and confidence it produces. The role of the district in supporting individual schools' writing programs and in developing the necessary organizational skills for enabling teacher and student are also aspects in proposals deserving serious attention.

BUILD IN APPROPRIATE ASSESSMENT AT EVERY STAGE. If results cannot be confirmed and replicated, the effort does not create capital. Assessment settles differences between "this ought to work" and "this is what did (or did not) work." The kind of hard evidence represented by random field trials and rigorous statistical analysis has great value. So, too, do softer forms such as systematic examination by qualified observers. They can build capital in areas such as practices based on values (for example, civic skill) that are reflected in school and classroom structure (such as age-appropriate student participation in decision making) and that show up in behavioral norms (for example, mutual respect). When validated, they can also count as capital. Such assessment may be supplemented by pencil-and-paper instruments, such as school climate surveys, but assessment should not be limited to surveys and objective tests.

To build educational capital, two kinds of assessment are helpful. One is tools that help ensure efficacy while a program is still being developed, that is, *formative* assessment—tracking and revising practice over time by steady evaluation and feedback. The other, *summative* assessment, lets us know if the claim of benefits is true—if the practice does what it says it does. It has many varieties. The gold standard—random assignment studies—stands at the head of a lineup of other types of quantitative and qualitative research. Each of these, practiced at the highest levels of care that the subject matter and classroom conditions allow, can improve the value and functionality of the initiative and helps certify new educational capital.

To become writerly in one's approach to writing—to understand and effectively use the qualities of good writing, that is, to think and work like a writer—requires that the assessment be integrated into the learning. Self-criticism is important, as is looking for just the right word and not resting until it appears, alternating sentence or paragraph structure to get the effect one wants, asking for feedback from others, and trying something new. In these and other writerly behaviors, evaluation takes many forms and occupies many pedagogical spaces, including those inside the student.

ENCOURAGE CONNECTIONS. Schools are organic wholes, and individual elements of capital function interdependently. Teacher professional development helps extract maximum value from the curriculum; school leadership requires district support for principals to be able to function as instructional leaders; and policies need to align with educational objectives if the policies are not to consume energy wastefully and derail commitments. The absence of these and other deliberate complementary connections undermines claims to be building educational capital.

In a writing program, the art and craft of writing as an expository or interpretive tool sends tendrils into the rest of the curriculum, upward through the grades, and out into the student's repertoire of talents and skills. Writing can spill into fourth-grade social studies via a paper on the Spanish influence in early California or into fifth-grade science in an analysis of the relation of binocular vision to food-getting behavior in animals. The skills acquired in elementary school need to be built upon and expanded in middle and high school. The student ideally internalizes both writerly skills and drives, using writing as a means of making her or his way in the world. For these things to happen well and consistently, capital elements must integrate with each other and with the school context.

Framing a Capital-Building Program

If the hypothetical foundation funded and followed through on an elementary-grades writing program according to the five criteria, it and the school district would at the end have the substance of a capital product. That substance would consist in a documented design and operating instructions for a program of proven efficacy in teaching K–5 students to write well. But let us step back to a time before such a foundation program objective gets developed, funded, and tested: What would it mean for a foundation to think in advance about how to frame a capital-building grantmaking program? How would it differ from what a thoughtful and experienced foundation does now? Where would one look for the influence of the five criteria on how the foundation came to this strategic priority?

One answer will, of course, depend on the expertise in its people and its style—in other words, the degree to which it is a learning organization. Nevertheless, we would expect to see influences such as these. First, the foundation would offer a commentary on the topic: what is known about it, why the foundation has given it a priority, and what it hopes its program will accomplish (expressed in educational-capital terms). Second, its guidelines would reflect the five criteria in terms appropriate to the topic and to the schools and districts toward which the program is directed. Finally, such thinking about capital building would influence the role of evaluation as both a steering and a validating tool, as well as how the grantmaker sees and acts on the potential for building on what has been accomplished, either alone or in concert with others.

At the end of the project, then, the challenge would be to document the program and put it into broader circulation, either to supply those already demanding improved writing or to create demand among those districts whose students are performing poorly in writing. Because even good ideas don't travel naturally from source to user, much of this challenge would fall to the foundation to make the existence of this new educational capital known and access to it easy. The district could continue as a demonstration and training center in a dissemination strategy. The foundation could have available to it intermediary organizations, public agencies (for example, county or regional offices of education), or the development of its own capacity to propagate the program. Whichever entity took this responsibility, it would in the process deepen and extend its own expertise and thus acquire some of the capital value of the program.

Where Foundations Can Build Educational Capital: Key Areas of Public Education

In our extended example of elementary school writing to illustrate the five criteria of educational capital, we used a project especially suited to our purpose. School improvement opportunities, however, do not often come so neatly packaged. Schools, whatever else they may be, are complex and demanding places requiring strength across many areas of personal, professional, and organizational capacity. Each component affects the others, and making changed parts into a changed whole will happen more reliably when parts are approached from a capital-building perspective.

Next, we look at eight substantive areas that depend on educational capital. These are the heart of school capacity and both internal and external interrelationships (about which Thomas Hatch has written cogently in Chapter Seven). These areas and the relationships among them are where foundations and K–12 grantees should and often do work together. We have framed these areas with their interactivity in mind and offer examples of projects that have built, or could lead to building, educational capital.

TEACHER PROFESSIONALISM. Teacher professionalism means *building, and building on, the characteristics that make teaching a more solidly professional undertaking by enhancing existing and developing new practices, skills, and aspirations that are the sources and stimuli of effective teaching and educational leadership.*

The range of opportunity is wide and includes improving teacher-preparation programs, strengthening tools for self-assessment and collective quality control, and providing career-long educational development. One capital-building project is the National Board of Professional Teaching Standards (NBPTS), which has developed high and rigorous standards for what accomplished teachers should know and be able to do and provides a national voluntary system for certifying teachers who meet those standards.[4] Another example is the work of the New Teacher Center, which is based at the University of California, Santa Cruz; the center developed locally and is expanding nationally a program of support for beginning teachers that enhances retention by building skills and confidence in the early stages of a teaching career.[5] These and similar efforts develop and confirm the elements of a profession that can be self-improving and merit the regard of the public.

When agencies such as these make substantive contributions to the means and ends of teaching, they also provide models for use by smaller foundations and at individual districts and schools, as well as in teacher training, where teaching careers begin. For example, the process for NBPTS certification enables local foundations to sponsor teachers engaged in that process and to work with districts to make effective use of the certified individuals. Turning those NBPTS standards into frameworks for teacher education would be another way of creating educational capital. It could make teaching an attractive challenge to more of the most capable undergraduates. In teacher development and elsewhere, the presence of educational capital can assist local foundations in making their work—when it reflects these more fully developed, validated, and documented efforts—more sophisticated and productive than it would otherwise likely be.

CURRICULUM. The area of curriculum refers to *ways of creating, selecting, ordering, and presenting material to students that are demonstrably effective, that transcend particular schools, and that are amenable to customizing by teachers, using their experience and judgment on how best to engage individual students.*

Curricular capital formation combines content and pedagogy with testable designs. Examples include the work of E. D. Hirsch Jr., founder of the Core Knowledge Foundation and advocate of the "coherent curriculum," in which students in elementary school acquire broad general knowledge as a basis for applying higher-order skills such as critical thinking, problem solving, and the like.[6] The work of Theodore Sizer's Coalition of Essential Schools—a whole-school reform design—is based on a set of ten "Common Principles," including learning to use one's mind well, the personalization of learning, and depth of coverage of subject matter rather than breadth for its own sake.[7] The coalition presents an alternative to more subject-matter-centered and structured programs. Science curricula developed by the National Science Foundation and by regional and often university-affiliated or independent science centers add to this list. The reader familiar with these and similar examples will also note that some are, or should be, validated in whole or in appropriate parts by research. Other validating elements, such as philosophical underpinnings or attitudes and beliefs about the relation of schooling to democracy or social justice, should, if they are to count as capital, rest on well-developed rationales that can stand up to public scrutiny and challenge. But all capital building does not have to be an exercise in forging consensus, though it can often move in that direction. When educators look deeply enough into each others' work to come upon practices worth adapting and issues worthy of joint study, the potential to build educational capital is considerably enhanced.

PEDAGOGY. The area of pedagogy refers to *ways of training teachers and expanding the craft of teaching that add to their repertoires elements that help them unpack and deepen skills, continuously learn new ones, and be able to reach all their students effectively.*

Although teacher professionalism extends to the unified whole of teaching, pedagogy is a particular teacher competency. Some of what appears to happen under this rubric, such as paying teachers to attend a Saturday-morning workshop on diversity, learning disabilities, or the use of computers, does not make the cut as capital. In contrast to this drive-by brush with ideas, when genuine educational capital is developed in pedagogy, long-term change and a deeper understanding of rationale and strategy are its hallmarks.

Examples include problem-based learning and the elements of critical thinking it engenders, various aspects of technology that develop skills in self-directed learning, and methods developed to take pedagogical advantage of small groups and of small schools. The work of the late Elizabeth Cohen on complex instruction shows how rich group work can be and how to deconstruct and recombine its elements to advance heterogeneous grouping, intellectual and social learning, and student efficacy.[8] Effectively merging pedagogy that presents subject matter with techniques that motivate and otherwise engage students in learning is, of course, at the center of good teaching. When it also accomplishes other objectives (as when classroom management becomes integral to an instructional strategy rather than an imposed structure), efficiency and effectiveness can be merged, creating an especially good foundation investment.

ORGANIZATIONAL ALIGNMENT. Organizational alignment refers to the *means for putting the system in the service of the classroom so that the environment of teaching and learning is conducive to both teachers and students doing their best work.*

Theater companies are distinctive in the degree to which all participants, from the box office to costume designers to scenic designers and directors and actors, know that it is the work on the stage that ultimately counts. Examples of activities attuned to making classrooms the critical stage on which all the backstage efforts eventually pay off are these: (1) leadership programs whose content develops new models or amplifies old ones (for example, helping principals learn the skills of instructional leadership and working with superintendents to clear an administrative path for them to practice those skills); (2) efforts to define, implement, assess, and refine learning communities in schools and districts where better ideas and practices travel, where educators provide professional help to each other, and where performance data and other forms of high-value information comprise much of the content of professional conversations; and (3) programs to develop teacher-leaders, equipping them to play farther-reaching roles in their schools and districts.

A leading example is the Broad Foundation's Superintendents Academy, which brings together corporate CEOs, government officials, nonprofit executives, and educators to build competence in prospective educational executives across topics such as planning, organizational leadership, student achievement, reinventing schools, and data-based decision making.[9]

Organizational alignment and policy are not usually the causes of improved learning but the conditions that support those causes. When, in 1996–97, California rushed to reduce class size in grades K–3, very little was done to help teachers learn and use instructional strategies that could capitalize on a setting of twenty students rather than thirty. Little improvement in learning has been attributed to that costly move (estimates vary between $1.2 and $1.6 billion). Conditions were confused with causes, and the capital-building and capital-using opportunities that small classes presented were largely squandered, at least in the short term.

SOCIAL CAPITAL. Social capital refers to *the factors that create trust, reciprocity, responsibility, and other qualities of community within and among school constituents.*

Although views on the implications vary greatly, no educator or parent fails to understand that schools are systems in which instruction and learning depend partly on social conditions inside and outside the school.

Norms about effort and achievement linked to perceptions of being physically and emotionally safe, cared for, responsible, and trusted are powerful intermediary factors in student and teacher effort—the more so in low-performing schools. The work of the Collaborative for Academic, Social, and Emotional Learning (www.casel.org), for example, promotes building school climate and teacher and student skills to make classrooms more productive than academic emphasis alone is likely to do. By conducting research and developing guides for parents and teachers, it builds educational capital.

Under this broad rubric of social capital, foundations can help educators learn how to improve the social environment in school. This is significant more as means than end, that is, not just for its own sake but for helping illuminate long-standing, controversial arguments about how to motivate students for academic success and promote knowledge, attitudes, and dispositions in preparation for employment, social, and civic roles as adults. The link between educational capital and social capital is shorter than is often imagined. That link has effects on instructional potential by influencing student academic attitudes, engagement, and performance. But it also has effects on correlated concerns such as students' drug, criminal, and sexual behavior, as well as other risk taking. Together, these aspects of the social capital—for example, school climate, mutual respect, caring, character, and the like—continue to be prime candidates for educational capital building. We realize that this is contested territory, but we also believe that all sides in these arguments have a stake and a constructive role to play in developing the practices and the evidence supporting them that acknowledge the many causal factors at work in classrooms that affect the learning taking place there.

POLICY. The area of policy refers to *grants defining and advocating for policies at all levels that support effective and interrelated practice.*

Achieve, Inc., helps "states raise academic standards, improve assessments and strengthen accountability to prepare all young people for postsecondary education, work and citizenship."[10] It needs supporting policies to enable that to happen. The work of the Education Trust gives priority to *equity* in finance and teaching and informs policies designed to that end. The National Center for Teaching and America's Future documents the paramount influence of teacher qualifications on educational outcomes. On regional and local levels, some organizations clarify complex school reform issues (for example, high school redesign or reading controversies). Others educate citizens about school finance, charter schools, English language learners, and the like. Still others publish on the Internet factual information on schools and districts, building a form of capital by equipping citizens to engage in the creation and assessment of educational policy.[11]

Policies can have unintended negative effects, including fragmenting practice when they emphasize competing goals such as developing teacher judgment versus tightly prescribing curriculum delivery. So policies must be monitored. Moreover, larger state and national policies (for example, teacher certification or No Child Left Behind) can become powerful determinants of local options and handcuff, purposefully or not, local boards. There is a special role for foundations in this regard. Education capital building requires cooperation, continuous inquiry and experimenting, and respect for evidence. These increase policy coherence and the beneficial effects on schools it produces. Foundations serve this end by the practices they themselves follow in assessing and funding grants for policy analysis and advocacy. When policy advocates argue and try to settle arguments by arguing harder, the educational capital value of the policies can end up tattered and torn. In such cases, foundations are in a position to repair that value by summoning new evidence, clarifying secondary effects, and expanding an argument from narrow advocacy to broad understanding and thus to influence.

RESEARCH AND RESEARCH TOOLS. This area refers to *projects that develop new knowledge, that extract meaning from other studies (meta-analyses), that assess particular projects, and that develop resources for advancing evaluation of practice.*

Sponsoring research taxes foundation capacity. Some foundations make it a priority and do it well; examples are Spencer and Russell Sage. But most do not typically invest, as do government funding agencies such as the National Institutes of Health and the National Science Foundation, in a peer-review network capable of evaluating research design, investigator capability, and the significance of the issue under study. As a consequence, foundations often settle for a grantee's self-assessment, decline to invest in larger studies with the intellectual depth, scope, and duration to produce noteworthy results, or, in their own grantmaking, pay little attention to how well-predicated on research the proposals they receive may be. Because research is also a cross-cutting element that is influential across teacher professionalism, curriculum, pedagogy, organizational alignment, and policy, foundations are major stakeholders in its improvement, widespread use, and integration into the policy, practice, and professional conversations— their own and those of their grantees—that influence educational improvement. And some foundations, reluctant to let a good idea languish, will pay to repeat the same findings over time in hope that news coverage will finally move the public. This may not build capital, however, until acceptance of evidence reaches a tipping point.

ORGANIZATIONAL LEARNING. Organizational learning means *ways of using and developing educational capital that enable schools, districts, and foundations to become learning organizations with the capacity for continuous improvement.*

A learning organization, according to Peter Senge, is one simultaneously aware of its present and future so that it can be causal in that future rather than the effect of external forces.[12] That is a tantalizing vision for over-regulated, financially strapped, and politically beleaguered school districts or the intermediary organizations that seek to influence and support them. However, because public schools belong, ultimately, to the public, we hold to a more modest vision of learning organizations than one that suggests ultimate control over one's future. We would modify that definition of schools, districts, and foundations that are learning organizations to read: *organizations that are continuously building, using, and refining knowledge to increase student learning.*

The examples of organizations that try on a "learning organization" identity are more frequent than those that establish it over the long run. One that has a long-run perspective is the National Writing Project, about which Ann Lieberman writes in Chapter Eight. A younger effort is that by Springboard Schools in San Francisco—an outgrowth of the Annenberg Challenge—that places "cycle of inquiry" at the center of its work with schools and districts.[13] Foundation efforts to become learning organizations themselves are often interdicted by changes in personnel and strategy. In school districts, external factors such as state and federal policy, student mobility, and budget stringency are formidable counterforces to long-term learning. These challenges do not make organizational learning less significant, just tougher, as Hatch delineates in Chapter Seven.

Improving Prospects for Building Capital

We are humble before the task of diagnosing foundations' effectiveness in K–12, first because there are always exceptions (though we might disagree with some who say "you must not be talking about us") and, second, because information about foundation effort is typically incomplete and filtered. That said, we turn now to challenges in grantmaking to build capital.

Conditions in Public Education

Unlike facilities, most other elements in the education system relevant to instructional outcomes make very difficult improvement targets. Policy, practice, skill, opinion, and social relationships are mutually influential, horizontally and vertically. Teacher competence and attitudes are influenced by training, policy and incentives, administrative and parental pressure, school norms, and peer support. What a teacher does with what effect on whom depends on students: their motivation, social skills, self-confidence, and the incentives they face as influenced by experience with other teachers, classmates, family members, and many others outside school in the past and present. Changing one element may require attention to the others, yet authority over those elements is diffuse, to say the least.

The public education system, albeit with exceptions for some charter and regular schools with extraordinary leadership and staffing, is hardly conducive to innovation or continuous improvement, particularly where low-income students are concerned. Hindrances include intense competition among perceived self-interests, as well as differing philosophical and budget priorities among and within key constituencies. Leadership and staff turnover eliminates memory and disrupts improvement underway. Schools have trouble identifying and reacting to high- and low-quality performance. Inertia and cynicism about reform, again and again, are common among teachers. Although they are growing, resources, staff time, and structures to support learning from experience are still inadequate. There is little capacity to show parents and the public how educators' learning effort improved student performance. Differing perceptions of staffing responsibilities can hinder teamwork. Conflicting views of the purpose of central office data and evaluation departments often pit routine data collection against whatever scientific inquiry might produce.

Improvement means that better practice replaces less effective practice, and effective people gain influence while less effective people lose it. This process has much less institutional support in public education than in many other fields. The growing research base on education, including great advances in understanding brain function and student learning needs, is impressive. Yet long-standing arguments about instructional priorities, methods—and especially spending—persist; advocates move in and out of leadership and board jobs, corroding the sense of confidence, predictability, and community from the local system to federal levels. As David Tyack and Larry Cuban write in their trenchant 1995 book, *Tinkering Toward Utopia,* even those who are close to public education and nearly unconditional in their support for it will concede that priorities are never safe from dispute and have been subject to cycling for more than one hundred years.

Grantmaking to Change Systems

Grantmakers who seek fundamental, sustained, and widespread changes know all that, sometimes through hard lessons. They recognize the importance of systems analysis to choosing goals and strategy. Ambitious foundations have long valued study and planning before launching strategies. They hire program officers, in part, for academic preparation and disposition, and they have budgets for consulting advice, publications, travel to visit their own grantees and exemplary organizations, attend professional meetings, and participate in grantmaker associations. They use "white papers" to justify, define, and budget for grants programs and get advice from educational leaders and other foundations about what problems to select and how to address them. They appreciate the importance of networks for themselves and grantees, and meetings are an important part of their strategies. They require evaluations of grants, and sometimes they evaluate program strategies over many years.

In the 1990s, a wave of systems—economic and other forms of rationalistic thinking—washed over the public and nonprofit sectors, including foundations. Foundations were moved by many factors: the well-publicized innovations in "new philanthropy" undertaken by young entrepreneurs and financiers, the gains made by advocates for privatizing schools through vouchers or through businesses that manage charter schools, the predilections of their own business-based board members and their staffs who, increasingly, had been trained in business or public policy programs. Around them, researchers and policymakers favored education reforms with rationalist attributes such as standards, policy alignment, and incentives that were becoming powerful elements in state and then federal education policy.

Foundations paid high prices for strategic planning and for organizational advisers who sensed a new market. They elevated planning standards, and proposal review became "due diligence." Foundations asked applicants to implement "continuous improvement" processes, using tools such as "theories of action" or "logic models" and did so themselves. More foundations hired evaluation staff to support grantees and increase the objectivity of the evaluation process. Some hired "knowledge managers" and installed network technology to organize and ensure easier staff access to in-house thinking, as well as material from the outside. Many increased spending on communications from Web sites, newsletters, and press releases to support goals and grantees. And they created associations to discuss and promote evaluation and organizational effectiveness.[14]

Systems thinking in grantmaking at the local level required strategies that were "comprehensive," as well as ever more assurance that grantees had put in place all the factors relevant to success. Foundations required intermediary organizations serving large numbers of local schools or educators to select clients only where conditions were favorable or to provide services to make the conditions favorable. They also increased efforts to inform, motivate, and get consensus among policymakers, parents, and the public.

Applicants and grantees found that the number of ducks they were required to line up steadily lengthened as donors tried to reduce failure risks. Experienced grantees felt the declining trust in their ability to deliver, of course, which explains a lot of the tensions in grantmaking relationships discussed in other chapters.

Most foundation people seem pleased with the increased rationalism and rigor in their work, though some regret the burdens on applicants, diminished role for intuition, and some risks.[15] However, it is not clear (even to many insiders) whether they are really getting better results or whether the results just seem better compared to more intuitive and trusting grantmakers. But some benefits seem sure, among them reduced jargon and resulting mistaken assumptions about what terms mean, as well as awareness of unstated or migrating assumptions, expectations, risks, and leaps of logic. Stronger planning promises a higher level of understanding, agreement, and commitment among all constituents of a program or grant and, perhaps, more agreement and satisfaction when grants are completed.

Building capital requires that grant-funded experience be credible and adequately detailed for a variety of audiences and that it be comparable to other relevant experience. We believe that foundations' greater emphasis on planning and learning makes capital building more likely but has a way to go before its full potential to build capital is realized.

In the next sections, we discuss four conditions that limit foundation effectiveness.

FRAGMENTED EFFORT, DELIBERATE AND NOT. As independent actors, foundations contribute to the turmoil of priorities and diluted efforts in public education. Public education is believed to be "crucial" to national defense and economic competitiveness, social cohesion and the sense of social justice, individual economic opportunity, reduction of social and health care costs, and environmental quality. That means any foundation donor, board, or staff member can find some personal philanthropic priority for which the schools are essential. And they do. One after another, they decide to focus on something a little or a lot different from each other as they pursue their own agendas using ever more powerful communication technology and techniques to mobilize pressure.

The reform field has become much more crowded and, notwithstanding the focusing effect of standards and high-stakes testing, more diverse. A large number of foundations and government grant programs independently pursue goals, different and similar, often affecting the same grantees. When grantmakers visit a superintendent whose district they support or a legislator whose support they seek, they seem not to notice when another grantmaker is leaving as they arrive. Donors' diverse goals are sometimes compatible with high standards and testing (for example, in math or literacy), sometimes in competition (for example, promoting subject matter that is not tested), and sometimes outright opposed (such as pedagogical methods thought to develop students' interest in learning but are inefficient in moving test scores). In many cases, even when goals are identical, foundations are competing for school or policymaker attention and resources. Adam Smith would have a hard time seeing a helpful, invisible hand at work under such poor conditions for nurturing innovation and continuous improvement.

Foundations seek niches where they can be leaders. Although grant strategies are typically based on careful white papers that take account of previous and, occasionally, parallel work, foundations usually follow their own stars. Yes, they occasionally cooperate by cofunding the same projects or working in consortia, say, to improve the scale and coherence of grant support in specific districts; sometimes superintendents are disciplined enough to refuse grants that do not fit their master plans. In general, however, foundations whose work is inherently interdependent make little difference to each other except in avoiding duplication.

INSUFFICIENT INFORMATION QUALITY, COMPARABILITY, AND ACCESS. Most of the information that foundation people currently share with each other (and almost all of what is published) is mainly about aspirations—problems that grants are meant to solve and the elegant designs of programs. Foundations are proud of their new strategies and grants; they are glad for publicity that heartens and, perhaps, attracts interest and money to their grantees. It heartens trustees who might have had reservations. And it is said by the Council on Foundations to increase public favor and weaken efforts to regulate or tax the foundation sector. However useful such information is in promoting priorities and grantees or even inspiring other foundations, it is not, by itself, useful for improving effectiveness.

Lack of candor is a problem, particularly with respect to information pertaining to judgments of success or failure. Almost everyone has a current or potential stake in maintaining a donor's good opinion. Strategy or grant evaluation reports are usually written by the foundation or grantee for lay audiences, often without detail that would be useful in capital building. Privately, evaluators say they sometimes filter reports for clients, knowing they will not be subject to rigorous internal review, let alone by peers. Public critique is usually about how foundations make choices (for example, arrogantly or in a herd) or priorities (say, not generally bold enough or no interest in school choice).[16] Those interested in foundation effectiveness are obliged to work from public material, not proposals and foundations' own documents, which are not available.

Cordiality, its benefit to cooperation notwithstanding, inhibits reality testing and other potential boons to effectiveness. Foundation interest in learning is growing, but standards are still generally low. Information on grants and strategies may be sufficient for the donor, but judging from published reports, it often is not good enough for others to believe and use, that is, for building capital. Normal business investment factors are often missing, for example, ex ante success criteria and full (versus grant-only) costs. Objectives and evaluation tools are not often easily comparable to those in past or current efforts with similar goals. Data elements defined for use by grantee and donor are not necessarily subjected to tests of interest and credibility among important audiences. This is not to say published grant and strategy reports are useless; they are just not very powerful. Some foundations subject some of their work to independent process and outcome evaluations, some of which becomes part of credible and influential research literature. We are arguing that in designing objectives and assessment mainly for their own and grantees' needs, donors neglect opportunities to increase the odds that results will have greater impact.

Many foundations offer "lessons" from their work at conferences or sometimes in writing. Standards for such lessons are low, too. "We learned it takes longer than we thought" is a common encouragement for patience that would be more useful with an estimate of how long it should take under favorable circumstances. Vague platitudes often pass for lessons: "You should select grantees carefully" or "you must have the superintendent's support." More interesting would be how to be more careful, what that costs, and how much better the grant results were, or possibly criteria for defining and testing superintendent support. Lessons sometimes simply restate the donor's prior assumptions ("we thought bringing various constituents of the project together to plan would be helpful, and it was"). It would be more valuable to indicate how much better were the results compared to previous grants and how much time, money, and political capital it took to bring people together to secure the benefits. Statements of the characteristics of effective programs are common, but advice on how to get ineffective programs and the people associated with them to do better is not. Lessons would be stronger if donors compared grant designs, process, and results to their own and to others' previous efforts.

OVEREMPHASIZING "GETTING SOMETHING DONE" OR "GETTING RETURNS." It is not surprising that board members, typically with business backgrounds, have different preferences from their well-schooled, expert staff. The strains thus produced can be productive, but sometimes board members' desire for tangibility, measurable progress, and expectation of business-style "returns" show up as a chronic tension, with staff tolerance for ambiguity, patience with complexity, and regard for the educators with whom they work. Such a sustained conflict of expectations can sour the atmosphere when grants or programs are up for renewal. There can be a payoff, however, when the tension can be resolved with respect for both views. Such a resolution is likely to be good for capital building as well.

Measurement problems exacerbate conflicts in expectations. Grants are investments, of course, but using a simple analogy to financial investment invites problems. In education, students' economic status, their attendance record, and their test scores are available and mostly credible and comparable. However, important mediating factors (such as family stability, student motivation, school climate) and outcomes that are important to many audiences (for example, eagerness to accept new learning challenges and skills for working with others) are not. Self-reports, if gathered at all, must substitute for objective assessments. Cost is a major constraint: teachers' opinions of a training program are much cheaper to assess than how the program affected teacher behavior and student response to it. That is why even most commercial training and curriculum products have little or no reliable effectiveness data for customers or donors.

The impulse to get something done ("we want to help kids and know what good our money has done") can short-change efforts to build knowledge. Knowledge building requires high respect for credible research's role in market efficiency; it is also costly, and it invites the pain of reviewing complex evaluation reports where findings are much more likely to be subtle rather than startling and compelling. In the end, though, detailed, credible, comparable documentation of effort and results is what enables a technical innovation or policy change to withstand and eventually erode opposition. Business-minded philanthropists must learn that the school world does not commonly beat a path to the better mousetrap, partly because they do not know about it and partly because they do not believe it is better. Techniques and programs matter, but ideas and the evidence that underlie them matter more.

INDIVIDUALISM AND PRIVACY AS CONSTRAINTS ON CAPITAL BUILDING. The realities in educational systems go a long way to explain foundations' disappointing strategic results; so do their own traditions and predispositions. The foundation sector's tradition of independence and privacy, which is the subject of the editors' recommendation for greater openness in Chapter Two of this volume, needs attention.

The celebrated pluralism in America's philanthropic sector owes much to foundation independence; applicants, especially entrepreneurs, always have "another door to knock on." The belief that competition among entrepreneurs is the best way to obtain societal improvement is deeply rooted in our culture. Moreover, the prospect of approval, not just helping, motivates donors to create foundations in the first place. And individualism and competition play no small role in motivating board members and staff, which is why niche work and the exhortation to "lead" are so compelling. Privacy is not only a right; by protecting foundations from criticism (not necessarily well informed), it encourages them to take risks that government and other donors would not. On the other hand, notwithstanding the high level of integrity, work ethic, and commitment to results that grantees and other observers routinely perceive among grantmakers, resistance to transparency is due, in part, to self-interest.

These benefits are real. So are the costs. Independence and privacy constrain and even diminish foundation effectiveness by discouraging opportunities for joint work on the shared problems that underlie their different goals and exacerbating competition for attention inside the education system. It also denies them the benefit of objective commentary and comparisons that are, presumably, required to make any market efficient.

It is not yet known how much learning is taking place and how much that learning has affected foundation strategies. Whatever the answer, we believe that the inadequate pace of educational improvement justifies foundations making trade-offs in favor of transparency and cooperation to learn and solve common problems.

Grantees have mixed feelings about foundation cooperation. They all relish the opportunity to knock on another door with a new idea. However, because foundations rarely provide enough money for their projects, grantees are obligated to patch different grants together and suffer the burden of meeting different reporting requirements. Grantees that require funds for the long term must constantly divide and repackage their work to attract new donors. Foundation cooperation can help, but that might invite complaints about "herd" or "cartel" behavior that limits funding to a preferred list. These and other changes can be made experimentally, in particular programs rather than across the foundation, and with selected partners. Some might worry that greater donor cooperation for capital building will send the foundation field down a slippery slope toward homogeneity and timidity.[17] The existing incentives for independence and privacy, we believe, are strong enough to forestall, or at least ensure early warning for, such a danger.

Recommendations for Building Capital

For those who have studied or even just read about processes of organizational learning and changing a field, the recommendations that follow should be familiar, if not easy to implement. For others, they sum up to a different way of thinking about grantmaking and school improvement— one that emphasizes interdependence. Our purpose is provocation, not prescription; we aim simply to cultivate better practices and an affinity for good work that builds on other good work to achieve cumulative results.

Internal Planning and Operations, and Cooperation with Peers and Grantees

Capital building depends on coherence and cooperation among multiple actors performing many related functions. The following nine recommendations aim to help foundations act more deliberately and more powerfully on the interdependencies among themselves and their diverse grantees.

1. *Design the criteria of capital building into grantmaking strategies.* Establish in guidelines for proposals and in periodic and final reports the foundation's clear intention to build knowledge and understanding within the grantee's own organization, as well as more widely in the field. Set objectives and indicators for capital building, including learning objectives that will be evaluated (in part so they will be taken seriously). Although the ripple effects of building educational capital are inherently difficult to predict, tools are available. For example, simulation may uncover possibilities, springboards, or obstacles for attention; using peers to

help assess proposals and results can reveal opportunities to enrich the capital-building potential of a proposal.

Capital-building strategies may require greater board tolerance for complexity and abstraction; for ambiguous, ambivalent, and delayed results; and more difficult attribution of results to the foundation's effort. It is, therefore, crucial that boards understand what capital-building strategies involve. Capital-building benchmarks may be essential to board commitment, and benchmarks satisfactory to one foundation could be of great use to other grantmakers. Regardless of who gets credit, foundations should plan to capture and celebrate examples of capital that has been built.

2. *Design strategies in which grantees are partners in capital building, not just in realizing the proposal.* Guarantee local districts and schools opportunities for intellectual engagement and leadership beyond their own sites.

3. *Balance prescription with flexibility, firm accountability with opportunity for surprises.* Specifying learning objectives up-front gets staff and grantees to think about what is important to learn, along with "whether the project worked." However, important results and valuable learning often come unexpectedly. The evaluation and the grant accountability process should be flexible so they capture results that are not predicted.

4. *Find partners to help solve common problems.* Foundations should be proactive about the interdependence of their varying goals, especially those that have common underlying challenges (for example, promoting student-centered instructional techniques that motivate or prepare students for standardized tests, or building student and school data capability and use for improved diagnostic and treatment decisions or facilitating stronger grant evaluations). As foundations already have common grantees, they should try developing common grant programs, based on their different expertise and angle of approach to problems. Foundations interested in improved subject-matter-specific instruction, for example, could do this with foundations that are interested in professional development methods or in teacher recruitment and retention. For many years, advocates for "progressive" approaches to solving social problems have marveled at the effectiveness of foundations on the right that "are strategic, coordinated, disciplined and well financed."[18] Why should the same not be said of efforts to improve public education?

5. *Ensure that key grant and program audiences outside, as well as within, grantees will find information about results interesting and credible.* Sustainability depends on the understanding and agreement, if not commitment, from many audiences within and outside grantees (parents,

teacher unions, community leaders, and the like). Foundations should name those audiences and ask representatives to help identify credible indicators for program and grant progress. Key audiences want to know not only if something is good and how it works; they want to know how much better it is, for whom, and at what cost in time, money, and political capital. They want help imagining what they could give up to get it. District finance departments, typically invisible when grants are negotiated, are often particularly important when demonstration grants are finished and continuation is about to become a district expense. Ambitious donors should structure projects to produce benefit and cost information that budget directors can believe.

6. *Experiment with better information for assessing strategies.* Foundations asked to stay the course on complex objectives need confident disciplines similar to those for stock buying, holding, and selling. Boards need benchmarks that are based on analogous previous experience, much as pharmaceutical and high-tech companies must assess strategies for creating new drugs or equipment.

7. *Do as you say.* Applicants will be glad for our recommendation that foundations impose on themselves comparable capital-building goals and planning and assessment standards to those they expect grantees to meet. Having one's own staff walk a mile in those shoes may improve mutual understanding and respect. Though foundations are removed from the work on the ground, they stand in a potentially highly productive relationship to all their grantees when it comes to putting developed capital into broader circulation.

8. *Gather and publicly display the research base that grantseekers are expected to use in preparing proposals.* User-friendly formats such as bibliographies, study or survey summaries, and meta-studies invite a different kind of engagement for projects otherwise focused on a local problem. They also help peers and applicants know what lies behind strategy and grant choices.

9. *Maintain educational capital and organizational learning in staff transitions.* Destruction of past learning should not be the price of new blood. In foundations, a strong internal learning capacity should keep track over time of program officer, program, and cross-program learning objectives and answers to questions. Staff should be charged and supported to meet this responsibility. Departing educators and grantmakers should leave behind knowledge about sustaining programs; those who enter should have, as an early responsibility, learning why a program is in place and concluding whether and how it can be improved.

Communications

The next six recommendations acknowledge the importance of communication in realizing capital-building goals. Communication must not only be clear, it must also attend to the concerns of key audiences and offer sufficient candor and detail (yes, complexity has a place) so that it will be persuasive and usable.

10. *Provide information that is useful for learning.* Expectations are important. Foundation strategies should carefully and honestly distinguish knowledge building from advocacy purposes and communicate about the work accordingly. Foundation and grantee publications should clearly distinguish hopes, measurable goals, and other statements of intent from results and relate grant results to progress on solving specific problems. For that, they need to compare designs and results among many approaches to similar problems. Foundations should also deliberately get such information into media that are trusted by key audiences. Several foundations working together can raise information standards for their peers. In attending more self-consciously to results, they can help the public appreciate progress on big problems and the techniques behind it. If foundations are precise about what they want themselves or others to learn, they are more likely to produce information, if not lessons, that adds value to the field.

11. *When spreading educational capital, be clear about non-negotiable conditions for success and opportunities for local tailoring.* Too-rigid requirements invite rejection; too-loose ones may lead to disappointment.

12. *Promote a perspective of continuous improvement in communicating about the foundation's work.* Americans, including press editors, are first interested in who won or lost and who is arguing. Help the public recognize the real, though incremental, nature of improvement by sharing credit for small steps on a long road, much as the media regularly reveals in science and technology.

13. *Speak across the fifty-yard line.* Most news about school needs and reform efforts are initiated by or responsive to permanent camps along the ideological spectrum. Stories including both sides tend to feature the polar opposites—not the blended, compromising middle where most citizens are. Foundations and grantees should learn to use terms, values, and images that communicate across divides, along with assuring that the concerns of diverse constituencies can be addressed when planning grant and program evaluations. For example, when describing efforts and results, foundations could indicate the arguments they are helping to resolve. Pro-

posals for and reports about curriculum and pedagogical innovation grants might attend both to academic objectives and to students' ability to use that learning to make better choices in terms of personal and social responsibility.

14. *Follow up.* The news media, chastened by complaints that they only offer negative news, now look for positive stories in public education. Unfortunately, much of the good news comes when a new policy or project is showcased as it is launched, with emphasis on the problem, design, and intentions. Journalists rarely compare the admirable programs they feature or relate them to schools that show notable progress to state or federal performance standards. Public mistrust of education reform has many causes, but one may be the dearth of information about the actual effects of once-publicized promising innovations. The news rarely gives audiences any sense that knowledge is building, as it does when covering natural science. Foundations can help reporters and commentators create longitudinal stories on educational process as they do on test scores.

15. *Signal cooperation.* Foundations publishing about themselves typically ignore mentioning other donors to the same projects or what they have learned from the initiatives of their peers. Grantees may list funders together but rarely show how different foundation interests coincide in their work. This habit of declining to interconnect credit seems to please individual donors and possibly supports the public's regard for the foundation field in general by keeping the matter of credit simple (even if incomplete). However, it also signals that foundations work and accomplish alone. Donors first (then grantees) might experiment with communication that signals interdependence and partnership rather than parallel or competitive effort.

Targeting the System's Capacity to Learn and to Reach Consensus

The pressures and priority conflicts that pervade schooling, combined with skepticism about data quality and its uses, can make organizational learning anemic even when there is reform going on. The priority for learning won't increase much unless school constituents receive information they consider complete, credible, and persuasive. This can't happen if investments in information are made entirely for "accountability" purposes.

16. *Support comparable and longitudinal data and communication among different databases.* Notwithstanding images of "investing" and "accountability" in foundation work, funders generally are not much

interested in improving data for clinical or research capability. It is true that cost, technical, and confidentiality barriers are high and must be borne mainly by the public sector. However, capital building, not to mention evaluation of foundation grants, would benefit enormously from better and more comparable data. In partnership with government or its agents, foundations can accelerate the development of longitudinal systems and encourage the inclusion of a wider range of valued indicators and outcomes captured in social service, criminal justice, and health systems.

Learning Among Foundations

When independence leads to insularity, interrupted by the occasional speech, panel presentation, or glossy report, foundations miss powerful opportunities to learn from each other. Looking over one another's shoulder is a start.

   17. *Use case studies in developing the craft of grantmaking.* Case studies and ongoing discussions focused on solving common operational problems have proven a very good way for teachers to improve.[19] Why not the same for foundations with overlapping interests? Given the problems of grant complexity and candor mentioned earlier, case studies will be most helpful if prepared by independent writers with diverse expertise. They will need access, not just to what contemporary staff and board members say but also to former staff and written records. Ideal cases might cover in greater detail topics such as how the foundation came to design its program by including arguments resolved or not; how the program was implemented (comparing internal and external views); results as compared against the foundation and grantee's stated expectations; projects with similar goals in the field, including ones the foundation rejected; how the foundation learned from grants and what it did differently afterward and whether the changes produced better results. There are many structures available now to facilitate shared problem solving and for obtaining peer review.[20]

Building Capital: Accumulation and Interdependence

All components of the education system, including its foundation donors, need to renew and improve continuously. There is no perceptible disagreement with this principle among foundations or the education leaders with whom they work. Implementation, however, needs a substantial boost. Welcome innovations in individual schools—private, charter, or just unusual—normally do not and perhaps cannot have broad and durable impact under current conditions in the larger public system. Priorities are always in conflict because values, funders, and vendors are in conflict. We advocate the approach of building capital because, unlike leverage, it features accumulation and interdependence; that is, the way progress comes about. Collectively, the foundation sector has the resources and strategic flexibility—in short, the capacity—to make greater incremental contributions to improving the K–12 system.[21] However, it needs to continue developing its disposition and capacity for learning and, for that, cooperation.

Many people have complained over the years that, in becoming "investors" and "venture capitalists," foundations have lost their philanthropic mission, that they regard themselves too highly, and that they naively deny the fundamental conflicts of values in public education made worse by rising expectations without commensurate funding. We do not believe that rational or economic thinking is a generally worrisome obstacle to foundation effectiveness, annoying as they sometimes are to grantees. Analytical techniques can be as powerful in serving public goods as private ones; pride motivates excellence. Pride, however, needs boundaries. Foundations should curb their disposition to see themselves as single actors and success in terms of their own private goals. By contributing innovation and variety in the K–12 field, private goals do tend to serve public purposes, but at a cost. Self-centered philanthropy denies, reduces, or delays learning. It precludes concentration of effort on key issues underlying diverse goals. In short, it hinders formation of capital.

The basis for more ambitious foundation cooperation would seem to be secure, save for the hold that individualism, ownership, and privacy have on the foundation culture. Foundations can loosen the grip without letting go. Given the stakes associated with strengthening public education, the potential benefits of greater cooperation are worth more risk.

NOTES

1. The number of two hundred "ambitious" foundations is estimated as follows: the Foundation Center found that one hundred foundations that make grants of $10,000 or more account for almost one-third of all foundation giving to K–12 (see the Appendix for more on Foundation Center data). Approximately two hundred foundations are members of Grantmakers for Education (GFE), which is dedicated to improving foundation effectiveness in education. Not all its members would stand at the top of the Foundation Center's annual grantmaking compilation. We have

conflated these estimates of the larger givers with those identified with GFE to suggest that much of the K–12 grantmaking horsepower is concentrated in a few foundations.

2. The "passing gear" metaphor is from Paul Ylvisaker—a widely admired sage in the foundation field at the time. "Social venture capitalists" came into fashion again while the stock and venture capital markets were booming in the late 1990s, and some wealthy technology entrepreneurs began giving away money. In the widely read "Philanthropy's New Agenda: Creating Value," *Harvard Business Review,* Nov.-Dec. 1999, Kramer and Porter argue that foundations must get extraordinary impact to justify their tax preference and the overhead costs associated with giving the money away (pp. 122ff).

3. The assertions and observations here and later come mainly from our combined experience working for and with foundations, from recent interviews with grantmakers, their consultants, and grantees, commentary at a Carnegie Foundation–sponsored conference on this book in November 2005.

4. This description was taken from the NBPTS Web site, last accessed March 30, 2006 (http://www.nbpts.org).

5. This description was taken from the New Teacher Center's Web site, last accessed March 30, 2006 (http://www.newteachercenter.org).

6. A provocative summary of Hirsch's views can be found in E. D. Hirsch Jr.'s "Not So Grand a Strategy," *Education Next,* Spring 2003, pp. 281–301, and Core Knowledge Foundation Web site (http://www.core knowledge.org/).

7. See Coalition of Essential Schools' Web site, last accessed April 23, 2006 (http://www.essentialschools.org).

8. See, for example, Elizabeth Cohen's *Designing Groupwork: Strategies for the Heterogeneous Classroom.*

9. See the Broad Foundations' Web site, last accessed March 15, 2006 (http://www.broadfoundation.org).

10. See "About Achieve" on Achieve's Web site, last accessed May 18, 2006 (www.achieve.org).

11. An example of the latter on a state scale is California's EdSource (http://www.edsource.org); on a national scale is the Standard and Poor's Web site (http://www.schoolmatters.com).

12. See Peter Senge's *The Fifth Discipline,* p. 14.

13. A description of the cycle of inquiry can be found on the Web site of Springboard Schools, an organization with which both coauthors are or have been associated (http://www.springboardschools.org).

14. The Pre-Collegiate Education Group was founded circa 1983 and was later reconstituted as Grantmakers for Education (http//www.edfunders.org). The Grantmakers Evaluation Network, founded in 1995, and Grantmakers for Effective Organizations, founded in 1998, merged in 2002 (http://www.www.geofunders.org).

15. See, for example, Mike Schmoker, "Tipping Point: From Feckless Reform to Substantive Instructional Improvement," *Phi Delta Kappan*, 2004, *85*(6), 424–432; available on Phi Delta Kappa Web site (http://www.pdkintl.org).

16. For example, *With the Best of Intentions: How Philanthropy Is Reshaping K–12 Education,* edited by Frederick M. Hess, is summarized on the American Enterprise Institute for Public Policy Research Web site (http://www.aei.org).

17. Grantees have mixed feelings about foundation cooperation. They relish the opportunity to knock on another door with a new idea, and one sometimes hears complaints about "herd" and "cartel" behavior that unfairly and unwisely reduces opportunity for innovators. On the other hand, because foundations rarely provide enough money for grantees to do what they want, grantees are obligated to sew many different grants together, with unwelcome work required to meet different reporting requirements and time frames. Grantees that require foundation funds for the long term to test or sustain an innovation must constantly divide and repackage their work to attract new donors.

18. The quote is from Rom Stein in "Goals Reached, Donor Closes Up Shop," *New York Times*, May 29, 2005. For a more extensive review of the "herding" concern, see S. Covington, "Moving a Public Policy Agenda: The Strategic Philanthropy of Conservative Foundations," National Committee for Responsive Philanthropy, July 1997. See also Chapter Fourteen of this volume.

19. Grantmakers for Education has just begun an effort to create case studies on grants in education. The programs of the Center of Philanthropy at Indiana University are good examples of such initiatives.

20. See, for example, the Breakthrough Series Collaborative, Institute for Healthcare Improvement Web site (http//www.ihi.org); "Peer Review in Philanthropy: A Road to Accountability and Effectiveness," P. A. Patrizi and others, unpublished paper for California Endowment and David and Lucile Packard Foundation, Sept. 2005.

21. We have heard estimates that more than $32 trillion in wealth will change hands between 1998 and 2052. The financial sector has responded, with firms like Fidelity Investments creating donor-directed charitable funds (that compete for donors with community foundations) and with a burgeoning army of consultants, helping wealthy people give money away "strategically" and initiate children into the philanthropic community.

REFERENCES

Calkins, L. *The Art of Teaching Writing.* Portsmouth, N.H.: Heinemann, 1994.
Cohen, E. G. *Designing Groupwork: Strategies for the Heterogeneous Classroom.* New York: Teachers College, Columbia University, 1994.
Senge, P. *The Fifth Discipline.* New York: Currency/Doubleday, 1990.
Stein, R. "Goals Reached, Donor Closes Up Shop," *New York Times,* May 29, 2005.
Tyack, D., and Cuban, L. *Tinkering Toward Utopia.* Cambridge, Mass.: Harvard University Press, 1995.

Chapter Five Overview

With long—and ongoing—careers in education, the authors of this chapter bring experience in foundations, educational institutions, and intermediary organizations, as well as work in policy and scholarship, to the topic of foundations and education. Writing with the insight and clarity their experience provides, they examine the significance, for school reform, of the differences in foundations' and school districts' organizational cultures. Because these differences originate in the ways the two kinds of organizations determine their priorities and are governed, operated, and held accountable, it is not surprising to find that the differences or mismatches result in difficulties in working together. To get around that frustration, a sizeable proportion of foundation support does not go to schools and school districts directly. Instead, it goes to intermediary organizations that can negotiate these differences in the service of outcomes beneficial to both.

Foundation reform strategies fit usefully, if somewhat uneasily, into a three-part typology: standards-based, market-based, and network-driven approaches. The authors show that the energy that impels each approach lies largely outside the schools. They observe that organizations with broader sweep than a single district and the capability to manage a change strategy are acquiring a significant role in the improvement of K–12. As with much else about school reform, however, the practical details deliver more understanding than simply naming a category of tools or agencies active in improving schools. The authors argue that because of the cultural divide, foundations and schools need intermediary organizations. At the same time, they are acute in their analysis of much unfinished business—how these organizations function and how they might take on appropriate forms of accountability to those they sit between.

5

FOUNDATIONS AND SCHOOL REFORM

BRIDGING THE CULTURAL DIVIDE

Nancy Hoffman and Robert Schwartz

OVER THE LAST DECADES, those charged with changing and improving organizations have given much more attention than previously to the idea of organizational cultures. The reason for this emphasis is that the rationalist approach to organizational change has had so little impact. This failure is often attributed to a lack of understanding on the part of the change agents as to how people in specific organizations were socialized to go about their work. In the literature on the subject, perhaps the best shorthand is to equate organizational culture with personality. (In the organizational literature, *personality* is used widely to stand for *culture*.)

And what could better exemplify organizational personality differences than walking through the door of the Rockefeller Foundation on the twenty-second floor of an elegant suite of offices on Fifth Avenue, versus the door of 26 Court Street—headquarters of the Boston public schools. At Rockefeller, as the visitor steps off the elevator, the glass doors slide back discreetly, allowing the petitioner into an urban Shangri-la where voices are muffled by the sound of a fountain, and tastefully printed publications lie invitingly arranged on low tables with their pictures of impoverished Africans. A nonbureaucratic-looking receptionist inquires, "Whom are you here to see?" But in Boston, the visitor puzzles about which entrance might be the front door, enters a utilitarian lobby, and finds herself before a desk labeled "information" that neither of us has ever seen staffed. The lobbies say, respectively, "high class on behalf of the poor" and "bureaucracy on behalf of everyone, or perhaps no one."

But organizational personality is more than skin or foyer deep. It is only the surface manifestation of the basic assumptions, values, and ways of operating that define an organization. In a classic definition,

> [Organizational culture is] a pattern of shared basic assumptions, that the group learned as it solved its problems of external adaptation and internal integration, that has worked well enough to be considered valid and therefore to be taught to new members as the correct way to perceive, think and feel in relation to those problems (Schein, 1992, p. 12). [Schein goes on to note in Chapter Two that levels of organizational culture include, along with basic assumptions, values, behavioral norms, patterns of behavior, and artifacts and symbols.]

We call attention to this definition because it focuses on how the work gets done. As foundations and school districts try to work together, even toward similar goals, the differences between the organizational cultures create tensions that often go unrecognized and unresolved. However, a new organization form—the intermediary organization—has come to play an increasingly important role in mediating tensions.

This is a positive development. In the two case studies that are at the heart of this chapter, we focus on the role of intermediary organizations in two large, multisite projects. One story has come to a close, and the problems that arose yield lessons in the use of intermediaries. The other story is still unfolding, and the role of the intermediary is still being invented and reinvented, but the lessons point to effective use of an intermediary organization. Together they suggest the potential of intermediaries and "translators," mediators, and creative forces in moving forward the agenda of school reform.

Sources of Tension

Looking at foundations and school districts from either side of the cultural divide, three sources of tension are most apparent: (1) the differences in these organizations' mission and goals, (2) their governance and decision making, and (3) accountability.

Mission and Goals

Foundations are in the research and development business, ideally focused on advancing a field and developing new knowledge. They are also, by definition, committed to "doing good" and are free to publicly promote their values and priorities—liberal, conservative, sectarian—for getting to where they judge society should go. School districts (a term we use to refer to large, urban districts serving mostly low-income young people) focus on the here and now, serving the students right in front of them; although they certainly intend to learn from practice, it is exceedingly difficult for districts to capture and harness new knowledge, let alone devote substantial resources to speculative ventures needed for good research and development. The knowledge development agenda and the service provider agenda are inherently in tension. In other words, one organization has as its primary goal producing the next best thing or beyond—a new paradigm entirely—whereas the other has a goal of making a system work "well enough" every day. These contrasting agendas shape daily practices and mind-sets, that is, the ways that work gets carried out.

For example, common and acceptable foundation practice is to fund the implementation of an innovative school design in multiple, geographically disparate communities to see where it will take and why. From the foundation's perspective, this is a wise experiment. Despite their seemingly Goliath-like power, foundations contribute only a tiny fraction of the budgets of large school districts. Thus their strategy is often to create "existence proofs"—demonstrations that a particular theory of reform can actually work on the ground and produce documentable results—and then to press for widespread adoption with public funds. The process of designing such demonstrations rarely requires either deep knowledge of a community or the necessity to contend with opposing perspectives and points of view. Indeed, what foundations often do is troll for promising examples of the innovation they would like to document and "prove," then work to strengthen the model and "scale it up." The two cases we offer in this chapter—projects funded by The Pew Charitable Trusts and the Bill & Melinda Gates Foundation—are examples of the strategy to create existence proofs to undergird the desired policy changes.

The chief academic officer of a large district may have a similar vision of what needs to happen next—what an ideal model of a school or a professional development practice would look like—but one such existence proof is likely to change little in a district. Although foundations often lament their inability to "go deep" or even proclaim that they are doing so with a particular reform, large grants sustained over periods beyond the standard three to five years only touch the surface of a district and rarely contribute to the unglamorous daily work, for example, of managing human resources or improving accounting procedures or collecting data. Much as school leaders might like to focus their energies on innovation and knowledge development, the reality of daily life, especially in urban districts, is work-a-day devotion to ensuring that no harm is done, that systems function as needed, and that incremental change remains on the agenda.

Governance and Decision Making

A second and profound source of tension between foundations and school districts pertains to those to whom each must answer, with what kind of decision-making process, and on what timetable. The differences here lead to major disjunctions in regard to governance and decision making. Private foundations answer only to themselves, which means to their trustees or benefactors. Grantees are rarely privileged to know how decisions are made and by whom, starting with decisions to fund their own projects, although they usually know with clock-like precision the day and hour of the board meeting in which a decision will be made. Because foundations take action in sealed rooms, their decisions have an air of authority, of edicts from above, with the rationale and mess of conflict hidden from view. And to seal the curtain around foundations, good program officers are schooled in decorum. They are socialized to be pleasant, to listen well and respectfully, and not to disclose doubt, confusion, or dissatisfaction. And the elegantly argued white papers on strategy that appear on foundation Web sites simply underscore the reserved, consistent messages of those with power, money, and choices.

School districts, by contrast, have multiple constituents they need to satisfy: school boards, parents, students, employees and their unions, special-interest groups, politicians, business leaders, and, increasingly, mayors, city councils, and the media. These groups rarely agree with each other, and they often use the rhetoric of entitlement: each believes it should be listened to, and each wants to own a piece of the agenda—the piece that pertains to its own agenda. Whatever their relationship to Foundation X's agendas and dollars, superintendents must first keep their jobs, so often they find themselves caught between mayors and school boards with mainstream ideas for improving schools (and too few dollars with which to implement these ideas) and foundations with risk-taking and controversial agendas.

In addition, school districts are mythologized as (and actually are) cornerstones of our democracy. This means that they are expected to act openly—in the sunlight, not in sealed board rooms—and to act fairly, taking into account multiple views and needs. And they are expected to be efficient. They are stewards, not only of the nation's young people but of taxpayer dollars.

Most of the school districts' constituencies, if they are aware of foundations at all, rarely see them as players, either as sources of dollars or of new ideas. Why is Boston moving to portfolios of small schools? Although district leaders were already committed to this general approach, few parents would know that the decision was encouraged and hastened by the Bill & Melinda Gates Foundation, whose dollars are supporting the new school design team on which those very parents and their children serve. In addition, although school districts can sometimes act quickly, their actions are often constrained by collective bargaining agreements, and they cannot afford to get too far in front of elected officials. School district decision making has nothing like the precision and predictability of foundation board meetings, where the docket appears just as advertised. How many morning papers recount the decision that *was not* made in a raucous school board meeting because no one could come to agreement or the proceedings were disrupted by citizens expressing their free speech rights?

K–12 education is a roughly $500-billion enterprise. Even the largest private foundation grants typically represent less than 1 percent of an urban district's budget. Leaders from the two sectors often have very different notions about how much reform private dollars can realistically buy in large, politically complex, urban systems. And foundations certainly have exaggerated notions of the amount of respect their dollars and wishes should be afforded. The tension, then, in regard to governance and decision making can be profound. Foundations tend to see themselves as key stakeholders whose dollars should give them a voice at the table; superintendents, on the other hand, see no meaningful way to incorporate foundation representatives into the school board's decision-making processes. Even if the superintendent and school board embrace the foundation perspective as a breath of fresh air—an external validation of the superintendent's "out-front" reform agenda—many districts struggle to explain how and why a group sending dollars from afar can be telling school leaders what to do. As we point out later in this piece, when they manage well, intermediary organizations can buffer between foundations and school districts, and absorb some of the resistance. They can write grant proposals as inside-outside players and represent the consensus foundation-district perspective at the district's decision-making table.

Accountability

Foundations and school districts have been talking more of the same language in the last several years. Both now see themselves as leading and advocating for change rather than simply managing the status quo. Both now speak the language of business, calling themselves *entrepreneurial* and using such terms as *leveraging* and *competitiveness* to describe their relationships with external organizations. Both have moved from input measures to outputs and use the terminology of accountability, and both promise a new era where all children are well served. Nonetheless, as one of the cases illustrates, with the stakes high and the results visible, foundations and school districts still remain in considerable tension with each other about who is accountable to whom and for what, and what constitutes realistic demands for the documentation of results.

School districts now operate in a test-based accountability environment, in which there is intense pressure to raise scores quickly and meet adequate yearly progress targets. Many states are imposing statewide school inspection, review, and accountability procedures that demand data collection, self-study, the hosting of visiting teams, and a public review process, often with little help for schools in preparing the documents for the review and inadequate support to address the problems identified.

Foundations have become increasingly enamored with their own versions of measurable results, but their measurement requirements are not usually about test scores and Adequate Yearly Progress formulas because these can be had from public sources; moreover, some foundations consider these relatively weak indicators of progress. Foundations want data, quite appropriately, showing the uses to which their dollars are put. For the newer, venture-style foundations, these data may need to be embedded in a theory of action, which leads to a theory of change, which result in metrics: how many students, for example, will complete Algebra I or how many teachers will change the nature of the assignments they make from less to more challenging.

Most school people are not trained to think this way. In addition, many foundations also employ professional evaluation firms and organizations that impose their own data-collection requirements. In keeping these firms at arm's length to ensure as much objectivity as possible, foundations may not know what data are being collected, and even the most responsible of external firms may be working at cross-purposes from grantees.

With "data consciousness" the mantra of both worlds, strapped school districts cannot meet the demands for information. Often districts complain that they are asked repeatedly by multiple players who do not communicate with each other for versions of the same data in different formats, at different points, and with different provisions for confidentiality. At the school level, many teachers are ill-equipped to collect and provide data; they have neither the electronic resources nor the time. What should be an exercise in self-reflection, with data used constructively for program and school improvement, comes to feel like a burdensome compliance exercise. As one of the cases shows, intermediaries can be helpful go-betweens in easing these burdens and in engaging grantees in making the rules of the game more transparent.

Foundations and Reform Strategies

How do these differences in organizational culture between the K–12 and foundation sectors affect the work of foundations in supporting education reform? In order to answer this question, we first offer a simple typology of the major K–12 reform strategies, with examples of foundation-funded initiatives associated with each strategy.

Given the size, diversity, and decentralized nature of the American education system, it should be no surprise that the education reform movement is hardly monolithic. Since the early 1990s, there have been at least three major strands, or wings, of the movement competing for attention and support, each with its own analysis of the core problem in American education and its own corresponding solution.

The dominant wing of the movement, at least in terms of federal and state policy, is the systemic or standards-based wing. For systemic reformers, the core problem of the schools is lack of specificity around goals and results. Systemic reformers believe that K–12 education will get better only by adopting the principles of organizational effectiveness from other sectors: setting clear goals, aligning all available resources toward the accomplishment of those goals, measuring progress regularly against the goals, using data to make appropriate midcourse corrections, and holding educators accountable for results. It has been governors, legislators, and business leaders who have been the principal advocates for this approach, and it is these ideas that underlie the education reform laws enacted during the 1990s in virtually all states, as well as the federal No Child Left Behind Act.

The second major wing of the reform movement might be characterized as market-based. Simply put, these reformers believe that the core problem of American public education is that it is a monopoly and that schools will get better only through the injection of competition, parental choice, and other forms of market pressure. Their strategy is to weaken the power of the monopoly by putting more power into the hands of the consumers, increase the supply of good new schools, and thereby compel existing schools to become more responsive to their customers or risk going out of business. There is a growing coalition of supporters across the political spectrum for this reform strategy, including some (for example, Chester Finn of the Thomas B. Fordham Foundation), who are also strong supporters of standards-based reform.

The third wing of the movement is a little harder to characterize, but we think of it as network-based reform. These reformers share with market-based advocates the belief that "the system" is the problem, that parental choice is essential, and that the school is the crucial unit of analysis in public education. Network reformers, however, believe that schools do best when they are organized into networks with others who share their philosophy and values and that voluntary associations of like-minded educators are more likely to produce meaningful school improvement than legislative mandates or bureaucratically organized state or district reform strategies. As is true of the other two reform camps, the network-based tent is broad enough to include under it educators with a wide diversity of approaches, such as those employed by the Edison Schools, Expeditionary Learning, Core Knowledge, and Essential Schools.

Although this way of defining the current education reform landscape is oversimplified, it provides a useful entry point for categorizing and analyzing the work of private foundations in supporting K–12 reform, for foundations have played a key role in promoting each of these approaches to reform. Although the major foundation players in K–12 education reform do not neatly align themselves into these three reform camps, one way to understand the work of foundations in this sector is to trace the role of foundation support behind one or two of the key organizations and initiatives in each wing of the movement.

Perhaps the organization that best exemplifies the network-based approach to school reform is the Coalition of Essential Schools (CES), founded and led for many years by Theodore Sizer at Brown University. CES evolved out of a late 1970s study of the American high school; CES was led by Sizer and funded by a consortium of foundations. The study produced a series of books, one of which—Sizer's *Horace's Compromise*—outlines a set of core principles around which high schools would need to be organized if they were to succeed in enabling all students to develop the habits of mind and heart envisioned by Sizer and colleagues. Launched in the early 1980s with foundation support, CES has grown over the years from a handful of schools to well over one thousand, now organized into regional networks that are tied together through national conferences, publications, and professional development offerings.

Although CES is probably the best-known example of a national network of schools organized around a common set of principles and led by a prominent university-based educational thinker and entrepreneur, it is hardly the only such example. Other prominent networks funded during the 1990s include the School Development Program, led by Yale's James Comer; Accelerated Schools, founded by Henry Levin, then at Stanford; and Success for All, founded by Robert Slavin, of Johns Hopkins University. Except for Success for All, which emerged out of a federally funded research center, the other projects all benefited from early development investments from foundations; CES and School Development Program networks were each helped to scale up through major gifts and sustained support from a single donor (Atlantic Philanthropies for CES, the Rockefeller Foundation for the School Development Program).

The systemic approach to reform is exemplified by two influential foundation-funded initiatives—the National Board for Professional Teaching Standards (NBPTS) and the New Standards Project. The proposal for a national board first surfaced in *A Nation Prepared*—a 1986 report from a Carnegie Corporation–sponsored task force on the teaching profession. The corporation followed up the task force's report with two major grants: one to help organize the national board; the other to support the initial research and development work needed to create a system to assess "accomplished" teaching. Once the national board was organized and the initial research and development work began, many other national private and corporate foundations added to the pot, as did the federal government, and NBPTS has now become a major force for raising standards in the profession.

The New Standards Project was a collaborative venture between the University of Pittsburgh's Learning Research and Development Center, the National Center on Education and the Economy, and nearly twenty states and large urban school districts to create a new national performance-assessment system. Although this project was conceived and developed by the codirectors of the two national centers—Lauren Resnick and Marc Tucker—the education directors of The Pew Charitable Trusts and the John D. and Catherine T. MacArthur Foundation were active participants in helping shape the project's design; the two foundations remained major financial supporters throughout the life of the project. Although the initial vision of the new national performance-assessment system adopted by a significant number of states never came to pass, the New Standards

Project's performance standards, assessments, professional development institutes, and national conferences have had a profound effect on both policy and practice as the standards movement has evolved over the past decade, and its products and services continue to occupy a small but influential niche in the education market.

In the market-based wing of the reform movement, it is difficult to single out one or two exemplary projects, given the highly decentralized nature of the activity in this realm, but here again foundations have played a central role. Without the advocacy and large-scale support of The Bradley Foundation, for example, vouchers and school choice, especially in Milwaukee, would not have been given a serious test. The charter school movement did not need foundation support to get started, but the investment of "venture" philanthropies like the New Schools Venture Fund in charter management organizations like Aspire and the Knowledge Is Power Program (commonly known as KIPP) has helped stabilize the movement and legitimize it in the eyes of policymakers.

The decisions of particular foundations to focus their education investments in one or another of these three reform strategies are inevitably idiosyncratic, reflecting some combination of foundation history, board ideology, and the policy preferences and professional experience of individual program officers, but one can still offer some generalizations about the foundations most prominently associated with each reform camp. It is important to note, however, that just as some key reform organizations and leaders cannot be located neatly in just one reform camp, so it is with foundations.

The foundations most likely to support network-based reformers are those, like the Carnegie Corporation, the Ford Foundation, and the Rockefeller Foundation, with a long history of involvement in K–12 education. They know the field well enough to have recognized such brand-name leaders of reform networks as Sizer, Comer, and Howard Gardner; they have a history of supporting curricular and instructional innovation, and they tend to be skeptical both about more systemic, top-down reforms and about the application of market-based reform ideas to public education. All three of these foundations have a strong commitment to equity and a long history of support for education advocacy organizations with an equity agenda, coupled with a deep belief in the democratic purposes of public schooling. Their goal is to make public schools work more effectively for all children, not to support the development of a parallel system or to open the door to privatization. To the degree that one can generalize about the values of senior program staff in these venerable foundations, they tend to be grounded in the community activism and social justice ideals of the 1960s, coupled with a healthy respect for the expertise of the kind of university-based education thought leaders around whom reform networks have been created.

The systemic reform camp, although the dominant one in terms of governmental activity and support, is today the most thinly populated by foundations. This is probably because the leveraging power of private dollars is less obvious here, at least now that the federal government and virtually every state have made substantial investments in this reform strategy. As we mentioned, in the early 1990s the Carnegie Corporation, The Pew Charitable Trusts, and the John D. and Catherine T. MacArthur Foundation were all major investors in building key pieces of a national institutional infrastructure to support the development of model learning and teaching standards and assessments—investments that have helped guide the work of states and districts in the last decade. In more recent years, the Carnegie Corporation and MacArthur have focused their systemic grantmaking on districts only, while the Trusts has focused its education work on the preschool years. The only major new player to have emerged in recent years with an interest in systemic reform nationally is The William and Flora Hewlett Foundation. As with the Trusts and MacArthur a decade earlier, the foundation's involvement in systemic reform has been driven largely by the prior governmental experience of its senior education officer.

If foundation interest in systemic reform has waned in the last several years, the opposite trend is apparent with market-based reforms. Support for choice and competition, not only in the provision of schooling but also in the development of alternative routes into teaching (for example, Teach for America, the New Teacher Project), the principalship (for example, New Leaders for New Schools), and the superintendency (for example, the Broad Superintendent's Academy) have flourished, principally from new foundations and venture philanthropic funds that have sprung up in the last decade. While some of the older conservative foundations like the Olin Foundation and The Bradley Foundation view their education grantmaking in the broader context of long-standing philosophical commitments to free markets and less government, the newer philanthropies like the Broad Foundation and New Schools Venture Fund (NSVF) are less driven by ideology and more by a desire to inject more entrepreneurial, risk-taking leadership into classrooms, schools, and districts. The newer foundations, created largely out of "new economy" money, are more likely to be staffed by people with MBAs than those with education degrees, and they are much more likely to look to the high-tech boom of the early 1990s for their inspiration than to the social activism of the 1960s.

For the older foundations committed to the view that low-performing schools will improve only under the threat of competition or that poor children will be better served in schools not under the jurisdiction of school districts, the question of how best to mediate the cultural divide between foundations and school districts is largely irrelevant. Their grant-making does not presuppose a working relationship with school district leaders, and their public stance is often overtly oppositional. For funders like NSVF and the Broad Foundation, however, and for foundations more typically committed to systemic or network-based reform strategies, the challenge of bridging the cultural divide is critical.

For that reason, among others, national foundations have increasingly turned to intermediary organizations to assist them in carrying out their reform initiatives, especially those that involve multiple sites.

The Role of Intermediaries

Although the work of intermediaries is significant, and the role they have come to play in the education reform landscape is one that helps to bridge the cultural divide between foundations and school districts, there is very little literature on intermediaries and no clearly established definition of the term. Although nonprofits working in different fields might define the key characteristics of intermediaries somewhat differently, all would agree on the function that leads to the name: intermediaries mediate and coordinate between organizations for the purposes of promoting innovation, improvement, and changes in practices. They are organizational "performance enhancers."

At their best, intermediaries mediate between organizations—in one case to be described here, between foundations and school districts; in the other, between foundations, other intermediaries, and only indirectly districts and schools. Intermediaries work to produce mutually acceptable visions and theories of change, theories of action, strategies for implementation, and accountability for results. While they may provide policy advice and technical services, or function as evaluators and critical friends, these discrete functions are important in that they add up to successful translation of the values and visions of the entities between which they work, so that the practices of one become (more) transparent to the other.[1]

Intermediaries are relatively new entities and are part of a growing and changing nonprofit sector. First launched in the 1960s by the Ford Foundation to extend the foundation's capacity to affect change in low-income communities, intermediaries now play important "go-between" roles in education, workforce development, youth development, health care, community development, and the like. In education, their growth has accompanied the development of large-scale reform initiatives, especially those focused on urban school districts. Here we make a distinction between intermediaries, as defined earlier, and "reform support organizations," or RSOs, as exemplified by CES or America's Choice.

What do intermediaries do for foundations, schools, and school districts? At the simplest level, they sometimes serve as fiscal agents for those foundations whose by-laws prevent them from funding governmental entities directly or whose boards prefer not to deal directly with large school district bureaucracies. At the other end of the spectrum of activities, intermediaries may be charged by foundations with designing an initiative for a foundation, selecting and funding grantees, monitoring performance, and assuming accountability for results, with only a light touch from the responsible program officer. More frequently, intermediaries manage some funds for their foundation clients, as did the intermediaries in the cases that follow, but their chief responsibilities include the kinds of work listed next. Note that while some of these functions primarily serve the funder, others strengthen and expand the capacity of schools and districts in the following ways:

○ Provide definition and conceptual coherence for initiatives working between the foundation and the grantee.

○ Goad to keep reform on track often being the prod to action—the timeline keeper.

○ Help the district or school see its innovation or change in national context while ensuring that the foundation appreciates local idiosyncratic conditions.

○ Provide informed outside perspective so the foundation is reminded of its perch on the twenty-second floor, while the district is reminded to see beyond the here-and-now.

○ Broker resources or provide technical assistance and professional development that models the goals and vision of the foundation for the district, showing what the change looks like.

○ Extend the capacity of schools by providing resources schools do not have, often joining the districts or schools in advocating with the foundation for extra dollars or reallocated budgets to meet new needs as they arise.

○ Engage schools in cycles of inquiry, finding common ground between foundations' need for knowledge development and the districts' pressure to move forward without stopping to collect and analyze data.

o Help build the capacity to sustain the foundation investment, especially by helping the district integrate the innovation into its budget and long-range plan.

Although the two cases we offer focus on national intermediaries that serve multiple foundations, these observations apply as well to the strongest local intermediaries that work with a single school district, especially such local education funds as New Visions in New York and the Boston Plan for Excellence.

Good intermediaries are "dual client organizations," with agendas and points of view of their own. They do not simply tailor their services to the needs of a school district or, for that matter, to those of a foundation. They insert a perspective that takes into account both the interests of the foundations that fund them and the schools and districts for whose improvement they share accountability. As "inside-outside" organizations, they both pull and push. They must be sufficiently in synch with their partner school districts to be able to build on a district's reform plan and strategy for implementation, but they must also be sufficiently independent to introduce ideas and practices that go against the grain, that disrupt business as usual and thereby create tension that often leads to change. They must also be willing to speak truth to power, pushing back against the sometimes unrealistic demands and expectations of foundations and helping program officers understand the messy reality of urban school district life. To be effective, they must be genuinely bilingual and bicultural, moving back and forth between Fifth Avenue and Court Street, to return to the initial contrast between the lobbies of the Rockefeller Foundation and the Boston School Department.

Intermediaries at Work: Two Cases

In the two cases that follow, we write from the perspective of participants. In the first case—the Pew Network for Standards-Based Reform, funded by The Pew Charitable Trusts—one of us was the senior foundation officer responsible for designing the initiative. In the second case—the Early College High Schools (ECHS) project, funded by the Bill & Melinda Gates Foundation and other major foundations—the other of us is the senior officer at the intermediary organization responsible for managing the project. If these stories were told from the perspective of the K–12 education leaders involved in the projects, they would undoubtedly have somewhat different emphases, but we have endeavored to represent the views of the other key organizational participants in our respective projects, as well as our own.

In the Pew Network, the focus was on supporting districtwide improvement. In the second case, the focus is on new-school development, and the role of school districts is barely visible. In this sense, these cases offer a contrast between foundations supporting different reform theories, with the Trusts being in the systemic camp and Gates (the major ECHS funder when the project began in 2002) straddling the network and market camps. As this and its other small-schools projects have developed, however, the Gates Foundation has come to realize the limitations of a school development strategy that bypasses districts and is now paying much more attention to systemic issues.

Case One: The Pew Network for Standards-Based Reform

This project owes its conception to the recommendations of an external review committee appointed by senior management of The Pew Charitable Trusts to review the grantmaking strategy of its Education Program in the early 1990s. During that period, the Trusts had been a major investor, not only in the New Standards Project but in several other national initiatives and organizations focused on standards-based reform. The external review team, chaired by the late Professor Donald Schön from the Massachusetts Institute of Technology, although generally supportive of the Education Program's funding strategy, argued that until there were some existence proofs that standards-based reform could actually succeed in dramatically raising student achievement, it would remain one among several competing theories of how to improve schooling.

Consequently, the staff of the Education Program decided to launch an initiative designed to demonstrate that well-designed implementation of standards-based reform in a variety of urban settings could, in fact, produce substantial gains in student performance. In early 1995, this unit of the Trusts began a process to find and select a small number of school districts that were not only committed to the core principles of standards-based reform but already had in place some of the key elements, that is, challenging standards, curriculum frameworks, and aligned assessments. After a multistage process involving the circulation of a prospectus outlining the specifications for the project, the nomination of candidate districts, the submission of letters of interest, and site visits to the most promising districts, eight districts were selected to receive planning grants.

Following the submission of implementation proposals and a second round of site visits in June 1996, the Trusts' board of directors approved the staff's recommendation to provide four years of funding support to seven of the eight districts. Two of the seven were, in fact, sub-units within large urban districts (Community District 2 in New York City; the San Diego High School Cluster in San Diego). The others were medium-size (15,000 to 50,000 students); they served diverse student populations, had stable leadership, and were committed to standards-based reform.

Right from the outset, the Trusts' Education Program staff realized that this initiative would be too large and complex to be administered directly by the foundation. Its first decision, therefore, even before launching the site selection process, was to select the Education Development Center (EDC) to serve as the intermediary organization for the initiative. EDC staff worked in concert with the Trusts' staff to select the sites, manage the planning phase of the project, and, ultimately, serve as the Trusts' re-granting agent for the implementation phase of the initiative. The Trusts selected EDC for this role because of its substantial expertise in professional development, which the Trusts' staff saw as the most important missing piece in much of the standards-based school improvement work to date, not because of any perceived expertise working with entire districts on systemic reform. In the authorization of the implementation phase of the initiative, EDC received $8.5 million, $5.5 million of which was designated for regranting to the seven districts. The remaining $3 million was for technical assistance and professional development support to the districts and for EDC's administrative costs. A separate evaluation grant for the project was made to the Bay Area Research Group and SRI International.

ONE PROJECT, TWO VIEWS. At the very first meeting of the superintendents of eight districts during the planning phase of the project, tensions between the goals of the foundation and the goals of the participating districts became apparent. The Trusts saw this as a demonstration project, in which the districts would commit to using the extra resources provided by the foundation in particular ways to strengthen their capacity to implement standards-based reform on the ground. One of the eligibility criteria for districts was that they be located in states that were partners in the New Standards Project, and one requirement specified in the prospectus was that districts would administer the New Standards Project's performance assessments, which were then just under development. This represented a prior claim on some of the funds that districts might have hoped to use otherwise and also served to underscore the fact that the foundation's bottom-line objective was to secure evidence on a common measure that student achievement was, in fact, improving in these districts.

The district leaders, while delighted to have been chosen for this initiative, had somewhat different hopes and priorities. Although they did not say this aloud, they were realistic enough to know that an extra $200,000 or so a year was unlikely to make a significant impact on student achievement. They saw the initiative as an opportunity to develop a "learning community" of peer districts to help one another address the challenge of how to improve teaching and learning in a standards-based environment, and they were eager to tap into a national pool of technical-assistance and professional-development experts that they assumed the EDC and the Trusts would make available to them. It was in this spirit that the district leaders proposed that the project be organized as a "network" and that the network leaders play a major role in governing the project. In order to gain the buy-in of the superintendents, the Trusts' senior education officer assented to this proposal—a decision that only complicated the role of the intermediary.

A few months later, when district teams came together in an institute to begin the real work of the project, these tensions again came to the surface, this time most sharply around the role and behavior of the intermediary. Was EDC there to serve the foundation or the districts? Was it principally an agent of control, there to assure fidelity of implementation to the Trusts' design principles, vague as they were, or was its job to respond to customized requests for assistance from the districts? This was particularly an issue because the funds for technical assistance remained with EDC rather than being part of the district grants, and EDC's first response to requests from the districts was invariably to offer up people from its own organization rather than drawing on a more national pool of consultants, as the districts would have preferred.

A WIDENING GULF. As the project developed, the gulf between the expectations of the foundation and those of the participating districts only grew wider, as did the tensions and dissatisfactions both parties had with the intermediary. These problems of accountability, governance, and goals—the very tensions we describe in the opening of this chapter—were then exacerbated by substantial turnover, first at the foundation (the two education officers responsible for the project left within months of the board's June 1996 authorizing vote) and then among the superintendents and the intermediary organization's staff.

THE OUTCOMES. After the loss of its own senior staff, the Trusts contracted with a respected senior statesman in the K–12 world to hold the project together, which he did admirably, but the project was the source of considerable anguish among the foundation's leaders; the sour taste left by the initiative may well have contributed to the foundation's decision, soon after the project closed, to shift the focus of its education grant-making to the preschool area.

From the perspective of the leaders of the network (mostly senior district administrators), the project did, in fact, provide an unusual opportunity for peer learning, for which they were grateful, and the network members themselves issued their own quite impressive final report summarizing the improvements under way in their own districts, as well as their own collective learning. As we all know now, the challenge of implementing standards-based reform in the classroom, across whole schools and districts, is vastly more difficult than most of us understood a decade ago, and the periodic evaluation reports from the project helped illuminate that challenge. The final report of the evaluators, while making a very useful correction to the then-dominant theory of change about standards-based reform, concluded that only one district—the district that had already made substantial investments in teacher knowledge and skills prior to the grant period—could demonstrate steady and impressive gains in student achievement. None of the other districts could show similar progress against the Trusts' bottom-line measure.

Case Two: Early College High School Initiative

In March 2002, the Bill & Melinda Gates Foundation, with additional support from the Carnegie Corporation of New York, the Ford Foundation, and the W. K. Kellogg Foundation, funded an out-of-the-box experiment to add to their growing portfolio of small-school networks. They granted $40 million to create seventy schools that combined high school and the first two years of college; the schools were to enable poor and poorly prepared young people to earn sixty college credits or the associate degree in fewer than the six years it would take to get from grades nine through fourteen. The Gates Foundation selected eight organizations to participate and designated one among them—Jobs for the Future (JFF)—to be what the foundation called the "co-ordinary."

Three and one-half years later, in August 2005, the Gates investment has grown to $114 million, with another $10 million from other national funders; thirteen organizations or institutions now serve as intermediaries, and about 180 schools are in the pipeline, with about 75 schools up and running in 24 states. The idea of schools integrating grades nine through "fourteen" has had considerable policy traction and has inspired states and institutions without external funding to plan such schools on their own. The jury is still out about results, but JFF and the Gates Foundation believe that within the next several years there should be sufficient documentation of school and student success to claim the first existence proofs.

THE ROLE OF THE NATIONAL INTERMEDIARY. In its work as the national intermediary organization charged by Gates with guiding, managing, and building policy change from the ECHS initiative, JFF has a number of parallels with that of EDC on behalf of the Pew Network for Standards-Based Reform. A large foundation chose a national intermediary with decades of experience to act as its extended staff in a multisite, multistate project with a bold goal: to create a network of new schools with a radical, untested design. The foundation intends that the project make an "argument" that underprepared high school students can succeed in college-level work; the increased achievement of the students in the schools is to be the existence proof, as improved achievement in the Pew Network districts is to be for standards-based reform.

The lead intermediary has a strong reputation in the field and has managed a wide variety of projects over the years. In this case, JFF was best known for advocating for and implementing projects to support young people and adults in transition to employment and family-supporting wages and was on the national radar screen for its leadership in the school-to-work movement of the 1990s. It had also just completed a project to identify schools working well for disengaged and poorly served adolescents, a number of which integrated high school and postsecondary education. Thus, like EDC, JFF's field knowledge made it a credible lead intermediary. In addition, strengthening and supporting intermediary organizations through peer learning was at the top of the organization's list of competencies. And also like EDC, the end point of the project—establishment of new schools—was not in JFF's history.

From the perspective of JFF, halfway through the demonstration phase of the project, there is much to say about the intermediary role. In working across the very different cultures of a wealthy foundation, the diverse intermediaries it chose to implement, as well as the schools, community-based organizations, districts, and postsecondary institutions that formed ECHS partnerships, JFF is engaged in a delicate and sometimes uncomfortable balancing act. For both the foundation and the intermediaries for which JFF is the co-ordinary, JFF serves as guide and provocateur, as buffer and shock absorber, as translator between multiple cultures, and, more recently, as assurer of quality.

The story of JFF's role comes in two parts: phase one, business as usual, in which JFF was more a support- or technical-assistance organization than true intermediary, and phase two, in which the JFF and the foundation together redefined the co-ordinary's work to have as one of its key responsibilities "performance management."

THE CHALLENGES OF THE PROJECT. The ECHS initiative was launched with much fanfare at LaGuardia Middle College High School, a pioneering small school on the LaGuardia Community College campus in Queens and one of Gates's inspirations for ECHS. Created in the 1980s, this school recruited young people at risk of failing in high school and used "the power of the site"—a community college campus—to extend their academic goals, elicit more adult behavior from them, and engage them in college courses for free as soon as they were ready. The second exemplar cited by Gates as evidence for the feasibility of early college was Bard High School Early College in New York City, which had opened with 250 ninth-graders and "eleventh"-graders in fall 2001, just a few months before ECHS was funded.

Beyond these two exemplars, there was a three-page paper by Tom Vander Ark, executive director for education at Gates, agreeing with the Commission on the Senior Year that the final year of high school was often a waste of time and proposing that low-income students should have the same options to attain college credit in high school that had long been afforded to wealthy ones. Although Vander Ark's idea represented exactly the kind of risk taking that gives foundations cachet and, in hindsight, it's clear he was dead-on about the important policy issues such schools could raise, the paper contained abstract principles, not an actual school design. With the exception of the Middle College National Consortium, it would be fair to say that the partner organizations (including JFF, National Council of La Raza, KnowledgeWorks Foundation, Woodrow Wilson Foundation, and the like) sought out by Gates, while flattered to be funded, had either not thought much about implementation, assuming that Gates knew what it was doing, or kept their reservations to themselves, assuming that the idea was such a stretch that it would be modified before anyone was in too deep trouble.

In addition, presented with the idea of accelerating into college young people who were behind in high school, almost all school people with potential to start schools were deeply skeptical, as were the potential postsecondary partners. So JFF, as lead, found itself mediating a credibility chasm—the foundation's risk-taking culture at some odds with the on-the-ground realism of the grantees.

As those involved in the initiative would discover during the start-up year, establishing and maintaining early colleges posed great challenges: academic, financial, structural, and political. Getting the curriculum right when it is accelerated and driven by the demands of postsecondary is hard enough without having to find permanent funds and establish secondary-postsecondary partnerships. Counterintuitively, it is also hard to hold back the tide of eager early adopters.

THE WORK STARTS. The first task was to create a cadre of "believers" and a statement about what the intermediaries had signed on to, using Vander Ark's principles as a guide. Within six months of the kick-off, JFF had written, circulated, and gotten sign-off on (though not full sign-on to) a core-principles document codifying what came to be called the non-negotiables: acceleration, two years of free college credit concurrent with the high school diploma, and elimination of the physical transition between high school and college. The group as a whole had a unified message and public goals.

The second task was to make the schools work. From the start, JFF was concerned about how the ECHS intermediaries would demonstrate that the students in the new schools met the goals in the non-negotiables. During the first year of the project, the players (Gates, JFF, and the intermediaries) took all the expected steps. The foundation busied itself with ECHS by sending out communications packets, setting up reporting structures, and affirming that it had made excellent choices in JFF and the other intermediaries. Responding to the excitement among states and school developers, Gates added several more intermediaries to the original network of seven, as well as more dollars to JFF for its support work. JFF convened peer learning sessions, established relationships with and coached the intermediary leaders, read proposals for schools, and produced "just-in-time" tools to build the intermediaries' capacities for starting schools. The intermediaries sent out RFPs, trolled the country for willing postsecondary partners, signed on their first schools and began school planning, and attended the JFF peer learning meetings.

Everyone put on a bold face in public about meeting the challenges they were facing. But it is likely that most network participants, including those from JFF, were questioning privately what they had gotten into while remaining polite and reserved with each other and up-beat with Gates. The power differentials, the diverse ways of doing business among the groups, and the lack of clarity about what steps were needed at each stage of school development contributed to an environment of self-protection in the network. This was business as usual.

REALITY SETS IN. However, at the end of the first year, at a meeting with leads of each intermediary organization, frustration burst into the open—mostly around the unanticipated problems of funding the schools. JFF had asked for school budgets; few had appeared. The partners said aloud to each other and to JFF that most had begun schools without a plan to pay for the postsecondary credits, books, and transportation. In December 2003, the foundation invited JFF to present its work to the foundation's senior leadership. JFF appeared at the meeting truly worried and ready to speak frankly against further expansion of ECHS. Some schools were on track to open, but a number were slowed down. During the prior year, JFF had identified significant state policy and financing barriers to implementing early colleges. In addition, demands for Gates funds to start additional ECHSs were coming in to JFF daily, taking up huge amounts of time and underscoring JFF's fear that it was attached to a truly generative idea with no evidence as yet to support it—one garnering attention far beyond its documented promise. These were facts that belonged on the table. JFF had its reputation at stake, and it wanted to be clear with Gates about what the project could deliver.

Early in the initiative, JFF had advocated with the foundation to create a student information system to track students longitudinally over ten years but had gotten little traction. At the meeting JFF pushed hard and got agreement with Gates about two issues: (1) the project would move from widespread seeding of schools to carefully planned and documented demonstration of the best case to be made for ECHS, and (2) Gates would fund the student information system. It was unusual in the grantmaking world that the grantee asked the funder not to do more but to agree to let the intermediaries focus on doing better what they had already begun.

Everyone got real; they pulled back from the brink of too-rapid expansion and shifted gears. JFF and the intermediaries would put all their energy into creating schools rather than to scaling up. And that meant figuring out strengths, weaknesses, gaps, and potential for growth among the partner organizations and making explicit plans to build each intermediary's capacity with regular check-ins to see whether the work was progressing with sufficient quality and timeliness. It also meant negotiating funding and enabling policy conditions prior to signing on new intermediaries.

REDEFINED RELATIONSHIPS. A year later, in the spring of 2004, JFF began, in a careful agreement with Gates, to transform its relationship with the intermediaries from support organization and advocate for the network to true intermediary; they negotiated between Gates and what the foundation was now calling "school development organizations." *Performance management* (the foundation's term for the new relationship it has), not just with ECHS but with other grantees, still rankles with some. However, the explicitness about roles and expectations and the accompanying more targeted support from Gates to JFF—and from both of these organizations to the intermediaries—signals much greater alignment between foundation, co-ordinary, and ECHS school developers.

Engaging the intermediaries in small working groups, JFF drafted benchmarks for schools and created technical-assistance plans for each partner. With the foundation, JFF implemented a yearly three-part review cycle with an annual report, a face-to-face three-hour conversation with the senior foundation officer and JFF, and a follow-up technical-assistance plan. In addition, all intermediaries agreed to have data from their schools and school districts entered into the student information system. The "performance management" phase of the work has resulted in refreshingly honest, though often painful, conversations among funders, JFF, and the intermediaries about what skill set and experience is needed to start early colleges and attain the intended results, and how the foundation and JFF can fill the gaps identified. These are as disparate as business planning, literacy coaching, and interceding with government officials. Although some intermediaries may end their relationship with the initiative once their funded schools are open because they do not want to be school developers, such a decision is not a sign of failure but rather an acknowledgment that the host intermediary has other goals to pursue and has decided not to develop the competencies required for scaling up.

JFF can now do a better job of bringing the public and private views of participants in this challenging project closer together. For a number of participants in the work, there is a sense of relief; no one can do this work perfectly, and telling the truth (or having it told through data collected from school districts) to the foundation is, ultimately, more productive than operating in what someone has called "a culture of nice" that plasters over the difficulties of achieving change. Transparency about expectations and straight talk cut through the differences in cultures, though not entirely. And to its credit, the Gates Foundation has adopted a public stance that is exceedingly helpful. They admitted publicly the difficulty of the work it has set out; they showed where results the foundation anticipated are as expected and where it is reasonable to readjust.

If one were to interview the intermediaries and school staff themselves and get some honest assessments, there would likely be mixed feelings.

Where the buck stops is, ultimately, in the ability of the schools to get underprepared youth through two years of college. A risk-taking idea that is filtered down (along with support) from the foundation to JFF and the intermediary organizations to schools is clearly not an idea built from the ground up; few would have been quite so ambitious. But because of the accountability now built into school development through JFF and the foundation's review process, there is greater honesty about what it takes to attain the enabling conditions, and the foundation will not be surprised in several years if only a certain percentage of students attain the goal of two years of college credit.

Lessons and Reflections

In these two examples of how national foundations have employed intermediary organizations to help them carry out large-scale, ambitious reform initiatives, we can see some points of similarity, as well as some obvious differences. In both cases, the foundations decided to work with and through intermediaries for several reasons. First, neither foundation had sufficient internal capacity to manage a complex, multisite initiative on its own. The Trusts, for example, had only two senior program staff with relevant knowledge and experience, and both already had substantial grant portfolios. The Gates Foundation was still in start-up mode, with barely enough staff to carry out the routine grantmaking functions required to meet the foundation's daunting annual Internal Revenue Service payout requirements.

Second, and more important, neither foundation had the expertise required to help the site partners address the very substantial implementation challenges posed by each project. In fact, one might argue that had the foundations had such expertise, the projects would have been designed quite differently, with longer timelines and substantially more realism about project outcomes. But the ambitious goals of these two initiatives put a huge premium on selecting intermediaries with appropriate knowledge, skills, and motivation to help the site partners translate the broad vision of the foundations into workable plans on the ground.

Given how dependent each foundation was on its intermediary for the realization of foundation goals, one might have expected these intermediaries to have been selected through a careful screening and vetting process. The reality, however, is that there are very few nonprofit organizations with the capacity to carry out projects of this scale and sophistication, and in both cases these initiatives were asking grantees to do things on the ground that very few people know how to do. Neither foundation went through a competitive process in selecting its intermediary. The Trusts selected EDC with its eyes open, knowing it was asking the organization to do a kind of district-level systemic work it had not done before; they also knew that EDC would have to draw on staff currently deployed in several different program offices to get the required expertise. Gates took even more of a gamble, selecting in JFF an organization whose reputation had been built largely on its work in the school-to-career field, not in the school-to-college transition. As it happens, however, Gates had significantly more success with its selection than did the Trusts. The question is why.

In answering this question, we see some lessons for foundations about the importance of investing time and care, not only in the selection of intermediaries but in helping build their capacity to become more effective partners in carrying out foundation initiatives.

Understand the Intermediary

The lessons from the Trusts' case have much more to do with the foundation's mistaken assessment of the culture of EDC than with the intermediary itself. At the time of its selection, EDC was an organization with a budget of $34 million and a staff of more than four hundred. Its revenue came entirely from grants and contracts; its fourteen centers carried out 250 projects all over the world. While it housed staff whose skills and experience, especially about professional development, were directly relevant to the goals of the Pew Network, these staff were spread over two or three different centers and were engaged in other ongoing projects. Despite the genuine interest of EDC's president in using the Trusts' initiative to strengthen her organization's capacity to do more systemic work, the bureaucratic structure and culture of EDC made that difficult, and the Trusts' funding, relative to the size of the organization, was an insufficiently powerful incentive to induce change. The Trusts, like many foundations, had a small education staff and considerable autonomy, and they could be nimble and inventive. Indeed, the Trusts' experience with EDC mirrored the frustration that funders often complain about with school districts: people in separate organizational silos seem to have difficulty coming together to carry out a coherent, aligned, systemwide reform strategy.

By way of contrast, at the time Gates selected JFF, it was roughly a forty-person organization with a $6 million annual budget. Like EDC, it was dependent for its budget on grants and contracts, but it housed only two programmatic units—a Youth Transitions Cluster and an Adult Cluster. The goal of the Youth Transitions Cluster was, and still is, to enable underserved youth to gain a postsecondary credential by age twenty-six.

Thus ECHS was not just another project, as the Pew Network was for EDC. ECHS presented a major opportunity for JFF to enact its theory of change on a national stage. Therefore, being asked by Gates to manage ECHS represented a big win for JFF and was exactly "on mission." In addition, more of JFF's work than that of EDC's was truly to intermediate; carrying out research, providing technical assistance, or developing new products was not.

Share Common Ground

A second point of contrast is that JFF, prompted by Gates, has come to play a much more aggressive and directive role than did EDC, both with the foundation and the partner organizations. Just prior to starting the project, JFF had engaged a strategic planning group specializing in non-profit development but using the tools of the profit-making sector. JFF was used to creating strategy documents, had a theory of change, and had incorporated ECHS into the broader goal and metrics for the Youth Transitions Cluster. The JFF staff used strategic thinking language in pushing the foundation to consider changing the work and the strategy for carrying it out. The foundation staff drew on JFF's own knowledge and experience, on what JFF saw happening on the ground as the partner intermediaries started up schools, and on what the foundation was learning from its broader education portfolio.

And fortuitously, this new foundation was also feeling its way and evolving, not just its thinking about ECHS but about all its work with high school reform. It, too, was moving toward results-oriented strategic thinking, which required constant revision based on lessons learned and changes in the external environment. Thus the biggest difference then between the Trusts' work with EDC and the JFF-Gates relationship is that JFF and Gates have invented and reinvented ECHS together and are continuing to figure out its future. To return to the frame, the culture of decision making at JFF was more like Gates than like EDC. In our view, the give-and-take between JFF and Gates, though not without its tensions, is an important part of the value added by an effective intermediary organization.

Use the Intermediary to Build Bridges

A foundation's interest in and need for intermediaries depends in large measure on the reform strategy the foundation has chosen to support. The Trusts' decision to launch the network came after five years of supporting systemic reform through national research and development projects (such as the New Standards Project) and through the work of the Pew Forum on Standards-Based Reform—an ongoing seminar and think tank widely credited with providing intellectual leadership and policy guidance for this emerging reform movement. At the same time, the Trusts was deeply invested in high school reform in the School District of Philadelphia—an experience that provided an almost daily reminder of the challenges and frustrations involved in trying to move an entrenched central bureaucracy and a resistant teachers union. At the Trusts, as at other large national foundations, there was increasing pressure from top management and the board for "measurable results"—pressure that program staff sometimes respond to by overpromising. One of the ironies of the Pew Network initiative is that, in some sense, the foundation and the grantees switched roles: the grantees saw the project primarily as a wonderful learning opportunity for themselves and a welcome respite from the bottom-line accountability pressure they were increasingly under from their states and school boards; the foundation cared principally about test scores and other evidence of increased student learning. An effective intermediary might have helped bridge this gap and at least enabled the foundation to appreciate the accomplishments of the project, but this intermediary was, unfortunately, seen by both parties as part of the problem.

The Trusts' subsequent decision to leave the K–12 field, like that of several other national foundations, can be seen as reflecting donor fatigue, or frustration with the agonizingly slow rate of improvement in urban education. For all the reasons we cite at the opening of this chapter, the mismatch in goals and expectations between the sectors is most apparent to those foundations committed to the systemic reform strategy, where virtually all the important levers for change are inside the system. The Gates Foundation's ECHS initiative is interesting in that while it is essentially a network reform strategy, it is also a market-based strategy, providing choice and competition in the high school sector. Because Gates's ambitions from the outset have been not simply to dramatically increase the supply of good high school options, especially for low-income and minority youth but, more important, to transform urban high school education nationally, its strategy is now becoming systemic as well. As the foundation's intermediaries, JFF included, are bumping up against the challenges of getting districts to own responsibility for the new schools that Gates funds have helped to create and to integrate these schools into the larger system in ways that will enable them to survive and flourish, some of the cultural tensions that plagued the relationship between the Trusts, its intermediary, and its districts are beginning to emerge. Whether JFF and the other partner organizations involved in the ECHS project will be more successful in managing these tensions is an open question.

Bridging the Cultural Divide: A Role for Foundation Dollars

The organizations on each side of the cultural divide need intermediaries. Foundations interested in large-scale reform and improvement of urban education need powerful, intermediary organizations to help them carry out their programs. As the staff and leadership of the Bill & Melinda Gates Foundation is now discovering, even foundations that think they are principally in the business of supporting reform networks or charter schools will ultimately face the need to engage the larger system if they want to institutionalize and sustain their projects.

Urban school districts need such intermediaries if they are to accomplish the ambitious reforms envisioned by the standards-based reform movement. Even the best organized and led urban districts have very little capacity to reflect on their work, to access external sources of expertise, or to address crucially important issues of organizational alignment and coherence. Good intermediaries can help districts do these things, as well as help them gain access to private funds, which are typically the only sources of flexible dollars available to urban districts.

Unfortunately, the supply of intermediary organizations that can perform these crucial brokering, assistance, and translation roles for both foundations and school districts is limited. Increasing the supply of such organizations should be high on the priority list of any foundation seriously interested in urban education reform.

NOTE

1. See McQuarrie, Guthrie, and Hess (2006). Their paper was funded by the Ford Foundation and the Social Science Research Council as part of an ongoing study of intermediaries. Drawing on Bourdieu's social theory, the authors of this unpublished paper make a significant distinction between organizations that carry out specific functions (such as professional development or business planning) and those that translate wholesale a mission, vision, and set of practices.

REFERENCES

McQuarrie, M., Guthrie, D., and Hess, A. "Intermediary Organizations and the Coordination of Social Practices." Paper presented at the ASA Annual Meeting, Philadelphia, Aug. 14–16, 2006.

Schein, E. H. *Organizational Cultures and Leadership.* San Francisco: Jossey-Bass, 1992.

Chapter Six Overview

Barbara Cervone served as coordinator of the Annenberg Challenge from January 1994 through September 2000. In this chapter, she reflects on Ambassador Annenberg's noble motives and extraordinarily ambitious goals. Responding thoughtfully to the editors' charge for this book, she analyzes the complex and difficult task of applying relatively unstructured grants to the pressing and contested terrain of urban (and to some extent, rural) public education.

The many facets of this grant program reflect the robust ambition behind its launching. Many experts were consulted (and returned conflicting advice in ample supply); the initiative's authors respected local ideas and encouraged other funders to join as codesigners, and they were unafraid to break from the sometimes timid norms of philanthropy. Among the driving motives was the press for speed. Urgent problems demanded action.

The ensuing story is one of intended pluralism among grantees—pluralism that sometimes looked like scatter and confusion. Yet in other places it looked like the full-bodied energy unleashed by the convergence of good ideas, capable people, adequate resources, and a mandate to make change happen. As Tom Hatch observes in Chapter Seven, although reform activity can nurture good ideas, it can also produce "churn." Churn returns a decidedly unfavorable ratio between well-intentioned activity and beneficial change.

In a trenchant closing section, the author deals with "lessons and dilemmas," asking shrewd questions and responding to them from within the Annenberg Challenge perspective. This analysis is enlightening in its own right. If one changes the lens, however, from one faithful to the Annenberg vision and the implementation that followed to one focused on opportunities for educational capital building, interesting questions arise. How might a $500 million gift have been designed if educational capital development had been its goal? Whether designed as such or not, how much de facto educational capital actually informed the strategies of the

Challenge overall and the several grantee sites? (We know, for example, that tested principles from the Coalition of Essential Schools, prior work in small schools, and some achievement-gap-closing ideas were built upon.) What is the relation of grant size and duration to building educational capital? How should multiple actors, such as schools, districts, intermediary organizations, and foundations, interact so that educational capital is the product? And how might scaling up and building educational capital be connected to spread better practices?

6

WHEN REACH EXCEEDS GRASP

TAKING THE ANNENBERG CHALLENGE TO SCALE

Barbara Cervone

Do we design what we believe? Do we enact what we design?
Do we get what we intend? Do we like what we get?
What do we need to rethink?

Donald A. Schön (1930–1997), principal investigator
for the Annenberg Challenge cross-site evaluation and professor emeritus,
Massachusetts Institute of Technology

LAUNCHED IN 1993, THE ANNENBERG CHALLENGE was the largest private grant to public education in our nation's history. Aimed at improving education in our country's most pressed urban schools, Walter H. Annenberg's $500 million gift was as idealistic as it was generous. Mr. Annenberg wanted to catch the public's eye, and he did, most of all in the selected cities where his challenge grants, some as large as $50 million, were concentrated. He wanted to raise hopes that even the most failing schools and school systems were capable of excellence, and he did, even though the private resources the Challenge provided were a drop in the public bucket for the large urban districts and schools it engaged.

It did not take long for the Annenberg Challenge to stir criticism along with hope, and one of the early and enduring criticisms was that it lacked focus and its goals were not clear. It is easy to see why this seemed so. From the start, the Challenge defied simple characterization, as it charted a course that embraced pluralism and crossed boundaries. The sites, eighteen in all, came in many stripes—from Chicago, where education activism was a long-standing tradition among local community organizations, universities, and foundations, to Chattanooga, where a vote to unite county and city schools offered an opportunity to think about school reform for the first time.

The geographical expanse of individual sites was often enormous: the three largest counties in South Florida, twenty-eight school districts in the San Francisco Bay Area, and over one hundred rural communities from Alaska to Louisiana. And the reform strategies reflected the full menu of what seemed promising at the time, from starting small schools to turning large-school feeder patterns into K–12 "families" to "place-based" education to making literacy a driver for change.

Not only was the Challenge hard to describe and grasp, but it was also hard to assess. Answering questions about impact with confidence can be tough in tightly focused interventions, even in one school. And tracing a specific intervention to a rise in student test scores—the Holy Grail—is rarely as straightforward as it sounds. With the Challenge, the hurdles to determining impact, most especially of the initiative as a whole, were for-midable. This was the case several years ago, when the sites that had received Annenberg Foundation grants reached the end of their funds, and it's just as true now, almost twelve years after Mr. Annenberg stood in the Rose Garden and announced his $500 million gift.

From the start, though, the Annenberg Challenge was crystal clear about one thing: the importance of going to scale. Looking back, the Challenge's determination to reach for *scale*—a term that seeped into the language of school reformers just as the Challenge began—seems its most distinguishing feature. When school reform activists and researchers met in the early 1990s to discuss what lay ahead, at gatherings like The Pew Charitable Trusts' Education Forum, they agreed that creating single, exemplary schools, or "fireflies" as Deborah Meier called them, no longer sufficed. The next and much larger task, they concurred, involved creat-ing an abundance of bright schools and ensuring that their lights did not dim. Funders of K–12 education were reaching the same conclusion. But few knew how to accomplish this exponential spread (there were no existence proofs that it could even be done) and, for better or worse, the Challenge became an early trailblazer.

When Challenge project directors and researchers gathered twice a year to compare notes and assess progress—cross-site meetings that were a first but are now customary in large K–12 foundation initiatives—they talked often about the struggle to balance breadth and depth as they reached for scale. Writing about the Challenge has always posed the same dilemma, and this narrative is no exception. "Would that this mammoth undertaking had just one or two story lines," a program officer whose foundation had contributed matching funds to the Challenge once sighed. "But it has more stories than we can know and tell, far more than we can analyze and understand."

One Man's Gift

As Mr. Annenberg, with President Bill Clinton at his side, unveiled his half-billion-dollar Christmas gift to America's public schools in December 1993, confidence in our public schools was at low ebb, and schools in big cities especially were beset by seemingly intractable problems. The tide of mediocrity in America's elementary and secondary schools that *A Nation at Risk* had warned against a decade earlier seemed to be rising unabated. Annenberg's message was simple: something should be done to stem this tide, and something *could* be done. He asked, too, that other Americans of wealth and other foundations join his crusade.

Behind a philanthropic initiative one-tenth this size often lie months of environmental scans and consultant reports, all leading to the setting of program specifications and proposal guidelines. Few foundations make large moves without embracing these preparations, even if their planning ignores the lessons learned by those before them in the belief that their idea is brand new. Annenberg launched his challenge without these preliminaries. They would follow, he insisted.

What Mr. Annenberg valued most in the two individuals he invited to help him think through his unprecedented gesture was the passion they shared—that every American child, regardless of his or her circumstances, deserved an excellent education, that public schools are, indeed, the balance wheel of democracy. Vartan Gregorian, then president of Brown University and a trusted friend of Annenberg's since Gregorian's days as provost at the University of Pennsylvania, championed public institutions at every turn, with New York City's Public Library, which he headed for seven years, taking center stage. Theodore R. Sizer, the founder of the Coalition of Essential Schools (CES) and the chair of Brown's Department of Education at the time, backed up these democratic ideals with firsthand knowledge of what it took to turn one school around and how to build a movement with school reform at its core.

Annenberg's reliance on two close advisers to shape the spirit of his gift and his eschewal of a corps of external planning consultants to hammer out the details (then as now, the foundation's program staff included a director and part-time program officer) might seem astonishing. But that is how Mr. Annenberg had always done business.

Abiding Principles

When Mr. Annenberg turned over responsibility for the Challenge to Gregorian and Sizer, after the Christmas 1993 White House announcement, the first thing both did was to seek input from as many educators, activists, researchers, and visionaries as they could cram into a six-month planning period. What, they asked, have we learned about improving schools? Where should an initiative directed toward the design of school reform lie—at the school level, at the district or regional or philanthropic level, or at some combination of these? What are the consequences of starting at a particular place or several places at once? What do we know about public engagement in school change? If improving teaching lies at the heart of improving schools, what contributes most to teaching quality?

The questions tumbled forth. The answers, often competing, came from CEOs of national education organizations like the College Board, community organizers like MacArthur Fellowship winner Ernesto Cortes, educational researchers like Richard Elmore at Harvard and Michael Fullan at the University of Toronto, charter school advocates like Theodore Kolderie, seasoned teachers and principals from school reform networks like the Accelerated Schools and New American Schools, and public engagement experts like Deborah Wadsworth and Robert Sexton.

Sizer and staff at the newly minted Annenberg Institute, who were charged with spearheading school reform nationwide along with coordinating the Challenge, also conducted what they called "reconnaissance" in Boston, Chicago, Detroit, and Los Angeles. They gathered local funders, political and business leaders, university faculty and deans, K–12 educators, and school reform activists for day-long discussions of possibilities and local circumstances. They also gathered leaders in rural education to imagine what a rural Challenge initiative might encompass.

This design phase could have continued for several more months, but Mr. Annenberg brought another distinctive element to his gift: a demand for speed. If the condition of public education in the United States was indeed urgent, then we owed it to students and their families to act with urgency. From these intense meetings and discussions, a set of six interlocking assumptions about what a good school looks like, how schools change, and how change goes to scale quickly emerged. They became the Challenge's abiding principles.

First, the grants awarded by The Annenberg Foundation had to be unprecedented in their size (more than in their number) if they were to win attention, achieve salience in the increasingly crowded field of school reform, and make a difference. The majority of the grant recipients needed to be big as well, embracing the largest school districts in the country; reform in these districts would potentially reach millions of students. The fact that the largest districts were often the most troubled was as much a plus as a minus. It meant the Challenge would prove itself in the hardest places and where the need for change was greatest.

A smaller portion of Challenge grant funds, however, would be reserved for special opportunities, most often triggered by one or more local foundations launching a major initiative that Annenberg would then match, creating, for example, a new countywide school system in Chattanooga, a unique teacher professional development center in Salt Lake City, partnerships between grassroots arts organizations and schools in New York City, and a cross-generational literacy program in Chelsea, Massachusetts.

Second, the grants had to harness, not supplant, promising local reform efforts. They should unleash new ideas and local creativity, too. Such bottom-up reform would honor local conditions and coalitions, reflecting Annenberg, Gregorian, and Sizer's large faith in democratic processes. It also seemed the best way to ignite the local ownership and energy required for reforms to take root and grow.

For New York City, this meant building on a decade of experience with small schools and doubling their numbers, as well as creating an experimental charter district where exemplary small schools would enjoy both autonomy and influence in the larger system. In Chicago, the Challenge would expand on the city's 1988 reform movement, which gave local schools more autonomy, and extend it through community partnerships that would bring new ideas to teaching and learning. As rural schools and communities struggled for their survival, the Rural Challenge aimed to revitalize both, nurturing connections that supported initiatives targeted at the local economy, environment, and culture.

Third, the Annenberg grants had to have a systemic impact, and the only way to do that was by engaging multiple players simultaneously: students, teachers, schools, parents, intermediary organizations, community partners, business leaders, local funders, ordinary citizens, education administrators at the district and state levels, professional organizations, and education policymakers. One of the first documents produced jointly by the research teams attached to each Challenge site was an "impact map" outlining the five levels each Challenge project hoped to affect. The first level comprised students themselves; the second, their schools and classrooms; the third, school networks and other "intermediate" structures; the fourth, district and other policymakers; and the fifth, the community, including parents.

Fourth, the grants needed to catalyze new philanthropic energy. When Mr. Annenberg announced his gift at the White House ceremony, he called on the nation's wealthy, saying, "I do not believe The Annenberg Foundation's $500 million Challenge grant over five years will do the whole job. This must be a challenge to the nation. . . . Those who control sizable funds should feel an obligation to join this crusade for the betterment of our country" (1993). All the Annenberg grants would thus carry matching demands, requiring sites to raise new private and public dollars to meet Annenberg, often two-to-one. Mr. Annenberg hoped that local funders not only would increase their financial commitments to K–12 education in their area but would also tie their contributions to the reform agenda contained in their site's proposal to The Annenberg Foundation—a radical break from the norm, where local funders encouraged and supported their own discrete projects. Even more, Gregorian and Sizer wanted local foundations to be active partners in developing their site's plan—a role to which they were largely unaccustomed.

Fifth, the grants would nourish schools working toward a shared definition of good teaching and learning. With CES's "common principles" as a guide, Challenge architects agreed that good schools were those that, in collaboration with their immediate community, arrange their resources so that each child is known well and then use this knowledge to shape each child's schooling, set uncompromisingly high academic expectations for all children, respectfully assess the progress of each student by means of a careful and continuing review of that child's actual work and then use that assessment to improve the child's learning, and exhibit daily the ideals of acting as a democratic and thoughtful learning community.

This vision of the "good" school influenced how the Challenge would measure its eventual impact on students. If the schools the Challenge prized were those that assessed students by multiple measures, then test scores alone were insufficient yardsticks of progress. The same was true of personalization and its impact on students or the student benefits that accrue when a school behaves democratically. Challenge planners also argued that "deep" innovations took time to show up in academic gains by students.

Sixth, to these principles Challenge planners added an organizational invention to oversee the reform work in each site: intermediary organizations. Although the Challenge was not the first philanthropic reform effort to employ intermediaries, the entities it imagined and then vigorously supported were distinctive. At the most basic level, they would provide fiscal oversight, ensuring that Challenge dollars would not simply move through existing bureaucratic channels and perhaps plug district deficits; awarding the grant funds directly to districts risked incurring one or both. Much more, they would position themselves as both outsiders and insiders, working neither solely within the system nor wholly outside it. If they were to succeed, Challenge projects and their intermediaries would have to transform attitudes and relationships among system insiders at the same time that they obtained significant new investments of creative involvement by system outsiders. They would also need to gain access to and exert leverage at crucial, "in-between" places where connection and dialogue are badly needed, yet largely absent.

No prior school reform effort had so explicitly designed itself to try this "inside-outside" strategy on such a large scale. Indeed, the Challenge's founders did not foresee the important organizational lessons that would emerge from their investment in intermediary organizations, including what it took to cross organizational boundaries and catalyze change up and down the system. They were extraordinary tasks: to inspire vision, to focus change efforts, to lend support, and to apply pressure.

More Than Challenged

Within nine months of the White House announcement, The Annenberg Foundation awarded its first Challenge grant: $25 million to a new organizational entity—the New York Networks for School Renewal (NYNSR)—to create a critical mass of small schools in New York City. Grants of $50 million each to Philadelphia, Chicago, and Los Angeles soon followed. By the fall of 1995, the list of Challenge sites had grown to include the San Francisco Bay Area, all of rural America, two arts initiatives (one in New York City; the other, national), Baltimore, and Chattanooga. Two years later, the entire $500 million had been dispersed. This total includes outright grants of $50 million to the Annenberg Institute for School Reform and New American Schools and $13.5 million to the Education Commission of the States. (Table 6.1 lists all the matching grants awarded.)

The ceremonies that attended the grant announcements in some cities were as grand as the dreams for "true reform" that they kindled. The hurdles of putting such sweeping programs in place followed closely. And the exigencies of pursuing scale felt like negotiating waves in an ocean: as soon as one wave passed, another appeared.

Table 6.1. Annenberg Challenge Matching Grants.

Site	Grant Name	Grant Award (in millions)	Date Awarded
Large Urban Grants			
Bay Area (CA)	Bay Area School Reform Collaborative (BASRC)	$25.00	July 1995
Boston	Boston Plan for Excellence— Boston Annenberg Challenge	10.00	Jan. 1996
Chicago	Chicago Annenberg Challenge	49.20	Nov. 1995
Detroit	Schools of the 21st Century	20.00	Nov. 1996
Houston	Houston Annenberg Challenge	20.00	Jan. 1997
Los Angeles	Los Angeles Annenberg Metropolitan Project (LAAMP)	53.00	Nov. 1995
New York City	New York Networks for School Renewal (NYNSR)	25.00	Jan. 1995
Philadelphia	Children Achieving Challenge	50.00	Jan. 1995
South Florida	South Florida Annenberg Challenge (SFAC)	33.40	Jan. 1997
Rural School Reform			
(National)	Rural School and Community Trust	46.75	July 1995
Arts Education Grants			
Minnesota	Arts for Academic Achievement	3.20	July 1997
(National)	Transforming Education Through the Arts Challenge (TETAC)	4.30	Sept. 1996
New York City	Center for Arts Education	12.00	July 1996
Special Opportunity Grants			
Atlanta	Urban Atlanta Coalition Compact	12.00	June 1997
Chattanooga	Chattanooga-Hamilton County Public Education Foundation	2.50	July 1995
	Leadership Development Initiative	1.50	July 1998
Chelsea (MA)	The Boston University/Chelsea Partnership	2.00	July 1996
Salt Lake City	Eccles-Annenberg Challenge	4.00	Dec. 1996
West Baltimore	Baltimore New Compact Schools	1.00	Apr. 1996

Logistics

The press for speed that characterized the design phase continued as Challenge sites began their work, and the first hurdle they faced was creating, overnight, an intermediary organization to head up their efforts. Although The Annenberg Foundation eventually allowed sites to extend their work into a sixth year, sometimes even a seventh, all began with the understanding that they had five years to get up and running, do their work, and then close shop. Most raced to file nonprofit incorporation papers, recruit a board of directors and staff, set up an office, and develop the requests for proposals and memoranda of understanding that would launch their work. Boston and Chattanooga were rare exceptions. There Challenge dollars flowed into an existing public education fund, giving them a jumpstart.

In addition to speed, The Annenberg Foundation favored lean administration—a stance they would later change. In the early years of the Challenge, the number of staff shouldering these burdens in most sites rarely numbered more than a handful.

Invention Versus Coherence

Balancing bottom-up invention with coherence and focus at the top was another immediate hurdle. The proposal guidelines The Annenberg Foundation and Institute gave prospective grant recipients outlined, in general terms, the Challenge's rules of engagement, goals, and vision of a good school. But they offered few specifics. For Gregorian, Sizer, and The Annenberg Foundation, this was as it should be. It matched their faith in reform plans designed by those closest to local action and their wish to encourage out-of-the-box ideas. However, it left local designers scratching their heads about what "Annenberg wanted" and resulted in a pluralism among the Challenge sites that defied consistency.

As the Annenberg Institute attempted to guide the work in individual sites (or, in the case of the last grants awarded, to aggressively shape the proposals submitted for approval), these tensions reappeared; it was then the institute that scratched its head. Local invention did not necessarily ensure clearly thought-out theories of action and effective strategies, and local ownership did not automatically secure buy-in, with key players joining enthusiastically in a common reform agenda. When "Annenberg Central"—the term the sites coined for the small staff at the institute who oversaw the Challenge—assumed the role of "critical friend" with each of the eighteen projects, it pressed for greater coherence and focus in most.

As the South Florida Challenge, for example, constructed a theory of change that centered on school-business partnerships, Annenberg Central worried that the strategy would produce a motley collection of small projects and little whole-school change. The only corrective at its disposal, though, was suasion. From the start, Gregorian insisted that the institute's role involve coordination and not direction, and that it had no authority in relation to the sites, which were independent.

At the site level, the tensions around local invention versus coherence centered on the plans that schools presented to win Challenge funds. Just as The Annenberg Foundation and the Annenberg Institute invited sites to develop reform ideas tied to their unique circumstances, sites extended a similar invitation to "their" schools. This ran counter to how most change initiatives worked, where plans and program specifications came from the top (the state or district) or the outside (community organizations, universities, and funders), and schools were recruited to enact these plans. When sites created a detailed but unified vision of the changes they sought to achieve and communicated these clearly to schools, the reform plans that schools offered were usually on target, if not robust. In the Bay Area, schools could apply for funds to support change only after they had presented a winning portfolio to the Bay Area School Reform Collaborative (BASRC), met its other requirements for membership, and participated in professional development activities. The Rural Challenge employed a cadre of experienced consultants who scouted out rural communities that "got" its vision of "genuinely good, genuinely rural schools" and then helped schools and townspeople craft plans finely tuned to this vision. Where focus and coherence wavered at the site level, however, the plans put forward by schools often headed in many directions at once and, sometimes, not in a convincing direction at all.

Breadth and Depth

With scale-up, the pursuit of breadth versus depth (the hope that one will lead to the other) always poses a dilemma. In the Challenge, the debate showed up most visibly in the number of schools to which sites awarded funds, which in turn were proxies, however rough, of breadth or depth. In Philadelphia, where Annenberg dollars flowed into Superintendent David Hornbeck's districtwide "Children's Achieving Challenge," every school (in theory) was a participant. In Boston, 48 percent of the city's schools received support through the Challenge, and in Chicago it was 40 percent. At the other end of the continuum, BASRC pursued a strategy that identified and invested in "leadership schools" and awarded grants to only 86 (7 percent) of the region's 1,214 schools. The Rural Challenge's scouts turned up two dozen or so schools and their communities, from Alaska to Alabama, where they made large investments.

District Relations

Annenberg's huge reliance on intermediary organizations to carry out the work made it seem as though there was no "district strategy"—that is, no hard plan for engaging districts as reform partners. The reality was far more complicated. In several sites, Challenge dollars actually supported a district-designed plan for change, with Philadelphia topping the list. In Boston and Chattanooga, the Challenge intermediary and the district had close working relationships, although this did not exclude pushing one another. The Boston Plan for Excellence regularly called the Boston Public Schools to task, as when it documented the district failures in professional development for teachers, but Superintendent Thomas Payzant valued these critiques.

In New York City, the mayor and school chancellor championed, from the start, the Challenge's citywide arts initiative led by the newly created Center for Arts Education. While still school chancellor, Ramon Cortines pledged to support the New York Networks for School Renewal's dream of creating a virtual charter district in which mature small schools would be given full autonomy in exchange for holding each other accountable to rigorous standards. Although the dream died under the next chancellor, Rudolph Crew, the Board of Education established an Office of New School Development and put one of the city's most experienced small-schools principals in charge. In Houston, what started as an arm's-length relationship between the district and the Houston Annenberg Challenge became collegial. In South Florida, representatives from Broward, Miami, and Dade districts, who had all been part of creating the proposal to Annenberg, sat on their local Challenge boards and applied for and received grant funds from the South Florida Annenberg Challenge.

The hurdle was not obtaining district engagement but turning that engagement into reform-friendly changes in policy and practice. In retrospect, the expectations in this regard were too high; initiatives like the Annenberg Institute's National Task Force on the Future of Urban Districts, which has district redesign as its sole target, underscore the enormous obstacles to making change in what most would agree are entrenched bureaucracies.

However, the urban school districts in which Annenberg worked were caught in churn as much as they were trench-bound. Revolving superintendents and school boards, changing state mandates, and managing the vagaries of funding kept them on edge, making them preoccupied, if not unsteady, partners in the Challenge's call for reform, even if they sincerely wanted to collaborate. Nowhere was this truer than in Detroit. The Schools for the 21st Century, which was Detroit's Challenge intermediary, repeatedly sought a close partnership with district leaders, but the district was in such turmoil (between bankruptcy and a state takeover that produced a succession of caretaker chief school officers and poisoned morale) that partnering became an obstacle rather than an aid to moving forward.

And the Challenge grants were, themselves, a source of churn. In those places and at those times when they seemed more like a conflicting than a measured strategy, "bureaucracy" proffered a countervailing railing, in the form (or guise) of safety, stability, and order. Balancing stability and churn, when the goal was change, demanded of both the Challenge intermediaries and the districts they encompassed unusual deftness in their relationships.

The enormous size of the Annenberg grants, ranging from $20 million to $50 million in the largest cities, also raised undue expectations about their systemic impact. Among school reform activists and others seeking large-scale change, it seemed that these grand sums would surely capture district attention and offer an incentive for public-private collaboration around an ambitious reform agenda. In fact, the Annenberg grants fell, as Gregorian loved to say, in "the arithmetical error" columns in these districts' annual school budgets, diminishing greatly the mystique surrounding their power. In New York, for example, Annenberg represented 0.05 percent of the city's school budget, in Los Angeles 0.09 percent, in Chicago 0.28 percent.

Philanthropic Participation

Every Challenge site met the private match requirement of its Annenberg grant. Some, like the Bay Area, Boston, and Detroit, came to The Annenberg Foundation with private funds already in hand and asked Annenberg to meet them. Private citizens, foundations, and corporations in Chattanooga contributed $5 million to match Annenberg's $2.5 million within a matter of weeks. Sites where there was little tradition of private giving to public education (notably Los Angeles and South Florida) took a full five years to make their match. Yet in their pursuit, they won contributions from foundations previously reluctant to become involved in public education. Annenberg's dream that his gift would inspire others was more than fulfilled.

However, the hope that local foundations would pool their contributions or make grants directly to their Challenge intermediary went mostly unrequited. Understandably, local funders insisted on remaining in charge of their K–12 contributions; they also wanted to continue to support programs they had launched or favored. Indeed, no one wanted to see local funders rob Peter to pay Paul. Thus, when their grant decisions more or less lined up with the Challenge agenda, as they often did, the awards counted as a (parallel) match. In sites hard-pressed to meet Annenberg's matching requirements, however, the temptation to embrace programs that strayed from the plan but carried badly needed funds presented yet another challenge to coherence and focus.

The Bay Area's full embrace of active philanthropic participation set it apart. Here, William R. Hewlett and his foundation gave BASRC its start with an unprecedented grant of $25 million. His generous example spurred other regional funders to contribute what they could, too. In turn, BASRC welcomed local foundations as full members of its collaborative, facilitating regular opportunities for them to meet, share information, and reflect together on the effectiveness of their K–12 grantmaking.

Evaluation and Research

Rather than recruit a national research firm like RAND to evaluate the Challenge overall, the institute asked sites to assemble their own evaluation teams, to be drawn from experienced school change researchers at nearby universities. This strategy suited the Challenge's complexities and pluralism. It also lined up with the principle of honoring local invention and ownership that characterized so much of the Challenge. Early on, a core of principal investigators and project directors agreed to use a theory-of-action approach to the evaluation. Local research teams then worked closely with project staff to elucidate their site's theories of action, select indicators of progress, develop a research design, and set up a system for providing formative feedback. In this way, sites would gain data that were tuned to their specific theories about change and were fine-grained and timely, allowing for midcourse corrections. Although the approach would not yield a summary evaluation of the Challenge as a whole, it would produce local reports that took annual stock of progress using an array of measures and, in some sites, seminal studies on specific issues like the quality of teacher assignments or the cost benefits of small schools.

This complicated evaluation strategy made it hard, however, to give a simple answer to the question, Has the Annenberg Challenge made a difference? The difficulties with providing a succinct answer left a void, as did the insistence that it would take time for the reforms the sites favored to show up in improved student test scores or changed school districts. Vocal critics of Annenberg declared the Challenge a failure long before the evidence was in; one *Los Angeles Times* opinion editorial asserted that Challenge sites refused to evaluate their work (Reilly, 1998).

Building Capacity

If intermediary organizations were the linchpin in Annenberg, then much of the Challenge's success rode on the capacity of their staff and boards to perform well. The fact that they were guardians of an extraordinary amount of private money gave them the power and credibility that large and successful nonprofit organizations take years to acquire. But raising, managing, and giving out money was only one of many areas where Challenge intermediaries needed to be expert. Most of all, they had to build the capacity of others—by providing vision, focus, support, and pressure at the right places and right times. And to do this, they had to assume roles that were largely new, with much of the learning coming through trial and error.

The intermediary organizations needed to become champions of reform, rallying teachers, administrators, parents, and community leaders around a shared vision of what was needed and how to get there. This required more than simply a good public relations effort. They needed to become educators, creating opportunities for professional growth among teachers and principals in the schools they funded. They needed to be political advocates, mediating among various political players, from state departments of education and school boards to unions and community activists. They needed to be program developers, recognizing special needs as they arose and then developing programs to meet these needs. Finally, they needed to become management coaches, turning visions into measurable goals worthy of the visions and seeding a culture of accountability. They also had to facilitate and respond to the university-based research teams they had recruited to assess their work.

It was a tall order, and the staff in Challenge intermediary organizations felt chronically overwhelmed. In Los Angeles, the day's agenda at the Los Angeles Annenberg Metropolitan Project (LAAMP) might include visits to three schools in South Central Los Angeles that were part of one of the twenty-eight school families supported by LAAMP, ironing out territorial concerns with the school reform organization (LEARN) that predated LAAMP, and a closed-door meeting with business and community leaders about becoming involved in an upcoming (and contentious) school board election. In Houston, the day's task list could include finalizing a professional development workshop on whole-school change for hundreds of teachers, meeting with the evaluators from the University of Texas-Austin to agree on which of the initiative's Beacon Schools would make good case studies, and planning a fundraiser that would attract additional donors.

Passing the Baton

One of the abiding principles of the Annenberg Challenge, as noted earlier, was that it would harness, not replace, promising local reform efforts. Similarly, as Challenge sites reached the end of their Annenberg funds, the hope was that they would take their strong suits and continue to advance them with new resources, possibly through a new organization. The Challenge, in effect, was the middle leg of a (marathon) relay race: sites would pick up reform ideas and activities that came before, build on those that had traction, and then pass the baton or reassemble their team for a new leg.

In New York City, the lead partner in the New York Networks for School Renewal—New Visions for Public Schools—continues to incubate new small schools. When the Annenberg grant ended, some 50,000 New York City students attended one of 140 small public schools sponsored or created with Challenge assistance. Since 2002, with $30 million from the Bill & Melinda Gates Foundation, the Carnegie Corporation, and Open Society Institute, New Visions has started more than one hundred additional small schools and has broken some of the city's large high schools down into smaller learning communities. The New York City Center for Arts Education, started in 1996 with a Challenge grant of $12 million, continues to support partnerships between schools and arts organizations in all five boroughs. In 2002, it won the Governors' Arts Award for outstanding contributions to the cultural well-being of the State of New York.

In the Bay Area, BASRC (which changed its name in 2005 to Springboard Schools) still puts its energy behind closing the achievement gap and giving teachers and administrators the tools they need to make ongoing improvements. The cornerstone, then and now, remains a "cycle of inquiry" that requires educators to reflect on their practice, make changes, and then reflect anew on what the changes yield. BASRC continues to serve as a researcher, developer, and convener in the Bay Area and to win major philanthropic support, including an additional $25 million from The William and Flora Hewlett Foundation and another $15 million grant from The Annenberg Foundation. Highlights of its work the past two years include launching an online course for teachers and school leaders on the cycle of inquiry, "focal district partnerships" that provide coaching to superintendents, principals, and teacher leaders, and a series of Best Practices Institutes.

The Rural Challenge (now called the Rural School and Community Trust) always saw state policies unfriendly to rural schools and communities as an enormous obstacle to increasing the number of "genuinely good, genuinely rural" schools. It was the only Challenge grantee to set aside a substantial portion of its annual budget for a full-fledged policy program with its own staff, in addition to supporting change efforts in schools and, in the case of the Rural Challenge, communities. In the years since, the policy arm of the Rural School and Community Trust, with generous grants from new funders, has commissioned and produced research on crucial issues affecting rural education like consolidation or the impact of long bus rides, filed amicus curiae briefs in key court cases, supported community organizing around funding inequities in a half-dozen states, and issued annual report cards on the extent to which individual states aid or abet rural schools.

Boston, Houston, and Chattanooga, as well as the intermediary organizations the Challenge supported in each, are all beneficiaries of the Bill & Melinda Gates Foundation and Carnegie Corporation grants to forge high school reform. Each has become increasingly adept at leading change in and with its school district, playing well its insider-outsider role. Two of the smaller Challenge sites—Minneapolis and Salt Lake City— continue the work they began with Annenberg, drawing on a mixture of public and private funds.

Challenge sites that never found their stride dimmed as their Annenberg funds ended. Wanting to spread the Annenberg largesse as widely as possible, Los Angeles began with a plan that provided insufficient vision, focus, support, or pressure; subsequent adjustments came too late, and the organization that received the handoff from LAAMP never really took hold. The Challenge in Philadelphia, which was one and the same as David Hornbeck's "Children Achieving" initiative, overreached in different ways, providing almost too detailed a vision and not enough focus, too much pressure and not enough support, adding enemies faster than friends along the way. It died with the end of Hornbeck's tenure as Philadelphia's school superintendent. The Chicago Annenberg Challenge never fully transcended its initial stance as a grantmaker and in its last year helped start a local education fund to which it bequeathed its remaining assets. In Detroit, the Challenge could never make up for decades of underinvestment in the city's schools or mismanagement among district leadership.

Regardless of its baton pass, each site brought to its last leg of the race heightened local conversation and awareness about good schools, scale-up, collaboration, professional development, standards and expectations, accountability and assessment, and district policies. "Whether they want to admit it or not, today's philanthropic reform efforts stand on the broad shoulders of Annenberg and the conversations about schooling it generated," observed a long-time stakeholder in Chicago school reform. "Never before have so many people, with such diverse roles, talked—or argued—so hard."

Lessons and Dilemmas

The Annenberg Challenge was never short on lessons and dilemmas. Most of the lessons have a familiar ring: school reform is painstaking work, teacher quality and professional development are critical to improving schools, students rise to high expectations, and leadership matters. Many of the dilemmas are also predictable and have been touched upon earlier in this case study: How do you balance depth and breadth, top-down and bottom-up reform, coherence and initiative, support and pressure?

Perhaps it is the reflections that get less attention that are best shared here, especially as they relate to K–12 philanthropic initiatives aimed at bringing reform to scale. Thomas Hatch's insightful 2002 article, "When Improvement Programs Collide," informs the thoughts and questions that follow.

○ *Can an initiative be too big for its own good?* Everything about the Challenge was large: the grants, the expectations, the cities and regions where the Challenge took up residence (for example, all of Los Angeles County), the number of schools participating (over 2,500). One could argue that it was *too* large. It was an enormous opportunity that often overwhelmed its actors: intermediary organization staff and boards, local funders, districts, principals and teachers, university-based researchers, community partners. This largeness also encouraged, if not rewarded, overpromising. The proposals that sites submitted to Annenberg were extraordinarily ambitious and, in turn, the proposals schools submitted to sites often overpromised, too. And then rather than help sites and schools negotiate down their plans to make them realistic, the institute introduced another layer: the expectation that key players be part of a cross-site community, with its own meetings, activities, and requirements. However rewarding this cross-site communication and learning, it added further demands. How then does an ambitious K–12 philanthropic initiative—large but probably not nearly as large as Annenberg—think and behave realistically while also setting high hopes and goals? Even small-school reform initiatives tend to over-reach in their quest for salience and impact.

The Annenberg Challenge also raises the chameleon character of "big." It may have been too big to manage effectively but, as noted earlier, when placed against the public budgets of schools and districts, its resources were infinitesimal.

○ *What do we mean by "systemic reform"? What are its goals, and how do we measure progress?* When the Challenge began, talk about systemic reform had just started to animate conversations about school improvement. More than a decade later, the discourse has grown louder, yielding as many questions as answers. How do funders and reformers outside the system forge strong relationships with the very bureaucracies they seek to change: districts, state departments of education, teacher unions, and teacher education programs? What theories of action seem most convincing? At what places and around what issues can outsiders exert beneficial leverage? How do changes in one part of the system affect another? How does one measure impact and against what yardstick?

Challenge sites chalked up what they considered substantial victories in their efforts to engage the system. In Los Angeles, for example, LAAMP created new-teacher preparation programs that linked its school families with the California State University to deliver fast-track, alternative credentials; the Rural Challenge provided convincing testimony to support universal access to the Internet for rural communities; its research on school size and student achievement continues to draw attention among policymakers. When Annenberg Central described these and many other wins as proof that sites were leaving "small footprints" in the systems of which they were part, it did so with both pride and realism. Skeptics, however, seized on the phrase as proof that the sites had failed to have a systemic impact.

○ *What are the liabilities of locally imagined and implemented change strategies?* From start to finish, the Challenge was a natural experiment on whether, or to what extent, school reform can rely on local invention and design. Prima facie, this localism meant pluralism, which inherently pushed against the values of consistency and coherence. This was a trade-off Annenberg was willing to make, for reasons described earlier (from wanting to build on ongoing reform efforts to fueling local ownership). However, this localism also assumes an inherent "goodness" in local design—that those closest to the action know best, and, in the special context of the Challenge, that the process of local collaboration and negotiation that produced each site's proposal to The Annenberg Foundation was inclusive. These are large assumptions, not always borne out in fact as one looks across the Challenge sites. When, for example, business leaders stepped in to help shape plans, as they did in several sites, the strategies they advocated typically lacked substantive knowledge of school change research. In cities where competing visions and organizations populated the local school reform landscape, the Challenge inherited these tensions; where there was a denominating reform agenda or organization, the planning process fell short of being inclusive and inviting new partners and ideas.

o *How do we build the capacity to build capacity?* In the Challenge equation, the intermediary organizations at each site were the key variable; their ability, as noted earlier, to provide the right combination of vision, focus, support, and pressure was pivotal. Most often, the staff at these intermediaries had not been part of the planning process, so the first test of their capacity was to understand the proposal Annenberg had approved and fill it out, even its frailties. Before long, Challenge intermediaries realized that to carry out what they had filled in, they would need to be not just program implementers and managers but also capacity builders—with all of their constituents, including the schools they funded. In addition, their role as being neither wholly outside nor exclusively inside the system required that they negotiate divergent views, act strategically, and find the in-between places that needed special attention.

However, this was new work for everyone involved, and the fact that the change strategies being championed were typically complex meant that they were also harder to learn. As K–12 funders move to large reform initiatives with multiple sites, the capacity of the intermediary organizations they tap to deliver the goods becomes urgent. It cannot be taken for granted. Sometimes, funders engage in wishful thinking in this regard, turning to organizations with a strong reputation in a different arena to become an intermediary for the project in question. Occasionally, the skills are transferable or easily gained; more often, they are not.

o *Finally, how do we build reform initiatives that take into account the ecosystems in which schools and school systems are inextricably a part?* In "When Improvement Programs Collide," Thomas Hatch writes:

> It may also be useful to view schools as part of an ecosystem in which many different entities are trying to co-exist. Viewed in this way, the initiatives of improvement programs, districts, and states cannot be considered as the "start" of change efforts. Changes are constantly under way. In this context, new initiatives, whether from the district, the state, improvement programs, or others, have to be carefully examined in the same way that we have to consider how new species and new developments will affect the ecosystems into which they are introduced. (p. 634)

The questions Hatch poses are the same ones the Challenge's principal architects would ask as they looked back. Was there sufficient capacity to absorb and carry out the new initiatives unleashed by the Challenge? Did they broaden and deepen efforts already at work? Were there high demands and hidden costs that may have produced harmful and not just positive effects? What was truly within Annenberg's sphere of influence, and what lay far beyond?

Donald Schön, an emeritus professor at the Massachusetts Institute of Technology who helped construct and then oversee the Challenge's cross-site evaluation until his death in 1997, once told the members of the cross-site group why he thought their efforts to reflect on their accomplishments and shortfalls were so important:

> When you have a community of reliable inquiry capable of drawing on strengths, on multiple sources of knowledge, and on multiple sources of intuition—in a context where something is at stake, and where our worry is how to take action, with a sense that we *have* to take action, and that there is a we here—under those circumstances there is the greatest grounds for hope, because it's there that we liberate our human capacity for understanding and perceiving. (1996)

As we continue our pursuit of schools that serve all children well, Schön's words seem as fresh as ever.

REFERENCES

Annenberg, W. A. Statement delivered in the White House, Dec. 17, 1993. The Brown University News Bureau.

Hatch, T. "When Improvement Programs Collide." *Phi Delta Kappan,* 2002, *83*(8), 626–634.

Reilly, P. J. "Annenberg's 'Challenge' Is a Bust: The Philanthropist's Big Grant for Public Schools Does Little Except Line Bureaucrats' Pockets." *Los Angeles Times,* Apr. 7, 1998.

Schön, D. A. Personal communication, Sept. 21, 1996.

Chapter Seven Overview

Seen from Tom Hatch's scholar's-eye view as a faculty member at Teachers College, Columbia University, foundations and the intermediaries they engage provide money and technical assistance to schools but at a high price for those schools, especially when juggling the demands of many agencies involved in a single school. Responding to their many (and often competing) requests and requirements, reassigning administrative and teacher time to the added effort that innovations soak up, and reallocating funds to continue a successful grant-begun program—all press heavily on the already burdened resources of a school. Third-party interest does not, of course, play into a patiently waiting school environment. Besides the intensity of daily demands, schools must continually respond to district priorities, as well as to state and national policy requirements.

In the face of what Hatch labels "turbulence," the course of reform is not likely to run smoothly. Relying on his research in six schools, he identifies characteristics—some in schools, others in the external environment, and still others in the relationship between the two—that critically influence the success or failure of foundation initiatives. Several characteristics point to educational capital. Some, such as creating professional development programs that respond to certain curriculum needs, designing a model for project-based instruction, or developing an inquiry-based model for school renewal, have direct relevance to the building or application of educational capital. Others—like mobilizing community support of the school's priorities, managing resources in order to allocate time to capital-based reforms, or building relationships between schools and districts to assure staying power of positive changes—are about the conditions that enable educational capital to gain traction.

With a degree of realism as welcome as it is scarce in school improvement schemes, Hatch demonstrates that compelling ideas connected to good intentions are only two legs of a three-legged stool. Without the third structural element—the *capacity to manage* initiatives—schools and foundations will struggle to secure for even well-developed educational capital the focus and attention sufficient to prove its local merit. For foundations, the message is that the passage from the glow of a potentially effective idea to the sober management of a successful grant obliges sympathetic attention to the grantee's capacity.

7

BUILDING CAPACITY FOR SCHOOL IMPROVEMENT[1]

Thomas Hatch

WHEN A NEW PRINCIPAL ARRIVED at Charleston High School in the San Francisco Bay Area in 1996, she found that the school was involved with four different local and national foundation-supported reform initiatives: (1) the Bay Area Coalition of Essential Schools (BayCES, now known as the Bay Area Coalition for Equitable Schools), (2) the Bay Area School Reform Collaborative (BASRC, now known as Springboard Schools), (3) Joint Venture Silicon Valley, and (4) Advancement Via Individual Determination (AVID), and there seemed to the principal to be "twenty-five subsets of those" (Hatch, 2001, p. 44). While each one of these initiatives helped to provide the school with needed resources and technical expertise, they also demanded significant time and attention from the principal and staff members; they often pushed the school in different directions at the same time; they required the school to meet a variety of different assessment and reporting requirements; and they left the school needing to raise additional funds or cut other programs in order to sustain their initiatives. At the same time, Charleston High School also had to deal with numerous district, state, and national improvement efforts that included implementation of new professional development programs, curricula, graduation requirements, tests, and assessments.

Charleston High School was not alone in struggling to try to coordinate a variety of different improvement initiatives. In fact, in a survey of all the schools in the same urban district in the San Francisco Bay Area[2] at that time, over half the principals (51 percent, with 77 percent responding) reported that their schools were working with three or more different improvement programs (funded by foundations or other outside sources). Of all the responding principals, 15 percent reported that they were involved with six or more different improvement programs. Surveys in one comparison district in California and two in Texas showed that 63 percent of the responding schools in all districts were engaged with three or more improvement programs and 27 percent with six or more. In one district, 18 percent of schools were working with nine or more different programs simultaneously (Hatch, 2002).[3] Like Charleston, these schools were working with all these improvement programs in a policy environment that has fostered a spate of new district and state initiatives that have to be aligned and coordinated (Fuhrman and Elmore, 1990; Spillane, 1996). In this kind of environment, foundation-funded initiatives can end up doing as much to undermine the capacity for improvement as they do to build it.

The Challenges of School Reform in a Turbulent Environment

Despite the interest and investment in "systemic" reforms at the end of the twentieth century, schools operate in a turbulent environment that makes it difficult for anyone—school members, funders, or the reformers they support—to align their initiatives with others. Constant changes in leadership and policies, the economy, and public expectations make it difficult to prepare for the future and foresee what will happen to current initiatives or to imagine what other initiatives may be launched. Furthermore, the turbulent educational and economic environment affects funders and reformers as well. They may experience sudden changes in their own funding, in their leadership, and in their own internal capacity that can lead them to change their strategies and even "pull the plug" when they would prefer to stay the course.

Finally, from the perspective of funders and reformers, the resources and assistance they provide and the strategies and outcomes they pursue may seem consistent with other state and local initiatives. But practitioners in schools may still feel themselves torn in numerous directions at once, with no clear sense of how things come together. In other words, funders and other external agents cannot legislate coherence in the minds of practitioners; they can only do so much to maximize their support and minimize the conflicts that may come with it.

In such a turbulent environment, schools must have the capacity to find the resources they need, to manage the conflicting demands and requirements they face, and to deal with the fact that many aspects of the environment around them—policies, leadership, funders, funding priorities, and the like—are going to change relatively rapidly (March, 1991). In short, schools need to be able to create the conditions for their own success. As Michael Fullan puts it, "Altering context is not up to others; all of us can, to a certain extent, change the immediate context around us—and this starts us down the pathway of transformation" (2003, p. 29). From this standpoint, the problem facing funders and reformers interested in education is how to make productive investments in education and provide useful assistance without adding to or intensifying the demands and turbulence that schools face.

Foundations and the reformers they support can approach this problem by helping schools develop the basic organizational functions that enable them to make improvements and sustain them over time. Doing so, however, requires a reconceptualization of the capacity that schools need to make improvements. To aid in such a reconceptualization, I offer here the experience of six schools (and of one school, in particular) that have demonstrated the ability to make some improvements and sustain their performance over significant periods of time. The experiences of these schools illustrate the challenges of building capacity, even among organizations that manage to make some improvements, and they demonstrate the need to rethink some of the conventional assumptions about school reform.

How to Build School Capacity by Managing Demand

What does it take for schools to deal with a turbulent environment, make improvements, and sustain them over the long haul? Consider an analogy to the evolution of strategies for building the capacity of municipal water systems. Early in the twentieth century, in order to meet the needs of growing populations and a newly industrialized society, cities needed a much larger supply of water. The initial response was to try to increase capacity by building more dams and reservoirs and increasing their size. Quickly, however, the economic and ecological costs made it clear that building more reservoirs and increasing the supply of water could not go on forever.

As a consequence, strategies for building water capacity expanded to include efforts to manage the demand for water by developing appliances and other devices that required less water and by educating the public about the benefits of conservation. By controlling the demand for water in this manner, the need for construction of new dams and reservoirs diminished. From this perspective, the amount of water available at any given time is only a part of the equation for determining water capacity; capacity is a function of the resources available (in this case water) and the demand that exists. Furthermore, water managers have to think about the water available throughout the system—not just in individual reservoirs, and they have to take into account a wide range of environmental factors that can affect the demand for water, including shifts in weather patterns, ecological changes, influences of new technologies, and the impact of changing populations. If they fail to act systemically or to address these factors, they will be unable to ensure that the entire system has the capacity required to serve the public over the long term.

Although vast differences exist between water systems and school systems, considering an analogy between the two highlights several key issues for funders and reformers interested in helping schools build their capacity to make and sustain improvements.

First, school capacity is not determined solely by resources and features that can be considered internal to the school. It also depends on the relationship between the school and the surrounding community: changing the demands placed on schools changes the amount of resources and the amount of effort schools need to achieve their goals.

Second, although we often think of the development of school capacity as requiring the addition of resources or the development of mechanisms within a school, schools can also deal with issues of capacity by trying to shape the demands that are placed on them. Thus, in this formulation, capacity reflects both a school's ability to receive and implement certain policies and practices and its ability to act on and influence the surrounding environment. Put simply, changing the demands placed on a school will change the resources and the amount of effort that the school needs to achieve its goals. Increasing demands for performance (raising standards, for example) may mean that some schools that were meeting previous demands will have to get new resources, put in place new structures, or engage in other efforts to increase their performance. Correspondingly, those schools that can manage the demands placed on them may not have to increase their capacity or expend substantial energy in trying to meet new goals.

Third, although research often focuses on the capacity required for schools to demonstrate certain levels of student performance, schools face a host of demands that they must have the capacity to meet (Hatch, 2001). These include explicit demands (in the form of regulations, contracts, policies, and so on) from the district, the state, support providers, and others to implement certain practices. They also face demands from board members, educators, community members, and the general public to conform to their expectations and operate in certain ways. Thus, managing demands entails not only managing demands for performance but also managing demands for compliance and conformity that may affect a school's ability to meet performance goals. Managing demands is particularly crucial for schools because they have such limited resources; they cannot turn on a spigot and suddenly produce more funds, more time, or more qualified teachers.

Fourth, this view of school capacity accentuates the fact that capacity has a temporal dimension. Policies and practices that aim to ensure that the supply of high-quality instructional practices meets the demand for improved performance at a given time may be quite different from policies and practices that seek to ensure that a certain level of performance can be maintained over a significant period of time. In particular, those policies and practices that seek to support a school's capacity over time have to go beyond examinations of internal resources and other characteristics to take into account changing external conditions.

In short, school capacity depends on a school's ability to take into account and influence the supply of resources and the demands placed on it and to make appropriate organizational adjustments and changes over the long haul. Put another way, schools that demonstrate the capacity for high performance are neither totally dependent nor completely independent of the demands, pressures, resources, and opportunities that exist around them. They are intimately tied to their environments and likely to be capable of shaping, as well as responding to, external demands and pressures (Fullan, 1999; Hargreaves and Fink, 2004).

How Schools Make Improvements and Sustain Performance

Findings from case studies of six schools in the San Francisco Bay Area that operate in different community contexts and regulatory environments and with distinct instructional philosophies illustrate what it takes for schools to make improvements and adapt to a turbulent environment. The cases focus on two K–8 schools in a diverse urban district (Emerson and City) and two K–5 schools in a wealthy suburban district (Dewey and Peninsula) that have had good reputations and records of performance over twenty-five years or more. Two of these schools (one in each district) began in the 1970s with an open school or progressive instructional approach; the other two were launched at about the same time to reflect a more conventional or back-to-basics approach. All four are "schools of choice," with participation determined by application and lottery. The study also included an award-winning, five-year-old urban charter high school (Horizons), with a focus on students with special learning needs and an urban bilingual school within the regular public system (Manzanita), known for developing and sustaining its own reform effort over the past eight years within a deeply troubled urban district.

Although these schools have reputations as being successful, making improvements has been a constant battle, not a one-time initiative. Over the past fifteen years, these schools have had to make changes in their practices and operations in response to changes in enrollment levels and the nature of their student populations, significant swings in funding levels, shifts in state and district-endorsed curriculum frameworks and assessment approaches, and the introduction of new policies like the reduction of class size in the lower grades and the virtual elimination of bilingual instruction. In turn, these changes have contributed to crises at these schools, including threats of closure, consolidation, and reductions in staff; turnover among staff and leaders (including, at one school, five principals in eight years); tensions among parents and staff; and periods when teachers closed their doors behind them and worked largely on their own. In other words, these schools do not necessarily avoid problems; neither do they always operate effectively. What distinguishes them from other schools is the fact that they have been able to make some improvements and overcome some of the inevitable problems that arise.

Although these six schools are unusual in many ways, looking across their experiences highlights six critical practices. These six practices may be worthy of further examination for any schools trying to build their capacity to make improvements. These schools do the following:

1. *Develop, monitor, and revisit broad, general missions.* These missions, as well as the periodic efforts to revisit them and share information about them, provide a basis for distributing leadership and enabling many members of the school community to make decisions that are consistent with the school's practices and approach.

2. *Find or create professional development opportunities that fit their needs.* When necessary, these schools establish their own internal professional development opportunities, including inquiry groups, meetings to reflect on student work, and case discussions based on the model of the "grand rounds" in medical education.

3. *Manage hiring and turnover.* Like the "great" companies studied by Collins (2001), these schools hire the "right" people and find ways to get those people into the right roles, regardless of the official positions or responsibilities assigned by their districts.

In addition to these three internal activities, staff members (and sometimes parents and community members, not just principals) engage in three kinds of activities outside the school that help them find resources and manage external demands: (1) building public understanding of the schools' mission and needs, (2) reshaping demands and negotiating with district administrators, support providers, and others, and (3) mounting collective efforts when the school faces particularly problematic demands (Honig and Hatch, 2004; see Figure 7.1 for a graphic representation of the practices).

As the figure suggests, these internal and external practices are closely intertwined. The internal practices make it possible for these schools to build public understanding of their work, to shape and reshape external demands and opportunities, and to mount collective efforts when necessary. In turn, the ability of these schools to manage external demands makes it easier for them to develop and sustain their mission, attract qualified staff, and obtain appropriate professional development. This circular relationship helps to explain why it takes capacity to build capacity. It also helps to explain why it is so hard to help schools that do not already have some capacity to manage external demands and meet their own goals (Elmore, 2002; Fullan, 2003; Hatch, 2001).

Figure 7.1. Key "Internal" and "External" Practices That Enable Schools to Make and Sustain Improvements.

A Case of Foundation Support and School Improvement

Some schools can carry out these activities largely without foundation support or considerable external assistance. In fact, the two schools in the wealthy suburb (Dewey and Peninsula) and the urban K–8 school with a traditional instructional approach (City) did not seek or rely on extensive outside support. The three urban schools with less traditional approaches, however, sought and received support from a variety of foundations or from support providers who benefited from foundation grants.

On the one hand, that support helped to build the capacity of these schools by providing them with some of the funding, time, technical assistance, and external connections they needed to develop their missions, establish their own approaches to professional development, and get the right personnel in the right roles. On the other hand, these schools already seemed to have the capacity to engage in a constant process of negotiation with their funders, support providers, and others in order to make sure that support fulfilled their needs.

The experiences at Emerson—the K–8 school in the urban district—provide a useful illustration of what it takes for a school to take advantage of and coordinate external support from a number of different sources in order to make improvements.

From its founding in the 1970s to the early 1990s, Emerson managed to cultivate a devoted following among a diverse group of parents who believed in the community-based approach to decision making that launched the school (which included the fact that the school had no principal, and, instead, relied on staff consensus and a rotating "lead" teacher to make decisions) and the progressive instructional philosophy it developed. At the same time, changes in the external environment, including shifting enrollment levels, an aging teaching force, and political and leadership changes in the area all contributed to pressures and periods of crisis that the school had to overcome. In particular, the school had to mount several intense lobbying efforts to get resources and to keep the school open in the face of threats of closure from the district (because of changes in enrollments and a lack of adequate facilities, among other issues).

Furthermore, after a long period with a fairly stable, veteran staff, in the 1990s the school began to struggle with significant teacher turnover: at one point, out of a teaching staff of nine, the school took on five new teachers (one of whom had to be hired just days before he began work in September because the district assigned additional students to the school). As Diane Kirsch, a former lead teacher at the school, explained it in comparison to the Emerson of today, "This was really quite a different school.

People still cared about kids, and there was still a sense of community and of family and of really knowing kids. And there were always multi-age classrooms, but it reached a point where people taught whatever they were teaching, and people really didn't have a clue as to what was going on in other people's classrooms."

Providing Support for Key Organizational Practices

As part of its response to these problems, Emerson began a series of initiatives in the 1990s that benefited from some foundation support and that were crucial to the development of the school's mission, instructional approach, and structures for professional development. These improvement efforts grew out of the school's use of district funds (earmarked for the development of site-based management, which was, essentially, already in place at the staff-run school) to engage in what one former staff member termed "the goals thing." The staff used the funds to meet together on weekends and during the summer and examine the history of the school and where they wanted to be in ten years.

Rather than a set of documents or a mission statement, however, the most significant result of those meetings was the decision to seek funding to implement a model for project-based instruction that a group of teachers (including one from Emerson), administrators, and researchers in Emerson's district had developed with the support of Project 2061—a national initiative of the American Association for the Advancement of Science (which has been underwritten by the Carnegie Corporation of New York, the John D. and Catherine T. MacArthur Foundation, The Pew Charitable Trusts, and others).

Although the school's proposal for funding from the state of California (through the initiative known as SB 1274) was not accepted, the school managed to find enough time, money, and support to develop and implement their own version of the 2061 model. In addition, the members of the school's staff got several small grants (on the order of $10,000) from organizations like the National Foundation for the Improvement of Education and the Noyce Foundation, which helped them launch related initiatives like an assessment project that contributed to the development of the schoolwide exhibitions that have become a key part of their project-based approach.

The project-based approach that the school managed to develop by cobbling together support from a variety of sources also spawned the development of a host of organizational practices and collective activities that now enable the staff members to carry out their own professional development as a regular part of their work together. In fact, before they began working on project-based instruction, the faculty held a weekly staff meeting that usually involved discussions of issues like field trips, social events, and school behavior. But as they began to develop the projects, faculty established an extensive meeting structure that eventually encompassed a meeting of the whole staff every Monday, weekly meetings of the faculty at each developmental level (K–2, 4–6, 7–8), and then bi-weekly committee meetings that are often used for planning purposes, including a "professional development team meeting" and a "lead team meeting."

In a kind of snowball effect, establishing a distinct identity as a progressive, project-based urban school attracted the attention of a number of other support providers and funders and helped to build the school's capacity to make improvements. For example, a growing association with Partners in School Innovation (PSI) provided the school with Americorp members who assisted the teachers and with PSI staff who provided outside (and neutral) facilitators for staff meetings in which significant differences of opinion about the development of the projects were addressed. After two years, however, PSI, which was experiencing its own financial pressures that limited its ability to work in large numbers of schools, chose to end its relationship with Emerson and concentrate its support elsewhere.

Emerson went on to establish close relationships with both BASRC (established by funds primarily from the Annenberg Challenge and The William and Flora Hewlett Foundation) and BayCES (now an independent organization working to establish small schools in the Bay Area). These relationships have helped the school get access to a wide range of technical assistance and new ideas that helped to launch new initiatives, such as an inquiry-based approach to professional development and a focus on equity. In addition, the funds that have come with these partnerships, as well as private funding from several additional sources, enabled the school to continue to underwrite some of their significant investment in their own meetings and staff development and allowed the school to create a "reform coordinator" position that "freed up" one teacher to provide help and support for the rest of the staff.

Building External Connections and Gaining Social Capital

As the school's reputation and local and national partnerships with major support providers grew, the school made connections with a wide range of other funders, volunteers, prospective teachers, journalists, and others who could help them advance their goals. Although far less tangible than the dollars the school received, these external connections helped give the school the social capital, not only to respond to the environment but to begin to influence it as well. For example, through the associations with powerful local and national organizations, the school sought to gain partners who could help protect them from policies or actions of a district that was pursuing far more traditional instructional approaches. "We needed outside recognition," Kirsch explained. "I felt like we were never really going to get support from the district and that we really needed to make alliances with people outside the district who were going to support the school so that we would not be in a position of ever having to fight being closed down again."

In addition, the information about the school that spread through the reform community helped the school manage hiring and turnover by influencing the pool of teachers who applied to the school. As a consequence, as jobs in the district became more plentiful, the school was able to hire teachers from outside the area who already knew something about the school and already believed in project-based instruction, thus lessening (though not eliminating) the need for the initial professional development and socialization of newcomers.

Finally, the staff gained numerous opportunities to meet with people outside the school and the Bay Area who could help them learn about the latest research, practices, policy ideas, and funding opportunities long before the members of many other schools. In a sense, these activities allowed them to "scan" the environment (Honig and Hatch, 2004) and to begin to take into account ideas and practices that might eventually be reflected in the policies and demands they faced from their district and others.

The Role of the School in Managing External Support

The external support that Emerson has received has come with a price. As Kirsch described it, when the school began its relationships with external partners in the 1990s, the staff members at Emerson, like many in their position, assumed that the external assistance "was not going to be a lot of extra work or take us in a different direction." Subsequently, however, staff members have had to expend considerable time and energy in fundraising, navigating grant requirements, reporting on their expenditures and activities, negotiating mutually beneficial arrangements with their partners, and meeting with the wide range of groups and individuals who want to know more about their work.

To some extent, they have managed to deal with these demands because the school already had the capacity to make some improvements before they got extensive foundation support and external assistance. They had a relatively strong community, a relatively unique and progressive orientation, and staff and community members who understood that orientation and were already connected, both educationally and politically, to powerful groups and individuals in the area. As a consequence, the members of the school were not simply waiting for support to come along. Crucial functions (often the sole province of strong leaders) like seeking funding, bringing in relevant technical expertise and personnel, and building understanding of the school's mission and approach were already distributed across a number of people, giving the school the ability to find the right partners and the power to negotiate with those partners when necessary.

Developing Shared Understandings and Shaping External Support

The funding and support that came as a result of their efforts to develop project-based instruction grew largely out of the involvement of one veteran Emerson teacher, Rosalyn Bird, in the meetings in the district sponsored by Project 2061. Through the meetings, Bird got an opportunity to get out of the school and learn from the expertise of experienced educators from around the district and across the country. At the same time, she was able to help these other educators (often influential and well-connected individuals) learn about the work at Emerson.

Staff members at Emerson also played leading roles in the development of BASRC and BayCES's work in the Bay Area. In the mid-1990s, both organizations were just developing some of their key initiatives; as a result, staff members at Emerson were able to benefit from these partnerships before the establishment of many of the explicit demands that these organizations now place on their partners. With BASRC, for example, Emerson worked on the development of a school-based inquiry process. As Kirsch put it, "They were figuring out what their tools were, so we got to figure it out with them." Furthermore, Emerson staff got to meet with and benefit from the expertise of the key leaders at BASRC who, at that time, were directly involved in working with a relatively small number of schools.

Although there was considerable flexibility at these early stages, BASRC was under significant pressure to expand their work quickly to large numbers of schools in the region, which made such "personalized" and flexible relationships with individual schools much more difficult. Eventually, BASRC established a formal process that specified a number of requirements that schools had to meet to gain support, including producing a portfolio to apply to for funds, engaging in specific forms of inquiry, and sharing results in a structured network meeting. In addition, senior leaders— who had the power and authority to allow for exceptions and flexibility in BASRC's requirements—had much less time to spend developing relationships with or learning about the needs of specific schools like Emerson.

Finding Time to Reshape Demands and Manage External Support

Even though Emerson was in a relatively strong position to find the right partners and take advantage of external support initially, the staff members still found themselves trying to deal with the problem of coordinating multiple initiatives and shaping them to their own needs and goals. In addition to Emerson's involvement with Project 2061, BASRC, and BayCES, by the end of the 1990s the school was getting grants from a number of other sources to provide funding for resources like math books, personnel like school counselors and the continuation of the reform coordinator position, time for staff development, and an outdoor garden run by parents.

All these grants took considerable time to manage, and Emerson staff members had to work hard to make sure that the support they did get met their own needs. Sometimes, those efforts paid off. In one instance, Terry Evans, the lead teacher at the time, explained that the staff suddenly realized that the school needed to pay for more time so that teachers could meet during school hours, but the staff members had not anticipated that need when they wrote a grant to a corporate foundation. In response, she chose not to take the time to seek an exception from the funder (or to risk that they would say no) and went ahead and reallocated the grant funds. "I just did it," she said. "And then when I sent in the Annual Report I explained it. And they said, 'That's fine. Next time you need to ask us beforehand.' But I probably won't do it," she continued, "because we don't know beforehand necessarily."

Even at Emerson, however, negotiations with funders did not always work out. In one instance, the school worked extensively with a corporation that had made a commitment to provide resources to schools in the district. The corporation wanted Emerson, because of its orientation and reputation, to serve as a pilot school for the use of its resources. The company wanted to put computers in every classroom. "We didn't want thirty computers in every classroom," Evans explained. "We had been really clear about what our priority was, and it was people. We didn't want technology without human support for it." Ultimately, however, after the relationship between the company and the district soured, the school got twenty computers for a media center in the library. "We don't want twenty computers in there unless there's someone who can take care of them," Evans continued. "I've totally refused to go look at them . . . I have yet to see them. But they're there."

Even when these relationships go well, they often lead to more work and take more time that is only sometimes accounted for or anticipated. For example, as their relationships with support providers have developed, Emerson staff members have taken on more and more responsibility within the networks of support providers. Emerson has served as a "lead school" that other schools can visit; the staff members have participated in critical friends' groups and gone on visits to provide support for others in the network; staff members have often served as models, presenters, or facilitators for the convenings and meetings of the various partners. As the school has gained notoriety inside and outside these networks, its partners and others naturally refer journalists, educators, funders, and others to visit and look at the school. Staff members have taken the time to participate in numerous research projects, including several dissertations, numerous evaluations, a video series, as well as this project—all involving countless interviews and observations.

Prospects for the Future

Although this case study shows that Emerson has demonstrated the capacity to make improvements in the past, the changing conditions and difficult times that the school faces at the beginning of the twenty-first century raise serious questions about whether or not the school will have the capacity to continue to make improvements in the future and whether many other schools can follow their example. In particular, a number of factors are conspiring to increase the need for more professional development and for different kinds of professional development than the staff has needed in the past. Emerson's new initiatives on inquiry and equity are requiring the staff to develop new skills and practices. Conducting productive inquiries and linking them to changes in classroom practice has proven to be extremely difficult for schools involved with both BASRC and BayCES and requires dedicated time and external assistance.

Furthermore, the combination of the departure of a number of veteran staff over the past five years and a growing reliance on new teachers or teachers with less than five years' experience means that the school has to find ways to provide more professional development to maintain the project-based approach that has served as the schools' signature practice for so many years. Simultaneously, the pressures on the young staff members and the stresses they experience have intensified: the district, state, and federal testing requirements and accountability demands have increased substantially, and the work on equity with BayCES has led Emerson to establish its own ambitious goals to ensure that no child in the school will be in the bottom quartile on the required tests. As a consequence, time and workload at the school have become crucial issues. "If we're dependent on single women without families who can stay until 8 o'clock four nights a week," explained Laura Carmichael, one of the school's BayCES advisers, "that's not a sustainable way to run a school."

Even if Emerson can meet these changing demands and continue to make improvements, the prospects for many other schools to get or use external support to make similar improvements seem dim. In Emerson's case, not only did the school get extensive external support but it got that support at a time when the economy and reform efforts were booming. The school benefited from early involvement in the development of several major regional initiatives. And in many ways Emerson already had in place a distinctive mission, a highly qualified and committed staff, and substantial external relationships that provided it with the capacity to develop and manage these relationships and also to take advantage of them to make improvements.

Capacity Through Relationships, Not Regulation

The experiences of all the schools in the study suggest that whether the schools are highly regulated (like the bilingual school) or generally exempt from district regulations (like the charter school) does not determine whether or not the schools will demonstrate the capacity to make improvements.

All six schools faced enormous pressures, and simply relieving the schools from some regulations did not suddenly give some schools more capacity to make improvements than others. In fact, Horizons—the charter school—expended considerable time and resources in developing a productive relationship with its surrounding district in order to get resources to address the wide range of students' learning needs that was at the heart of their mission. Conversely, even Manzanita—the bilingual school in a highly prescriptive district—has earned some flexibility in its curriculum, assessments, and professional development activities. It has done so because the principal, teachers, and parents have all worked hard to get waivers from district policies they consider problematic, to develop their own alternative practices, and to align themselves with local reform providers and community leaders who share their instructional philosophy and serve as advocates for them with the district.

Far more important than the degree of regulation that the schools faced was the "fit" between the goals, instructional approaches, and organizational practices of these schools and those of their districts and other support providers and funders. Since the instructional approaches of the more traditional schools like City and Peninsula match those of their districts, they have survived and done well while relying largely on the resources and trainings available to them through the district and made do without much external support. However, of the other four schools in the study with philosophies and instructional practices that distinguish them from many of the other schools in their districts, only Dewey has shown the capacity to manage external demands and make improvements without significant external support.

Implications: Rethinking the Role of Foundations in School Improvement

The experiences of schools like Emerson suggest that taking advantage of foundation support and using external assistance effectively is no easy task. Part of what makes the task so difficult is the fact that the capacity to make improvements depends on finding the resources necessary to meet the demands that exist at any given time; most support also brings new demands that many schools may not have the capacity to meet. As a consequence, it should be no surprise that the schools that seem to benefit the most from foundation support often seem to be those that already have some capacity to find resources and manage external demands.

Although this analysis points out some logical and intractable problems with traditional approaches to providing funding and external support to schools, the experiences of Emerson and the other schools in this study also suggest that there may be other ways for foundations to approach the challenges of school improvement.

First, these case studies point out that even successful schools go through periods of considerable organizational turmoil and times when performance targets are not achieved. Rather than evidence of their failure, these instances reflect the reality of work in turbulent conditions. Too often, policies and programs ignore these conditions. To deal with these conditions, funders, policymakers, and practitioners have to shift the focus from implementing, scaling up, and monitoring specific policies and programs to helping schools develop the basic organizational functions that enable them to manage the shifting demands and opportunities around them.

Second, the examination of school capacity suggests that the capacity to meet performance targets at one moment in time is not the same as the capacity to make and sustain improvements over long periods of time. Funders, policymakers, and others need to recognize that specifying narrow outcomes, monitoring, and holding schools responsible for them often creates short-term demands that many schools do not have the capacity to meet. Such short-term pressures may make it particularly difficult for low-performing schools to make the long-term investments in the basic organizational practices of managing staff, developing thoughtful professional development, and mission building that contribute to a school's capacity to make improvements and sustain them.

Third, this analysis suggests that the schools in this study could make improvements because they have distinguished themselves from others, escaped from burdensome requirements and inflexible monitoring, and captured scarce resources, including such things as effective teachers, strong leaders, high-quality professional development, capable external assistance, political influence, and foundation support. In most cases, these are not the kinds of resources that can be scaled up. As a consequence, many other schools cannot be expected to substantially improve their performance until those resources are more widely available and more equitably distributed. That may require foundations to focus on improving the basic economic, organizational, and political conditions that contribute to major public policy problems like how to manage the equitable distribution of expert teachers.

Fourth, the recognition that schools face all kinds of demands, including demands to conform to public expectations, reinforces the need for foundations and others to focus on developing public understanding, not just swaying public opinion or publicizing data on school performance. Public understanding serves as a crucial driver of many of the demands that schools face. If schools are trying to make changes that are not well understood, then the external demands only grow more difficult, and the schools have to devote more and more time, attention, and resources to managing them. Conversely, even if policymakers and others strive to increase the pressure on schools to improve their performance, many schools, particularly schools in more advantaged communities, can satisfy public demands by continuing to operate in ways that conform to public expectations, even if they do not always perform at the highest levels or enable all of their students to reach high levels of achievement. If the wider public does not understand or demand a teaching force that truly delivers high-quality instruction to all students or that produces high levels of learning for all students, describing most teaching as "high-quality" and labeling low levels of performance as "proficient" or "adequate" will continue to suffice.

Of course, it is easy to see why many foundations might find it difficult to focus on basic organizational functions, long-term performance, and the development of public understanding. Investing in these areas would make it harder for foundations to point to specific programs or interventions that they contributed to or to show direct causal links between their investments, specific initiatives, and measurable changes in student achievement over the short term. And foundations operate under some of the same constraints and face the same economic, political, and public pressures that contribute to current demands for accountability and demonstrations of quick, measurable improvements.

Furthermore, foundations have to be willing to fail. That means that foundations, their leaders, boards, and critics need to be able to distinguish between the kinds of predictable failures that should have been avoided and the kinds of productive failures that lead to new lessons and new learning. Although the failure to achieve specified performance targets is often viewed as a reason to end funding, in some cases at least, failure may be a sign that even more support is required.

In particular, schools trying to do something different—something that does not conform to public expectations or political demands—may need more support and more latitude rather than tighter controls and more demands for more results in less time. One way to distinguish between efforts that may help build the capacity to make improvements and those that may not is to look at whether schools and other organizations are using foundation investments to put in place the people, mechanisms, and external relationships that will allow them to develop, monitor, and revisit meaningful missions and goals, to find qualified staff, and to get appropriate professional development when they need to. Ultimately, foundations may be the only organizations in the educational arena that can tolerate—and possibly even cultivate—the failures that are an inevitable part of improvement.

NOTES

1. The work described in this chapter was supported by The William and Flora Hewlett Foundation, The Spencer Foundation, and The Carnegie Foundation for the Advancement of Teaching. For help and assistance in the development of the project and the manuscript, I would like to thank

Lee Shulman, Ann Lieberman, Ray Bacchetti, and Thomas Ehrlich. The conclusions are solely mine.

2. Pseudonyms have been used for the district, all the schools, and all members of the schools.

3. This survey asked principals to report only on their involvement in forty-four improvement programs listed at the time of the survey in the *Catalog of School Reform Models* (Northwest Regional Educational Laboratory, 1998) or well known within their local area. It did not attempt to take into account other programs, projects, or partnerships with businesses, universities, community programs, and others in which schools were involved.

REFERENCES

Collins, J. *Good to Great: Why Some Companies Make the Leap and Others Don't.* New York: HarperBusiness, 2001.

Elmore, R. F. *Bridging the Gap between Standards and Achievement: The Imperative for Professional Development in Education.* Washington, D.C.: Albert Shanker Institute, 2002.

Fuhrman, S. H., and Elmore, R. F. "Understanding Local Control in the Wake of State Education Reform." *Educational Evaluation and Policy Analysis,* 1990, *12,* 82–96.

Fullan, M. *Change Forces: The Sequel.* London: Falmer Press, 1999.

Fullan, M. *Change Forces with a Vengeance.* New York: RoutledgeFalmer, 2003.

Hargreaves, A., and Fink, D. "The Seven Principles of Sustainable Leadership." *Educational Leadership,* 2004, *61*(7), 8–13.

Hargreaves, A., and Fullan, M. *What's Worth Fighting for Out There?* New York: Teachers College Press, 1998.

Hatch, T. "It Takes Capacity to Build Capacity." *Education Week,* 2001, *20*(22), 44, 47.

Hatch, T. "When Improvement Programs Collide." *Phi Delta Kappan.* 2002, *83*(8), 626–634.

Honig, M., and Hatch, T. "Crafting Coherence: How Schools Strategically Manage Multiple, External Demands." *Educational Researcher,* 2004, *33*(8), 16–30.

March, J. "Exploration and Exploitation in Organizational Learning." *Organization Science,* 1991, *2*(1), 71–87.

Northwest Regional Educational Laboratory. *Catalog of School Reform Models.* Portland, Ore.: Northwest Regional Educational Laboratory, 1998.

Spillane, J. P. "School Districts Matter: Local Educational Authorities and State Instructional Policy." *Educational Policy,* 1996, *10,* 63–87.

Chapter Eight Overview

As one of the country's longer-running teacher professional development programs, the National Writing Project (NWP) offers a wealth of insight into the stuff of longevity. One factor is the unusually dynamic and complementary roles played by foundations over NWP's thirty-two-year (and counting) lifetime. Large national foundations helped begin the project and have nourished it through grants for evaluation and program development. Smaller foundations enabled local advocates to begin and take advantage of the NWP model for linking college and university faculty and K–12 teachers in ways that improved the teaching and learning of writing in, at last count, 189 sites nationwide. Foundation support helped generate state and federal funds in an exemplary public-private strategy for building writing capacity in K–12.

Ann Lieberman, over a long career at Teachers College, Columbia University (with shorter stays at the University of Massachusetts, Amherst, and the University of Washington) and now at The Carnegie Foundation for the Advancement of Teaching, has paid special attention to the ways in which educators work together. She brings that sensibility to her chapter, along with an eye for how a variety of strategically significant elements fit and function together. Peeling back the onion of time and place, she traces how the interplay of program strength and funder acuity, woven together over more than three decades, have yielded a writing initiative that has certified what worked and purged what didn't.

Lieberman's chapter illustrates how what we are calling educational capital can be uncovered in a retrospective look that did not set out with the motivation to find it. When the five criteria of educational capital, as delineated in Chapters Two and Four, become lenses for viewing this case study, elements of all are readily apparent.

Of special interest in this case study of NWP is the way it combines *hard capital* (the knowledge and skill that teachers have, keep developing, and willingly share) with *soft capital* (the working relationships that encourage collaborating and support risk taking). In the best educational programs, these two kinds of educational capital are integrated, and the personal, professional, and intellectual aspects of teaching and learning are, in reality, all of a piece.

8

THE NATIONAL
WRITING PROJECT

COMMITMENT AND COMPETENCE[1]

Ann Lieberman

DESCRIBING THE GROWTH AND FUNDING HISTORY of the National Writing Project (NWP), arguably the most successful K–12 professional development project ever in the United States, is like unpacking a Russian *matrushka* doll. The current NWP, as well as its support base, is layered and integrated from the local level to the national, each layer a separate entity yet connected to the larger whole. But if we trace the development of this network over the past thirty-two years, we see that three themes dominate the development of the NWP over time and help explain the growth of this complicated, long-lived network:

1. The power of the intellectual and social practices of the writing project nourishes extraordinary loyalty and commitment from teachers.
2. The eventual joining together of private and public funding has helped create the national network and helped local writing project sites spread and deepen their work.
3. The importance of local funding for writing project sites allows for a diverse and complex local support base tied to local goals and interests.

The interplay between these themes provides a way of understanding how development and financial support has grown over the writing project's thirty-two-year history. From the beginning, when the network was established, all the local sites have used "the model," making them similar, yet unique in history and context.

Foundations and the Early Growth of the NWP

Over a period of five weeks in 1974, a new approach to professional development was born, rooting itself in the work of teachers' knowledge rather than only that of outside experts. Jim Gray, founder of the NWP, brought together a group of teachers on the University of California, Berkeley, campus, calling the effort the Bay Area Writing Project (BAWP). This first summer institute was funded by the University of California, which was committed to improving the writing skills of incoming students, as well as providing outreach.

The basic elements and core activities of what was to become "the model" for the writing project's "summer invitational institute," although refined over time, were present in this first institute. Teachers (elementary through community college) demonstrated to their peers successful approaches to teaching writing. They wrote and met in small groups to receive feedback. And they read, wrote, and discussed research and literature together. Soon these teachers were at work in their local communities providing leadership and professional development for their colleagues in the schools. The writing project model became a visible and transportable example of how teachers could become involved in their own development and how a community of learners could be mobilized as part of a school-university partnership.

BAWP gained almost immediate visibility in the writing and composition community, and Gray and his colleagues were contacted by other universities and composition scholars who wanted to set up a writing project site. While early writing project leaders focused on refining the model and developing ways to support others in starting their own projects, conversations with a range of funders led to the decision to raise money to expand the project. Two years after the first institute, the National Endowment for the Humanities (NEH) provided the first grant to help establish eight writing project sites throughout the state of California, giving birth to a state network of sites, as well as three sites in other states. NEH gave small grants ($15,000) that required a one-to-one match. The resulting funds were sufficient for each school-university partnership to conduct a summer institute. Although some funding from NEH continued through 1984, the basic pattern of awarding start-up funds and then requiring sites to develop their own financial base from a mix of local sources continued and became the established pattern for expanding the network. For the first ten years, foundation support was essential to the development of new writing projects. In turn, the initial seed money supported the raising of matching funds from local university, school district, and foundation sources.

The early development of the network drew attention from other funders as well. In 1976, two years after the first summer institute, the Carnegie Corporation of New York provided a different type of initial support when it funded a three-year proposal to evaluate BAWP. The idea was to find out why the writing project was so attractive to teachers and to understand the impact of its work. In summarizing the evaluation, Michael Scriven—an eminent evaluation researcher at the University of California, Berkeley—stated: "The writing project appears to be the best large-scale effort to improve composition instruction now in operation in this country, and certainly is the best on which substantial data are available" (Gray, 2000, p. 113). The extensive evaluation work established a strong base of findings for the NWP network from its inception and garnered even more attention for the project. Carnegie Corporation of New York eventually extended its early support to six years of funding, from 1977 through 1983. NEH also made the Andrew W. Mellon Foundation aware of the writing project, and together they provided ongoing support for nine years during this early period.

Thus, the funding story began with foundations playing a most significant role in helping create new writing project sites on university campuses across the country, allowing what might otherwise have been just a demonstration project to become a widespread, ongoing network. Yet despite these funding sources, Gray described the early years of the NWP as ones marked by concerns over funding:

> In spite of our numerous funding sources, we had a constant need for more money, and it seemed we were always on the edge of a precipice. The project kept growing and we were writing new grant proposals and new amendments during the first three years of NEH funding just to keep up with the demand. (Gray, 2000, p. 134)

The fullest expansion of the network would require ongoing support from public monies and local funders. Public and private funders stepped in at this point to support the growth of the network in their geographical areas of interest. Just five years after the first summer institute at Berkeley, state funding created thirteen additional sites in California. Both universities and schools were to gain by these partnerships, which helped make the writing project an attractive package to sell. Writing projects in other states attracted various patterns of investment from state sources and university budgets. This first decade of growth resulted in a loosely connected network of largely autonomous writing project sites throughout the United States, and the same mix of funding sources continues to support the work of local sites to this day.

The Intellectual and Social Practices of the NWP

Consistent financial support, however, cannot explain the ongoing demand for and commitment to the writing project on the part of educators. To continue this look at the growth and development of the NWP, it is important to take a look inside the network to see how it works, and, more important, why it works.

A number of people have written about the NWP, and each has tried to describe the practices that have made it so successful (McDonald, Buchanan, Sterling, 2004; St. John, 2004; Lieberman and Wood, 2003; Fancsali, Nelsestuen, and Weinbaum, 2001; Gray, 2000). What stands out in the accounts is that teachers come to the writing project most often as individuals who are isolated in their schools and essentially struggling alone with the inevitable dilemmas of teaching; they leave the summer institute as a member of a supportive professional community.

Less apparent are the common practices at the yearly summer institutes.[2] These practices, known as "the work" or "the model" to insiders, are critical to understanding why the writing project "hooks" teachers and commits them to a way of being in the world. The work at the summer institute is nothing short of an enactment of a culture that helps teachers gain a transformed vision of what it means to be a professional teacher and a colleague (Lieberman and Wood, 2003).

Every year, at every site in the country, teachers apply to attend a five-week summer institute on the campus of a nearby college or university. Every summer, at every site, each institute offers the "summer fellows" who are selected three core activities; they are the same activities of the first summer institute in 1974. How these activities are enacted during the institute, the participants say, is what makes the institute like "magic": "It's changed my life outside my teaching, inside my teaching. It's literally changed my whole life. It's given me a support system; it's given me friends; it's given me my writing back; it's given me my classroom back" (Lieberman and Wood, 2003, p. 32).

The directors of each site organize the institute by creating a climate of inordinate respect for the knowledge of teachers as a *starting* point for learning. And they do this on the first day by literally modeling what is to go for the remainder of the institute. By the second day, teachers are teaching each other their best strategies, reading first drafts of a piece of writing and receiving critiques from their colleagues, reading and discussing research, and perhaps hearing from one of the experienced teacher consultants (TCs).[3] Seamlessly, the participants start running the institute, as they learn, over time, how to take an interest in their own and their colleagues' thinking, challenges, and practice. The curriculum is shaped by the expertise of the institute fellows, guided by their current knowledge in the field of literacy. In the best of senses, the curriculum stresses learning as a social phenomenon and teaching as a collective responsibility (Lieberman and Wood, 2003).

Teaching demonstrations give teachers an opportunity to share a classroom strategy or approach. Veteran TCs coach teacher participants, demonstrating how to present to colleagues, how to engage an audience so that they are best positioned to learn together, and how to blend practical discussion of the realities of teaching with theoretical perspectives on why certain teaching approaches are effective. As these demonstrations unfold, the fellows, recognizing collective professional expertise, often rethink and revise their own practices. The activities of writing and response, teaching each other within the context of inquiry and study of research, and sharing and receiving feedback on their work, encourage and support teachers' knowledge and perspectives, even as they surface teachers' questions and problems in teaching. These activities lay the groundwork for an important set of social practices that, over time, bind people together in a professional community that provides support, sharing, and learning. The rituals built into the institute also create an expectation that learning in a professional community is critical to one's own growth and development. For many of the participants, this is the first time they have felt part of such a community, and it is understandable why many think of their experience in the institute as magic and state that it is "transformative."

In addition to the summer institute, all local sites carry on two other core activities: (1) in-service activities in their local service area and (2) continuity programs that help enrich the site and also keep the focus on problems that teachers are encountering in their particular context. Some sites participate in national programs that support the development of new competencies, for example, in technology or in the particular support of new teachers, or are connected to national special-focus networks that closely address the site's concerns. These networks focus on English language learners, rural and urban contexts, and, more recently, on teacher inquiry. The interplay of local resources and needs, supported by national learning opportunities and support, creates distinct portfolios of work for local sites.

Learning and Leadership in a Community of Practice

Wenger has written about "learning as social participation," stating that participation in communities of practice "shapes not only what we do, but also who we are and how we interpret what we do" (1998, p. 4). These communities become places of professional learning because people imbue activities with shared meanings, feel a sense of belonging, and create new ways of thinking about their own identities. In the NWP, "the social practices convey norms and purposes—what it means to belong to a community—and in the process, these practices shape professional identities" (Lieberman and Wood, 2003, p. 21). In such a community, teachers learn to open up their practices in the teaching of writing to their colleagues; they search for ways to better meet the needs of their students, and they find peers to join them in this collective search. Many find that they enjoy teaching others what they have learned in their classrooms.

These myriad activities form a set of social practices that, at the same time, help create the climate of collaboration and professionalism:

o *Approaching each colleague as a potentially valuable contributor by honoring teacher knowledge.* Teachers teach each other in workshops, conferences, and the like. Teachers learn to share what they know and take seriously what others know.

o *Creating public forums for teacher sharing, dialogue, and critique.* Key to breaking teacher isolation is learning how to go public with one's work. In time, public presentation, critique, reflection, and self-critique become community norms.

o *Turning ownership over to learners.* In the institute, teachers learn that internal accountability comes from being responsible for taking ownership of their own development. In the process, they live the idea that professional learning and student learning are mutually dependent and intertwined.

o *Situating human learning in practice and relationships.* It quickly becomes clear to teachers that learning is both active and relational. Learning-by-doing and learning within relationships begin to serve as guideposts for professional development.

o *Providing multiple entry points into the learning community.* Teachers come to the summer institute for different reasons: to write, to get resources, to find community, because they heard the writing project was good professional development, and the like. This brings a variety of perspectives, interests, and talents, all of which enrich the community.

o *Guiding reflection on teaching through reflection on learning.* Teachers come to see that they are learning, not because they were explicitly taught but because they had time and space to talk about books, research, and writing in the context of a learning community.

o *Sharing leadership.* Participants take turns demonstrating teaching strategies, being a teacher one day and part of the audience the next. Rotating leadership responsibilities becomes the norm in the community.

o *Promoting a stance of inquiry.* Fundamental to good teaching (and learning) is the idea that questioning and searching is an attitude that helps teachers stay positive, despite difficult contexts and tough teaching problems. The stance helps participants develop a reason to improve rather than complain about difficulties.

o *Rethinking a professional identity and linking it to professional community.* Teachers learn to collaborate and go public with their teaching. This kind of learning changes the way they think about what it means to be a colleague and shows them that professional knowledge can be collectively owned (Lieberman and Wood, 2003).

The work of the NWP, then, is about learning what it means to continue to learn and to help others learn, to go public with one's work, and to continually ask questions of it.

The summer institute not only provides the starting place and practice of these norms, but it intentionally provides a chance for leadership to emerge. This leadership, in turn, helps the site grow and develop, but also affects the professional community and the subsequent work with schools. The resulting capacity for educational improvement has been the focus of interest from foundations at many levels, local to national.

Work at the Local Level: Building from the Ground Up

By starting with local sites, we begin to see how each local culture is grown, what the teaching and learning practices are, how leadership is nurtured, and how foundations continue to be involved in their development.

The growth in local sites teaches us about the incredible variety of contexts and the constancy of the model, despite these differences. It also gives us a sense of how the different sites created different funding arrangements and of the role that foundations with more local interests have played in the growth and stability of local sites.

This—the story of the founding of the BAWP and its national expansion—is but one story. In reality, there are 189 different stories—one for each site—in this loose, yet tightly integrated national network.[4] To understand the NWP, it is important to start with where and how the work gets accomplished, namely in the local site, and build upwards to the eventual formation of the national office. Unlike other organizations, the writing project work and the socialization of the participants into the culture all happen at the local level. And in an important way, leadership learns the "writing project way" in local sites. In the words of McDonald and others (2004), this is a professional development project that has learned to "scale up" by "scaling down."[5]

It is important to note that although most NWP sites are successful, quality and capacity do vary. Problems can arise through the changes in the host institutions, leadership transitions, or failure to implement the model. For this reason, all sites are subject to an annual review. Each site must file a narrative and quantitative report that includes the previous year's activities, prospective plans, budgets, and commitment letters from local partners and host institutions. A team at the national NWP office and peers review the annual reports to analyze strengths and weaknesses and to identify sites that might not be in compliance with the model or who might need extensive support. Sites are identified for technical assistance or, in more extreme cases, are reorganized. On rare occasions, sites are not re-funded.

For a flavor of how sites develop and find the necessary financial resources, consider three different local sites: (1) the New York City Writing Project (NYCWP), (2) the University of California, Los Angeles (UCLA) Writing Project, and (3) the Mississippi State University Writing/Thinking Project. The differences, as well as the similarities, of these local sites demonstrate the importance of context, as well as the core activities of the writing project, and reveal how much these contexts find their way into the life of their districts, states, and universities.

New York City Writing Project

In 1978, Gray invited Richard Sterling, currently the NWP executive director and in 1978 a faculty member in composition at Lehman College of the City University of New York,[6] and colleagues John Brereton and Sondra Perl, to replicate the BAWP model in New York. With a grant of $15,000 for the first summer institute, the NYCWP began its work. It was clear from the beginning that this would never be enough money to sustain the writing projects unless they could find other funds. The early money was just barely enough to start a new site.

In New York, Sterling and several of the teachers from the first summer institute began to offer workshops for the New York City schools to keep alive the professional community begun in the summer, and to modestly fund the new activities of the writing project site. In this way, the project began to fund itself by providing fee-for-services professional development, creating the "in-service" part of the model. A number of the teachers who had experienced the summer institute became the TCs who provided in-service programs for schools and districts. The in-service work, in turn, provided a new focus for the summer institute. In effect, the goals of the summer institute became not only a learning experience for teachers but a way of developing teacher leadership as well. This leadership is key to the growth and development of every site, as it builds the capacity of a site to provide a variety of learning experiences and adapt to the local needs and circumstances of the context.

During the early years of the NYCWP, several foundations awarded grants to pay for additional professional development opportunities for teachers during the school year. The Rockefeller Foundation and Chase Manhattan gave grants to support what they deemed an interesting approach to the teaching of writing, but developing, sustaining, and expanding the work was still very difficult. In 1980, the NYCWP applied for a $300,000, three-year grant from the federally funded Fund for the Improvement of Postsecondary Education (FIPSE).

This three-year grant supported the Writing Teachers Consortium, which brought the writing project to a number of high schools in all five boroughs of New York City. This ongoing partnership, which includes in-service courses, in-class coaching, and leadership training is one of the largest sustained efforts of any writing project site (Mintz, Stein, and Wolfe, 2002).

In each case, New York's Board of Education matched the grants and agreed to release a handful of TCs to work during the school day to implement the new strategies for teaching writing. This gave the NYCWP the opportunity to begin developing leadership across the city. The Board of

Education released the teachers to conduct professional development in high schools in all five boroughs, and the university-based NYCWP worked with the teachers to improve the teaching of writing in their classrooms.

Not only was the model taking shape as a school-university partnership, but a connection was evolving between the universities and funding sources, with the school district paying for services, while the university offered its new approach of having expert teachers work with schools. This kind of outreach in the largest school district in the country increased the visibility of the project. It meant that an intermediate group—neither school nor university but representing both constituencies—could mount professional development that engaged both K–12 teachers and university personnel. Furthermore, it appeared that the model could travel to different contexts without losing the power and prospects for its success.

University of California, Los Angeles (UCLA) Writing Project

The power of the model to travel to and adapt to diverse contexts is possible, even within the context of a coordinated state network. The UCLA Writing Project was founded in 1977 as one of the first sites in California to follow the BAWP. Beginning as part of the Academic Center for Institutes and Programs—an off-campus program housing several subject matter projects—the UCLA Writing Project benefited from early start-up funds in the 1970s and the supportive context of significant state funding in the 1980s. Like NYCWP, the UCLA Writing Project also earned income from in-service programs and fees for institutes and conferences.

In 1995, however, the UCLA Writing Project moved onto campus and into Center X, within the UCLA Graduate School of Education and Information Studies. Center X, created as a response to the inequities that had been exposed in South Central Los Angeles during the previous decade, looked directly at the unequal playing field that low-income children of color face in our schools. The rich resource base and intellectual context of the university provided a foundation for the continuing development of the project. Through Center X, both the California Subject Matter Projects and UCLA's Teacher Education Program were supported to create programs that would address the specific context of Los Angeles.

It is not surprising, then, that the focus of the UCLA Writing Project has been on serving the diverse population of Los Angeles. The city's size, complexity, and diversity make this a multilayered, rich context. And although the writing project leaders adhere to the core principles of the NWP, they have also made some important adaptations for their context. They offer a five-week summer invitational institute, but they have also developed an invitational institute delivered over a six-month period, designed for teachers in year-round schools who work during the summer. These teachers meet on Friday nights and Saturdays over the course of a year. The site leaders have also designed a Spanish invitational institute that is held during the academic year and given entirely in Spanish. Taking their local community seriously has encouraged the site leaders to expand the core work, reach out to other populations of teachers, and make the writing project fit the needs of both an expanding and diverse population while adding new topics of concern to the agenda.

Over the course of its history, the UCLA Writing Project has relied on the steady support of its local university and state and district resources. It has also benefited from participation in a variety of foundation-funded NWP programs, such as Focus on Standards, which enabled it to develop new approaches to linking district and state standards to local curricula. And most important, it has been able to realize a deep partnership with the university, drawing on and contributing to the intellectual resources there, and to put that partnership to work in the Los Angeles public schools.

Mississippi State University Writing/Thinking Project

The NWP came to Mississippi in 1984 when Sandra Price Burkett, through a grant from the William E. Walker Foundation, secured funds to begin the first project—the Mississippi State University Writing/Thinking Project. From the outset, Burkett planned for a state network of writing project sites and invited each state university to submit a proposal for a new site that would eventually become part of the network. By 1986, there were writing project sites at the four largest state universities, and word had spread that this professional development network was making great strides in improving the teaching of writing with Mississippi teachers and students. So it was not surprising that by 1987, the Mississippi Department of Education, having committed to a proposal for the federal Job Training Partnership Act, called together the four writing project site directors and twelve teacher leaders to design a curriculum; they were also to design and conduct a related program of staff development for teachers of at-risk, low-income students ages sixteen to twenty-one. The condition of the funding was that students were to show a combined gain of eight months in achievement in math and reading skills after completing an eight-week summer session (Burkett and Swain, 1987).

The directors and the teachers provided a one-week set of workshops during the spring and four half-day sessions during the summer for the teachers. Emphasis was placed on writing, reading, problem solving, test taking, and writing in mathematics. The 1,500 students who were part of this program showed combined gains in reading and math of three years, four months. Not only was this impressive to the state and federal government, but it served as the beginning of a state partnership with the writing project that exists to this day. Seven writing project sites in Mississippi now represent a collaborative network called the Mississippi Writing/Thinking Institute (MWTI)—a unit of the Center for Educational Partnerships in the College of Education at Mississippi State University. Through the years, the state network and its sites have benefited from the support of the Phil Hardin Foundation, the Mississippi Power Company Foundation, the Weyerhaeuser Company Foundation, the Foundation for the Mid South, the Rural School and Community Trust and, most recently, a partnership with Mississippi Public Broadcasting.

Through legislative appropriation, the Mississippi State Department of Education contracts with the Writing/Thinking Institute to conduct professional development programs that are consonant with the principles and guidelines of the NWP. By 1995, the MWTI was providing 108 programs of professional development for over 3,500 teachers in the state.[7] By 2004, the MWTI had grown tremendously, serving 4,587 teachers throughout the state and conducting over 250 multiple-session programs for Mississippi teachers (Mississippi Annual Report, 2004). Each of the seven sites works on a variety of programs, including writing, reading, science, history, mathematics, and programs tailored and designed to meet special needs.

The Role of Funding

From the beginning, foundations made it possible for the writing project to grow in a variety of places throughout the country. Foundation money supported the spread of the writing project, both in California and in other parts of the country. Although the funds were modest at first, varying from $10,000 to $20,000, they were initially enough to help create a summer institute in a growing number of sites. In time, as the effectiveness of the local sites and the national coordination became apparent, the level of local funding increased, as did state and national funding.

Evidence Leads to Federal Funding

The early success of the writing project model in California and Mississippi made a compelling case for federal support to both Senator Thad Cochran (R-MS) and Representative George Miller (D-CA). The enthusiasm of teachers and the evidence from classrooms, along with the steady growth of the network since 1974, resulted in authorization of the NWP as a federal program and an appropriation of $2 million in 1991. In turn, this bipartisan-supported federal grant was to significantly change the way the writing project organized itself.[8]

For the NWP, the investment of $2 million in 1991 meant that it was now possible to begin to think about a national organizational infrastructure. The funding was intended to expand the national office as a center for support and accountability and to support the development of additional writing project sites in underserved areas. But federal funding came to mean much more. The money from the federal government also came with mandated yearly assessments and a much stricter accountability of where and how the money was to be spent. How many teachers were being served? What was the nature of the activities? The NWP established a rigorous peer review process built on evaluation tools used in the California state network to gather data for a networkwide accountability system.

Working with bipartisan support in the Congress, the NWP has become known as a significant player in both literacy and professional development circles. The federal connection has also pressed the NWP into ratcheting up its accountability mechanisms, collecting both qualitative and quantitative data on student achievement. In the process, the NWP has shifted from being a cottage industry to a full-fledged national network that numbered 189 local sites in 2005.

The Ongoing Role of Foundations: Deepening the Work of the NWP

Now that the NWP has achieved national reach through federal funding, is there still a role for private funding or foundation support? The answer is clearly yes, as in its maturity the NWP network illustrates the importance of a mixed portfolio of support, with diverse funders playing important roles in deepening the work of the NWP and supporting continuing research and development that enhances the model. The tradition of this sort of investment began just before the start of federal funding and continues to the present.

In 1990–91, the Institute for Literacy Studies at Lehman College (the umbrella organization and research unit that houses the NYCWP) applied for funds from the DeWitt Wallace-Reader's Digest Fund (now the Wallace Foundation) to support a coordinated set of inquiry activities to be conducted by the Urban Sites Network—a special-focus network of urban writing projects across the country that had been meeting informally since the mid-1980s. As proposed by Richard Sterling, then director of the NYCWP, the idea was that the network would receive the money from the foundation, administer a set of program activities, and disperse support funds to local sites. The objectives of the funded project of the Urban Sites Network were (1) to develop and document knowledge of the issues facing teachers in urban classrooms, (2) to increase the diversity of teachers in urban writing project sites, both as participants and as leaders, and (3) to broaden the understanding of the needs of English language learners in urban communities. The participating sites would explore these issues in a local, yet national effort. Foundation support for this network-driven design helped the NWP establish a design for national programming that continues to this day.

The development of the Urban Sites Network of the NWP was a very important landmark for the writing project, not only because the amount of money was substantial ($3 million over three years) but also because the foundation money was to be used to deepen and expand the knowledge of the writing project in an area of growing concern: the plight of urban schools. Ten urban writing project sites were eventually involved in this initial work, including UCLA and New York City. The award of a large grant to a local site of the NWP signaled the fact of common experiences to draw on and enough similarity across sites to work on a common theme. With this grant, foundations began a new round of investment in the national network of writing project sites.

Although much was learned across the writing project sites that participated in the Urban Sites Network, there was more to be accomplished. The leaders who emerged from the Urban Sites program work had begun to think in a national fashion about the health of the NWP network and the capacity of local sites. NWP proposed to continue the work of supporting sites to tackle challenging issues of equity and access through Project Outreach—a new initiative sent to the DeWitt Wallace-Reader's Digest Fund that would reach an additional eighteen writing project sites, including the Mississippi Writing/Thinking Project. The foundation once again responded by providing an additional $2 million of funding over three years. By this time, the foundation had developed a partnership in the work and had a vested interest in its continuing success.

These two significant investments changed the NWP in substantial ways. They provided enough funds to work intensively on a particular set of problems, and they helped to create a new model for the work of the writing project network. Writing project sites could create special interest networks within the NWP, which could focus on particular issues, develop leadership, and learn how to deepen the model to fit the particulars of local contexts. Soon after the funding of NWP's Project Outreach, similar program designs for rural communities were supported by the Annenberg Rural Challenge. The Annenberg-funded program, called Writing for the Challenge, inaugurated a similar program of investment, development, and programming for NWP's Rural Sites Network.

Public and Private Funding: A Mixed Portfolio

It was becoming clearer that foundations could sponsor what the federal government could not. The foundations could sponsor new initiatives that provide greater depth and value to the "model," while federal funding continues to expand the number of writing project sites, to support quality control and accountability measures, and to provide resources for dissemination of lessons learned. In an important way, this melding of public and private funds continues to provide opportunities for the NWP to do what healthy networks do: constantly "troubleshoot," be self-critical, and work on problematic issues. Like any other healthy network, NWP develops commitments to the network by providing a core set of ways of working and constantly solving problems that arise so that the core work can be enriched. This way of working makes networks—these "third spaces"—important and attractive models for change. They are new entities—local site partnerships—neither owned nor controlled by the bureaucracies in which they reside, yet they serve them in ways that appear to be more flexible, fluid, and dynamic (Lieberman and Grolnick, 1996; Lieberman and McLaughlin, 1992).

All three sources of funding—federal, state, and private—have been important to the development of the NWP. The federal money has clearly made possible the development of an infrastructure for this national effort. State funds have not only been an important source of financing for sites but have opened the way for the NWP to have a voice in state policymaking through the growth of statewide leadership. The foundations continue to help the network deepen its work, adding significant value as well as helping to build its organizational capacities. In fact, the NWP has been so successful that there are now efforts to expand its work into new territory; here again, foundation support has been significant.

Rather than allow funders to grow weary of an old idea that has been around for thirty years, the writing project has continued to expand its reach through additional foundation grants. There is now research evidence that writing project teachers have significant effects on their students' writing (Fancsali, Nelsestuen, and Weinbaum, 2001). In addition, researchers have found that what teachers learn in the summer institute is implemented in teachers' classrooms (Lieberman and Wood, 2003; St. John and others, 2001), adding evidence of the effectiveness of the NWP's approach to professional development and local networking. With the basic design of the model in place, foundations have continued to support the kind of national programming initiatives described earlier. These programs are coordinated research and development efforts involving local sites that extend the work and knowledge base of the writing project to address new challenges and important areas of service.

During this current phase of foundation involvement, other projects have included a Stuart Foundation grant for the Focus on Standards project, which includes the UCLA Writing Project, and a grant from the W. Clement and Jessie V. Stone Foundation supporting writing project work with new teachers. More recently, the Carnegie Corporation of New York has given a three-year grant to the NWP to support writing project work with adolescent literacy. In another case, with approximately $80,000, the Rockefeller Foundation supported a planning grant to study teacher leadership across the network. In this way, the NWP has continued to stay current with the changing needs of the day, while it has consistently used its core model as a means for solving new problems.

What This Case Teaches Funders and Educators

Although this case is only a brief description of the NWP, it begins to make evident how teachers get socialized into a supportive professional community and how this community grows through the work of the site director and the teacher consultants. Although I describe only a sample of local sites, they give a flavor of how (although the core work sits at the center of the site) each partnership is nuanced and shaped by its local context. Finally, one can see that through flush and lean times, the network structure and leadership, the core work, and the commitment of teachers makes the NWP an extraordinary example of a professional development project with important lessons for us all, funders and educators alike.

Lessons Learned About the NWP

o *Professional development matters.* The professional development that takes place during the summer institute and through the academic year starts with the teacher as a learner and a potential leader. The teachers learn about their own practice by teaching it to others, that writing is a process, and that their peers have many ideas that can help them in their teaching. In a word, this professional development *respects* what teachers know. It is this respect that helps teachers go public with their work and engage in their own development, and it is the social practices that help them become professional colleagues in a community of peers.

○ *A model of teacher learning and leadership must be transportable.* The core work of the summer institute provides the frame for the kind of activities that engage participants. Both the core work and the social practices can be used in any context. This is a remarkable feat for the writing project. Most good ideas are eaten away by the exigencies of the context. In the writing project, the core activities provide the design for professional development, allowing ample room for nuance and shaping of local context issues.

Foundations saw how sites could be developed in different contexts and how the core work could be transportable. This was a puzzle that few projects have been able to solve.

○ *A network of school-university partnerships can be effective and sustainable.* The local partnerships in the NWP are really local networks; they are an organizational structure that can be independent of, yet attached to, schools and universities. They are flexible and more informal; they provide opportunities for teachers to both consume and generate knowledge, and they work to develop a variety of collaborative structures, often encouraging risk taking in a supportive environment (Lieberman and Grolnick, 1996). This network-like quality of organizing helps teachers stay connected, either as TCs or as members of a new "community of practice." It is this interorganizational quality that is attractive to funders. Funders can support activities that are visible; they can see how local sites expand and how they spread their influence throughout a given context. They are funding both schools (and teachers) and higher education without getting involved in either of their formal organizations.

○ *Network leadership is critical.* The NWP has been fortunate in having only two executive directors in its thirty-year life. Network leaders learn to facilitate cross-cultural brokering, foster facilitative relationships, and act as embodiments of the culture. Collaboration and consultation are important in network leadership, as is the fact that leadership is nurtured in all parts of the network (Lieberman and Grolnick, 1996). Perhaps the most important part about the NWP leadership is that it is exemplified at every level. Teachers, teacher consultants, and directors all learn to facilitate for others, start where the learners are, and build community among their participants. Networks stay vital and continue to grow to the degree that the tensions that hold them together are constantly negotiated. Leadership is dispersed throughout the network, always working, however difficult that may be, toward a democratic ideal.

Lessons Learned About Funding

○ *Foundation funding is key to getting started and building capacity.* This case clearly shows that foundation funding has come in two significant ways and at two important times in the life of the writing project. In the first years of the writing project, foundation funds provided seed money to create new sites all over the country. In fact, several foundations provided multiyear grants, as they were convinced that this was a project worth supporting. Besides these significant multiyear grants, foundations have played an important role in building the capacity of local sites to work on their problems and expanding the idea into other areas. Foundations continue to be interested in the writing project, helping it push the boundaries and using the tremendous infrastructure to do new work. The role of the foundations cannot be underestimated here. Without them, it would not have been possible to develop the model and the network to a scale and capacity worthy of federal funding.

○ *An intermediary organization and matching funds are both critical within a school-university partnership.* Two interrelated lessons from the writing project are significant here as well. Housing the writing project sites within a school-university partnership turned out to be a very significant step in the maintenance and growth of the NWP. In this case, both schools and universities have a common interest in students knowing how to write. Capturing the imagination of two organizations, yet creating an intermediate one to serve them both, has been critical for foundation support. There is a bounded entity to receive their money and the flexibility of an intermediate organization to do the work. This gives foundations confidence that their money will be spent on what it says in the proposal.

The second lesson here is that to require matching funds at the local site is a powerful strategy. It not only provides for doubling the money at a local site but it (in concert with being at a university) provides for a flexibility and localness for a national project. Local funds can be raised as local people become invested in their own context. Although this does not alleviate times of stress, it does provide for a steady base for a local site's operation. In addition, matching funds show foundations that the locals not only support the project but have an investment in its continued success.

○ *Support for implementation is critical.* The writing project was luckier than most, in that it had funding for a period of almost ten years in its infancy. Even then it was growing new sites and not spending time thinking about the work, the model, teacher participation, or impact. But it is during the process of implementation that much learning goes on in an improvement project of this kind. Most foundations do not want to pay for the "learning time." Yet this is the critical period when most projects learn the real depth and breadth of their work. The writing project was fortunate that their participants were so committed to the project that they persevered through lean times because they had a vested interest in the project's continuance. There was so much more to the writing project than learning to write.

○ *Commitment and competence can be built at low cost.* In the final analysis, the development and sustenance of the NWP turns out to be quite an inexpensive way to provide for the professional development of teachers, considering the fact that there are sites in every state in the country and that each site is a partnership with a college or a university and that over 100,000 teachers are served every year (St. John, 2004.) This network has found the way to nurture and gain the commitment of teachers to constantly improve their practice. Money cannot buy this, but respecting and involving the participants on their own behalf can.

NOTES

1. I would like to acknowledge the enormous help I received from numerous people in the NWP. Most specifically, Richard Sterling, Judy Buchanan, and Elyse Eidman-Aadahl were helpful in the organization and conceptualization of the ideas and with facts and figures.

2. A site grows out of a school-university partnership; the university is the contractual agent and host of the site. Each site receives a basic grant and must document both summer institute plans and the nature of the continuing work throughout the year.

3. Teacher consultants are those teachers who have already completed the summer institute and have been active in providing professional development for their schools and districts. Many become expert in a given area, such as assessment or working with a heterogeneous classroom, and they come to the summer institute as experts and fellow teachers. They form the leadership cadre of each site.

4. This is not meant to be an organizational history of the writing project, nor can it do justice to the struggles that have made the NWP an extraordinary

model of professional development. Its longevity, stable leadership, and continued growth and development is a story that must be told over and over again to understand its layered history.

5. This idea of "scaling down" is in opposition to the current idea of scaling up. In the NWP, spreading and developing new sites (scaling down) is what enlarges the NWP and hence the growing number of participants (scaling up).

6. In 1994, Sterling was to become the second executive director of the NWP, following founder Gray.

7. Documentation of programs, participants, and contact hours are required in an annual report for the federal grant given to the NWP. This figure is taken from the 1995 annual report of the Mississippi Writing/Thinking Initiative.

8. The federal grant has grown to over $20 million annually, with the future hope from bipartisan sponsors that every teacher in the nation will have access to a writing project site.

REFERENCES

Burkett, S., and Swain, S. "Final Report: Development of Instructional Management Plan, Staff Development, and Evaluation for Summer Youth Remediation Program." Sharkville, Miss.: Mississippi Writing/Thinking Project, Mississippi State University, 1987.

Fancsali, C., Nelsestuen, K., and Weinbaum, A. "NWP Classrooms: Strategies, Assignments and Student Work." In S. Swain (ed.), *National Writing Project Evaluation: Year-One Results.* New York: Academy of Educational Development, 2001.

Gray, J. "Teachers at the Center: A Memoir of the Early Years of the National Writing Project." Berkeley, Calif.: National Writing Project, 2000.

Lieberman, A., and Grolnick, M. "Networks and Reform in American Education." *Teachers College Record,* 1996, 98(1), 8–45.

Lieberman, A., and McLaughlin, M. W. "Networks for Educational Change." *Phi Delta Kappan,* 1992, 73(9), 673–677.

Lieberman, A., and Wood, D. *Inside the National Writing Project.* New York: Teachers College Press, 2003.

McDonald, J., Buchanan, J., and Sterling, R. "The National Writing Project: Scaling Up and Scaling Down." In T. Glennan Jr., S. Bodily, J. R. Galegher, and K. A. Kerr (eds.), *Expanding the Reach of Education Reforms: Perspectives from Leaders in the Scale-Up of Educational Interventions.* Washington, D.C: RAND Corporation, 2004.

Mintz, N., Stein, A., and Wolfe, M. "Models of Inservice On-site Consulting: New York City Writing Project." *National Writing Project at Work,* 2002, *1*(2), 1–33.

Mississippi Annual Report. Sharkville, Miss.: Mississippi Writing/Thinking Institute, Mississippi State University, 2004.

St. John, M. "The Legacies of The National Writing Project (NWP): 30 Years of Developing Working Assets for Ongoing Improvement." Talk presented at the NWP Annual Meeting in Indianapolis, November 2004.

St. John, M., Dickey, K., Hirabayashi, J., Stokes, L., and Murray, A. "The National Writing Project: Client Satisfaction and Program Impact: Results from a Follow-up Survey of Participants at Summer 2000 Invitational Institutes." Inverness, Calif.: Inverness Research Associates, 2001.

Wenger, E. *Communities of Practice: Learning, Meaning, and Identity.* Cambridge, UK: Cambridge University Press, 1998.

PART THREE

HIGHER EDUCATION
AND FOUNDATIONS

Chapter Nine Overview

Charles T. Clotfelter's chapter probes the ways in which foundation grants have impact in higher education, with primary emphasis on the role of foundation funding in support of university research. Clotfelter is professor of public policy studies, economics, and law at Duke University and directs Duke's Center for the Study of Philanthropy and Volunteerism. He examines the characteristics of research universities and major foundations and considers ways in which their interests are conflicting.

Though their aims are competing, Clotfelter finds a largely productive relationship between the research function of universities and the related aims of foundations. His portrayal of mainly harmonious relations between foundations and institutions of higher education is at odds with the comments we heard from some leaders of both foundations and higher education in our initial conversations at the outset of the project that is the basis for this book; it is also at odds with what we heard from a number of the participants at the Centennial Conference on Foundations and Education. This chapter offers a good caution, lest we too quickly assume that those comments necessarily represent permanent rifts between foundations and institutions of education.

It is true, however, that academic research, particularly in the health and natural sciences and in engineering, is an arena where educational capital is built by universities individually and collaboratively much more readily than in teaching and other student-centered functions of higher education. Perhaps for that reason, it is also an arena where the interests of foundations and those in universities seeking support from foundations are much more naturally aligned.

9

PATRON OR BULLY?

THE ROLE OF FOUNDATIONS
IN HIGHER EDUCATION[1]

Charles T. Clotfelter

PRIVATE FOUNDATIONS AND INSTITUTIONS OF HIGHER EDUCATION are large and entrenched subsectors of the American economy. In 2003, there were some 59,000 such private grantmaking foundations.[2] Their combined assets amounted to $399 billion, and they made grants totaling $22.6 billion (Foundation Center Web site, "FC Stats" table on "Change in Independent Foundation Giving and Assets, 1987 to 2003). Higher education has many fewer entities; depending on how multiple campuses are counted, there are between 3,000 and 4,000 colleges and universities (U.S. Department of Education, 2003, table 171, p. 209). Their collective endowments are roughly two-thirds the size of private foundation assets.[3] Although the dollar value of foundation grants is large, their share of total college and university revenues is small, amounting to less than 3 percent of total revenues.[4] This small share naturally prompts this question: *Can a source of funding this small represent anything more than a marginal influence on the direction of American higher education?*

Foundations' Influence on Educational Institutions

Evidently, private foundations can be influential, judging by what scholars of American higher education have written. In one history covering the early decades of the twentieth century, Hollis (1938, p. 294) concludes that foundations affected the development of higher education by supporting activities at the cusp of cultural change. In a more recent effort to assess the aggregate effect of foundations in higher education, Cheit and Lobman (1974) opine, "Among the important patrons of higher education, none has had more influence per dollar spent than the private philanthropic foundations" (p. 1). They conclude by noting that "foundations have been not only significant but in many cases key contributors to the progress of America's colleges and universities" (p. 1).

As evidence of their transformative role in higher education, observers have argued that foundations were the driving force behind a number of important developments, among which are the transformation of medical education; the creation and sustenance of colleges for African Americans in the South; the development of modern, empirically based social science research; the establishment of a national faculty pension plan; the development of modern biological research; the application of Web-based technology to the storage and dissemination of published research; and the fostering of new interdisciplinary fields such as area studies, city planning, women's studies, urban studies, and public policy studies. In some of these efforts, observers have perceived a facilitating role, wherein foundations have supported innovations that government was unprepared to pursue.[5] Foundations have been seen as providing higher education's "venture capital," making possible needed reforms (Curti and Nash, 1965, p. 214).

In truth, higher education has not been particularly receptive to certain kinds of reform that some foundations have urged. In matters of teaching and learning, for example, higher education has been reluctant or unsuccessful in attempts to improve the "production process" in the way that education policymakers have aimed to do at the K–12 level. Nor have colleges and universities shown the same enthusiasm for institutional change schemes as that demonstrated either by K–12 education or business; whether this reluctance is wise remains an open question.

Not everyone has taken a sanguine view of the role foundations have played in higher education. For example, there are perennial complaints that foundations are fickle in their interests, choosing new fads over sustained support.[6] More fundamentally, some have viewed foundations as stout defenders of the status quo, or at best timid sustainers of established institutions (Nielsen, 1972). A darker interpretation sees foundations as active handmaidens of the ruling class, working specifically in the area of higher education to harness universities to serve the aims of the rich and powerful; from this perspective the vast foundation support for historically black colleges and universities has been interpreted as support for

Jim Crow educational patterns.[7] Others, noting the ways in which university research buoys the established economic order, have adopted a perspective advanced by Italian political theorist Antonio Gramsci, who argued that the ruling class can exert its influence indirectly but effectively by shaping intellectual thought.[8]

As of this writing, the relations between foundations and higher education are not everywhere pacific. Some conservative foundations, for example, have complained that university faculty overwhelmingly demonstrate a liberal bias.[9] Strains have also arisen concerning the conditions placed on grants to universities.[10] More generally, as the editors note in the introduction to this volume, some observers have perceived a growing rift between these two sets of institutions.

I do not share the editors' dismay over current foundation-university relations. This difference in outlook may arise from our different foci: whereas the editors are most concerned about foundation support for teaching and general administrative functions of colleges and universities, my focus here is on foundation support for university research. When it comes to research and policy-related activities, foundations and higher education have achieved a rather productive interaction. Foundations have offered resources, and university actors have responded in sensible ways— sometimes in ways that strengthen organizations outside universities altogether. In the realm of research, therefore, I believe the foundation-university relationship is, for the most part, a productive one, but it is not one that lends itself to simple assessment.

With these differing perspectives as the backdrop, let us take a general look at the role played by foundations in higher education, with an emphasis on research universities and the research function. Whose interests are ultimately being served by foundations and universities? In asking this question, we must consider as given such structures as the tax code and the related requirements imposed on foundations and the basic structure of colleges and universities. Thus refined, the question is this: *Given both existing law and the nature of foundations and universities, how can we usefully think about the effect of foundations on institutions of higher education?*

Pertinent Institutional Characteristics of Universities[11]

In his 1973 analysis of the university as an organization, James Coleman contrasts two organizational types: the community and the corporation. Communities, he notes, are characterized by a lack of hierarchy and therefore a certain decentralization of control. In contrast, the corporation exhibits a strong hierarchy, in which leaders exert their will among sub-ordinates. As an organizational form dating from the Middle Ages, Cole-man argues, the university is, in many important ways, more a community than a corporation. It is not so much that all decision making is in the hands of the faculty but that university leaders are severely limited in the extent to which they can command the troops.

This observation manifests itself in the following four features: (1) the independence of the faculty, (2) the influence of the academic discipline, (3) the power of university administrators, and (4) the unboundedness of institutional aspirations.

Independence of Faculty

In his analysis, Coleman argues that the defining fact about university organizations is that the quintessential university worker—the faculty member—is not an employee in the usual sense. Although their paychecks bear the university's name, faculty members may think of themselves more as independent contractors than as ordinary employees. According to an oft-repeated story, this fact was brought home to Dwight Eisenhower soon after he had been installed as the president of Columbia University in 1948. Immediately after Eisenhower opened his first meeting of the fac-ulty by addressing those present as "Employees of Columbia," a senior professor rose to correct him, saying, "Mr. President, we are not employees of the university. We *are* the university."[12] In important ways, the loyalties of faculty are often as much or more to their disciplines and professional associations as to the institutions where they work—a characterization that is most true in research universities.

A structural feature that bolsters the independence of faculty is, of course, academic tenure, which goes a long way to rob much of the hierarchical punch from top-down commands in colleges and universities. But the inde-pendence of faculty is also honored in other ways, including the traditions of departmental votes on faculty appointments and promotions and the use of faculty committees to advise administrators on university issues.

Influence of Academic Discipline

Academic disciplines, such as economics, physics, or English, play a role of fundamental importance in higher education, and their influence has particular relevance in an assessment of the role of foundations. As out-lined by Geiger (1986), the academic disciplines began to coalesce in the last decades of the nineteenth century in a process of professionalization of scholars that paralleled that of the so-called learned professions of law, divinity, and medicine (pp. 20–30). Much more than do the members of those professions, however, academics need colleges and universities in order to practice their disciplines. The members of the academic disciplines thus formed themselves into national communities, each based on an area of inquiry, each establishing "some degree of authority over the standards of that inquiry" (p. 29) and each establishing national organizations that were remarkably similar in form. In their influence over the structure and behavior of colleges and universities, they exert a double influence—one manifested in administrative organization and one showing up in the behavior of faculty.

In terms of administrative structure, disciplines provide the logic for a large chunk of what passes for university organization charts. For example, virtually every university has a department representing economics, physics, and English, and the same goes for several dozen other disciplines. Much of the same goes for the learned professions, which typically take the organizational form of schools rather than departments. Whether they are called departments or schools, these discipline-based units make important decisions about course offerings and graduation requirements. Equally important, the departments and schools are central to the recruitment, retention, and promotion of faculty members. For these decisions, faculty members look to scholars in the same discipline who work at other institutions, not only because of the importance of impartial judgments regarding academic merit but also because of the relative scarcity of scholars who specialize in a particular field.

Another source of disciplinary influence in the university applies to the faculty's independence. Owing both to the tendency for faculty to become rather specialized in their research expertise and the resulting thinness of the national market in any particular special area, faculty tend to develop professional connections with like-minded scholars at other institutions. National and international professional organizations, conferences, and journals are typically organized along disciplinary lines. The discipline becomes an important reference point for determining standards of scholarship and issues worth studying. In his presidential address to the American Economic Association in 1961, Paul Samuelson stated, "the economic scholar works for the only coin worth having—our own applause" (1962, p. 18). Whether this seemingly insular attitude fosters high scholarly standards or merely an ivory-tower insensitivity to practical problems, Samuelson's view is common among all the established disciplines. Moreover, it is strengthened in the process of graduate education, thus ensuring that the discipline's principles of scholarship are passed on to newly minted scholars. It is also the discipline that supplies qualified commentators on the quality of a research paper or a job candidate. Thus disciplinary connections are fundamental to the tradition of peer review, which, in turn, is central to the conduct of scholarly research.

The influence of disciplines may, however, be a double-edged sword. Although they offer a ready scheme for organizing the university and providing quality control through recruitment and promotion functions, disciplines can also present an organizational problem, especially for a university administrator who wishes to carry out any major reform. For one thing, the pull of discipline lessens the ties of loyalty to the local institution, thus strengthening the inherent independence of faculty members. Perhaps a more serious problem is that departments, like any semi-autonomous unit in any organization, can become narrow-minded defenders of turf when resources are scarce. Nor can the disciplines, which are the guiding stars for their respective departments, be depended on to appreciate the importance of emerging fields of study, especially those arising at the boundaries between traditional disciplines. This disciplinary worldview may be especially vexing for the man and woman from the world of practical affairs—a possibility suggested by the pejorative use to which the term *ivory tower* is usually put. As Geiger (1986) observes, "the gradual accumulation of an esoteric knowledge base places increasing distance between the trained scholar's understanding of the domain and lay appreciation of the subject" (p. 30).

Power of University Administrators

Notwithstanding the unusual degree of autonomy that faculty members enjoy, deans, provosts, and presidents do, in fact, have power. In most institutions, at least one of these officials has a veto over who gets hired and who gets tenure, although this right is seldom exercised when faculty are solidly behind a candidate. These administrators also set salaries and therefore can reward favored faculty and, over time, penalize others. Budgetary resources can be doled out or held back, though ordinarily only on an incremental basis. But a principal source of power, when it is available, lies in discretionary money—funds that can be used to fund a new initiative or add to favored ones—in short, to influence an institution's direction.

To be sure, it is not easy to point a university in a new direction. Doing so has been compared to trying to change course on a giant ocean liner; it can be done, but only with difficulty and not very rapidly. One reason is tenure. Another is the large influence of faculty and the mores of scholarly life, made more potent because these administrative leaders, at least most deans and provosts, typically come out of the faculty ranks, having been imbued with the beliefs and practices of disciplinary scholars. When those administrators intend to return to the faculty following their administrative service, this influence is all the more potent. So in the attempt to achieve desired institutional objectives, it is usually unwise to make faculty too angry, such as by cutting existing budgets. Infinitely preferable is to have access to otherwise unclaimed resources—a predicament similar to that faced by executives at every level of government. As political commentator Irving Kristol has wryly noted, "like everyone else, university administrators prefer an untroubled life" (quoted in Nielsen, 1972, p. 432).[13] This is one reason central administrators might welcome the additional funds made possible by foundation support.

One further source of affinity between university administrators and foundations may arise because they share some characteristics. Both are more oriented to the world of action than to the ivory-tower world of study and contemplation. Both sets of leaders thus tend to be interested in the practical and policy importance of research. To have an impact, they may have to get around departments, if not the disciplines themselves. Being "above" departmental organization, university administrators are more likely than rank-and-file faculty to see established academic departments as barriers to the unbounded institutional aspirations that often occur at the margins of disciplines. Thus the provost stands ready to launch the initiative that will catch the next big academic wave, if only the money can be found.

Unbounded Institutional Aspirations

What is the college or university's ultimate organizational aim? Coleman (1973) argues that universities really have no aim other than to award degrees. Cohen and March (1974) express this view more starkly: "The American college or university is a prototypic organized anarchy. It does not know what it is doing. Its goals are either vague or in dispute" (p. 3). If this is true, the administrators have not been informed, because they often speak as if they do know the aim, albeit a rather vague one. This aim is simply to be "the best."[14]

No provost worth his or her salt lacks a list of projects worth funding— ones that will improve the quality of her institution, add to its prestige, make it a more attractive place to work, and contribute to the demand for its offers of admission. Especially when it comes to initiatives not entrenched in existing budgets, these central administrators constantly hunger for new funding. One reason is the competition constantly at work among colleges and universities, especially those that are near to each other in the prestige pecking order. Although few will admit it, they look to rankings such as those published by *U.S. News & World Report* to demonstrate to their trustees or legislators and to members of their communities that their universities are beating the competition.

Pertinent Characteristics of Foundations

More numerous than colleges and universities and decidedly more heterogeneous, private foundations occupy a favored niche in America's institutional landscape. Subject to relatively few legal restrictions, these organizations are able to operate quite freely, in perpetuity if that is their desire, in pursuit of their chosen missions. Especially striking is the small number of "aye" votes required for approval of any action, certainly compared to any piece of legislation passed by an elected body with comparable resources. Foundations are required by law only to distribute a minimum percentage of their assets each year in grants; they must not pay excessive amounts of compensation or engage in financial arrangements that amount to self-dealing, and they are to make grants only to certified nonprofit organizations. This freedom of action, combined with their significant financial resources, heightens the need to ask the question that economist James Duesenberry endorsed for social science investigation in general: "Who are these guys and what do they want?"[15] In answer, two features of private foundations seem to be especially pertinent: (1) their overall objectives and (2) their practical orientation.

Impact, Not Revolution

A perusal of published foundation annual reports and Web sites reveals great variety in the ways that corporate objectives are expressed. Some have mission statements. Others quote from their founding documents. Still others suggest their objectives only implicitly, by describing the kinds of activities they support. But in one way or another, all seek to have an impact—to "make a difference." For some of the most established general-purpose foundations, such as the Carnegie Corporation of New York, the Rockefeller Foundation, and the Ford Foundation, the founding purpose was quite broad: to contribute to the advancement of knowledge and to improvements in the general human condition (Arnove, 1980; Geiger, 1986, 1993). In recent years such objectives have been restated as a "core value" of foundations, spurring some of them to engage in "impact analysis" (Bernstein, 2003, p. 36).

Beyond such broad objectives, what kind of impact would a foundation desire? What seems to be beyond debate in the case of the vast majority of private foundations is that their objectives are fully consistent with the maintenance of existing social, political, and economic institutions.[16] Their governing boards are, in the words of Nielsen (1972), "a microcosm of what has variously been called the Establishment, the power elite, or the American ruling class" (p. 316). In this respect, of course, they are not unlike many universities, especially the wealthy and private ones. Whether this verifiable fact means that foundations then pursue agendas that serve the ruling class or merely maintain the existing system is another question, and not one I mean to address here.[17] Whether it reflects the life histories of board members or their desire to deal with the best practitioners, however, foundations are quite at home in dealing with elite institutions. At the same time, the large private foundations have also displayed an unmistakable reformist orientation, if not missionary zeal, bringing to mind the progressive movement of the early twentieth century. These dual themes of elitism and reformist inclination are discernible in foundation dealings with higher education.

Practicality

A second characteristic of foundations that deserves notice is their practical orientation, as contrasted with the abstract ivory-tower perspective often associated with universities. The donors who established foundations were usually captains of industry or finance, and those who serve in foundation boardrooms also tend to be men and women who have been successful in the world outside the academy. Although such trustees may have been trained in very prestigious colleges or universities, and the large foundations often employ program officers with academic backgrounds, few governing bodies of foundations are dominated by those with academic careers.

This practical orientation has two visible manifestations when it comes to foundation support for higher education. First is a marked tendency to focus on real-world problems when setting priorities for support. This kind of problem-centered thinking often does not come naturally to scholars who normally derive direction from the internal questions that are debated within disciplines.

A second consequence of foundations' practicality is an abiding, if not universal, skepticism about the ability of universities to set reasonable institutional priorities. Despite their tremendous potential, universities are sometimes seen as more or less clueless when faced with the task of bringing about real-world change. For example, the Ford Foundation concluded, in the words of one program officer, that "universities were paying scandalously little attention to what was going on in American cities" (Pendleton, 1975, p. 3). The foundation believed that "the universities needed to be turned around" on this issue (p. 8). The W. K. Kellogg Foundation expresses a similar sentiment on its Web site, explaining why it launched a program to "transform" higher education: "There was a belief—and much concern—amongst philanthropic institutions, that colleges and universities were slow to change and responded only to direct threats to their own institutional interests." The reason for this collective ineptitude? One obvious culprit is the faculty. Thus Bernstein (2003) points an accusing finger at "pockets of well-entrenched faculty who can act as tough barriers to institutional change" (p. 37). To be sure, not all foundations share this degree of skepticism, as illustrated, for example, by the Andrew W. Mellon Foundation and the Spencer Foundation—two foundations whose leadership and areas of interest are closely tied to higher education.

A Model of Competing Interests

How do these two types of organizations interact with each other? It is relatively easy to observe the components that make up the dealings of private foundations with universities: proposals are solicited, submitted, and considered; grants are approved; funds are paid; projects are carried out; outcomes are reported. The revenues of universities are expanded, and the annual reports of foundations are added to. If the interaction were instead an ordinary market transaction, like the purchase of office equipment, it would be a simpler matter to identify the supplier and the customer. The notion that one party was exerting undue power over the other would not occur to us if we believed the market for office equipment to be reasonably competitive.

But the competitive market model turns out to be ill-suited for the present application. Instead, for the kind of interaction we observe between foundations and universities, economics offers several, more useful models. Two of these are *bilateral monopoly* and *oligopoly,* both of which model conflict between agents and neither of which produces the kind of definite solution so familiar with competitive supply and demand. Instead, the outcome depends on the bargaining power of the two parties.

Another model involving interacting parties is the *principal-agent model.* Here, a principal sends an agent to do his bidding, but the agent has ideas of her own and thus may not undertake transactions exactly as the principal would have wanted. More generally, economics offers a host of situations that may be analyzed through game theory. Often the outcomes are not predictable. In each of these types of models, the parties have objectives they wish to achieve, which opens the possibility of competing interests.

In the case of foundations and higher education, it is helpful to think of three rather than two different actors. In addition to the foundation, we can think of faculty and university administrators as separate actors. Of course, reality is much more complicated than that. For one thing, the numerous colleges and universities compete with one another for grants, faculty, students, and prominence. There are also many foundations, each keeping at least one eye on the decisions of its sister foundations.

For the moment, though, consider just one foundation, along with one university's faculty and administration. In this simplest of models, one must acknowledge that the interests of these three parties are not necessarily the same, although they could be. The foundation probably has certain broad objectives and even strong preferences about the form of programs it wants to finance. The university administration (personified, let us say, by the provost) has projects that he believes will enhance the quality of his institution, for which money is necessary. This list may include new scholarships, the renovation of a classroom building, or a new academic program. Finally, the faculty, composed as it is of many individuals, can be thought of as having research agendas that are shaped to some large extent by the direction of research in each person's own discipline and specialized field, which naturally encompasses research being done around the country and the world. Faculty members are thus interested primarily in research within their own special area; seldom do their wish lists include the kind of institutionwide projects on the provost's list.

Since faculty members are the workers in universities who do the research, any foundation-supported program involving research must inevitably involve faculty. But faculty members are essential for a second reason: quality control. In order to do a competent job of evaluating any proposal, a foundation must turn to experts able to judge the quality of its potential product. Since few foundations employ staff members who have this expertise, foundations must rely on the recommendations of scholars to advise them on the merit of individual proposals.

One ready source of expertise is the academic department. Because these are already established in universities, foundations can simply make grants directly to departments, leaving it to them to allocate research dollars to the most worthy uses. But for most foundations this is an unattractive option, for the same reason it is unattractive to provosts: they both have reason to distrust the university's academic departments to make the best use of additional funds. They believe departments will be reluctant to make hard choices, to venture outside their home disciplines, or to pursue emerging lines of inquiry using the newest research methods. Funds given to departments, they fear, will simply result in business as usual rather than significant advances.[18] One way that foundations reconcile their general distrust of disciplines with their dependence on faculty is to provide support in forms that cannot easily be used by academic departments in traditional ways.

Another consequence of the conflicting interests among the three actors described here is a somewhat adversarial environment for negotiation. Thus in dealings between the foundation and either of the university actors, the following principle applies: *each university actor wishes a grant to have the least possible collateral effect on his or her actions, that is, the minimum possible impact on otherwise planned projects.* On the other side of the coin, the foundation wishes its funds to have the *maximum* amount of effect on behavior. One way by which foundations attempt to achieve this is by providing "seed money" for novel programs, at the expense of ongoing operating support (Cheit and Lobman, 1974, p. 74; Frumkin, 2000, p. 40). Indeed, some foundations make it a rule, formally or informally, not to fund any activity for more than three to five years or not to provide funding for endowments, thereby maximizing its control over how its funds will be used. According to one of its former program staff, one of the largest foundations quite deliberately maintained such a time limit on most of its grants, reasoning that most grantees would otherwise, over time, begin to forget about the grant, its source, and its original purpose.[19]

Two Approaches to Improvement

Foundations have taken two broad approaches in their attempt to improve the functioning of higher education's institutions that seem to be in need of help. One is to provide support for universities more or less as they are. The other is to provide support in forms that necessarily require significant modifications in operation, if not in structure. Although not always clearly distinguishable in practice, some examples will serve to distinguish them.

Strengthening Institutions as They Are

One approach to the aid of higher education has arisen from a view that, with all their strengths, colleges and universities lack the necessary infrastructure, administrative wherewithal, or self-understanding to make the kinds of hard choices required by changing circumstances and limited re-sources. One form of such support is through general institutional grants, such as those described by Cheit and Lobman (1974) as "sustenance" (p. 12). Prominent examples are the handful of foundations that make long and sustained grants to particular institutions, such as the Duke Endowment to Duke, the Woodruff Foundation to Emory, and the Weath-erhead Foundation to Harvard and several other universities.[20] Other foundations have focused on particular aspects of infrastructure, such as the Carnegie Corporation of New York and the Andrew W. Mellon Foun-dation's support of university libraries.[21] Similar in effect is Mellon's JStor project, established in 1995 to collect, store, and make available back is-sues of academic journals in electronic form. Using optical character-recognition technology, the stored records provide an exact replica of the original journal pages, making it unnecessary for university libraries to store back issues and greatly reducing the time required to retrieve arti-cles. Although not manifested as grants to individual institutions, this project bolsters the infrastructure of universities in general.

Closely allied to these forms of financial support are foundation-supported studies designed to strengthen institutions by improving techniques of admin-istration and general understanding of the enterprise itself. For example, in 1933, as the American Depression was pushing universities to the financial brink, The Carnegie Foundation for the Advancement of Teaching published *Economy in Higher Education,* with the express aim of presenting "a rea-soned compendium of pertinent knowledge" to help guide colleges and uni-versities through the crisis (Hill and Kelly, 1933, p. vi). This is but one of many studies published by this foundation that are devoted to general issues facing colleges and universities. In the 1970s the Carnegie Commission on Higher Education sponsored numerous studies covering various aspects of higher education.[22] Taken together, this effort is credited with a profound influence in how higher education is conceptualized.

In choosing institutions to support, foundations have displayed a decid-edly elitist orientation. From the early decades of the twentieth century they have concentrated support, especially for research, on elite institu-tions.[23] An illustration of this elite bias may be observed in the relative stability in patterns of foundation support over time. Table 9.1 at the end of this chapter lists the universities that received the most in grants over roughly the first third of the twentieth century from the nine large foun-dations that gave most of the support for higher education (Hollis, 1938). What is immediately obvious from this list of familiar names is that they are, by and large, still among today's most prestigious universities, and this impression is supported by the high rankings these universities enjoy using these criteria. It is readily apparent that most of the institutions favored in the early decades by these foundations are today among the country's premier universities—a correlation that, as Geiger (1993) notes, suggests both cause and effect.

Redirection and Reform

The alternative approach that has marked foundations' support of universities begins with a different presumption—that the missing ingredient is not so much financial strength as it is the clarity or wisdom necessary to make improvements. Given this dim view of universities' ability to chart a productive course, it should not be surprising that foundations have sought ways to impose reform from the outside. One way to do this is to commission studies that will show the way to reform. The famous Flexner Report, financed by The Carnegie Foundation for the Advancement of Teaching, did just that for medical education, spurring its transformation from a parochial form of vocational training into the science-based profession we know today.[24]

An important consequence of the reformist orientation exemplified by these efforts was to create new entities within universities that were independent of traditional academic departments. These structural changes were one instrument by which foundations, allied with university administrators, could wrest some control from entrenched academic departments without losing the necessary participation of faculty themselves. For much the same reason foundations also found ways to bypass university structures altogether by turning to independent research-oriented bodies.

Four Illustrative Cases

Four cases illustrate these two approaches: (1) the National Bureau of Economic Research; (2) the Rockefeller Foundation philanthropy, social science research, and the Social Science Research Council; (3) the Ford Foundation's challenge grants; and (4) the funding of university-based centers.

NATIONAL BUREAU OF ECONOMIC RESEARCH. A view held among business and some academic leaders in the decade before 1920 was that public debate about issues in economics needed unbiased information, in part to offset what was perceived to be a rising tide of socialist and anarchist opinion. According to one such leader, Henry Pritchett, "the antidote to these movements must be found in a dissemination among the mass of people of simple, fundamental economic facts, told in understandable form" (quoted in Lagemann, 1989, p. 55). Thus was born the National Bureau of Economic Research (NBER), which was chartered in 1920 as a "fact-finding agency" and supported, in part, by grants from the Carnegie Corporation of New York, the Commonwealth Fund, and the Laura Spelman Rockefeller Memorial.[25] Having been founded on principles of quantitative research and impartial judgment, and explicitly abjuring policy recommendations, the NBER appointed economist and business-cycle expert Wesley C. Mitchell of Columbia as its first president.

In 1930, the agency commissioned a study on national income by Mitchell's student, Simon Kuznets, that would become the basis for national income accounting. Although it has university representatives on its board of directors, the NBER has always been independent of any university. Yet it involves many university faculty in its research activities. In 2005, the NBER had some 850 economists and other social scientists, virtually all of whom held university faculty appointments, affiliated with it as research associates or faculty research fellows.

ROCKEFELLER PHILANTHROPY, SOCIAL SCIENCE RESEARCH, AND THE SOCIAL SCIENCE RESEARCH COUNCIL. At about the same time that the NBER was being organized, Rockefeller philanthropy in the form of the Laura Spelman Rockefeller Memorial and later the division of social sciences in the Rockefeller Foundation actively sought to build up sociology and other social sciences, stressing the importance of empirical, problem-oriented, and interdisciplinary research. It utilized newly created special research institutes both inside and outside universities.[26] Examples of the former include the Local Community Research Committee at the University of Chicago, the Institute for Research in the Social Sciences at the University of North Carolina at Chapel Hill, Harvard's Department of Social Relations (which is now defunct), the Russian Institute at Columbia, the Institute of International Studies at Yale, and the Institute for Social Research at Michigan.[27] From their creation, these units were distinct from existing departments; only the Department of Social Relations would assume a status in its university comparable to conventional departments.

Of the special institutes outside universities, the most prominent for social science was the Social Science Research Council (SSRC), which relied on committees of university professors to shape research agendas and award fellowships and other support. The SSRC was dominated by faculty from the country's elite universities. In the years between the world wars, for example, over 70 percent of those receiving postdoctoral fellowships came from just eleven universities: Chicago, Harvard, Columbia,

Stanford, Yale, the University of California at Berkeley, Wisconsin, Minnesota, the University of Pennsylvania, Michigan, and Cornell (Fisher, 1993, p. 199). Through its support of the SSRC, according to Fisher, the Rockefeller funds attempted to transform the way social science research was done by erasing the boundaries between the disciplines. The SSRC, in turn, hoped to "obstruct the long-term trend" in the established disciplines, an objective that was at best only partly achieved (Fisher, 1993, pp. 237–238).[28]

FORD FOUNDATION'S CHALLENGE GRANTS. In the wake of the near quadrupling of its assets in the late 1950s, the Ford Foundation made a series of large capital grants to private colleges and universities for the stated purpose of shoring up the financial well-being of higher education's private sector. The bulk of these grants were in the form of challenge grants, which required the institution to match, at a three-to-one rate, the foundation's grants with institutional fundraising. The top beneficiaries—Chicago, Columbia, Stanford, and NYU—each received $25 million in grants to match another $75 million from its own donors. Besides the infusion of money itself, according to Geiger (1993), the lasting effect was to invigorate the fundraising enterprise by demonstrating the potential returns from aggressive efforts. In light of the contemporary tendency for universities to conduct virtually continuous capital campaigns, this demonstration seems quite significant.

UNIVERSITY-BASED CENTERS. Following the pattern of other foundations that had established university-based research centers, in the 1960s and 1970s the Ford Foundation attempted to reform universities by funding efforts within and across institutions to boost research on topics related to urban areas, foreign countries, and women. In a bold attempt to focus the attention of universities on the problems of urban areas, Ford launched several major efforts to foster related research and to encourage universities to become interested in local policy questions. These included short-lived "urban extension" units at a few public universities and research centers connected to another dozen mostly private universities, allowing them to establish, among other things, endowed professorships. Complementing the research done in these centers, Ford also funded a research-oriented group of economists called the Committee on Urban Economics, administered by Resources for the Future (Pendleton, 1975).

Ford made similar efforts to entice universities to go into international studies and women's studies. Following an explicit strategy that began with individuals—both prominent faculty and promising students—and then moved to institutional support, Ford helped to create area studies research and centers (Magat, 1979, pp. 103–106). Likewise, Ford supported women's studies by creating fellowships for faculty and graduate students, following the pattern it had followed in area studies. By 1990, Ford and other foundations also supported the creation of special research centers on college campuses, beginning with one at Stanford funded by Ford and one at Wellesley funded by the Carnegie Corporation.[29] By 1990, over six hundred colleges and universities had established women's studies programs.

Recent Patterns in Foundation Grants to Higher Education

To illustrate in more detail the types of grants foundations now make to colleges, universities, or scholarly organizations for faculty and research, I classify by purpose a portion of the grants made by private foundations in 2003 (see Table 9.2 at the end of this chapter). In an attempt to achieve a reasonable representation of grants, I selected the twenty-six foundations making the largest value of grants in each of four subject areas tracked by the Foundation Center—education, health and medical research, public affairs and society benefit, and social sciences. When these foundations provide information on individual grants on the Web, I checked the grants against the center's description.[30] I obtained brief descriptions of all grants of $200,000 or more. This level of giving, imposed to keep the tabulation effort manageable, surely biases the results by undercounting smaller grants, which may be predominantly made up of fellowships and research grants made to individuals.

Four foundations made large grants to higher education of over $50 million: the Lilly Endowment, the Bill & Melinda Gates Foundation, the Andrew W. Mellon Foundation, and the Robert Wood Johnson Foundation. Another twelve foundations gave at least $10 million. Two of the foundations on the list—the Duke Endowment and the Woodruff Foundation—are closely associated with individual universities: Duke and Emory. Table 9.2 is hardly a complete listing of all foundation giving to higher education. Neither does it include all foundations giving the most, but it represents the patterns of giving to higher education from the largest foundations supporting higher education.

Table 9.3 (also at the end of the chapter) offers a more in-depth look at these grants. Based on the very brief descriptions typically listed in foundation reports, I divided the grants in Table 9.2 into twelve categories. Several of these categories are self-explanatory and were, in fact, rather straightforward to apply in most cases, despite the brevity of the available descriptions: "undergraduate scholarships," "graduate and postdoctoral support," "faculty support," "construction," "libraries," "computer and communication systems," and "support for other organizations." To be sure, this brevity might well lead to some incorrect classifications. Some grants surely contain funds spanning more than one function, such as program development grants that included money for construction or research grants that included money for community outreach.

Table 9.4 (also at the end of the chapter) shows that grants in four categories have such potential for error in interpretation: (1) individual research projects; (2) general research support, through research centers; (3) other programs internal to the institution; and (4) other programs external to the institution. Because they are not neatly classified and because of their quantitative importance, they are worth a closer look.

In the category of individual research ("individual" because the available evidence suggests that they were specific topics with not more than a few principal investigators, rather than support for larger research efforts) are over a dozen topics in social science and medicine. Support through established research centers, as well as other collaborative efforts with an apparent research focus, funded research of a similar broad variety, with areas as diverse as international security and coastal mariculture.

Grants that primarily supported programs within institutions other than research included funds for curricular changes, a summer transition program, and a new department. In contrast, non-research grants deemed external to the institution supported collaborative programs, such as one to recruit undergraduates to become professional librarians, or community outreach and advocacy, such as an international program to prohibit biological and chemical weapons.[31]

These examples illustrate, first, that classifications, even with the help of short descriptions, are at best very inexact, and second, that foundations support a tremendous range of university projects.

Within this diversity, Table 9.3 offers a rough idea of the relative importance of the broad categories. The roughly $640 million that these grants represent falls approximately along the following lines. About one-third of all the grants in this snapshot supported research, most of that going for general research support to central administrations or to free-standing research units. Another third went for non-research projects that are not otherwise classified in the remaining categories. The greater part of the support devoted to projects in this category was dedicated to activities internal to institutions, including curriculum and teaching; the remainder involved outreach to the community and world.

The next-largest category is financial aid—for undergraduates, graduate students, and postdocs, amounting to one-sixth of the total. The only other category accounting for as much as one-tenth of the total is construction and renovation. Although infrastructure thus received a significant share of foundation support to higher education, the largest categories of grants represent research and other new programs. Very little support, it must be added, was directed to academic departments. It was much more common for funds to be sent to independent units, either within universities or outside their walls.

Implications

In light of these various observations, the model of competing interests yields four implications for foundation-university interactions, which I discuss in the next sections.

Faculty Are Necessary; Departments Are Not

For any project involving research, both foundations and university administrators need card-carrying research scholars, most of whom are employed as university faculty. These faculty members are needed, not only for doing the research but also for evaluating research done by others. Just as provosts employ outside scholars to assist them in making tenure and promotion decisions, foundations use university faculty to provide quality-control advice. By using faculty to advise them in this way, foundations can take advantage of the disciplinary standards, the ready supply of specialized experts, and the lines of communication that are essential parts of the existing national professional associations. Most commonly, this quality-control function takes the form of peer review—a familiar technique used in the grantmaking process of such government agencies as the National Science Foundation and the National Institutes of Health.

   Despite the necessity of using university faculty to provide the quality-control function, foundations have been disinclined to go to the academic departments where faculty members are housed. Whether or not this is motivated by the view of departments as defenders of the established academic order and therefore not ideal conduits for initiatives that involve institutional change, foundations have often chosen to support university research centers that are independent of departments. Foundations can bypass university strictures altogether by employing such organizations as the SSRC or the NBER, whose imprimatur provides something like a "*Good Housekeeping* seal of approval" certifying that grant money is being used for worthwhile projects undertaken by reputable scholars.

Thus foundations can solve the problem of evaluation without having to operate its own review apparatus.[32]

Although this dependence on intermediary institutions for quality control has the effect of weakening the power of academic departments, it does not necessarily weaken the influence of disciplines. By maintaining the standards of research and establishing the issues worthy of study, the disciplines continue to exert an influence over the kinds of research that foundations support.

Foundations Prefer the Comprehensible

Owing to the pragmatic bent of their leaders and their general desire to have an impact, foundations evince a decided preference for the visible, the practical, and the comprehensible, as distinct from the abstract, the theoretical, and the esoteric. One corollary to this orientation is the tendency to favor expenditures that are relevant to the experience of all college students, such as buildings and scholarships, as opposed to those that mainly touch the lives of doctoral students and faculty. Such expenditures may have special appeal for the kind of private elite institutions from which many foundation officers graduated. Their high tuitions make scholarship aid especially important, and the lack of public funding for construction and renovation makes them particularly needy in this respect (Geiger, 1986). As shown in Table 9.3, scholarships and fellowships accounted for one-sixth of the large foundation grants tracked, and another tenth went to construction and renovation projects.

When it comes to research, foundations are more interested in solving the world's problems than in settling debates among scholars. Research into the esoteric questions debated in disciplinary journals or the methodological approaches that figure prominently in required graduate courses is unlikely to be supported by foundation grants. This orientation often leads in the direction of research that spans disciplinary boundaries, such as area studies, American studies, urban studies, women's studies, and public administration.[33] Not surprisingly, the established academic disciplines rarely embrace such interdisciplinary efforts. For example, Stigler (1967) opined that the area-studies institutes established at some universities with foundation support have made "no important contribution to economic theory or to research methodology, nor, in close relationship, have those institutions attracted or trained two economists of the very first rank" (p. 273).[34]

Although it may have prevented explicit forays into disciplinary dialogues, this pragmatic mind-set may, nevertheless, have led to important advances that would come to be embraced in the academy. One of the explicit aims of the Rockefeller funds in the 1920s was to encourage the development of a new brand of empirically based social science research. In economics, foundation support of large-scale projects within universities (including Wassily Leontief's input-output analysis at Harvard) or outside them (such as Simon Kuznets's work on national income accounting at the NBER) paved the way for a radically different scale of research projects and new ways of thinking about the economy (Stigler, 1967).[35]

Rivals Weaken One's Bargaining Position

Just as the existence of competitors weakens a firm's ability to raise its selling price above marginal cost, the existence of similarly situated rivals will tend to weaken a player's bargaining position. This is perhaps easiest to see in the case of universities. Even the most prominent of universities has rivals that would be willing and able to undertake a given activity were the funds available. Thus in preparing its proposal to Foundation F, for example, University A will be constrained in its requests by the knowledge that Universities B and C could easily undertake a similar program. But if University A has no rivals in a particular area—is, in effect, a monopolist—it will enjoy greater bargaining power. Faculty members, in their negotiations with foundations, are essentially in the same position.

In either case, the existence of potential rivals makes the grant applicants more interchangeable and thus expendable, from the standpoint of the foundation. But what is good for the goose is also good for the gander. Where there are multiple sources of funding for a particular kind of activity (this can include government agencies and corporations, as well as other foundations), the provost or the faculty researcher wishing to get funding for a proposed project should be in a better position to secure the funding without having to compromise. Stigler (1967, p. 283) writes this about competition between foundations:

> The competition is in at least some part a competition for the projects of distinguished scholars, and to this degree increases the scholar's role in the formulation of projects. Both the acceptance of general professional opinion and the competition for scholars work to reduce the directive influence of the foundations. Their influence becomes secondary to the values and goals which the science itself produces.

If our foundation is the only game in town when it comes to supporting a certain type of program, however, applicants will be in no position to call the shots, and thus the foundation will be in a stronger position to set the agenda of research.[36]

Interaction Discourages Candor

As with other forms of bargaining, the interactions surrounding foundation grantmaking inevitably have built-in incentives encouraging puffery or outright misrepresentation—most of it on the side of the applicants. Virtually all grant applicants responding to a request for proposals will take the time and trouble to emphasize how the proposed project will conform to the granting agency's wishes. Basic self-interest urges the applicant to identify—if not accentuate—these areas of overlap. Beyond this, the temptation exists to employ rhetorical devices that might otherwise be classified as exaggeration, if not worse. To be responsive to foundations' focus on new projects, for example, universities will have an incentive to describe proposed activities as new initiatives rather than as continuations or revisions of old ones. Observers such as Stigler (1967) and Frumkin (1998) believe that such re-labeling does in fact occur.

A qualitatively different but effectively similar variant of this kind of incongruence between proposal and action is a kind of fund substitution sometimes called triangulation. In the same way that any budgetary unit can subvert the intent of funding intended to pay for a specified initiative, a recipient can dress up an existing activity as a new one. It can then use the funds received to pay for another activity—one not mentioned in the grant. If successful, this ploy converts a targeted grant into unrestricted revenue. After the Ford Foundation directed substantial funding in the 1960s and 1970s to graduate departments in elite universities for the purpose of reducing time-to-degree, some of its officers felt slightly snookered when average time actually increased. They felt that the departments had used the grants as general funding without trying hard to make changes (Geiger, 1993). In whatever guise, the incentive to engage in deception of any kind will likely be reduced to the extent that a university and a foundation have repeated dealings with each other.

A Relationship That Works, After a Fashion

The relationship between grantmaking private foundations and higher education cannot be characterized accurately by either of the terms suggested in this chapter's title. Perhaps like the teenager who is both dependent and willful in relations with the parent, the modern university takes advantage of foundations' largess, all the while attempting to minimize the amount of control that foundations exert over them. Somewhat like parents, foundations often believe they know what is best for universities, and they do what they can to exert that benign influence. In addressing the subject of this chapter, I model this relationship as a stylized interaction pitting foundations against university faculty and their central administrators. All the participants attempt to pursue their own objectives to the extent possible, but not everyone can be completely successful because the participants' aims are not entirely compatible. Still, it is reasonable to conclude that, as in most ongoing relationships freely entered into, both sides benefit.

NOTES

1. I am grateful to William Bowen, Joel Fleishman, Craufurd Goodwin, Ellen Lagemann, Michael McPherson, Henry Rosovsky, Al Slivinski, Margaret Wyszomirski, and the editors for helpful discussions and comments on earlier drafts; to Robert Malme for research assistance; and to the Center for the Study of Philanthropy and Volunteerism at Duke for research support. The views expressed here are my own and certainly should not be ascribed to any other person or institution.

2. I exclude here community foundations, corporate foundations, and operating foundations.

3. A survey of the 723 colleges and universities with endowments of at least $1 million in 2003 yielded a total value for their endowments of $231 billion. See the National Association of College and University Business Officers' home page (http://www.nacubo.org/x2321.xml), last accessed Dec. 20, 2004.

4. Foundations were responsible for 28 percent of total voluntary support for higher education in 2003 (Council for Aid to Education, *Voluntary Support for Education, 2003* [http://www.cae.org/]). As a percentage of current fund revenues, private gifts, grants, and contracts were 4.8 percent for public institutions in 1999–2000 and 9.5 percent for private institutions in 1995–96 (U.S. Department of Education, National Center for Education Statistics, *Digest of Education Statistics 2002* [Washington, D.C.: U.S. Government Printing Office, June 2003], tables 330–332, pp. 372, 374). Assuming these percentages are stable over time, foundation support was roughly 1.3 percent of total revenues for public institutions and 2.7 percent for private institutions.

5. See, for example, Horowitz and Horowitz (1970, p. 227).

6. See, for example, Frumkin (2000, pp. 40–41).

7. See Anderson (1980, p. 10).

8. See, for example, Fisher (1980). For opposing views, see Bulmer (1982) and Karl and Katz (1987).

9. See, for example, Horowitz and Horowitz (1970, pp. 168–227) and Bauerlein, 2004.

10. See Strom, 2004.

11. For more general discussions of the characteristics of universities and their faculty, see, for example, Geiger, 1993; Clark, 1995; Rosovsky, 1990; Clotfelter, 1996.

12. Quoted in remarks made by Hunter R. Rawlings III, Cornell University, State of the University Address, June 7, 2003 (http://www.google. com/search?q=cache:MuK-84t5MSAJ:www.news.cornell.edu/campus/ stateofuniv0306.html+%22Eisenhower%22+%22Columbia%22+%22 president%22+%22faculty%22+%22discipline%22&hl=en), last accessed Dec. 21, 2004.

13. Feldstein (1993) makes a similar point—that university leaders have little incentive to make unpleasant choices because, unlike their corporate counterparts, they can expect few rewards and many costs for making efficiency-enhancing changes (p. 38).

14. For an extended argument along these lines, see Clotfelter (1996, pp. 253–254).

15. Reflections shared in an economics department roundtable in May of 1970 at Harvard University.

16. Colwell (1980) adds to the evidence for establishment connections the observation that there exists a considerable amount of overlap between foundation donors and trustees, on the one hand, and, on the other, the boards governing think tanks and other intermediary institutions (p. 422).

17. For arguments in favor of class-favoring activity by foundations, see, for example, Fisher (1980, 1983, 1993) and Arnove (1980). For contrary interpretations, see, for example, Bulmer (1982) or Karl and Katz (1987).

18. Two exceptions to this avoidance of departments have been attempts to streamline graduate training undertaken by the Ford Foundation and the Andrew W. Mellon Foundation. In both cases, grants were made to departments with, in the latter case, important strings attached. See Geiger (1993, pp. 227–229) and Bowen (2005, p. 4).

19. Novelty also implies a distinctive purpose; thus a related tendency is to shy away from activities that are otherwise well positioned to receive financial

support from other sources, such as research in fields where National Science Foundation grants are plentiful. See Kohler (1987, p. 163) and Geiger (1993, p. 100) for examples.

20. In the case of the Duke Endowment, the bulk of its aid of higher education is specified by its charter in the form of specified percentages of income to be directed to four colleges and universities. These institutions, along with the percentages of total income assigned to each in the Duke Endowment's original indenture, are Duke University (32 percent), Davidson College (5 percent), Johnson C. Smith University (4 percent), and Furman University (5 percent) (http://www.dukeendowment.org/pdf/ind.pdf), last accessed Dec. 26, 2004. For a description of the Weatherhead Foundation, see the *Harvard Gazette,* Nov. 6, 1997 (http://www.news.harvard.edu/gazette/1997/11.06/WeatherheadsDev.html). The Ford Foundation's Challenge Grants, noted further down in text, were similarly unrestricted but were not sustained over a long period.

21. See, for example, Radford (1984).

22. The range of issues covered by studies sponsored by the Carnegie Commission on Higher Education is illustrated by a selection of study titles: *Higher Education: Who Pays? Who Benefits? Who Should Pay?; Governance of Higher Education; The Campus and the City; Reform on Campus; The More Effective Use of Resources; Changes in University Organization, 1964–1971; The Future of Higher Education; The Rise of the Arts on the American Campus; The University as an Organization; Professional Education; The Multicampus University; The New Depression in Higher Education; The Finance of Higher Education; The Economics of the Major Private Universities; A Classification of Institutions of Higher Education.* Web site for The Carnegie Foundation for the Advancement of Teaching (http://www.carnegiefoundation.org/publications/publication_archive.htm#commission), last accessed Mar. 28, 2005.

23. Lagemann calls them "trend-setting universities" (1989, p. 154). This view is also illustrated by the sentiment in such foundations as Rockefeller and Carnegie to "make the peaks higher." See, for example, Kohler (1987, p. 151) or Seybold (1980, pp. 27–34).

24. For discussions, see Lagemann (1983, chapter 4) or Wheatley (1988).

25. The quotation is from Wesley C. Mitchell's notes (Lagemann, 1989, p. 59). See also Fabricant (1984, p. 30).

26. For discussions, see Bulmer (1982, pp. 186–191), Fisher (1983, p. 219), and Kohler (1987, p. 142).

27. For the history of these units, see Curti and Nash (1965, pp. 231–233), Bulmer (1982, p. 189), Robinson (1984, p. 78), Nielsen (1972, p. 41), and Lagemann (1989, p. 166).

28. See also Bulmer (1982, pp. 186–191).

29. See Proietto (1999) for an analysis of the impact of this support.

30. To construct my list of foundations, I began by looking at those foundations listed in the top ten in total giving for 2002 in the following four categories: education, health and medical research, public affairs and society benefit, and social sciences (*Foundation Giving Trends 2004*, table 6). I supplemented that list by adding any other foundations in the top twenty-five in total giving to higher education in 2002 ("Top 100 Foundations Giving to U.S.-Based Recipients for Higher, Graduate, and Professional Education and Educational Institutions, Circa 2002," unpublished table copyrighted by the Foundation Center, 2004). In order to simplify the tasks of collecting data and classifying grants, I adopted the dollar minimum cited in the text. I searched the foundations' Web sites for lists of grants distributed for the year 2003 (or 2002 if 2003 was not available). Descriptions and amounts were collected for all grants to higher education, or research organizations. Of the twenty-six foundations listed in table 2, nineteen appear among the top thirty, and another four are among the next thirty, in the Foundation Center table, "Top 100 Foundations Giving to U.S.-Based Recipients for Higher, Graduate, and Professional Education and Educational Institutions, Circa 2002." The remaining three are The Atlantic Philanthropies, Richard King Mellon Foundation, and the Howard Hughes Medical Institute.

    Those who are familiar with the information compiled by the Foundation Center point out that the reliability of these data is limited by the accuracy of the underlying reports from individual foundations, which form the basis for the center's tabulations. Because foundations differ in their ability to produce accurate and properly classified grant figures, both the list of top foundations and the amounts assigned to them are subject to error.

31. Assignment to categories was based on the information that foundations make public describing their individual grants. Given the brevity of these grant descriptions, it was not always easy to distinguish between general research support and other programs external to the institution.

32. For historical treatments of the use of intermediary organizations, see, for example, Hollis (1938, pp. 250–251, 274ff), Seybold (1980, p. 285), and Fisher (1993, p. 206).

33. While generally avoiding strictly disciplinary research, foundation leaders often hold disciplines in high regard. See Pendleton (1975, p. 15), for example.

34. It may be that this scorn of interdisciplinary approaches is particularly strong among economists. See Leonard (1989) for a related discussion.

35. Also see Bulmer (1982, p. 190) and Fisher (1983, p. 219) for discussions of the importance to some foundations of empirical and practical research topics.

36. A possible corollary to this third principle is the tendency for foundations to direct their funding toward areas with relatively fewer alternative funding sources. Since medicine and the natural sciences receive comparatively generous funding from government agencies such as the NIH and NSF, foundations probably are inclined to look elsewhere for perceived "gaps" in support, for research to support. Kohler (1987) documents this tendency (p. 163).

REFERENCES

Anderson, J. D. "Philanthropic Control over Black Higher Education." In R. F. Arnove (ed.), *Philanthropy and Cultural Imperialism: Foundations at Home and Abroad*. Bloomington: Indiana University Press, 1980.

Arnove, R. F. "Introduction." In R. F. Arnove (ed.), *Philanthropy and Cultural Imperialism: Foundations at Home and Abroad*. Bloomington: Indiana University Press, 1980.

Bauerlein, M. "Liberal Groupthink is Anti-Intellectual." *Chronicle of Higher Education*, Nov. 12, 2004 (http://chronicle.com/temp/reprint.php?id=taz1fjbe3lt4y13h2lgyjjc3pgh2fd7), last accessed Dec. 20, 2004.

Bernstein, A. R. "Is Philanthropy Abandoning Higher Education?" *The Presidency* 6 (Fall 2003), 34–37.

Bowen, W. G. "President's Report," Andrew W. Mellon Foundation, provisional draft, Feb. 2005.

Bulmer, M. "Support for Sociology in the 1920s: The Laura Spelman Rockefeller Memorial and the Beginnings of Modern, Large-Scale, Sociological Research in the University." *American Sociologist*, Nov. 1982, *17*, 185–192.

Cheit, E. F., and Lobman, T. E. *Foundations and Higher Education*. Berkeley, Calif.: Carnegie Council on Policy Studies in Higher Education, 1974.

Clark, B. R. *Places of Inquiry: Research and Advanced Education in Modern Universities*. Berkeley: University of California Press, 1995.

Clotfelter, C. T. *Buying the Best: Cost Escalation in Elite Higher Education*. Princeton, N.J.: Princeton University Press, 1996.

Cohen, M. D., and March, J. G. *Leadership and Ambiguity: The American College Presidency.* New York: McGraw-Hill, 1974.

Colwell, M.A.C. "The Foundation Connection: Links among Foundations and Recipient Organizations." In R. F. Arnove (ed.), *Philanthropy and Cultural Imperialism: Foundations at Home and Abroad.* Bloomington: Indiana University Press, 1980.

Coleman, J. "The University and Society's New Demands Upon It." In C. Kaysen (ed.), *Content and Context.* New York: McGraw-Hill, 1973.

Curti, M. E., and Nash, R. *Philanthropy in the Shaping of American Higher Education.* New Brunswick, N.J.: Rutgers University Press, 1965.

Fabricant, S. "Toward a Firmer Basis of Economic Policy: The Founding of the National Bureau of Economic Research," 1984. Paper posted on NBER Web site (http://www.nber.org/nberhistory/sfabricantrev.pdf), last accessed Dec. 16, 2004.

Feldstein, M. "Comment." In C. T. Clotfelter and M. Rothschild (eds.), *Studies of Supply and Demand in Higher Education.* Chicago: University of Chicago Press, 1993.

Fisher, D. "American Philanthropy and the Social Sciences: The Reproduction of a Conservative Ideology." In R. F. Arnove (ed.), *Philanthropy and Cultural Imperialism: Foundations at Home and Abroad.* Bloomington: Indiana University Press, 1980.

Fisher, D. "The Role of Philanthropic Foundations in the Reproduction of Hegemony." *Sociology,* 1983, *17,* 206–233.

Fisher, D. *Fundamental Development of the Social Sciences: Rockefeller Philanthropy and the United States Social Science Research Council.* Ann Arbor: University of Michigan Press, 1993.

Foundation Center. *Foundation Yearbook.* New York: Foundation Center, 2004.

Frumkin, P. "The Long Recoil from Regulation: Private Philanthropic Foundations and the Tax Reform Act of 1969." *American Review of Public Administration,* Sept. 1998, *28,* 266–286.

Frumkin, P. "Philanthropic Leverage." *Society,* 2000, *37*(6), 40–46.

Geiger, R. L. *To Advance Knowledge: The Growth of American Research Universities, 1900–1940.* New York: Oxford University Press, 1986.

Geiger, R. L. *Research and Relevant Knowledge: American Research Universities Since World War II.* New York: Oxford University Press, 1993.

Hill, D. S., and Kelly, F. J. *Economy in Higher Education.* New York: Carnegie Foundation for the Advancement of Teaching, 1933.

Hollis, E. V. *Philanthropic Foundations and Higher Education.* New York: Columbia University Press, 1938.

Horowitz, I. L., and Horowitz, R. L. "Tax-Exempt Foundations: Their Effects on National Policy." *Science,* 1970, *168,* 220–228.

Karl, B. D., and Katz, S. N. "Foundations and Ruling Class Elites." *Daedalus,* Winter 1987, *116,* 1–40.

Kohler, R. E. "Science, Foundations, and American Universities in the 1920s." *OSIRIS* (second series), 1987, *3,* 135–164.

Lagemann, E. C. *Private Power for the Public Good: A History of the Carnegie Foundation for the Advancement of Teaching.* Middletown, Conn.: Wesleyan University Press, 1983.

Lagemann, E. C. *The Politics of Knowledge: The Carnegie Corporation, Philanthropy, and Public Policy.* Chicago: University of Chicago Press, 1989.

Leonard, R. "To Advance Human Welfare! Economics and the Ford Foundation, 1950–1968." Duke Center for the Study of Philanthropy and Voluntarism Working Paper, Mar. 1989.

Magat, R. *The Ford Foundation at Work: Philanthropic Choices, Methods, and Styles.* New York: Plenum Press, 1979.

Nielsen, W. A. *The Big Foundations.* New York: Columbia University Press, 1972.

Nielsen, W. A. *The Golden Donors: The New Anatomy of the Great Foundations.* New York: E. P. Dutton, 1985.

Pendleton, W. C. *Urban Studies and the University.* New York: Ford Foundation, 1975.

Proietto, R. "The Ford Foundation and Women's Studies in American Higher Education." In E. Lagemann (ed.), *Philanthropic Foundations.* Bloomington: Indiana University Press, 1999.

Radford, N. A. *The Carnegie Corporation and the Development of American College Libraries, 1928–41.* Chicago: American Library Association, 1984.

Robinson, M. W. "Private Foundations and Social Science Research." *Social Science and Public Policy.* May/June 1984, *21,* 76–80.

Rosovsky, H. *The University: An Owner's Manual.* New York: W. W. Norton, 1990.

Samuelson, P. "Economists and the History of Ideas." *American Economic Review,* Mar. 1962, *51*(1), 1–18.

Seybold, P. J. "The Ford Foundation and the Triumph of Behavioralism in American Political Science." In R. F. Arnove (ed.), *Philanthropy and Cultural Imperialism: Foundations at Home and Abroad.* Bloomington: Indiana University Press, 1980.

Stigler, G. J. "The Foundation and Economics." In W. Weaver (ed.), *Philanthropic Foundations: Their History, Structure, Management, and Record.* New York: Harper & Row, 1967.

Strom, S. "ACLU Rejects Foundation Grants over Terror Language," *New York Times,* Oct. 19, 2004, p. A17.

U.S. Department of Education, National Center for Education Statistics, *Digest of Education Statistics 2002.* Washington, D.C.: Government Printing Office, 2003.

Wheatley, S. C. *The Politics of Philanthropy: Abraham Flexner and Medical Education.* Madison: University of Wisconsin Press, 1988.

W. K. Kellogg Foundation. "Kellogg Forum: Higher Education for the Public Good." (http://www.kelloggforum.org/forum_history.html), last accessed Mar. 10, 2005.

Table 9.1. Institutions Receiving the Most Grant Support from
Nine Foundations, 1902–1934 and Their Contemporary Rankings

Institution and 1902–1934 rank[a]	Contemporary rank based on		
	Federal grants, 2000[b]	Foundation grants, 2001[c]	U.S. News & World Report, 2005[d]
1. University of Chicago	3	28	14
2. Vanderbilt University[e]	40	—	18
3. Carnegie Mellon University[f]	62	58	22
4. Johns Hopkins University	2	19	14
5. Columbia University	10	4	9
6. Yale University	22	25	3
7. Harvard University	13	3	1
8. Cornell University	6[g]	32	14
9. Duke University	28	5	5
10. California Institute of Technology	1	93	8
11. Washington University	20	48	11
12. University of Rochester	51	—	37
13. Princeton University	50	18	1
14. Tulane University	91	87	43
15. University of Iowa	38	—	58
16. Stanford University	5	17	5
17. University of Pennsylvania	7	1	4
18. Swarthmore College	—	—	—
19. New York University	52	15	32

[a]Hollis, 1938, table XII, p. 274.
[b]Rank based on revenue from the federal government in 1999–2000 (U.S.
Department of Education, Digest of Education Statistics 2002, table 341, p. 383).
[c]Rank based on "Top 100 Recipients of Grants Awarded to U.S.-Based
Organizations for Higher, Graduate, and Professional Education and
Educational Institutions, Circa 2002" (Foundation Center, 2004).
[d]"America's Best Colleges 2005, National Universities: Top Schools."
Downloaded from www.usnews.com, Jan. 11, 2005.
Swarthmore ranked number two for liberal arts colleges.
[e]Includes Peabody College.
[f]Rank for 1902–1934 for Carnegie Institute of Technology.
[g]Rank based on total grants received by medical, endowed, and
statutory schools.

Table 9.2. Grants to Higher Education and Scholarly Organizations
of $200,000 or More in 2003, Selected Foundations

Foundation	Number of grants	Total value of grants ($ million)
Lilly Endowment, Inc.	42	$95.5
Bill & Melinda Gates Foundation	17	$87.2
Andrew W. Mellon Foundation	103	$76.0
Robert Wood Johnson Foundation	78	$59.7
The Starr Foundation*	48	$38.2
Robert W. Woodruff Foundation	9	$36.8
The W. K. Kellogg Foundation	13	$31.8
The Duke Endowment	36	$31.1
The Ford Foundation	38	$23.6
David and Lucille Packard Foundation*	39	$22.8
The Atlantic Philanthropies	19	$19.2
The John D. and Catherine T. MacArthur Foundation	16	$17.8
The Alfred P. Sloan Foundation	23	$13.6
The William and Flora Hewlett Foundation	17	$12.2
The Whitaker Foundation	52	$12.1
The Rockefeller Foundation	20	$11.8
The Brown Foundation	8	$ 9.2
Richard King Mellon Foundation	8	$ 8.2
Lumina Foundation for Education	12	$ 7.4
Howard Hughes Medical Institute	14	$ 7.0
M. J. Murdock Charitable Trust	12	$ 5.5
The J. M. Olin Foundation	14	$ 5.4
The Spencer Foundation	8	$ 3.0
The Annenberg Foundation	2	$ 2.9
Carnegie Corporation of New York	5	$ 2.7
The Pew Charitable Trusts*	1	$ 0.5

Source: *Foundations' Web sites.*
*Note: *Totals are for 2002.*

Table 9.3. Grants to Higher Education and Scholarly Organizations of $200,000 or More in 2003, Selected Foundations

Grant category	Amount ($ millions)
Research support	$202. 8
General research support, research centers	$136.2
Individual research projects	$66.3
Financial aid	$104.1
Undergraduate scholarships	$62.4
Graduate fellowships, postdoctoral support	$41.7
Construction and renovation	$69.8
Faculty, including salaries and leaves	$19.1
Computer and communication services, other than libraries	$11.4
Libraries, other than construction	$9.0
Other programs	$206.8
Internal to institution	$119.2
External to institution	$87.6
Technical support organizations (for example, JStor, ArtStor)	$8.5
Other professional organizations	$10.2
Total	$641.4

Source: *Foundations' Web sites; author's calculations.*

Table 9.4. Examples of Specific Foundation Grants to Colleges and Universities, Four Categories, 2003

1. Research support: individual research projects

The role that race and ethnicity play in transition from high school to college

The role of religion in U.S. African immigrant communities and their civic engagement

To better understand the perceptions of and access to financial aid information by low-income youth

To support research on the effects of affordable housing on children's well-being

To develop model approaches to reduce student high-risk drinking

For research on barriers to Native American substance abuse treatment and welfare system

For development of best practices for treatment of depression in primary care

For comparing the effects of Internet-based cardiopulmonary disease-monitoring program

To support a study: Does Hospice Save Medicare Money?

To support a study: Success in the Making: Life Course Patterns of Urban Youth

To support a study: Contact Between Two-Year Colleges and Employers

To support a study: Neuromechanical Determinants of Postural Responses

To support a study: Photoencapsulation of Stem Cells for Cartilage Tissue Engineering

To support a study: Magnetic Resonance Flow Imaging for Congenital Heart Disease

To support a study: Stem Cell Driven Regeneration of Craniofacial Sutures

To support continued development of a firearms injury national reporting system

2. Research support: general research support, research centers

For support of the Center for Retirement Research for assessing older adults' employment opportunities

To advance interdisciplinarity in the biological sciences, particularly life sciences

To understand better how faculty develop and use interdisciplinary knowledge

For the Coastal Resources Center to strengthen sustainable development practices of coastal mariculture

To strengthen the capacity of the university's Civil Rights Project to disseminate new research

For collaborative work among African American, Caribbean, and women faculty

For a collaborative research project on religion and transnational migration among immigrants of Florida

To expand the Institute of Population and Reproductive Health

In support of the Consortium on Chicago School Research analysis of Chicago Public Schools

In support of scientific and technical training and research on international security by the Security Studies Program

In support of research by its Center for Urban Economic Development

3. Other programs: internal to the institution

To support a permanent endowment for undergraduate humanities research program

To support core programs in the humanities

To support the summer transition program

To establish the Molecular Genetics and Microbiology Department

For the National Young Leaders program at the Kennedy School of Government

For medical education and research

Precollege science education grant for institution

To support curricular revisions

For program to support the development of experiential education programs

To support the development and deployment of a peer-to-peer network infrastructure for academic purposes

To support the design of new models of foreign study for undergraduate students

4. Other programs: external to institution

To support a program of assistance to Latin American libraries and archives

To launch a planned collaborative program to recruit undergraduates to the library profession

To support the implementation of a consortial post-retirement medical insurance agency

To support collaborative research with Appalachian colleges

To increase Trinity's academic engagement with Hartford youth and health groups

To implement the Bay Tech Standard Campaign at twenty-six community colleges

To assist in establishing a statewide interdisciplinary telehealth program for improving child health

To support the Primary Care Children's Mental Health Initiative

Table 9.4. Examples of Specific Foundation Grants to Colleges and Universities, Four Categories, 2003, *continued*

To develop partnership with SC Network of Children's Advocacy Center concerning child abuse treatment

For the Center for Justice, Tolerance, and Community to expand its research and public education programs

To convene an international symposium on contraceptive research (Institute of Medicine, NIH)

To support strategic planning activities

To establish a self-sufficient network of colleges and universities with accelerated degree programs for working adults

In support of the Network of Youth Mental Health Care

In support of the Stanford-Harvard Preventive Defense Project by the Belfer Center for Science and International Affairs

In support of the Harvard-Sussex Program to promote global prohibition of biological and chemical weapons

For technical assistance and direction for Developing Leadership in Reducing Substance Abuse program

For addressing substance abuse treatment for hard-to-employ women on welfare

To continue the Youth First Project in Pakistan

To continue efforts to improve early abortion services in the United States

To assist in developing a Caring Communities Program to aid health care programs

To improve the wellness of children in the residential homes in the Carolinas

Source: Foundations' Web sites.

Chapter Ten Overview

This chapter takes a different tack from the one preceding it. Clotfelter focused primarily on relations between foundations and major research universities, and his attention was directed particularly at funding for research. This chapter examines relations between foundations and institutions of higher education in terms of funding for teaching and learning.

That foundations should have difficulty with higher education around the improvement of teaching and learning in some ways reflects the problems higher education has with itself. At any moment on many campuses in the United States, one can observe arguments over teaching versus research, conflict over the value and credibility of both peer and student evaluation of teaching, the poor record of universities in training Ph.D.'s in teaching, even though that is where the lives of many will take them, and the persistence of the lecture, despite evidence that few lectures are inspired and few students are inspired by them.

Bringing more than forty years of experience in higher education (mostly at Stanford) and foundations (mostly at Hewlett) to the task, Ray Bacchetti looks through the lens of organizational behavior at why these organizations sometimes talk to and sometimes talk past one another. Some of those reasons trace to different functions, some to different traditions, and some to structural characteristics that keep the focus on the mirror rather than outward and empathetic regarding the worlds, motives, and accountabilities of the other realm.

Yet these institutions need each other far more than they admit. It is in their mutual interests for higher education to be continuously improving undergraduate education and for foundations to leverage their relatively small investment in improved teaching and learning. Enhancing the working relationship will require some changes in both parties, but none that threatens their core characteristics or essential priorities. Bacchetti analyzes these issues and then uses the concept of "educational capital" and other recommendations from Chapter Two to propose approaches that will be useful, both to foundations and to institutions of higher education.

MANY MOTIVES, MIXED REVIEWS[1]

FOUNDATIONS AND HIGHER EDUCATION
AS A RELATIONSHIP RICHER
IN POSSIBILITIES THAN RESULTS

Ray Bacchetti

FOUNDATIONS AND INSTITUTIONS OF HIGHER EDUCATION can behave like carnival bumper cars in the ways they career, collide, momentarily lock together, and then move off cheerfully in new directions. The drivers are independent and friendly, collegial and judgmental—and accountable, but not to each other. Listen in on these several conversations and imagine how and where world views overlap. Or don't.

Conversations

The foundation's board of directors had met earlier in the week. The staff follow-up meeting is beginning, where the president will communicate the board's decisions and discuss its concerns. "All the grant recommendations were approved," he reports, "but there was some pretty tough discussion about higher education."

Tension has been building for a while, so the president's announcement comes as no surprise. The problem has been particularly serious in the higher education program itself, where the emphasis is on broad institutional interests such as teaching and learning, liberal education, diversity, new program development, and the undergraduate experience. Grants have seldom produced strong and lasting changes; evaluation, if done at all, has been done grudgingly and without the rigor that faculty apply to their disciplinary work; proposals have seldom demonstrated a basis in research; each grantee institution has wanted to go it alone, despite the commonality of the issues. And institutional interest usually sags or disappears once the money runs out.

The president is silent for a moment. Then he speaks: "This is the question the board put to me at the end of the meeting: *Should the foundation continue to fund its higher education program aimed at teaching, the student experience, and new program development, or end it, with future support for colleges and universities channeled to advance our other program priorities?*"

Across the city, a comprehensive university's dean of undergraduate instruction is struggling with how to keep building more systematic attention to the improvement of teaching. Her goal is helping faculty shift from gate-keepers to enablers of student success. She knows that relying on department chairs is a low-octane approach. Colleagues at other places have well-regarded centers focusing attention on improving teaching; philanthropy helped virtually every one get started. But she recently learned that a peer institution had decided to move the teaching-improvement role from a long-standing center back to departments. Budget problems were the stated reason, but she knows that budget problems don't make decisions. Deans and provosts do, and they base them on priorities. Will this move be read by foundations as the end of a trend and spook them? And what if foundations want to see results? How will the faculty respond to efforts to demonstrate that a center generates better teaching? (Silently, she answers her own question: not willingly or well.)

First to speak at the foundation meeting is the junior program officer in higher education. He expresses his frustration with past proposals that pranced into the foundation, surrounded in the high rhetoric of institutional commitment, only to have the grant-launched program blown away on a breeze of budget problems some years later. Asked for an example, he cites a popular-with-students interdisciplinary program at an Ivy League university. It had cut across three professional schools to focus on undergraduate education in human biology. "We even renewed the initial grant," he added, "but one day the program just disappeared." It wasn't a high enough priority when the university's budget needed trimming.

"Are these kinds of events exceptions or the rule?" the president asks.

"That's a complicated question," he replies. "The event was an exception, but the conditions that allowed it to happen are part of every grant we make in higher education. Colleges and universities are sovereign, and they should be, but they give their word lightly, and it's difficult to know whom to believe on matters of institutional commitment."

Down the highway, at a community college, a young faculty member is putting together a proposal to use technology to give students more ways to get into subject matter through problem solving, Web searches, online dialogue with experts, and other ways of learning on their own outside class. They are, after all, highly mobile, hard-working individuals who represent a broad range of educational preparation, language and cultural backgrounds, career aspirations, and learning styles. He hopes that a foundation will see the merit in his idea, give him a program-validating grant, and provide him with the means to offer financial incentives in order to pull in more faculty and develop the idea. The college's new president has advertised her interest in innovation. Maybe she'll help open some foundation doors, since he doesn't know where to go knocking.

Entering the foundation conversation, the senior education program officer notes another dimension of higher education's reluctance or inability to see foundations as other than income sources. "Colleges and universities are mightily indifferent to goals the foundation might have. We say to them that our goals pertain to sets of institutions. But they can't seem to see beyond their individual campuses. In developing a project and the proposal we get, it's a rare institution that cites the work of others or that cares about propagating its success. We end up reinventing wheels, and each college and university can be counted on to think its wheel is unique."

At a distinguished university a couple of states away, the chief academic officer is opening a development office retreat. The invitation asked him to discuss the "university's first principles." He gives top billing to autonomy. "The institution's primary obligation," he says, "is to hire the best faculty and then support them in doing what it is they determine is most worth doing. In their teaching, they bring to undergraduate and graduate students both their comprehensive disciplinary background and their knowledge of where the leading edge of understanding is taking them" ("and us," he adds). "To enable these individuals to advance their work, the university needs financial support that does not attempt to steer them elsewhere."

"The university," he goes on with emphasis, "has been around for a long time and changes very deliberately. Don't let donors think they can short-cut that process." For example, he reminds them, the university's now-established Center for Teaching and Learning was a favorite with several donors and a national foundation, but it took many twists and turns before becoming an accepted feature of the academic landscape— and only when it had influential faculty champions. Even now, he adds, it operates as a voluntary resource, not an instrument of deans, provosts, or department chairs.

Wrapping up the foundation conversation, the senior education program officer sits up straight, looks around the room, and says, "Thanks for letting us ventilate. But don't let us confuse you with our frustration. This foundation needs higher education for the expertise it brings to our several program areas, and we need colleges and universities to do a better job in undergraduate education, diversity, and the development of faculty as teachers. Those and similar areas have been our priorities. The foundation's specialized programs, as well as the civic health of the nation, depend on the sort of intellectual and social sophistication that lukewarmly educated generalists or narrowly educated careerists can't provide. So we have a modest proposal. Give us three months to see if we can, working with some of our more acute higher education colleagues, redefine and re-energize both our aims and strategies. Then let us present those ideas for your—and then the board's—critique."

The president agrees. Colleagues make a few friendly suggestions. The meeting adjourns, and the education group's challenging work begins.

———— o ————

Listening in on these several meetings, we begin to scratch the surface of how broadly motives sprawl, how isolated the parties are from one another, and how little information publicly circulates about interesting and successful work outside the disciplinary agendas and networks. As a foundation program officer and as a university official, I have heard people take each of the positions I fictionalized. Although those positions are not universal, they are common. Each small choir, however, is being preached at (or complained to) by itself.

When we look for an effective connection between foundations and higher education institutions, a decidedly mixed picture emerges. At one end of the spectrum is a set of relatively productive relationships between foundation program interests and disciplines and their often problem-area-focused centers and institutes. But at the other, when we get into the more organizationally complex areas of teaching and learning, the character of the undergraduate program, the social role of higher education, and the development of new programs, things get tangled and untidy.

Conversations are often hollowed out—in higher education by the search for funds and low intention levels regarding significant change; in foundations by aspirations to be influential and by naiveté about the power of the status quo.

Higher education generally wants gifts and grants that will nourish an ecology of possibilities, whereas foundations frequently seek more of a problem focus and a result they can see. The university views intellectual excitement as legitimately episodic—the value of every idea does not hinge on whether it leads to a new teaching program, research emphasis, or center. Higher education likes to keep a steady pace; foundations want to see results in a limited time. (As one newspaper story recently put it, foundations want results "now, more, better, faster.") The foundation, unhappy with seeing its grants evanesce, wants to influence the institution or the field; faculty may agree but, as one savvy development officer put it, they do not know how to deliver. Promises to spread ideas about undergraduate education and the other kinds of initiatives designed for wide institutional effects are not easily put into a strategic package, especially by faculty inexpert in institutional change. A college or university, knowing how many moving parts (including hearts, minds, and attitudes) it is working with, is happy to have a project jostle the institutional environment, softening it up for other ideas later on. The foundation thinks that avoiding impact assessment ducks accountability.

In prior generations, foundations found higher education somewhat more supple and collaboration more welcome. One does not have to read far in the small but illuminating literature about foundations and higher education to appreciate that many consequential shifts in higher education had their origins in foundation initiatives. The transformation of business schools from vocational schools to research-based powerhouses, the introduction of international studies cutting across established disciplines, advances in medical education and the sciences, support for quantitative approaches in social science, and the many aspects of diversity, among other major shifts in higher education, have the fingerprints of foundations distinctively on them.

The passage of time has raised the profile of the truly consequential foundation initiatives, while many others have disappeared into the background. Data are not readily available at the level where one could reliably assess foundation giving according to reasonably well-defined objectives. It is plausible to conclude that much of what foundations have done is written with disappearing ink on the ledgers of higher education.

As close as I could get to a pre-disappearance look at that ink was to examine summaries of foundation aims and sample grant titles submitted to the Foundation Center. A survey of the one hundred largest funders of higher education revealed that only fifty of these are national in reach, and only ten support college and university programs aimed at institutional issues such as the efficacy of undergraduate education or academic innovation. Another ten institutional-issue funders operate in only one or a few states or express their approachability "by invitation only." The other eighty national, regional, and state funders make grants to higher education for scholarships or facilities or in support of specialized program interests. Examples are medical or scientific research, environment, youth development, and the like—where colleges and universities develop and provide expertise and training. Going further into foundation Web sites, one finds some helpfully informative and user-friendly ones, but there is little comparability among them as to the information they provide. Some provide very little. Of the top one hundred foundations that fund higher education, one-third maintain no Web site at all.

As a consequence, tracing changes over time at some meaningful level of disaggregation was a more extensive task than we could take on in this project. Word on changes in foundation priorities is often reported in the *Chronicle of Philanthropy* and other publications and, of course, on grapevines of variable veracity. In recent years, several foundations that had been mainstays of *institutional* initiatives have stopped or attenuated such funding. Among them are The Atlantic Philanthropies,[2] The Pew Charitable Trusts, The William and Flora Hewlett Foundation, the W. K. Kellogg Foundation, and The James Irvine Foundation. The Ford Foundation has shifted a share of its higher education funding interests overseas. The reasons for this shrinkage in foundation interest in *institutional* issues, which this chapter examines, quite likely extends to many foundations outside the top one hundred.

The admirable efforts of some foundations to develop and publish theories of change or logic models as guidance for hopeful grantees fit poorly with higher education. The formality of a logic model's stages (that is, resources and inputs, activities, outputs, outcomes, and impact; see W. K. Kellogg Foundation, p. 5) means the model doesn't mesh easily with a college's interest in trying a new idea and judging it on the basis of the faculty's response. The warm assertiveness of the new venture philanthropists and their intention of working with grantees to produce results confront cool aversion in higher education.

Tracing causal chains in higher education is doubly difficult. On the one hand, the operational landscape is too complex, interwoven, and multifaceted to support the metaphor of a chain. A public service program fluttering into life at Stanford and, fifteen years later, public service becoming a graduation requirement at Mount St. Mary's College may be in some way related. But the explanation is more likely to be a narrative rich in sophisticated inference searching for plausibility rather than analytical rigor.

Colleges and universities seldom go looking for connections, however. During my foundation tenure at times too numerous to recall, proposals would refer to their animating ideas as *unique*—a word meaning unparalleled or incomparable. Sitting where I sat, I would know that others had tried the idea, worked out its bugs, and had it up, running, and ready to be shared (or had found it wanting and abandoned it). But the observation begs the question. Hopeful grantees usually aim to frame appealing proposals by making distinctive claims. Causality is not high on their list. And reconstructing a chain or even a web of influences after the fact is brain-spraining work.

There is a lot to look at if one wants to understand the awkwardness in the foundation–higher education relationship. To be sure, notable success is no stranger to this relationship. But neither is the leaching away of the value of scarce foundation dollars by failure to agree on what each party in a grant transaction can expect from the other.

Before moving on, however, I stress two points. First, whatever quarrel I have with either higher education or foundations is a lover's quarrel. These are vital institutions that need each other. When they do their best work, it is superb and makes the ground move under us. Second, the variety and complexity of these entities is so great that all generalizations are suspect. Raising timely, provocative, and ultimately useful issues is enough of an ambition.

Impressions from the Field

How well do foundations and colleges and universities understand each other? At some level, of course, they do pretty well. Foundation staffs are college and university products, and college and university faculty and administrators often share the general interests of foundations. Nevertheless, it is probably fair to say that no foundation has a comprehensive grasp of higher education, and few in higher education understand foundation motives and styles. The variety is too great, and both sides are changing as the social conditions in which they operate change. Most foundations focus on one or more subsets of institutions (the historically black colleges and universities, liberal arts colleges, research universities, or religious institutions, for example). Or perhaps they focus on subsets of the subsets—or a suite of issues like service learning, diversity and inclusion, liberal education, or other programmatic goals and objectives related to disciplines or cross-disciplinary themes. Foundations look outward at issues affecting multiple institutions; a college or university looks inward at issues affecting itself.

Before entering foundation work, I had at some level always known how diverse higher education and foundations were. I soon realized how paltry my sense of that diversity was, compared to the real thing. I knew a fair amount about universities (from attending two and playing administrative roles in three), less about community colleges (where I had served as a trustee), a bit about a mixed set of others (from accrediting service), and not much else. I had to learn about Alverno's ability-based curriculum, Colorado College's "block plan," and Macalester's intern program. And I had to learn about the California State University system's plans for making already diverse campuses more genuinely inclusive; programs in Chicago, Berkeley, New York, Austin, and Los Angeles for great universities to work with public schools; how geographically isolated colleges differed from urban ones, and so much more.

Each of these projects had a history behind it, a set of institutional arrangements supporting it, and a range of unfinished business for which it sought foundation support. One of a program officer's first jobs is to make sense of this rich and scattered universe so that his or her grant recommendations add up to an intelligent, coherent, and effective program deserving approval from the foundation's board.

Because the program staff members are, to a considerable degree, the eyes, ears, and direction finders of their foundations, their differences contribute to foundation differences. These individuals often come, as I did, after substantial proportions of their careers are behind them. They hail from a variety of places such as policy positions, higher education roles as faculty members, administrators, deans, and presidents, and officer posts in national education associations and scholarly institutes. As a group, foundation program officers represent a considerable intellectual resource. Alone (which is how they typically work), each is stuck with what she or he already knows (which varies) and whatever on-the-job training can be drawn from advisers or extracted from contacts with actual and potential grant applicants (a rich resource if used well). In a survey of educational and foundation leaders as part of this study, some of our respondents in higher education thought (no doubt reflecting their own experience) that foundation program staff were generally clueless as to the facts on the ground. A few vouched for the opposite: shrewd and perceptive program officers. Of course, no one really knows how to characterize the field because there are no entry requirements, few shared professional standards governing it, and no agreed-upon notions of grant-making effectiveness.

Differences That Matter

Among the many other differences between higher education and founda-tions—differences that help account for some of the tension and angular-ity in their relationship—are communication, time, and accountability, which I discuss in the sections that follow.

Communication

The dialogue in grantmaking often rides a rhetorical "up" escalator. The potential grantee sells into a competitive market. With often quite unself-conscious ingenuity, college or university representatives see the positives of their proposals clearly; understandable confidence and optimism obscure the downsides. The foundation program officer, after a period of tough and skeptical questioning, makes a decision to encourage the proposal or decline it. Once settled on a yes, the program officer, like the institutional representative, has a stake in being proven right. This often-elaborate dance tends to relegate scrutiny to the beginning stages of a relationship and affirmation, as well as a subconscious advocacy, to the later ones. Objective assessment is always difficult, but difficulty is not normally the main issue. Rather, the main issue is will. And there is seldom much will when it comes to hard-nosed grant postmortems.

Time

Foundations' time horizons are nearer than those of higher education insti-tutions. Colleges and universities are deeply conservative institutions. And they should be. Their task is to preserve and conserve knowledge, as well as to transmit and advance it, so haste runs counter to the cultivated instincts of faculty and to institutional natures. But foundation staff mem-bers are expected to show accomplishments quickly. Their grant budgets are renewed annually, in part on the basis of results. Boards normally want to lead flexible foundations and prefer not to encumber grant budgets too far ahead. This produces grant durations of one to three years far more often than four years or more. Colleges and universities measure time dif-ferently. Although pilot projects, explorations, and experiments can be sized to three years (seldom fewer), plans intended to be institutionalized take longer. Short grants with long intentions are often disappointing if effort expires, as it often does, when the money is gone.

Accountability

As accountability has climbed in the foundation hierarchy, it has applied to program officers as much as higher education grantees. This introduces a subtlety into relationships captured in a comment made to me by a distinguished professor at a leading university: "Program officers should be chosen on the basis of whether they find joy in the triumphs of others. Once they start seeing themselves in the mirror of their grants, that's trouble." However, in the demanding life of an accountable program officer, the expression "my program" shades into "how well am I doing?" The relationship between doing well and taking low risks, favoring prestigious institutions, living within foundation-set parameters rather than college or university timetables and organizational distinctiveness, accentuating positives, and seeking program coherence over institutional differences is a subtle but real one. Not all bad, but not as self-effacing as the quoted professor would prefer, either.

With these many factors at work, what sorts of ideas is a foundation likely to receive? The individuals in higher education and foundations reflect their venues. College and university people, like their foundation counterparts, seldom talk outside home base about the sort of *institutional* issues that this chapter focuses on.[3]

As a result, there exists a profusion of ideas. Many are variations on a theme (say, improving undergraduate education), and many bear little connection to others. The result is a kind of anarchy. For example, one year's worth of my foundation's grants to improve teaching and learning in liberal arts colleges, totaling about $1 million, spread across ideas to develop software to personalize student learning; bring critical thinking to public, real-world, issues; spread quantitative analysis through the curriculum; integrate technology into curriculum design; assess the outcomes of the core curriculum; and revitalize a self-designed major program.

These ideas may carry an institutional imprimatur and reflect an organized and poised implementation plan. Or they may have received institutional permission and an endorsing letter, leaving it to the proposer to cultivate participation and, if successful, to seek backing to continue the work. It is difficult for a program officer to tell which is which—the institution that is poised and determined or the one that expects well-expressed intentions to substitute for a plan. Occasionally, a proposal may reflect sectors of higher education that are receiving contemporary energy and focus, for example, diversity, service learning, or interdisciplinarity.

Another likely ethos-of-origin is an individual's action on his or her agenda. Initiatives to bring undergraduates into research, to introduce freshmen to disciplinary differences in methods of inquiry, or to experiment with the case method as a way to cultivate leadership, as well as learn problem-solving skills, are all instances of faculty-instituted endeavors that may or may not outlast the initiator's engagement with them. Other foundations' programs with which I was familiar reflected a similar spread of program intent and content.

On my side of the transaction, I unintentionally abetted this anarchy. My guidelines were broad and respectful of institutional differences. In those guidelines, I stated confidently that "the diversity of institutional character [contributes to] the vitality and quality of American higher education." Challenges to this point of view did not come either from inside the foundation world or, of course, from the hopeful and successful grant-seeking institutions. They came from a slowly building and personally nagging frustration that my grants were not adding up to a great deal. Aside from nominal similarities, such as having the improvement of undergraduate education as a common theme, these grants had little synergy with one another. Unlike a hundred proximate candles lighting their region with one hundred candlepower, these were like one hundred, one-candlepower lights, each in its own closet. I like to think that a substantial chunk of the grants I recommended had respectable half-lives, but I was too busy making the next round of recommendations to examine how long those half-lives might have been or to help in extending good ideas to other institutions. Occasionally, I knew and could prove that I had chosen successfully—that a well-designed and well-executed grant made a difference worth making. But only occasionally.

An outside evaluator of grants made during my tenure observed that interesting overlaps and similarities in those grants created the potential for synergy. However, the foundation, she went on to say, was not set up to tap into that potential; nor do the college and university grantees have very sophisticated models for thinking about how one thing leads to another. Even so, I concluded that my on-the-job learning took too long, and what wisdom I acquired came late in my foundation experience. I met colleagues during my tenure and since that time whose struggles were similar to mine and who, like me, contributed to the anarchy that felt good at the time but left too thin a legacy.

A full account of the challenge of making a difference has to acknowledge that far more people know the vocabulary of teaching, student development, and academic innovation than understand the dynamics of institutional change in higher education. Many individuals in higher education believe change obeys two rules: (1) good intentions open the path to institutional change, and (2) good ideas make it happen. Both are, at worst, wrong; at best they are faint approximations of what needs to occur. The customs and practices that make institutional change so difficult exist for many good reasons—reasons that have their downsides. For every reason to revere college or university features that have been honed and seasoned by decades, sometimes centuries, of practice, there are others that have more to do with mindless inertia, turf protection, and the comfort that comes from occupying a privileged place in the social structure.

Looking through many windows into foundations and higher education brings into view some of the complexities of doing good work in both domains. Behind this scatter of differences of person, place, motives, and goals lie some explanatory notions of why misperceptions and tensions exist—notions taken up in the next section that will again come into focus in the final section on recommendations.

Where the Problems Come From

This catalogue of angularities—of bumps in the road and troubles in the relationship—reflects the workings of organizational cultures. Each side is socialized into perspectives, patterns, and expectations without any serious reference to the other. They often meet, if not as strangers, at most as acquaintances who have not seen each other in a while. The people in higher education tend to see foundations as sources of funds for carrying out the college or university's purposes. It would come as news to most faculty that foundations have purposes of their own and see higher education in instrumental terms in relation to those purposes. Their counterparts in foundations know higher education from having been students, sometimes all the way to a Ph.D., and perhaps as former faculty or institutional officers. But their foundation job is about change more than securing the status quo. They are, moreover, unlikely to know well other kinds of institutions than the ones in which they have studied and served. To see where the impulse for their on-the-job predispositions originates, we need to look deeper into the core of both higher education and foundations.

But let me first acknowledge that the problems in the relationship are the flip sides of the strengths of the partners. My emphasis will be on their independence and semi-sovereign natures. Sometimes this leads to great gains when people and ideas connect in the right way, place, and time. Such events, I would argue, are more exception than rule. Let us look first at higher education and then at foundations. What are some of these inbred and explanatory characteristics?

Higher Education

To all outward appearances, colleges and universities are open, connected, talkative, and worldly. The reality behind the appearances is substantial in everything except organizational culture and the educational program—what I have been calling the *institutional* issues. There the focus is inward for reasons with deep historical roots and important contemporary relevance.

INHERENT SELF-ABSORPTION. Higher education is an intense, personal business. In this respect, colleges and universities show many parallels to theater: auditioning over and over for students and for gifts and grants; performing to audiences of various levels of sophistication; learning new disciplines and polishing technique; making sure the supporting scenery, lighting, props, and so on are in place; working on pricing the product appropriately for the audience to be served and the expenses to be covered.

The analogy cools off in the realm of responsiveness. Theater people get feedback at every performance, and when audiences vote negatively with their feet, the play closes. For colleges and universities the outside world issues various report cards from time to time but otherwise is essentially a vague and often inarticulate factor in respect to its views on institutional performance. Reputations shape perception and are slow to change. Moreover, demand outstrips supply in higher education and is likely to continue to do so. A seller's market seldom pays serious attention to signals that improvement is needed.

The analogy warms up again when artistic integrity is put side-by-side with academic freedom. Academic freedom stands for more than certain rights of faculty members. It spreads to the edges of the institution where it signals resistance to external influence, as well as regulation. As I have argued elsewhere (Bacchetti, 2004), the intellectual independence of higher education is both a source and an instance of a free society. It is what permits colleges and universities to be trustworthy (and sometimes troublesome) critics of society and sources of ideas for dealing with problems great and small, as well as for imagining alternative futures. No small virtue.

To maintain this independence, colleges and universities control what happens in teaching and research. This inward focus on institutional concerns implies that energy flows centripetally; the mirror and microscope are the preferred tools rather than binoculars and radar. As one research university put the matter in a proposal about improving general education, the basis for its endeavor was, "the specific insights and goals expressed *by members of our community.*" (Italics added.) This sort of unself-conscious comment was typical. Inner direction rules. What others may think and have done about the topic counts for little.

Almost a clinical syndrome, this self-absorption makes what happens in the educational program at home significant and what happens away irrelevant. The institution takes on a self-contained and distinctive culture so that all institutional problems are local and all the resources needed to solve them are, by definition, close at hand. The well-known "NIH syndrome" is self-absorption's sibling; if it is Not Invented Here, interest slumps. All in all, a high degree of self-absorption inheres in the nature of the institution.

When a professor who would never consider doing an experiment that had no application beyond itself turns to a project exploring some aspect of undergraduate education, a different mind-set obtains. In science, replicability of the experiment to reproduce the findings is a critical test. Predictability is the job of science, that is, to learn how A can lead to B when specified conditions are met. But an inquiry into some aspect of teaching seldom shares those ambitions. Its aims are local. It usually turns on work with known colleagues and focuses on students of a particularly local sort. It is consistent with an institutional character that is meant to carry some comparative advantage (if admission is competitive) or some distinctive identity (if it is not). One can expect to hear deans observe, "Science is the world's business; teaching is ours."

Like many behaviors that are understandable but exaggerated, higher education's self-absorption can exact a stiff price in terms of the value and leverage of foundation grants. This egocentric view means that an institution will usually struggle alone with its institutional issues, with diversity, with introducing freshman seminars, improving teaching, designing interdisciplinary programs, introducing technology, and with many other matters whose family resemblances are very strong across comparable institutions. When it seeks foundation support, what it then proposes will, whatever its virtues, have two limitations: (1) its problem analysis and proposed solution will be limited to what those inside the institution know and are able to do to improve matters, and (2) no lessons learned by others will be sought to inform and enhance projects and enable the kind of cumulative improvement that comes from building on the work of others.

The irony of the second point deserves amplification. Institutions of higher education study just about everything else, send their faculty to meetings of their disciplinary peers, belong to national organizations, and often, after they have gotten a center or program running and foundation money spent, join the practitioner networks. But they seldom build the *institutional* programs for which they seek foundation support on a basis of comparative study. It just does not occur to them to do so. Self-absorption is like that. The ingredients of one's project are so near, and they are manifested in people one knows and often cares about. The elements in each project—the goals, strategy, logistics, time commitment, and the like—will have to be worked out with those same people. One wants, therefore, to devise solutions with sensitivity to the people involved and within parameters sensitive to the institution. That is understandable for the institution but discouraging to foundations seeking solutions that can be generalized and that are better than those preceding them.

The easy (and some would add wise) path for the foundation is to fund what institutions decide to do—an attractive course because many of the presented options will be good ones (colleges and universities may be self-absorbed, but they can also be focused, strategic, and smart). One university development officer told me that "when a foundation pushes, it is likely to get a transitory response"—her diplomatic way of saying that the project will stop about the time the money runs out. Some foundations make such alignment with institutionally self-generated goals a key element of their strategy—a sort of sustainability insurance. This is a good strategy for strengthening already valued processes; it is a weak one for stimulating change.

ORGANIZATION. In the organizational behavior literature, colleges and universities are often described as entities whose interior parts (for example, academic departments, student affairs offices, athletics, and administration) retain identities that link only loosely to each other and to the organization overall. For example, departments neither need another's permission to innovate nor are they obliged to acquiesce in anyone else's innovation. Many a green dean has muddied his credentials by assuming that good ideas could, like seeds, be broadcast and take root. To move an idea cross-ways in a college or university requires building coalitions and incentives, and other forms of cultivation. Bold ideas resist such conditions. Countervailing interests usually whittle and reshape the individually "bold" into the communally "acceptable."

At the level of individual faculty, a successful career generally depends on some combination of achievements, the nature and proportion depending on the institution. These include the ability to teach, as well as the ability to follow intellectual leads, apply for (and get) grants, and publish textbooks and scholarly articles and books. The individual professor needs to have several arrows in her or his quiver, and most faculty stay close to their academic specialties. Institutional programs and purposes command attention in some institutions, especially community colleges, but in most they are invited from or proffered voluntarily by civic-minded faculty. Such initiatives can also be withdrawn voluntarily and often are when other needs press or opportunities appear. This is not to say that faculty members are feckless; rather, it is to say that very little besides their own intention binds them to a course of action. Taking the individual faculty member as the unit of analysis showcases the centrality of independence. As a factor that permeates from faculty to institution, independence reflects an organization that runs more on broad custom and individual initiative than on plans, broad agreements, and long-term commitments. The latter matters are in play in government grants and contracts, when the college or university functions as a legal entity, and in some other domains—but seldom in relations with foundations. The agreements there are chiefly based on good faith, with unhappy partners walking away rather than attempting to enforce terms.

In such organizations, it is difficult to know who is in charge, who speaks for the institution, and whose word can be depended upon on matters related to education, student life, and the overall objectives of undergraduate or graduate education. Some institutional issues, such as general education, seem to belong to everyone—and thus to no one. Whatever the idea, no matter whose it is, tradition keeps a thumb on the scale, as does faculty and departmental autonomy, the cultivated inexperience of most department chairs, the influence of the disciplines, the lightness of accountability, and the subtle features of the relationship of teaching to learning. With so many thumbs, true weight remains elusive.

From community colleges to research universities, higher education resists change in its institutional features. Even when there is a will, hardly anyone knows the way. Practically everyone in a higher education institution has some power; no one has enough to make much of a difference alone. The collegial notions of faculty clash with the hierarchical tendencies of administration. The business savvy of trustees abrades the highly personal and intellectual professorial life. Colleges and universities are—and wish to be seen as—organizationally unique. They want to be taken on their own terms. But often even they do not completely understand whether and how those terms might be translated into terms associated with a theory of change or of action, accountability, logic model, business plan, or any of the other terms that now pepper foundation language.

EVIDENCE. A frosty attitude toward assessment of key elements inside the education program is one aspect of colleges and universities that seems like an anomaly from the outside but not from inside. In these institutions, where so much else rides on evidence and proof, the reluctance to assess their core functions of teaching and learning is a norm. In support of this norm is the genuine difficulty of understanding the complexity of learning and its relationship to teaching—a reason but hardly an excuse for not trying. The generally half-hearted acquiescence of colleges or universities in foundations' expectations that programs will be evaluated leaves the foundations in a peculiar place. They are asked to fund programs that purport to achieve particular objectives—for example, to make a difference in a student's academic career through a freshman seminar or a course on different ways of knowing—but the program's leaders are unlikely to generate more than anecdotal evidence on that difference. By the time the significant differences are likely to show up (or not), those involved will have moved on to other interests, and the programs begun with foundation support will have been institutionalized (or not). Often the extent of the evaluation will be an elaboration on the response a professor once gave me when I asked whether a new seminar program was a success. He replied, "The students like it and the faculty like it; what more do you need to know?"

Shifting perspectives, Roshomon-like, we can look at how even good evidence is perceived and used, in this case, in a university. Having once made a grant to a university college of education to gather, appraise, and publish evidence on best teaching practices in various K–12 subject areas, I, as a new program officer, opined out loud to the dean that a happy byproduct of this project would be its influence on the college's own teaching of teachers. Momentarily taken aback, he quickly recovered and reminded me that professors are the judges of what they teach. It would be entirely up to them, individually, to use any of the theories or practices that their college was certifying in print as "best." This is the position one would expect a dean to take. Higher education embeds into its identity freedom of inquiry, thought, expression, and publication, and it is wary of orthodoxies. But failure to teach what one's college is confirming as best practices circumvents what those outside the academy would likely view as common sense. This is the sort of distinction that foundations despair over.

The often casual college and university use of evidence in institutional matters while foundations are ramping up their expectations about research-based practices in those same matters creates inevitable tension in the relationship. Wanting research does not make good and relevant research easy to come by. But failing to approach these *institutional* matters with an evidentiary impulse is likely to fall increasingly short of foundation expectations.

Foundations

In a curiously ironic way, foundations show parallels to colleges and universities on their side of the relationship.

PROPRIETARY SELF-ABSORPTION. While self-absorption is in the culture of colleges and universities, in foundations it is in the genes. Given life by a donor's goals, as well as his or her money, foundations build deep into their structures the signature of their origins. They stand for different things. Their styles vary. On occasion foundations may collaborate in a cross-foundation initiative; more often they may simply find themselves engaged in the same project with other foundations. The creators of these pseudo-collaborations, however, turn out to be the grantees who successfully secured multiple supports for their projects. What one foundation starts, another foundation may continue funding, but this is unlikely. To do so may feel like disloyalty to the dispositions each has to make its own difference, not finance another's priorities.

Because their goal is to give money away to those who can advance their purposes, foundations generally maintain small staffs whose members, even if inclined, have little time left over from grantmaking to collaborate with others, do research, convene grantees, and the like. As a result, they may come to depend on the steady flow of proposals as a key source of information about developments in the field. That is not necessarily a bad source, but it is an uneven one. If a program officer does not have a broad background as context or is unable to keep up with the field independently, the assessment of proposals tends to center on their perceived intrinsic merit rather than whether they reflect an advance over similar prior efforts. This is not a particularly good way to exert leadership or even indirectly to advance the field or the knowledge on which it is built.

Let us consider why one long-running priority has produced such mixed and sluggish results: the substantial foundation sums spent on diversity. Foundations have funded developing inclusive campuses, improving retention and success rates of underserved undergraduate and graduate students, framing freshman orientation programs to begin a four-year process of building intercultural fluency, and similar efforts. These have been part of higher education for over forty years—more for some institutions, fewer for others. Large investments by, for example, the Ford Foundation, enabled many grants, convenings, and Internet-supported resources and networks for participants. Programs by national organizations like the Association of American Colleges and Universities (AAC&U) and the now-defunct American Association for Higher Education (AAHE) have sought to embed tools and strategies in their work in the field. But the sharing of useful information, serious collaboration around common goals, and joint assessments and reviews based on these results have been rare outside these larger programs. Foundations have often been enablers of the institution-by-institution approach. They have made grants supporting institutional introspection, trial-and-error undertakings, and efforts in which colleges and universities recapitulate the sequence of discovering what works and what does not—a sequence repeated with minor variations in hundreds of institutions.

Boards, by design, are usually self-perpetuating and turn over least frequently of the three internal constituencies of directors, executive leadership, and program staff. When there is turnover, it is usually partial, leaving ample opportunity to socialize new members to the norms and ethos of the foundation. One would hardly expect it to be otherwise. What board continuity provides in benefits, however, it can exact by impatience for results and a short attention span. Although staff turnover and the tendency to embark on program reviews or strategic planning exercises can point a foundation in a new program direction, it is a rare case that opens wide windows of opportunity to do business in a radically new way. The pull of the foundation's identity is steady and strong.

MARKETING. It is no easy matter to decide what kinds of programs to fund, whom to inform about grant possibilities, and how to express foundation intentions in terms that both focus and leave latitude at the same time. Some foundations let their broad statements of purpose carry the freight of communicating intent, issuing neither guidelines nor deadlines that would allow comparative assessments of merit. Most will say more. Even when the writers of program guidelines do their very best to be clear about the foundation's interests, those guidelines do not reach all those who might have an interesting or important response to make. When the writing reaches a reader, that reader often dons glasses whose prescription is ground to search for the college or university's interests, not a mutual relationship that will also advance the foundation's objectives. From time to time, foundation writer and proposal-potent reader connect authentically. It is a bit like whales mating: they can do it if they can find each other, but the search is not easy; it is a big ocean.

Because foundations generally maintain small staffs, it can be difficult for proposers to get clarification. Most foundations, in self-defense, discourage visits from college and university officials who want to assess foundation interest in their initiatives. When such interviews do occasionally occur, they are often awkward events—the higher education visitor hoping to make a connection and cultivate an inside track, the foundation program officer trying to be informative and noncommittal. Across the table, when foundation staff members execute their due diligence, it is seldom possible to go confidently beyond the quality of the animating idea to assess the probability of successful execution. A tendency to fill this void with institutional reputation may go part way to explaining why the top one hundred higher education grant getters in 2004 received 70 percent of the $2.077 billion granted in that year by the one hundred top foundations making grants to higher education.

The challenge of getting good information also partially explains why personal contacts are so precious and well guarded. Being able to broker a contact between a foundation and a grantseeker can be as sophisticated as the foundation itself. Savvy brokers are as valuable as self-promoting ones are hazardous. But brokers, however well they do their work, make a difficult-to-penetrate system even more so for all but those with insider connections.

INCONSTANCY. Given their self-absorption, one might imagine foundations to be stable, reliable, and consistent. They are in some respects; they also tackle challenges of great scope and complexity. But foundations put unrealistic timeframes around many of their ambitions. Sometimes a foundation will explicitly state its funding timetable; more often there will be an unpublished norm. Published or not, durations are generally short—in the three-year range. Some foundations are hospitable to renewal requests; others are not, believing that a good idea should generate enough momentum to enable advocates to secure funding elsewhere after the initial investment. When policies on the duration of funding are flexible, and the limit is a soft norm rather than a rigid ceiling, there is little room for complaint. Foundations cannot, by their nature, become revenue streams for a set of grantees unless they intend to close shop and pipe the money to a chosen few. But limiting projects to a fixed term, irrespective of the complexity of the problem being tackled, violates the rule of form following function. It obliges grantees to solve problems within arbitrary time limits set independently of the problem.

Besides issues of the duration of funding for particular initiatives, foundations often change their program priorities. This makes a certain sense from the foundation's point of view. It may have accomplished what it set out to do, it may perceive new issues as more vital and promising than older ones, or it may simply be feeling stale and looking for program revitalization. Change may also be evidence of some initial uncertainty about program direction, the significance of the goals sought, and practicality of the strategy employed. If one develops reservations about a program, it is often easier to walk away from it than to fix it. Not sticking with tough issues that have transformative potential but whose surface manifestations change, such as the many variations on the theme of instructional technology, often short-circuits a penetrating look in favor of an episodic contribution more apt to deal with superficial than significant matters.

It would be nice if these several issues could be debated. We should not hold our breath. Candor is seldom an invited visitor where gifts or grants are concerned. To their credit, a number of foundations have begun, with the Center for Effective Philanthropy, to survey grantees' perceptions of foundation administrative performance. Those are important matters but not the sort raised here. What the six characteristics just sketched (three of higher education and three of foundations) and others like them describe are norms, ambitions, priorities, organizational features, and definitions of purpose that make finding common ground problematic. If colleges and universities resist foundation purposes, they will lose a good deal of the research and development money available for innovation and improvement in the core teaching programs, the social roles of higher education, in building inclusive campuses and producing inter-culturally fluent graduates, and in exploring new combinations of academic content and talent. If foundations turn partially away from colleges and universities in respect to those same core functions, they will contribute to a stalling of progress on which much of the other strengths of higher education and society depend. The relationship of foundations to higher education floats so high above everyday awareness, and it changes so slowly that most have not noticed a deterioration, though it is well advanced. Rebuilding it, then, is likely to be as slow as its deterioration was.

So What? And What's Next?

Higher education spreads across a broad economic map. Wealthy private institutions, rich in capital of varying kinds, can ride out most cycles. Public research universities share in federal funds and private gifts; they get by, despite lukewarm state support. Comprehensive universities, tuition-dependent private institutions, and community colleges struggle to keep student numbers and educational quality in a tolerable balance with stalled or shrinking resources. The financial problems of the public sector dwarf foundation resources—which have never been a substitute for core state support. The endowed institutions, as successful as they have been in securing foundation funds, place much more reliance on gifts from individuals. For institutions in the middle, which have not seen much of foundation funding, their struggle on all financial fronts will continue. If foundations lose interest in making grants for institutional change and improvement, as contrasted with grants in support of their own problem-based and specialized program priorities, so what?

We can say, with some assurance, that neither side will suffer immediately. Foundations will focus elsewhere, do good, and only later begin to notice that liberal education keeps giving way to career-oriented programs, the improvement of teaching slips down the institutional priority lists, and the intellectual design of colleges and universities finds a groove and becomes less venturesome. Learning will increasingly become a private good as its public value and public role shrink. Foundations will have to work a little harder in their other program areas as such problems manifest themselves in less imaginative graduates and fewer new ideas. The colleges and universities will follow the money, let learning settle to a respectable level, and occasionally get a private gift that can light a small fire to temporarily warm teaching. As David Kirp has observed, "the student as acolyte whose preferences are to be formed [becomes] a consumer whose preferences are to be satisfied" (2003, p. 7). The independence of colleges and universities that foundations understand and cherish may erode as corners of higher education go on sale.

Among the values that will go missing in this scenario is the vision of the possible that foundations provide. Even the varied and transitory interests that foundations put forward can alight in an institution in ways that cause or catalyze change. When they do so, they supply a kind of energy without which educational institutions breathe shallowly and venture less. While most colleges and universities attempt to supply some of the oxygen that new ideas and experiments in teaching and learning require, they are hard-pressed to do more than token amounts. For a long time, higher education has looked to outside funds to finance much of its institution-level research and development.

On a still deeper level, foundations and higher education have a lasting stake in each others' vibrancy because each is an animating factor of a free society and an example of how such a society sustains its own renewal. Nowhere does, or should, this happen more consequentially than in teaching and learning and in the institutional arrangements that support student development. Colleges and universities can powerfully influence the judgment, ethics, and humanity of their students—who are not as crassly careerist as some contemporary observers make them out to be. College is for many a transformative experience. Incoming students have a fledgling sense that what they seek in college is to become more fully developed as self and citizen and more capable of defining the future rather than being simply swept along by it. Four years later, more fully fledged with possibilities, they know more. Reminding graduates of these aspirations, Stanford's president in the 1980s, Donald Kennedy, would end his commencement-day talks with an Adlai Stevenson quotation urging them not to forget "when you leave why you came."

What would it take for our hypothetical foundation to give an affirmative answer to its not-so-hypothetical question about continuing to fund institutional change in higher education? A makeover of either or both parties is not the answer. Each in its own way is distinctive, significant, and precious. And, to be sure, the variety even within each sector sprawls broadly. They are also largely set in their ways, they can be frustrating to deal with on such institutional matters, they only occasionally want the same things, and they need each other but do not seem to know how to articulate that need. If we look, then, for significant changes that move in the right direction and do not expect transformation as the price of doing business, what might those significant changes be?

An initial step would be to convene the parties in some representative conclave to identify and begin work on the issues that most discourage them in their relationship. Chief among these would be better ways to understand foundations in terms of their importance to colleges and universities and vice versa. Though the value of this relationship is often uncritically assumed, the lack of understanding is apparent when, as now, foundations sour on grants to encourage critical analysis and change in institutional characteristics across a broad swath of higher education and, instead, funnel support mainly to the leading universities to supply the knowledge and people that the foundations wish to see employed in their other program areas. Topics irking colleges and universities would likely include the short attention spans of foundations, the low and vague levels of information they provide, their lack of openness and transparency, and their complaints about wheel reinvention while taking no action to alter the conditions that lead to it. For their part, foundations might ask for clearer understandings of who can bind the institution, exit strategies that continue successes and discourage effort that is coextensive with foundation funding, and the grounding of projects in research so that progress in the field, rather than local repetition, is the result of a successful grant.

Other recommendations that respond to the issues and characteristics described in this chapter include those I've placed into Groups I and II and discuss next. Several recommendations overlap and can be seen in combination with others, and each applies in some way to both foundations and to colleges and universities. Group I reprises recommendations from Chapter Two, with emphasis on their higher education relevance. Group II brings in further ideas.

Group I

When it comes to teaching and learning, higher education's insularity interdicts the spread of ideas, despite swaths of commonality in the problems those ideas address. In this realm the needs for educational capital would be much the same across many colleges and universities.

BUILDING EDUCATIONAL CAPITAL. Consider just the chapter headings of Ken Bain's splendid little book, *What the Best College Teachers Do*:

> What do they know about how we learn?
>
> How do they prepare to teach?
>
> What do they expect of their students?
>
> How do they conduct class?
>
> How do they treat their students?
>
> How do they evaluate their students and themselves?

Each chapter's topic invites capital building that can find its way into a preparation-for-teaching aspect of doctoral training, into the resources made locally available to faculty by centers for teaching and learning, into the workings of departments that elect to make themselves learning communities in respect to teaching and learning, and into appointment, promotion, tenure, and salary decisions. An elaboration of the educational capital concept can be found in Chapter Two.

(In Appendix A at the end of this book, our colleague, Russ Edgerton, has permitted inclusion of his short and trenchant piece on ideas for improving teaching and learning in higher education. It presents numerous opportunities for reflecting on the relevance of and need for educational capital in this uncommonly important area.)

BEING OPEN. Cyberspace crackles with information, but too little reaches influential faculty and administrators on how to improve teaching and learning. Openness, as described in Chapter Two, can lead to more documentations and collaborations. Useful and useable information, which is widely and freely available, can promote networking and learning communities among those sharing similar challenges. The open courseware and open-content projects that began with MIT and now involve more than seventy universities are examples of how openness can feed on itself, enabling more institutions to participate while costs go down and demand goes up. Foundations working with greater openness, from guidelines and proposals to grants and results, and institutions of higher education doing the same, can enlarge and enrich the improvement of teaching and learning.

OFFERING PROFESSIONAL DEVELOPMENT. The idiosyncratic hiring practices for foundation staff are hopelessly out of date. Without training programs such as those beginning in a few places, the chance that much will be different about the relationship ten or twenty years from now is slight. (On its Web site, Independent Sector lists thirty-six U.S. "Academic Centers Focusing on the Study of Philanthropy." Many spread across the nonprofit sector as well. A small number offer courses, certifications, or degrees.)

Foundation and academic leaders, brought together with experts in organizational behavior, organizational development, and pertinent social sciences, could produce a much-needed curriculum. Along the way, the effort would necessarily generate important explorations into the effectiveness of the foundation–higher education relationship, as well as a beginning set of professional standards.

Similar programs for college or university development staff could amplify their skill and acuity in building relationships with foundations, not in simply being good at what many foundations, perhaps unfairly, think they are: members of a marketing department.

USING EXTERNAL REVIEW. Some foundations use external review to assess proposal merit and, in the process, necessarily draw reviewers into the more expansive dialogue about issues and priorities. More foundations should do so. But colleges and universities rarely ask colleagues from elsewhere to assist in solving problems and designing programs that draw on viewpoints and know-how outside the institution. Such convenings could lead to collaborations, the sharing of results, and the spread of successful ideas. A version of external review would substantially crack the insularity and self-absorption that so frequently thwart the hatching of high-impact ideas and giving those ideas legs.

As an example, a program such as the one I ran on pluralism and unity would have benefited greatly (and likely produced educational capital) had I had the wisdom, instead of going it alone, to gather together a cross-institutional group of acknowledged experts and potential applicants to probe "pluralism" and "unity," as applied to increasingly diverse campuses, share what each knew already about the topics, determine foresighted priorities within each, explore intra- and inter-institutional strategies and tactics, and plan to capture and spread what was learned. This same group or a subset of it could then have helped me select the proposals most likely to make a difference at home and across like institutions. In the process, the participating individuals would have continued to learn things that would be useful on their own campuses.

COLLABORATING. Foundations generally develop distinctive means to attack general issues. That can produce scattered and piecemeal results. But it need not do so. If foundations work together to identify a complex issue on whose importance they agree and then, according to their comparative strengths, take responsibility for different parts of it, they might ensure that the whole on which they collaborate will be greater than the sum of the parts if they work in isolation. Suitably rearranged, a similar logic would work for different grantees who would bring different intellectual resources and a variety of experimental locales in which to address a constellation of related issues. An investment by one or more foundations in a cohort of colleges and universities funded as co-creators of an experiment signals a good start at creating educational capital. Then providing resources for an infrastructure to manage the collaboration and ensure that its findings are documented and disseminated in a form useable by others could confirm the asset potential of the project. A similar result could be produced by working with regional or national associations to pool ideas, compose expert teams, design and implement innovative projects, assess results, and disseminate findings to a broader community.

Group II

Making good grants is important and hard but episodic work. Those grants enrich institutions, sometimes place (and win) a high-risk, high-gain bet, and encourage initiative. But foundation priorities, people, and grantees change. Learning can die out and progress stall. Utilizing a capital-building strategy addresses some of those challenges, but it's not the only way.

BUILDING OPERATING CAPACITY. If foundations were to devote a corner of themselves to an operating foundation-like structure, they could take on and stay with more substantial, farther-reaching, and complex strategies—the kind that can have systemic qualities, tackle deeper challenges, and produce more consequential results.

A foundation that, for example, was determined to focus for ten to fifteen years on re-imagining the interface between high school and higher education, so that instead of a boundary it became more bridge or inclined path for underserved students, would be poorly advised only to give grants to a variety of grantees. If, instead, it built its own capacity or that of an intermediary organization to explore research, identify and analyze innovative variations, frame experiments and pilots, connect with allies, seed and nurture the practices that emerge, and publish not only reports but multimedia materials for practitioners interested in attempting change but unable to make the investment to learn the what and how from the bottom up, there is a good probability that the problem would become less formidable and the field—and students—better off.

BEING A LEARNING ORGANIZATION. Drawing both intellectually and pragmatically on its experience, a foundation that can become a learning organization should be able to substantially increase its effectiveness. As a learning organization, it could give up cycling through planning exercises that merely replace current staff and old priorities with newer ones—a practice many on the outside see as arbitrary behavior, as well as the sacrifice of institutional memory. Not only could foundations-as-learning-organizations then build educational capital, but they themselves would benefit from it by being able to base future plans more deliberately and effectively on past learning. By adopting continuous learning as an operating characteristic in areas of core interest, they could become more powerful instruments of change. The welcome casualty in this would be wheel reinvention. The beneficiary would be innovations built on experience and ideas ranging beyond a single institution.

Adopting this recommendation would make a foundation more like what it hopes its grantees will become: evaluators of practice in order to improve continuously. Changes in organizational norms, procedures, and possible staff configurations would likely follow. These would make possible and eventually natural the use of tools where aspirations are given descriptive form and performance is steadily reviewed against them.

DISSEMINATING KNOWLEDGE. The existence of the Web makes possible communication strategies that would have been science fiction not long ago. Original information, along with links to other sites and sources, networks of faculty engaged in common endeavors, and commissioned meta-analyses, could provide the subject matter. Then the foundation could make reference to and use of that information a necessary condition of any proposal it would be willing to consider. Consortia of foundations with similar program interests could collaborate on both the content of the site and the function of the necessary conditions. Such a site, moreover, could become a source of ideas for would-be grantees who correctly pull from it notions on where important work remains to be done. This could be an integral part of the foundations' growing as learning organizations themselves and in more securely grounding and extending their work. Foundations could also create partnerships with regional and national organizations to pool learning on important topics and fund such organizations to propagate these findings for the benefit of wider audiences.

Foundations, only slightly less than their grantees, are guilty of shelving grant results and moving on to new projects that will produce their own to-be-shelved results. If a foundation were to make a point of, for example, organizing reports or studies relative to its interest in, say, quantitative literacy or undergraduate capstone experiences, it could then become a Web site of choice for all with similar interests and strengthen the means to its own aims.

Information passively displayed relies on voluntary action to come alive. For some institutions, the incentive to improve may be enough. For others, some financial incentive shrewdly applied may catalyze change. If a foundation made a condition of eligibility that proposals build on what has been done before, they oblige would-be grantees to do what few do now, which is to examine existing evidence and add to or use it rather than recapitulate it. If recapitulation is a college's goal, then it has, at best, a weak case for external funding.

More Conversations

Three months of hard work have gone imaginatively as well as methodically by, and the education staff has returned to a foundation staff meeting with the results of their consultation and reflection and, with enthusiasm, their recommendations. They propose that the overall theme of the program will be "rethinking liberal education for the early edge of the twenty-first century." They describe why they believe this will engage a set of issues that leaders in the field identify as critical, among them making the path from high school to college equitable and intellectually potent; paying increasingly sophisticated attention to student learning and the conditions that enhance it; making civic, social, and ethical, as well as academic development, part of the constellation of values informing undergraduate education; and taking "learning to learn" from cliché to a skill and habit of mind.

The staff's roles will emphasize negotiated relationships and collaboration among both foundations and colleges and universities, as well as between them, and will stress the importance of the application of findings beyond individual grantees. Indeed, one of the operating principles of the program, they report, will be that mutual benefit must be evident to both grantmaker and grantseeker if a proposal is to get across the foundation threshold.

But the centerpiece of the program will depart dramatically from the customary role of grantmaker. It instead calls for treating the higher education program budget like an investment portfolio. The foundation will be investing in the creation of educational capital that can then return increased faculty and student interest and educational dividends to and beyond the participants. It will implement the liberal education theme and incorporate the values and approaches noted earlier, while becoming more focused, proactive, collaborative, and oriented toward important issues and significant change. Its substance will be derived from its theme, and its program aims, guidelines, and priorities would be crafted accordingly. These will be embodied in a four-part strategy whose essential elements, allocations of dollars and effort, and time frames would be as follows:

1. *Grants*. Grants will be based on foundation-initiated guidelines and awarded competitively to the best proposals in each round. A panel of carefully recruited colleagues from higher education and foundations will help design the guidelines and rate the proposals. In order to reinforce the foundation's educational-capital-building investment emphasis, the program will favor collaborative proposals and will, itself, seek out foundations with shared interests.

o Allocation: 60 percent. Time frame: four to eight years, with four to five years as the modal grant duration. (This will be most like the current program and present the least shock to the community of past and future grantees. Even so, it would have significant new aspects to it.)

2. *An operating arm*. The foundation will create an operating unit that will provide shared leadership, technical assistance, and grants for one or two major liberal education initiatives, bringing together other foundations, a selected set of colleges or universities, and such other agencies as might contribute experience and expertise to the effort. The aim will be to create,

test, implement, and build on educational capital. To shape this initiative, staff will seek counsel from individuals and organizations with a record of deep study and forward-looking involvement in liberal education.

○ Allocation: 20 percent. Time frame: five years initially, with the potential for renewal after a review during the fourth year.

3. *Associations as instrumental.* A program of grants to regional, national, and scholarly associations interested in explorations into the deep structure of liberal education in support of the foundation's aims.

○ Allocation: 10 percent. Time frame: four to eight years, with four to five years as the modal duration.

4. *Dissemination and application.* A project will be organized to develop Web-based and other materials in partnership with grantees in order to make tools, findings, ideas, and developed educational capital available in ready-to-use form. The foundation will also encourage their use through small exploratory or seed grants as incentives to faculty and institutions to try them on.

○ Allocation: 10 percent. Time frame: five years, with a review then to determine whether to make permanent.

Their colleagues are impressed. In the discussion that follows, good questions get answers that run from the plausible to the persuasive. After a full hearing, the president sums up: "You've accomplished a great deal in three months. Your ideas are fresh, make sense, and will further aspirations that I know our directors have. Only one thing worries me. You've grown these ideas out of abstract soil—earnest and intelligent conversations but not genuine trials. There's a requirement for making it all work: that each (the foundations and the colleges and universities) give up a corner of their independence in order to shoulder a new level of responsibility and work together each to accommodate the other in order to advance a joint agenda. I'd like to think that will work. I believe we can make it work here. But I'm not sure about the rest of our universe."

NOTES

1. Much of this chapter reflects my fifty-year education career, mostly in higher education, then in foundations, and now in research. For eight years as a foundation program officer, I read and responded to proposals from

colleges and universities. During that period, I recommended more than three hundred grants worth just over $47 million in response to several times that many proposals, plus other letters of intent that never materialized into proposals. I got to know, on the surface and sometimes deeper, a number of other foundations and their program people. Before that, I had thirty-five years of experience in and around higher education as an administrator, trustee, and accreditor. Most of that time was spent at Stanford, where I was vice president for budget and planning when I retired. In my current role in research at the Carnegie Foundation, I studied Web and library materials and interviewed a wide variety of experienced people about foundations and higher education to test and amplify my own experience. Of inestimable importance to me was the wise counsel of my colleague and partner in this project, Tom Ehrlich. The responsibility for the contents of this chapter, however, is mine alone.

2. Atlantic Philanthropies, which ended its higher education program in 2002 after twenty years and $1.5 billion in funding, is domiciled in Bermuda and, therefore, does not appear in the data gathered and published by the Foundation Center.

3. Think italics when you see "institutional" as an adjective modifying "issues." I shall use *institutional* primarily to refer to those issues that stretch across a college or university, particularly those that surround and concern teaching and learning and the undergraduate experience more broadly. The intended contrast is to specialized program issues, when foundation support is sought for graduate training and research; discipline-, area-, or problem-focused centers; and the like.

REFERENCES

Bacchetti, R. "Independent to a Fault: Why Foundations and Higher Education Frustrate Each Other and What Might Be Done About It." *Change,* Jan.-Feb. 2004.

Bain, K. *What the Best College Teachers Do.* Cambridge: Harvard University Press, 2004.

Kirp, D. *Shakespeare, Einstein, and the Bottom Line.* Cambridge: Harvard University Press, 2003.

"W. K. Kellogg Foundation Logic Model Development Guide." Battle Creek, Mich.: W. K. Kellogg Foundation, 2001.

Chapter Eleven Overview

Edgar F. Beckham spent his life working in higher education, initially at Wesleyan University and later in foundations, mainly at the Ford Foundation. He had a remarkable career devoted to opening the doors of higher education to those of diverse backgrounds. In the months before he died in 2006, he brought his experience to bear in writing a case study of a successful partnership between the Bildner Family Foundation and its founders—Allen Bildner and his wife, Joan—two intermediary organizations, and a number of New Jersey colleges and universities.

The project started with the important idea that diversity of racial, ethnic, and religious backgrounds and perspectives could be a powerful educational asset and that a willing set of institutions might develop programs designed to educate their students with the understandings, skills, and values needed to use diversity as a resource for strengthening and extending democracy.

The foundation founder turned to two intermediary organizations—The Philanthropic Initiative (TPI) and the Association of American Colleges and Universities (AAC&U)—to help shape the idea into a project. They operated as a partnership (the Bildners, TPI, and AAC&U), and each had a role in thinking through how best to encourage and further the project goals. They crafted a set of criteria to qualify for financial support from the project. The partnership then worked with interested institutions and, over time, chose a group of eight for funding. During the next four years, the partners worked closely with the group of institutions to help them learn from each other, as well as to strengthen their student learning. In retrospect, the process clearly built educational capital for use by others, as well as by the group.

The case study highlights the particular benefits of using intermediary organizations, as well as some of the challenges. Each of the organizations that were partners in the project brought special strengths, but it required continuing attention to be sure that they were always on the same page. Each campus also had its own special needs, and the project sought to enable campus leaders to meet those needs while also being part of a whole that included more than eight separate campuses. The case study illustrates how a broad objective—in this case, diversity—can be promoted through a number of different campus-based approaches.

WORKING THROUGH INTERMEDIARIES

THE NEW JERSEY CAMPUS DIVERSITY INITIATIVE

Edgar F. Beckham

THE ISSUE CAN BE OF CRITICAL IMPORTANCE, and the funder's commitment to addressing it can be deep and abiding. But urgency and passion alone may not make a project work. As the experience of the New Jersey Campus Diversity Initiative (NJCDI) illustrates, a grant program's effectiveness can be greatly enhanced through careful planning and the cultivation of strategic relationships. Even when the work is directed at a large, complicated issue, modest funds can make a major difference if the design and the key actors are right. The NJCDI case is remarkable because it positioned a family foundation to address, on a statewide basis, an issue of national significance—and to do so at the cutting edge.

In 2002, the Bildner Family Foundation launched the NJCDI, with grants to eight New Jersey colleges and universities. Each institution was eligible to receive up to $225,000 for a three-year project designed to improve intergroup relations, reduce prejudice and bigotry, and demonstrate the value of diversity to the life and mission of the institution.

Diversity as a Critical Issue for Higher Education

Although the history of diversity in American higher education can be traced back to the efforts of Harvard College in the seventeenth century to transcend its Puritan roots, diversity became a more pressing concern about forty years ago, when the civil rights movement prompted many predominantly white colleges and universities to recognize that they had been complicit in denying educational opportunity to the sons and daughters of slavery. Institutions in the North were particularly sensitive to the suggestion that their condemnation of racial discrimination in the South was hypocritical in the light of the racial homogeneity of their student bodies. In response, during the mid-sixties, several of the most prestigious institutions launched affirmative campaigns to recruit students of color.

Over the years, *diversity* became the common term identified with these newly recruited students themselves and with all the issues associated with their presence, including their academic achievement, their environmental comfort, their social relations, and their identification with institutional ethos. This perspective on diversity was grounded in notions of social justice and sought to redress past wrongs. Over time, as the idea of diversity matured, institutions also discovered the benefits of diversity, not only to institutional conscience but also to the educational environment, to learning outcomes for *all* students, and, ultimately, to American society. This more recent perspective values diversity because of its educational impact. One of the great challenges that American higher education still faces is to bring these two perspectives into single focus.

By 2002, when the Bildner Family Foundation launched the NJCDI, much had been accomplished toward that objective. A growing body of research supported the view that a diverse educational environment improved educational outcomes, dramatically more so when diversity was put to intentional use as an educational resource. Efforts were under way to create a unified understanding of academic excellence that included both high achievement and inclusion. *Inclusive excellence* had become an accepted term to designate this intention. But despite the evident gains, there is still a residual tendency to separate the two perspectives, to think about equity in regard to minority students, about education in regard to students in general, indeed sometimes to refer to minority students as "diversity students" and to students in general as "students." In other words, when treated separately, the social-justice impulse can have the unintended consequence of further marginalizing the very students it had set out to bring into the mainstream.

A Funder's Commitment to Diversity

Allen Bildner dates his interest in diversity from a day in the fifth grade. On the way home from school in Summit, New Jersey, he was assaulted, called a "dirty Jew," and taunted with shouts: "Go home, Rabbi! Go home!" It was his first encounter with anti-Semitism, and though the physical hurt healed quickly, he remained confused for a longer time about his Jewish identity and felt impaired in his capacity to assert it.

Although Bildner's interest in combating prejudice and bigotry took shape at an early age, it was not until the late sixties, when he became aware of the demographic shifts taking place in the United States, that he began to appreciate the social relevance of his personal passion. He continued to invoke the language of prejudice reduction and intergroup relations, but they were no longer ends in themselves. They served a higher purpose: securing the future of America.

As the CEO of Kings Super Markets, Bildner saw strength in the diversity of his company's workforce. The company devoted time and money to helping its associates learn about each other's religion and culture, and, in his words, "as a result, to enjoy each other's differences." In short, as a businessman, Allen Bildner became a "diversity practitioner"—someone who saw diversity as an asset and set about to make the asset perform, for his colleagues and for the company.

Partners in Philanthropic Action

In 1993, Bildner and his wife, Joan, first mentioned their interest in directing their philanthropy toward intergroup relations to Peter Karoff, founder of The Philanthropic Initiative (TPI). TPI offers development and implementation services to philanthropic clients; TPI conducts research, explores fields of endeavor related to a donor's interests, helps to refine philanthropic objectives, and performs the multiple management tasks involved in moving funds from donor to grantee and ensuring that the funds are used for purposes spelled out in the contractual agreements. It also provides its clients with opportunities to educate themselves in the arts of strategic philanthropy—philanthropy designed not only to do immediate good but to do it in a manner likely to produce lasting change.

From that point forward, Karoff and TPI vice president Joanne Duhl served as management consultants to the Bildners, identifying a number of philanthropic options for them. These included a proposal to fund teachers in K–12, a scholarship program for students transferring from community colleges to four-year colleges, and a plan to create one or more state centers for intergroup relations. Several of these ideas resulted in individual grants from the Bildners.

A Third Partner

In 1996, when the Association of American Colleges and Universities (AAC&U) sponsored a national conference on "Diversity, Learning and Institutional Change," a staff member from TPI attended and brought back information about AAC&U's capacity in this area. A national association that has been the voice of liberal education for ninety years, AAC&U has focused explicitly on diversity in higher education for decades. It has partnered with major national foundations, other national education associations, and hundreds of individual institutions to increase minority participation in higher education, generate research on the positive educational effects of diversity, and develop evaluation strategies for diversity initiatives. AAC&U has also been a convener of national and international conferences on diversity and learning, and on the role of diversity in educating students for a diverse democracy and an interconnected world.

By connecting the Bildners with AAC&U and, in particular, with senior vice president Caryn McTighe Musil and program director Daniel Teraguchi, TPI helped the Bildner Foundation identify higher education as an area where grant funds, used effectively, could transform diversity into a powerful educational resource.

From 1990 to 1998, I coordinated the Ford Foundation's Campus Diversity Initiative. Beginning in 1992, AAC&U was a prominent partner in the initiative, playing a leadership role in shaping the foundation's collaboration with colleges and universities across the country, and participating in the design and implementation of the foundation's multiyear public information program to increase public awareness of campus diversity. The aim of the broader Ford initiative was to encourage colleges and universities to value diversity as an educational asset and to put it to use as an educational resource. The objective of the public information program was to increase public appreciation of higher education's efforts. By the time I joined the staff of AAC&U in 1998, it had added substantially to its capacity to frame and support diversity initiatives.

Alan Bildner's interest in diversity had been stimulated by strife. So was the Ford Foundation's. While its concern with social justice and issues of equity, especially in education, is more than a half-century old, the foundation renewed its focus on campus diversity in 1990 with a call to colleagues in higher education to pay attention to the alarming rise of intergroup tension on campus. *Race relations* and *diversity* were twin terms in the early formulations of the initiative at the Ford Foundation, just as *intergroup relations* and *prejudice reduction* would eventually be joined with *diversity* as goals of the NJCDI.

A Partnership for Success: The Triangle

The partnership that was established in 2001 to support the NJCDI can best be described as a triangle. The occupants of each angle—the Bildners (and, in time, the NJCDI advisory committee) at one angle; TPI's Karoff and Duhl at another; and AAC&U's Musil, Teraguchi, and Beckham forming the third—have brought something different to the initiative. The Bildners, although fervent about reducing prejudice and improving intergroup relations, also see diversity as a social asset. The TPI staff has experience with philanthropic options, a keen sense of how to transform intentions into productive action likely to benefit society lastingly, and knowledge about managing grants. AAC&U understands diversity as an educational strategy for preparing students for purposeful engagement in a diverse democracy. Joining the angles created the triangle and produced a strategic vision. Our pooled experience has informed strategic choices for both the design and execution of the initiative.

Another benefit of the triangle: it has allowed the Bildners to manage their active participation in the NJCDI through the intermediary roles played by TPI and AAC&U. The Bildners' presence in the initiative has been experienced as generative by nearly all participants. Indeed, the word *Bildner,* as noun, adjective, and even verb, has entered the language of diversity practice on these campuses in some playful, but always positive ways. Through this three-way relationship, the Bildners have been able to track the progress of the NJCDI and influence it at crucial moments in productive ways.

Over time, the Bildners, TPI, and AAC&U would develop implementation strategies collaboratively, through regular e-mails, frequent conference calls, and occasional meetings. Together we would work out some decisions in rather minute detail. But just as frequently, the Bildners would sign off on an overall plan and leave it to TPI and AAC&U to refine and execute it. TPI handled tasks related to management; AAC&U took responsibility for programmatic matters. However, although the division of labor was straightforward and well understood, communication among the three parts of the triangle was frequent.

A Funding Challenge: Designing an Effective Program

At the Ford Foundation, the relationship between race relations and diversity was never clarified as the basis for a program of grants. In 1990, the focus of efforts to address campus race relations was nearly exclusively on students' lives outside the classroom (and often the responsibility of the office of student affairs). The Ford Foundation, however, saw the value of diversity centered in the curriculum and in the intellectual culture of higher education. The solution was simple. "Race relations" was gradually de-emphasized in the language of campus diversity grant recommendations, whereas "diversity" was brought into closer association with such time-honored educational values as critical thinking, intellectual inquiry, civil discourse, civic engagement, artistic expression, and spirituality. By asso-ciating diversity with educational values, the Ford Foundation could assert that American higher education was engaging diversity in ways that were good for students, good for institutions, and good for American society.

Once the triangle was formed in 2001, Musil, Teraguchi, and I brought the lessons learned from the Ford Foundation's Campus Diversity Initia-tive and from AAC&U's work into the NJCDI conversation. Recognizing that advocates of diversity approach it from multiple perspectives (social justice, cultural pluralism, civil society, education), the Bildners, TPI staff, and AAC&U staff developed our own "simple" solution. The Bildner Family Foundation would allow applicants—colleges and universities—to approach diversity from a variety of vantage points but also would insist that each approach be aligned closely with institutional mission. This strategy, we thought, would ensure alignment with educational val-ues and ultimately produce educational outcomes supportive of the orig-inal social goals. The NJCDI was born.

We also identified our roles. Musil, Teraguchi, and I would serve as advisers to the Bildners and TPI. We would also advise the individual institutions on conceptual and programmatic matters related to diversity in higher education. TPI, with staff skilled in implementation, would man-age the grants; the Bildners would make the final decisions. Ironically, the very clarity of our different roles facilitated many a rich discussion of the multiple perspectives we represented. It was not unusual for the occupants of the three angles to engage in conference calls in which grant management, educational issues, and funding decisions were intermixed.

A Key Strategy: Linking Each Project to Institutional Mission

In 2001, Allen Bildner sent a letter to the presidents of forty-five colleges and universities throughout New Jersey describing the initiative and ask-ing for letters of interest. The thirty-three who responded were invited to send representatives to a one-day meeting.

At the meeting, Allen Bildner, Karoff, Duhl, Musil, and I outlined our expectations for proposals. It was at this meeting that we made our first vigorous attempt to subsume the language of intergroup relations under the language of education. We made the point that whatever an institution proposed, it would need to relate demonstrably to that institution's central educational mission. However worthy the activity might be in its own right, if it appeared to be an adventitious add-on, related only incidentally to educational mission, it would not be favored.

This is still a difficult message for American educators to hear, for diversity, at least in recent decades, has been understood primarily as an add-on, involving the incremental admission of students who had previously been excluded and a flurry of well-meaning attempts to assimilate them. As a result, diversity has existed primarily "in the numbers"—as "structural" or "compositional" diversity.

We wanted the institutions to see diversity as an educational asset, and because we assumed that an educational asset would perform educationally, we were, in effect, asking the institutions to demonstrate the linkage between the uses of diversity and their educational mission. Institutions are used to being asked *how much* diversity they have. They are not used to being asked how they *put diversity to use* for educational purposes.

We took three additional steps to communicate the foundation's intentions. First, we asked the institutions to submit a short preliminary proposal; we then reviewed these and offered comment for each institution to consider in developing its final proposal. Next, for each of the preliminary proposals we formulated a set of "clarifying questions," which we invited the institutions to address in their final proposals. These clarifying questions gave us another opportunity to emphasize the importance of aligning diversity as educational strategy with the educational mission of the institution. Because each set of questions was tailored to a specific proposal, we were able to use the questions to call attention to weaknesses that we hoped would be addressed in the final proposals.

Finally, we encouraged the institutions to define diversity broadly, to include all the dimensions of group identity to which members of their communities lay claim: gender, ethnicity, race, religion, social class, sexual orientation, national affiliation, and any others that might be pertinent to their circumstances.

Several considerations, which the Bildners, TPI, and AAC&U developed together, guided our evaluation of the final proposals. We believed that the grantees should

- Serve as models for other New Jersey institutions
- Demonstrate evidence of taking institutional diversity work to new levels
- Understand their own institutional history regarding diversity

○ Be aware of their current environment

○ Have a strategy for gaining buy-in from others

○ Have located diversity centrally within the institution

○ Represent a variety of institutional types, demographic profiles, geographic locations, and rankings within the higher education community

We also identified the following seven criteria for a fundable project:

1. The proposal presents a clear and achievable plan of action.

2. The project builds on prior activities and results from thoughtful analysis of internal strengths and weaknesses.

3. Key constituencies were involved in developing the proposal.

4. The project has the support of the administration and the involvement of key faculty and staff.

5. The project has the potential to have a substantial programmatic impact on the institution.

6. The project is innovative and ambitious and has the potential to inform the work of other New Jersey campuses.

7. The plan for assessing the project is well defined and comprehensive.

Eight institutions met the criteria for funding: Bergen Community College, Bloomfield College, County College of Morris CCM, Princeton University, the Richard Stockton College of New Jersey, Rowan University, Rutgers University (the campuses at Camden, New Brunswick, and Newark), and the University of Medicine and Dentistry of New Jersey. The projects ranged in focus from guiding faculty and staff in understanding the potential of diversity to contribute to positive educational outcomes to curriculum development and from community outreach to student engagement.

The project summaries that appear at the end of this chapter show the variety of institutions and programmatic intentions that were initially part of the NJCDI. The pooled experience of the Bildner Family Foundation, TPI, and AAC&U made it possible to respond flexibly to this institutional and programmatic diversity.

Diversity as an Educational Strategy

On a site visit to Rowan University, Allen and Joan Bildner attended a class titled "Environmental Ethics." Joan Bildner wondered what the course had to do with diversity. She got her answer as the class began to discuss the probability that toxic dumps and other unfriendly sites would end up close to poor and minority neighborhoods.

I experienced a similar sensation at Rowan when I learned about a course titled "The Leadership of Ideas." Described as a course in critical thinking, its connection to diversity became apparent when I learned that students would be asked to explore their own social transition from high school to college, to identify the social groupings that characterized their high school environments, compare them to their current situations, examine likenesses and differences, and research the way social groups are formed. In other words, the students would be asked to invest aspects of their own diversity in the learning process, thus making themselves and their knowledge of familiar social structures available to the entire class for examination and analysis. Diversity, as this course illustrates, is not just a topical matter within a course; diverse people and their social experiences are the subject matter of the course. In short, using diversity as a resource can mean engaging diverse people as active crafters of their own learning experience. And as we know, active learners learn more.

When diversity is the strategy that informs curricular change, the texture of change is rich and complex. It will not settle for mere representation of multiple cultures, each cloaked in its own terms of reference, but rather insists on critical interrogation, on intercultural interaction, on cross-cultural communication. For example, students from Rutgers-Newark went into the Newark community to collect oral histories. The students then shaped the oral histories into theatrical presentations that, by including multiple histories, transformed the oral monologues into dialogues in which personal histories became resources for interpersonal communication. The transition from monologue to dialogue parallels the movement from passive cultural representation to active intercultural engagement.

Several years ago, at an international conference on diversity sponsored by the Ford Foundation, Justice Albie Sachs of the Constitutional Court of South Africa observed that, in our diversity, "we are different and the same." He used the phrase several times as he wove the story of his life— as a white South African, a Jew, a freedom fighter who lost his right arm and nearly his life in the struggle for the soul of his country. By the end of his quietly stirring talk, his audience had begun to understand that standard dictionaries are wrong about "diversity." It does not just mean variety and differentiation, for it always seems to toggle back to a potentially unifying context. In Justice Sachs's view, the diversity of South Africans encompasses both their differences and their shared context.

To put Justice Sachs's point in social terms, when we realize that we are both different and the same, we can use our differences to contribute to the common good. Potentially, everyone becomes a performing asset within the common context.

The ultimate translation of the language of prejudice reduction and intergroup relations is into this rich relational texture in which self and other, difference and commonality are seen as complementary. This may be society's highest hope for the pathway we call higher education. And higher education should be understood broadly to include the curriculum, the co-curriculum, and the campus culture, that is, the lectures and concerts, workshops and training programs, the dialogic learning that takes place in a variety of settings, and the experiential learning that occurs in many structured and unstructured arenas.

Strategies to Support Implementation

The Bildners, TPI, and AAC&U appreciated that because the institutions would be working at the cutting edge of diversity as an educational strategy, they would need a variety of supports. That support included two institutes for learning with and from each other, annual reports that would push the schools to keep articulating their goals and progress, and annual site visits from an AAC&U consultant. In addition, AAC&U kept up a steady flow of electronic communication with the group, and during the first year, in particular, regular telephone consultations.

Intercampus Dialogue

The NJCDI brought the campus teams together for two institutes, the first in June 2002, the second a year later. The first institute was designed to introduce participants to the latest thinking about diversity as an educational strategy, to encourage them to think of diversity as a set of educational practices attached to desired educational outcomes, and to envision those outcomes as the kind of learning all students need, regardless of major or career path. Conducted over four days, the institute provided an opportunity for team leaders to share their institutional plans with the group. Campus teams also met on their own or with a consultant to refine their plans. The institute included seminars on four large issues related to diversity work in higher education: higher education in a diverse world; the intersections of identities; immigration, migration, and citizenship; and engaging communities locally, nationally, and globally. Workshop topics included global struggles for human rights, assessing diversity initiatives, bridging community divides, structuring intergroup dialogues, fostering intergroup understanding, and connecting the dots for institutional transformation.

The second institute featured the teams' shared progress reports. Teams regrouped into cross-institutional thematic clusters focused on areas of interest: intercultural centers and programs, curriculum development, faculty development, campus-community partnerships, and assessment. Practical workshops built skills such as structuring intergroup dialogues, honing a public message, and sustaining institutional change. As with the first institute, there was time for team meetings and consultations.

Presidential Engagement

During the first year of the initiative, Allen Bildner suggested that we do more to encourage active presidential involvement in the NJCDI. After thorough discussion within the triangle and some initial planning by TPI, Bildner invited the presidents to attend a meeting in September 2003, hosted by president Edward J. Law of County College of Morris and led by Jack Noonan, president emeritus of Bloomfield College. As a result of the meeting, the presidents agreed that they should intervene strategically to ensure that diversity was understood and appreciated as a core educational and civic value. In the course of their conversation, they addressed a number of challenges common to their institutions. They also expressed concern about the continued prevalence of hate crimes and bigotry, the uncertain future of diversity work in the wake of the U.S. Supreme Court's closely divided decision in the 2003 University of Michigan Law School case that upheld the right of universities to consider race in admissions procedures in order to achieve a diverse student body. The presidents agreed to meet again the following spring to explore ways to be more public in their advocacy of the lessons learned from diversity work on their campuses.

Most team leaders considered their presidents' participation in the meeting a positive event. They were so enthusiastic that they urged a second meeting in which chief academic officers and chief student affairs officers would meet at the same time. President Shirley Tilghman hosted the second meeting on the Princeton University campus. The chief academic officers and chief student affairs officers met jointly the same day.

At their second meeting, the presidents discussed approaches to delivering a public report on the work of the NJCDI. They agreed that colleges and universities throughout the state should be informed of the initiative's accomplishments.

The meeting of the chief academic and student affairs officers was designed to highlight the value of more intentional collaboration between professionals in student affairs and academic affairs. Individual attendees described notable successes in working collaboratively to plan curricular and co-curricular events that were mutually reinforcing. They also affirmed the importance of dismantling the barriers to collaboration.

These meetings of presidents and senior officers called additional attention to the importance of diversity—as educational strategy—to institutional life. They gave a boost to the morale of the teams on each campus and validated their efforts to relate the work of diversity to institutional mission.

On several campuses, presidents have found additional funding to support their projects into the future. Two institutions sent teams to AAC&U's "Greater Expectations" institute in June 2005 to plan activities that would "build on Bildner." Rowan University has awarded honorary degrees to Allen and Joan Bildner. These activities give both substantive and symbolic support to the work of the NJCDI.

Flexibility

One of the most generous characteristics of "the triangle" has been its consistent openness to change. Over the first two years of the initiative, institutions were urged to look critically at their initial designs and to signal a need for change as soon as they discovered it.

SUPPORTING MIDCOURSE CORRECTIONS. A number of institutions took full advantage of this flexibility to make important, midcourse corrections. For example:

o During the second year, Bergen rethought the structure, focus, and governance of the Center for the Study of Intercultural Communication, expanded its programming, strengthened its ties to the community, and obtained additional support from the president and the board of trustees.

o Stockton's initial plan was to infuse diversity materials and issues into existing courses. Disappointed with the results of the first year, the project team replaced the infusion method with a dedicated diversity course that would be taught in seven sections, all meeting at the same time. It worked well in the fall of 2003, even better in the fall of 2004, and was taught for the third time in the fall of 2005. Moreover, the diversity course has provided a model of course management that has been emulated by other courses. Stockton was able to respond so quickly because it had developed assessment instruments that allowed it to determine how effective each iteration of the course had been.

o The University of Medicine and Dentistry of New Jersey (UMDNJ)'s progress was slowed substantially in the first year by a personnel change because of miscommunication with the agency that oversees research involving human subjects. AAC&U worked with UMDNJ to resolve the communication problem and get the project back on track.

SUPPORTING SUCCESS; DEALING WITH SETBACKS. As the NJCDI headed into the third and final year in 2004, most of the projects felt flush with success. The teams anticipated that if they used their third-year funding prudently, they would have money left over. Could they use it in a fourth year? Could we advise them on strategies for finding other sources of funds?

But not every project was in that condition. One was at a delicate turning point. If institutional decisions fell a certain way, the project's goals would be secured and supported going forward. If not, the project would most likely be stuck, unable to use its good work for the benefit of the institution.

As Musil, Teraguchi, and I planned the all-project meeting held in April 2004, we decided to meet the needs of the majority at the meeting and deal with special problems on a case-by-case basis. Taking this course has meant more site visits, more written submissions, and more telephone conversations. But within the triangle, we think it is paying off. For example, the institution at a crossroads has traversed the turning point and now seems to be headed in a more productive direction.

The foundation declined to fund one of the eight institutions for a second year, but it allowed the institution to keep the unexpended funds from the first year and to use them for project objectives in the second. When Allen Bildner read the second-year report, he was so impressed with the institution's apparent recovery that he asked TPI and AAC&U to take a closer look at the progress and consider a recommendation for additional funding. TPI and AAC&U worked together to plan a site visit and set criteria for an additional proposal. That proposal was approved by the triangle, and the institution has received additional funds to continue its work.

Regrettably, in another case we were not able to find such a happy solution. After two years, the Bildners, TPI, and AAC&U lost confidence in the capacity of one institution to meet the objectives of the original proposal. Together, we worked diligently to try to satisfy ourselves that a third year of funding would promote the original objectives of the grant. When we were unable to do so, we reluctantly decided to terminate the grant.

Thinking Early About What Happens After the Program Ends

Since 2004, the main focus of managing the initiative has been on such practical goals as

○ Benchmarking and celebrating progress

○ Strengthening capacities to meet campus goals

○ Increasing the capacity to assess the impact of diversity work

○ Collaborating across institutions and learning to learn from and help each other

○ Focusing on longer-range sustainability of diversity work

Giving the Grantees Tools for Continuing the Work

As early as the second summer institute, AAC&U developed plenary sessions and workshops focused on identifying the products of the initiative and describing them in ways that appeal to others. AAC&U also described assessment strategies that can help produce the evidence that the work is valuable.

The all-project meeting in November 2004 was even more focused on the future. It was about sustaining institutional change, using stories to promote change, using stories as an assessment tool, and going public with best practices. In addition, AAC&U explained how to create consulting teams that could help transfer knowledge about diversity work to other institutions outside the program. There is enthusiasm for the idea, and several teams have been formed.

The final meeting of the NJCDI was held in April 2005. It was devoted to developing strategies for communicating the substance and value of diversity work to a variety of constituencies, including those internal to the institution (students, faculty, administrators, and staff), as well as external constituencies that have a vested interest in the institution. The local community, the parents of students, alumni and friends of the institution, potential donors, and those who influence pertinent public policy were among the audiences identified. At the end of the meeting, the teams identified the next steps in developing a comprehensive communications strategy for advancing their work.

Moving into the Mainstream

From the outset, the triangle has encouraged institutions to think strategically, which entails projecting their work into a future that may not look like their project. The results are encouraging. Most of the projects include structures that generate change: new courses, modifications of existing courses, pedagogical strategies, collaborations. In a number of cases, the structures will be continued after the grants have expired. And even where they are not, they will have spawned new and durable ways of thinking about diversity's role in education.

The faculty-staff seminars at Bloomfield College are a case in point. Over five semesters, these seminars have produced a cadre of faculty and staff who are enthusiastic about putting diversity to work for educational purposes. They have already created a minor in Latino/Latin American/Caribbean studies, a concentration in international business, a "learning community" in which students will be asked to use the richness of their own backgrounds as subject matter, as well as an honors seminar on culture, community, and identity. The faculty and staff have also revised courses at the pre-freshman level in general education, as well as in major programs, including history, the arts, the social and behavioral sciences, business, English and communications, religion, mathematics, science, and nursing. They have added and expanded library programs, and the staffs of academic affairs and student affairs have collaborated on a variety of programs, including one designed to help students apply diversity knowledge to the workplace.

Stockton offers another interesting example. In the third year of its project, the team was approached by a professor of psychology who proposed to organize his course using the project's course as a model. Similarly, a professor of education at Rutgers University-New Brunswick has proposed to use the project model as a platform for revitalizing the entire education curriculum. She has already enlisted additional faculty, who have received grants to modify additional courses.

At Rutgers-Newark, the Intercultural Fellows supported by the NJCDI are viewed by the dean and the provost as representing the core values of Newark as an urban research university. At UMDNJ, the new president views the work on cultural competency as integral to his strategic vision for the institution. At Rowan, faculty members who have participated in the workshops count them among the most rewarding intellectual experiences of their careers at Rowan. During my site visits, several spoke of the way their experiences in Rowan seminars are influencing their teaching in other courses. At CCM, the thirty-seven proposals for course revision that were approved and implemented will be published and widely distributed, including to the board of trustees.

Achieving Alignment: The Key Expectation and an Environment for the Idea

That the projects have "taken" in this way is due, in large part, to the triangle's insistence that the campus project be linked directly to institutional mission. Also, the idea is ripe: the institutions are not trying to foster change in a social vacuum but rather in a historical and cultural context that favors them. Rutgers-Newark was committed to its image as an urban research university before the NJCDI was conceived. The professors in the education department at Rutgers-New Brunswick can think grandly about revamping the whole curriculum because education departments across the country are under increasing pressure from accrediting agencies to do so. UMDNJ's advocacy of cultural competency in the delivery of health care places it on the crest of a national wave of concern about the economic and moral cost of health care disparities that correlate with race, class, and gender. Both Bergen and CCM are increasingly aware of their role in helping their communities utilize diversity productively.

And let us not forget that in New Jersey, already one of the nation's most diverse states, diversity is growing—in complexity, as well as in numbers.

In other words, as Allen Bildner discovered long ago in his business, social reality is motivating us to put the power of diversity to work in behalf of our social well-being. As the NJCDI is illustrating, one way is through education that uses diversity as subject matter and as pedagogical strategy to produce graduates who are prepared to discern the world, engage it, and make it better.

New Jersey Diversity Initiative: Campus Projects

o *Bergen Community College* established a Center for the Study of Intercultural Understanding to build on and connect diversity initiatives dispersed across the campus; offer diversity-related educational and training opportunities to faculty, staff, and students; and begin to strengthen campus-community partnerships that would deepen intercultural knowledge and skills.

o *Bloomfield College* developed a series of five semester-long seminars, each involving eight faculty and staff. The seminars focused on issues of teaching, learning, and research; personal and cultural identities; cross-cultural communication; and globalization. Throughout the seminars, participants examined ways to incorporate new content, insights, perspectives, and skills into their courses and programs. Bloomfield also expanded its Center for Cultures and Communication, which already offered a Diversity Training Certificate.

o *County College of Morris* (CCM) used the first two years of the grant to assess the curriculum. It then developed an action strategy for curricular renewal that has thus far infused diversity content into thirty-seven courses, ranging from children's literature to precalculus. Its objective is to integrate diversity and global awareness education into every degree program offered. CCM also sought to increase community outreach efforts that promote diversity as a community asset.

o *Princeton University* used a major portion of its grant to support dialogue initiatives, including Sustained Dialogue—a program that had begun at Princeton several years earlier. Sustained Dialogue used group discussion techniques to focus attention on controversial topics that contribute to social division. Princeton matched a smaller proportion of the grant to provide financial incentives for diverse student groups to collaborate in sponsoring programs devoted to intergroup issues.

o *The Richard Stockton College of New Jersey* provided a coordinated set of new courses and co-curricular activities designed to increase students' intercultural awareness and expose them to cross-cultural settings in the community, either through service-learning or an alternative experiential component. Stockton has employed an elaborate set of evaluation tools to assess the effectiveness of the process and document the outcomes.

○ *Rowan University* used a series of faculty development workshops to create twenty-four interdisciplinary team-taught courses, called Rowan Seminars, for first-year students. The courses focus on diversity and democracy.

○ *Rutgers*, the State University of New Jersey, has supported course development and co-curricular collaboration on three campuses: Camden, New Brunswick, and Newark. The intention is to make intercultural interaction central to campus life, both in and outside the classroom.

○ *The University of Medicine and Dentistry of New Jersey* focused on cultural competency in delivering health care. It first conducted an intensive assessment of the need for cultural competency and then sought to translate the need into instructional interventions for students, faculty, and staff.

Chapter Twelve Overview

Pat Hutchings has devoted her professional life to promoting better teaching and learning in higher education. First as a professor of English at Alverno College, then as a senior staff member at the American Association for Higher Education (AAHE), and now as vice president at The Carnegie Foundation for the Advancement of Teaching, she has been a national leader in the movement to strengthen undergraduate education.

During Hutchings's years at AAHE she helped design a project to test how well the idea of peer review of teaching might work as a way to improve the quality of teaching at research universities, and, in a second phase, at liberal arts colleges. This case study examines that project and draws some intriguing lessons from its story. Two foundations—The William and Flora Hewlett Foundation and The Pew Charitable Trusts—gave financial support for the project, and AAHE served a key coordinating role. At the time, Ray Bacchetti, coeditor of this volume, was education program officer at the Hewlett Foundation, and Bob Schwartz, coauthor of Chapter Five, was education program officer at Pew.

Hutchings's chapter offers some wisdom in thinking about how to have an impact on undergraduate teaching and learning. The peer review project was designed to provide operational examples of peer review as a strategy for documenting, critiquing, and improving teaching.

This chapter is also a wonderfully rich illustration of the power of a collaborative project that builds educational capital. The case study suggests how both foundations and institutions of higher education can benefit from the effective work of an intermediary organization. AAHE played the key role throughout the project; the project could not have happened, let alone succeeded, without the continued involvement of that organization.

12

FROM IDEA TO PROTOTYPE

THE PEER REVIEW OF TEACHING

Pat Hutchings

IT IS JUNE OF 1994, and seventy-five faculty members from twelve research universities across the country have converged on the Stanford
campus. With chemists from Michigan, historians from Syracuse, mathematicians from Nebraska, nurses from Kent State, engineers from Wisconsin, and faculty in English from Stanford (to name just a few of the
institutions and disciplines represented), it is a diverse and prestigious
group. Amazingly, the task that has brought these stars together is the
design of new strategies for the peer review of teaching—not a topic, it
seems fair to say, likely to warm the professorial heart; the classroom has
typically been seen as a private space, and many faculty are nervous about
opening the classroom door to colleagues.

Indeed, there is more than a hint of nervousness in the air at Stanford.
But there is energy, too. Participants are eager to talk about the preparation they have done for the meeting: reflective writing with colleagues
about their teaching and their students' learning. Over the next week, in
spite of sweltering nights in un-air-conditioned dorms and disgruntlement
about how little free time appears on the schedule, they meet in discipline-
based teams to talk about the teaching of their fields, the "pedagogical
thinking" behind the design of their courses, and their evidence of impact
on student learning. Over the next four years, they work together to create an array of strategies for documenting, critiquing, and building on

their work as teachers, whether in the hiring process, for purposes of ongoing improvement, as part of curriculum development and assessment, for promotion and tenure, or for post-tenure review, thus moving peer review, as the project's title declares, "from idea to prototype."

This case study, written as part of the Carnegie Foundation's centennial study of the relationship between education and foundations, explores the effort launched by that Stanford meeting: a four-year project (in two two-year phases, from 1994–96 and 1996–98) cofunded by The Pew Charitable Trusts and The William and Flora Hewlett Foundation, and coordinated by the AAHE. Titled "From Idea to Prototype: The Peer Review of Teaching," the project involved twelve research universities[1] (and several liberal arts colleges in the second phase), with two-person faculty teams from three departments on each of those campuses, and participation by disciplinary and professional societies with which those faculty were affiliated. The total budget for both phases of the project came to just over $1 million. As senior staff person at AAHE, I was the project director.

My aim in what follows is to explore what the project is a case *of* and what it can tell us about the relationship between foundations and educational institutions. But one insight bears mentioning at the start: it turns out that the dynamics of education grantmaking and project shaping are, like teaching itself, all too likely to "disappear like dry ice" (Shulman, 1993, p. 7). Since the project began, I have moved several times and my records are not, shall we say, what they might be; files at AAHE are deep in an archive I chose not to excavate. Both Hewlett and the Trusts have purged many of the files from that period of grantmaking, though they generously retrieved and shared what they had retained.[2]

Much of the relevant history, however, was *never contained in any file.* It is interpersonal, serendipitous, fugitive. To help fill in the picture, then, and to refresh my memory, I have interviewed the project's codirector, Russ Edgerton, who was at that time the president of AAHE, as well as our wonderful partner in the effort, Stanford University professor of educational psychology (and now president of the Carnegie Foundation), Lee S. Shulman. I have also interviewed the two program officers who worked closely with us on the project—Ray Bacchetti from Hewlett, and Ellen Wert from the Trusts. I had already interviewed many of the project participants during the four years of the project (see Hutchings, 1996). What follows, then, is not *the* story of From Idea to Prototype but an amalgam of stories, woven together to raise more general issues and recommendations.

The Intellectual Backdrop

The early 1990s were marked by rising attention to the work of faculty. At issue was not so much how hard they worked as it was choices about what work was most worth doing (Edgerton, 1993). From outside academe, there were growing calls for greater attention to the teaching of undergraduates, which was seen as neglected in the face of research interests and ambitions. But within academe, too, surveys indicated that faculty valued their work as teachers and wanted to see greater balance between teaching and research; 62 percent believed that teaching should be the primary basis for their evaluation (Carnegie Foundation, 1989; Gray, Froh, and Diamond, 1991). Questions about faculty roles, about the value of the various kinds of work faculty do, and especially about the priority of teaching were prominently and increasingly on the national landscape.

A key feature of that landscape was the 1990 report from the Carnegie Foundation, *Scholarship Reconsidered*. In it, Ernest Boyer argues for an enlarged vision of scholarship, encompassing not only basic research but other faculty work as well, including teaching. Boyer's report prompted hundreds of campuses to reexamine faculty roles and rewards; in a 1994 survey, 80 percent of provosts reported that their institutions either had recently reexamined their systems of faculty roles and rewards or planned to do so (Glassick, Huber, and Maeroff, 1997, p. 12), and many scholarly societies assembled special commissions and panels to do the same. Thanks in part to AAHE, which served as a clearinghouse for such documents, and also to Syracuse University's Bob Diamond, who collected disciplinary statements (Diamond and Adams, 1995), these documents circulated in the higher education community, and new ideas about how to elevate and improve the scholarly work of teaching spread quickly from site to site. Thus when the 1991 report of the University of California System Task Force on Faculty Rewards recommended that "peer evaluation of teaching be given the same emphasis now given to the peer evaluation of research," it was no surprise to see similar declarations in documents at Northwestern, the University of Wisconsin-Madison, and the North Carolina University System (where the peer review of teaching was mandated for all institutions).

The peer review of teaching was not, it should be said, a new idea. Neither was it a widespread practice; nor was it one that had been particularly useful or welcome in many settings. Typically undertaken as a kind of "parachute drop" in which a senior colleague or administrator landed in one's classroom, checklist in hand, peer review was more likely to raise hackles than to improve instruction. But the growing sense that higher education needed to pay more attention to the quality of teaching and learning brought new importance to the topic. It is worth quoting from AAHE's proposal:

> This is not to say that there isn't lots of good teaching on campuses today, or that faculty do not care about the effectiveness of their work with students. It *is* to say that as long as teaching remains a private enterprise, one in which there's little possibility for serious collegial interaction, improvement tends to be *ad hoc*, mostly a matter of individual inclination rather than larger shared purpose and resolve, unlikely to last, and often inadequate to the job of educating today's increasingly diverse and often underprepared students. (American Association for Higher Education, 1993, p. 4)

In this context, peer review could be seen as a way to signal a greater seriousness about the quality of teaching and learning. Doing so was a felt need on campus, as indicated by the growing number of reports and recommendations—and many faculty were attracted to the idea that teaching could be treated as scholarly, intellectual work. Moreover, AAHE's Teaching Initiative had involved a number of faculty and campuses that were designing appealing new ways to document and share what happened in the classroom. The challenge was to give visibility to these new approaches, to invent and test out additional "prototypes," and to get campuses to tackle what Bacchetti (borrowing a term from the corporate arena) later dubbed "a Big Hairy Audacious Goal" (Collins and Porras, 1997). The time and the issue were right for a wider, multicampus effort where peer institutions could go down this challenging road together. Or so AAHE was ready to argue.

Converging Perspectives

When asked about the genesis of the project, Edgerton begins by recalling a meeting during a higher education conference early in 1993, where he "first pitched the idea" to Bacchetti, the then-new education program director at the Hewlett Foundation, whom Edgerton knew through previous connections at Stanford. "I knew he was new," Edgerton says, "and might be looking for ideas" (all quotes from the Edgerton interview, Nov. 4, 2004).

That pitch no doubt filled in some of the national scene as noted earlier, but Edgerton also had a story to tell about AAHE's track record in advancing the agendas of teaching as scholarly work. An individual membership association of 8,200 members (this in 1993; the number approached 10,000 by the end of the project), the association had a reputation for taking up tough issues and framing them in ways that were intellectually engaging. A lively annual conference and a growing publications program provided forums for thoughtful exchange and the spread of new ideas. The association had always been dedicated to good teaching, and it was a clear leader in embracing the assessment movement, not as a form of bureaucratic reporting but as a route to improved teaching and learning.

Building on this work, in 1989 a new program was created; the AAHE Teaching Initiative entailed a variety of special projects and events aimed at helping campuses create a culture in which teaching was talked about, inquired into, reflected upon, and continuously improved. A first effort, with funding from the Lilly Endowment, entailed the development of case studies to prompt substantive discussion and exchange among faculty about the teaching of key disciplinary concepts. A second explored and promoted the idea of teaching portfolios as a tool for documenting and evaluating the scholarly work of teaching (Edgerton, Hutchings, and Quinlan, 1991). Much of the thinking behind the Teaching Initiative has its genesis in the work of Shulman, who argued (as he put it in an AAHE conference presentation) that "we need to change the status of teaching from private to community property" and make "the review, examination, and support of teaching part of the responsibility of the disciplinary community" (1993, pp. 6, 7). In short, for anyone following the issues and agendas of the Teaching Initiative, it was clear that peer review was "a natural," just waiting in the wings to make a more major appearance.

Meanwhile, AAHE was preparing to launch what it called the Forum on Faculty Roles and Rewards (FFRR). Supported by the Fund for the Improvement of Postsecondary Education, FFRR took up the challenge of the Boyer Report, working with campuses and other groups to reexamine the work of faculty and how it is evaluated and rewarded. As the hub for such work, AAHE ran a special annual conference, issued publications, nurtured networks, and ran projects around more specific issues under the larger roles-and-rewards umbrella—for instance, about career pathways and about post-tenure review.

In short, by the time Edgerton met with Bacchetti in 1993, he had a powerful story to tell about the place of peer review in the emerging movement to bring greater prominence to teaching—and, most important, about AAHE's ability to take the lead in that work. Peer review was not seen as an add-on or a bureaucratic form of quality control; it was part of an emerging vision of teaching as intellectual work and of faculty as agents of its ongoing improvement; as such, peer review promised to be an important engine for fostering more significant, lasting forms of student learning. And with preliminary commitments from a number of highly visible campuses already in place, the project was ready to shift into gear—if Hewlett would warm to the idea.

Formerly a vice president at Stanford, Bacchetti had joined the Hewlett staff in February 1993. His account of that transition is an important part of this story (all quotes from Bacchetti interview, Nov. 4, 2004). "I was coming at it from a wholly different perspective," he recalls. New to the business of education grantmaking, Bacchetti did not bring to the project the larger backdrop painted by Edgerton during their initial conversation. His concern was much more immediate, "because as a new program officer one of my tasks was to establish my credentials . . . and to put my stamp on the program." As Edgerton surmised, Bacchetti saw in the peer review project a possible way to do that.

But there were obstacles. For one thing, the project did not neatly fit any of the existing program categories and guidelines (which Bacchetti would rewrite the following year). "So part of the question was how I was going to judge this grant and then use it to help establish myself as someone who could bring important and useful work to the foundation." The internal review process was arduous. Staff from the six or seven program areas, along with the foundation's president, would meet and comment on proposals put forward in each area. "They were polite but they were tough," Bacchetti recalls.

Happily, both Bacchetti and the peer review project survived this rite of passage. The "range and prestige of the institutions that had already signed on" was a selling point. Also important, "the project had a story I could tell my colleagues." In short, Hewlett was potentially on board, but full funding for the effort would require a second partner.

With this in mind, Edgerton turned to Bob Schwartz, director of the Education Program at The Pew Charitable Trusts, which had recently funded a major initiative at AAHE on K–16 transitions. The Trusts' priorities at that time included several items specific to higher education, including a focus on "strengthening the priority given to teaching in the promotion and tenure process" (The Pew Charitable Trusts, 1993, p. 14). As it turned out, the timing was right in several ways for the kind of project AAHE was proposing.

As explained by Wert, Schwartz's colleague and the staff person assigned to see this proposal through the internal review process, the Trusts was "moving toward a new way of doing business" (all quotes from Wert interview, 2004). In 1990, the Trusts' grantmaking in education (indeed, all areas of the foundation's funding) had been reorganized to focus on strategies for addressing issues, rather than on response to institutional requests. What changed, Wert recalls, was not only the colleges and universities being funded (for the first time public institutions were eligible for funding through the Trusts' Education program) but the more basic rules of the game. "The grants, which had once supported the priorities of a small group of private colleges and universities, now helped institutions act on new ideas to improve higher education." It was in this new spirit that the Trusts funded the Preparing Future Faculty project, in which clusters of institutions collaborated under the leadership of two higher education associations to prepare graduate students for the range of institutional types in which they might eventually pursue their careers, and a multiple-campus initiative to strengthen the first two years of the undergraduate experience, coordinated by Karen Romer at Brown University. (I was the evaluator on that project, so I had worked closely with Wert.)

Increasingly, the Trusts, which, like Hewlett, had the leanest possible staff, was working through "constituent organizations"; they had created several of these over the years, including the National Policy Center on the First Year of College, and the Pew Forum on Undergraduate Learning. The peer review project thus fell into place, with its focus on ideas and its multicampus design and coordination through AAHE. "The project was typical of the Trusts' new way of supporting change," Wert observes.

By December 1993, the project was a "go," with funding from Hewlett and the Trusts in hand and twelve campuses on board. Though exact dates are impossible to pinpoint a decade later, it is safe to say that this process— from a gleam in AAHE's eye, to first conversations with Hewlett and the Trusts, through multiple drafts of the proposal, ongoing visits to and negotiations with campuses, and final arrangements for project management— took over a year. Such convergences do not happen without persistence and commitment by everyone involved.

From Idea to Prototype

As indicated by its title, the project began in an idea—a vision of peer review that dictated the activities of the participants. As AAHE's proposal argued . . .

> A broader cast needs to be put around the peer review of teaching. (Indeed the term itself may throw up obstacles to the kind of activity we most want to promote, and we may need to invent other, more useful

language in the course of the project.) What's at issue is not thumbs-up, thumbs-down decisions, or any single mechanism for gathering evidence, but varied occasions and processes whereby teaching becomes public and available for collegial observation, study, debate, and improvement. (American Association for Higher Education, 1993, p. 9)

Our central strategy was to develop a menu of strategies, shaped and adapted to different purposes, disciplines, and institutional contexts. In the formative period of the project, our most important task was to articulate this idea and get others to rally around it.

This process began as we worked to identify and bring on board a right set of campuses. Clearly, we wanted institutions whose prestige and distinction would engender aspiration: Michigan (say) was much more likely to come on board if Stanford were in the mix (and vice versa), and where Stanford and Michigan led, others would want to follow. Such places also had the advantage of being "hard cases" that would allow the project to serve as an existence proof: if the country's most vaunted research institutions could tackle the peer review of teaching, it could work elsewhere as well.

But high prestige is a double-edged sword. Precisely because so much institutional and individual energy went into research, the peer review of teaching was likely to be a hard road in the most research-intensive cultures. For the project to succeed, it would need campuses where teaching was more clearly central, and, frankly, where signals from provosts were more readily heeded. Thus we approached several institutions that had made a name for themselves as places committed to new thinking about teaching and learning. These places (Indiana University-Purdue University Indianapolis, the University of North Carolina at Charlotte, and Kent State University) were, in fact, a good match with Schwartz's interests. While the involvement of top-tier research universities was clearly a selling point for the project (one of the features that caught Bacchetti's eye), Schwartz saw the regional public institutions as crucial players—indeed leaders—in educational reform, and they would be very important in the peer review project.

More concretely—or beyond our general sense that we needed a mix of institutions in terms of profile and mission—the process of inviting and securing commitments from *particular* institutions meant studying campus documents (recent reports about faculty roles and rewards, for instance), negotiating with provosts (around the question, for instance, of department selection), and visiting campuses (where we would be able to take the temperature of faculty). Our aim was to find places where there was already momentum for the agenda we were pushing.

The process of identifying campuses went on throughout the fall of 1993, both before and after funding was secured. Then in January 1994, at AAHE's FFRR conference, we brought together the provosts and their designated project coordinators. This was an important occasion for clarifying expectations, raising aspirations, and confirming campus commitments to support a project coordinator, to host an initial campus event to put the project on the map and then a later one to showcase and discuss what the project accomplished, to cover the costs of travel, and to put in place appropriate incentives and rewards for faculty participation. As it turned out, there was a useful kind of peer pressure on this last point, as provosts quizzed one another about the levels of support they were providing to departments.

Involvement by the provosts was key, we knew, and they came together a number of times during the project, often as part of their campus team. But as the provosts themselves made clear, their ability to direct the interests of faculty was low. The project would rise or fall, depending on our ability to capture the intellectual interests of the faculty themselves. This was the heart and soul of the project, central to our conception of peer review, and it shaped activities in three key ways.

First, in everything we did we underlined that teaching was intellectual work, not just technique. This principle had several sources, but first among them was Shulman's work. Rather than try to persuade faculty to adopt particular pedagogical practices (to promote, say, collaborative learning or service learning), we declared ourselves agnostic about methods and instead invited faculty to bring the same spirit of inquiry that they brought to their other scholarly work to *whatever* classroom approaches they used. Thus, for example, in advance of the first meeting at Stanford, faculty were asked to prepare a reflective memo examining one of their courses as a reflection of their conception of their discipline or field:

> Every course we craft is a lens into our fields and our personal conceptions of those disciplines or interdisciplines. Give careful thought to the shape and content of your course as if it were a scholarly argument. What is the thesis of the argument, and its main points? What are the key bodies of evidence? How does the course begin? How does it end? Why does it end as it does? Most scholarly arguments carry the intention to persuade. What do you want to persuade your students to believe? Or question? Or do you want them to develop new appetites or dispositions? (Shulman, 1995, 2004, pp. 176–177)

Many participants found this (and the two follow-on "exercises" done in preparation for the inaugural faculty gathering at Stanford) a deeply intriguing set of questions—an exercise that established the project as an intellectual and scholarly endeavor.

Second, we aimed to engage faculty by focusing on the importance of the disciplines. The focus was not, that is, teaching in general but the teaching (and learning) of chemistry or nursing or English. Small grants were available for faculty to work with their scholarly societies, and representatives from those groups were present at many of the project gatherings over the four years of work.

Such gatherings were the third strategy for keeping faculty engaged. Meetings like the one at Stanford provided opportunities to meet and work with respected peers, both within and beyond one's own discipline, and to find new colleagues. Coming together as a full group twice a year helped to build real intellectual community and engagement that was, much more than any financial support, the key to motivation in the project.

What exactly did participants *do* during the four years of the project? In brief: each department team left the Stanford gathering with a detailed written plan for peer review in its own setting. Those plans were then implemented (and of course revised) during the next several years, and results were shared with the larger campus community and in disciplinary and professional communities. Meanwhile, at "project central," the task was to articulate the central ideas and vision of the project, organize meetings, broker communication across sites, solve problems, share successes, and inspire.

At the end of the two years, we had made good progress on some fronts, but the need to continue was evident. The result was a second proposal to Hewlett and the Trusts, with a focus on expanding the number of departments and disciplines (which campuses were keen to do), ratcheting up work with the scholarly societies, and focusing on sustaining campus change. We also added several additional campuses, most of them liberal arts colleges, in order to try out our ideas in a wider variety of institutional settings. Throughout, in both phases, the participation of the Trusts and Hewlett was vital not only in providing financial support but in giving the work legitimacy and creating a kind of "demilitarized zone," where it was possible for faculty to explore what was, after all, a contentious topic looked upon by some colleagues with deep skepticism.

Outcomes and Upshots

In the ongoing conduct of the project, both foundations were deeply respectful of the need to modify plans in light of evolving needs and opportunities that emerged. This flexibility was important because AAHE's style was, in some sense, to let ideas take their natural course, to see what worked, what would catch on. Thus the project was begun with a broad vision of success—a determination to invent, adapt, test out, and showcase useful, do-able strategies through which faculty could document their own teaching and their students' learning and put that work forward for review. The central focus, that is, was on the development of prototypes.

Of course, we were also eager to see campuses begin to use these prototypes, and our funders were a significant force in shaping clearer goals and expectations for our partner campuses. In feedback on the original proposal, Bacchetti was already pushing us to think more carefully about "the end game." What exactly will you have at the end of the project? he wanted to know. What were the campuses, and the provosts in particular, promising to *do*? How would the campuses be different, and what could we do to ensure that they would stay that way? The Trusts, for its part, urged us to do (and to have it fund) more formal evaluation of the project and its impact—on faculty practice as teachers, on departments, and on campus policy. Toward this end, we conducted a survey of participants toward the end of the first two years; in the second phase, we contracted with Jim Wilkinson, director of Harvard's Bok Center for Teaching and Learning, to conduct a review of the work in the spirit of a "critical friend." This sharp focus on outcomes from both foundations arguably pushed the project toward more concrete goals and toward better evidence (positive and negative) of their accomplishment. Several outcomes are important to highlight here.

First, the project helped put the idea of the peer review of teaching more prominently on higher education's radar screen. Increasingly over the years of the project, and beyond it as well, AAHE heard from campuses seeking assistance in starting their own programs of peer review. Project publications sold briskly and were reprinted a number of times over the years. Copies of a brochure capturing key lessons about the peer review of teaching were requested in bulk by scores of campuses. Project participants were much in demand on conference programs and for visits to other campuses seeking consultants. In short, From Idea to Prototype created a market for an idea that was previously very much on the margins.

Second, the project developed prototypes—a "menu of strategies" as the culminating AAHE publication put it—for nine different ways in which faculty could learn about and be helpful with one another's teaching, including teaching circles, mentoring, reviewing students' work collaboratively, holding a "pedagogical colloquium" as part of the hiring process, and developing and reviewing course portfolios. The AAHE volume in which these strategies were described—*Making Teaching Community*

Property—provided brief reports from project participants (and a few from outside the project) about how the strategy was used in their particular institutional and disciplinary setting, and to what effect (Hutchings, 1996; Hutchings, 1998b; Bernstein, 2001). Moreover, we learned that the use of these strategies (and no doubt the more general experience of talking and working with a larger community of colleagues dedicated to peer collaboration and review) changed what went on in classrooms. More than half of the participants reported that the project "changed my behavior in the classroom with students" (American Association for Higher Education, 1995, p. 7).

Third, the project developed an energetic group of idea champions—individuals who "got it" and became powerful spokespersons for the peer review of teaching and, perhaps more important in the long run, the larger vision of teaching as scholarly work. The development of such champions is, in part, something that happens because of chemistry that no one can completely engineer, but leadership development was also an explicit goal of the project and one of its most consequential outcomes, vital to the project's impact. For starters, the project served as a development experience for a graduate student working with Shulman; Kathleen Quinlan focused her dissertation on the work of the project (1996) and has since gone on to work in settings in which the agendas of the project have been further advanced. Furthermore, over half of the project's faculty participants reported that the work "allowed me to take a leadership role" (American Association for Higher Education, 1995, p. 7). Many became active in efforts to elevate the status of teaching as scholarly work in their scholarly and professional associations; many also became leaders (some eventually in administrative positions) in promoting peer review on their campuses.

That said, the impact of the project on campuses was, to put it gently, variable. In the survey done midway through the project, most participants reported that support from the provost was "about right," and where that was true it was possible to see significant changes, or beginnings of change, in institutional policy (at Nebraska-Lincoln, for instance, peer review of teaching became a requirement). But even where such changes occurred, the impact did not always make its way down to the department. Participants were asked to rate "the project's impact on/benefit to your department thus far" on a scale of 1 ("a nuisance") to 5 ("culture changing"), and almost half responded at a level 2. Clearly, department impact lagged far behind individual engagement. By the end of the project, more progress had occurred, but it was still uneven and still disappointing to many faculty who had dedicated significant time and energy to the project and were deeply invested in its agendas.

On the other hand, the project spawned a number of major follow-on projects: an initiative on the peer review of course portfolios directed by Daniel Bernstein, one of the participants from the University of Nebraska-Lincoln (an initiative that continues today with campus funding); a project on problem-based learning at Samford University that was very much informed by our work on course portfolios; and the Visible Knowledge Project at Georgetown, which, though it has its own history and provenance, is at least second cousin to the peer review project. Thus an important product of the AAHE project was a next set of projects, and this was not, as Wert emphasizes, simply a happy accident. "We were actively looking for next project ideas," she recalls, and she attended many of the project meetings with an eye to spotting new prospects and leaders like Bernstein. Indeed, at the conclusion of the peer review project, Wert, Edgerton (who was about to assume Schwartz's position at the Trusts), Shulman (who had recently moved to the presidency of the Carnegie Foundation), and I met to plan the "daughter of peer review," which was launched the next year as the Carnegie Academy for the Scholarship of Teaching and Learning. But that, as they say, is another story (Hutchings, 1998a; see also Huber and Hutchings, 2005).

Lessons and Recommendations

The interviews done as background for this case study were unanimous in pointing to a lesson about the value of collaboration as a condition for change and knowledge building. As Bacchetti argues in Chapter Ten of this volume, institutions of higher education are naturally inward-focused and even self-absorbed. If left to their own devices, it is unlikely that even the most forward looking among them would—or could—have taken on the prickly agenda of peer review in isolation from peer institutions; if they had, the results would likely have been slimmer, the range of strategies less varied and robust. Without the opportunity to compare notes, to calibrate ambitions, to learn from work in other settings, peer review is precisely the kind of agenda that was likely to stall. In this sense, From Idea to Prototype points to the need for foundations to take up bold ideas and to set in motion the kind of larger, collaborative, multicampus activity that is needed to make progress on such issues. As we learned from the midproject survey, the single most important condition in allowing the campuses to continue their work was the presence of one another working under a national project umbrella. Hard work needs good company.

The case draws attention to the valuable role that intermediaries—"constituent associations" (as Wert calls them)—can play in educational change. Both Hewlett and the Trusts had (and still have) the leanest of staffs; both program officers were at one point or another monitoring more than fifty projects (see, for example, William and Flora Hewlett Foundation, 1993), and there must have been days when even *remembering* all of them would have been daunting. Organizations like AAHE—(higher education associations, that is) and groups like the scholarly and professional societies—thus take on a particular importance as coordinators, connectors, and catalysts: moving campuses toward work that has wider usefulness, overcoming the dynamics of localism and inward-lookingness, spreading the word and giving credibility—situating the work (as Edgerton did in his first conversation with Bacchetti) in the larger sweep of emergent ideas in higher education. With links to a larger membership or constituency, as well as access to publication vehicles and conferences, these organizations can sometimes leverage small-scale efforts and turn them into larger movements. In this spirit, an argument might well be made for funders to provide such groups with organizational-development support, not only grants to run particular projects but resources to strengthen their general capacity and reach. Indeed, some observers argue that this strategy has been used by conservative foundations to fund a "distinct set of think tanks and linking organizations," that have had significant influence on policymaking (Covington, 1997; Shuman, 1998).

The case may also tell us something about collaboration *between* foundations. Both Bacchetti and Wert report that their organizations saw partnership with another foundation as a kind of ratification of their own choices. That said, they were careful not to tread on each other's territory; with a few exceptions, communication went through AAHE. That was as it should be, I suspect, keeping AAHE in the driver's seat. But what is clear from the Trusts-Hewlett partnership is that quite modest forms of collaboration and cooperation can make a real difference. The agreement to use a common reporting schedule (though their funding cycles were different) saved hours of work that could then be put into the project itself. In addition, it was agreed that the budget could be treated as an aggregate; the Trusts, that is, did not insist on paying for one kind of thing and Hewlett another. Such modest accommodations can be a significant help to those in the project trenches, and it would be good to see more of them.

At a more ambitious level, one might well imagine collaborations that actively promote, document, and disseminate the work, for instance by using their Web sites to share important products (including otherwise fugitive but helpful documents such as proposals and end-of-year reports) and to link with related efforts by other foundations. Doing so would help to mitigate the dilemma I discovered as I began this case study: that much of the work is written, as Bacchetti says in Chapter Ten, "in disappearing ink."

The project holds several lessons about impact. For starters, it points to the key role of academic departments in the change process. Individual faculty (and not only those who were directly tapped for participation) were clearly engaged and changed by the strategies of documentation and exchange promoted by the project. At least some of the campuses altered personnel policies, and many either invited or required more robust evidence of teaching effectiveness in the evaluation of faculty. What was missing was the all-important middle—the academic department where the rubber of new ideas and policies must meet the road—or fail. Over the last decade there has been increasing attention to the department as a lynchpin of campus change; that focus should continue, and both funding guidelines and educational reform agendas could profitably take much more account of departments as sites of impact.

At the same time, From Idea to Prototype may argue for a broader conception of impact. Foundation guidelines typically ask about grantees' commitment to continuing the work beyond the funding period, and it is heartening to hear, as I still do today, about campuses that continue to use the strategies developed through the project. ("Existence proofs are a dime a dozen," Bacchetti said in our interview.) The project reflects a philosophy, however, that appears to be on the rise today, in which the goal is not simply to change the local setting but to generate ideas, materials, tools, and structures and human capital (leadership, a next generation of scholars, and so on) that can help build the larger field and contribute to knowledge (Hirschhorn and Gilmore, 2004). Both kinds of impact are important, and, of course, they are linked. Work that does not "take" locally is unlikely to catch on more widely. But if knowledge and field building are to be taken more seriously as goals, we will need to rethink our theories of change and the indicators used to evaluate impact.

Moreover, different conceptions of impact may imply different time frames. Projects in higher education are typically funded for two or three years (this, certainly, was the norm for Hewlett during many years), and that is arguably enough time for a campus to get a new curriculum (for instance) off the ground in ways that should be self-sustaining. But a commitment to field and knowledge building may require a longer attention span. Funders want to know what institutions learn and "institutionalize" from the projects they fund. But those are reasonable questions for the foundations, as well. (I recently heard a program officer, not at Hewlett or the Trusts, quip that foundations get the money out the door and then go on to the next thing.) To what extent do foundations do what Wert described of the Trusts: scouting for next ideas, using one project as a platform for others, sticking with an agenda over the long term? Many of the forces reported in Bacchetti's chapter in this volume certainly work against a longer trajectory of commitment.

I end with a lesson captured in a comment from one of the AAHE project participants—a chemist, as I recall—at the inaugural meeting at Stanford. Following a presentation about the rationale for the project (pressure for accountability, a more scholarly view of teaching, and the like), he stood and asked with some disgust: "Is this a project about evaluating teaching? Because if it is, I'll go home." What he was interested in, he announced, was "doing something that will improve my students' learning." The two goals are not mutually exclusive, of course, and our original vision of success presumed a connection between the two. But over the next few days and increasingly over the four years of the project, it became clear that it was a focus on student learning that really energized participants and brought them together across disciplinary and institutional boundaries. It was student learning they wanted to talk about and look at. And it was student learning that they believed should be the core and centerpiece of the peer review of teaching (the project should be renamed "the peer review of learning," some lobbied).

If I could redo the project, I would find a way to make this focus clearer and more explicit from the beginning and to *involve students themselves in the work of the project.* Doing so would not only catalyze faculty involvement but provide a powerful experience for students—an occasion to think about their own learning, to become more thoughtful about the educational process, and to develop their own pedagogical intelligence (see Huber and Hutchings, 2005). The involvement of students in educational reform is a possibility that foundations and higher education could embrace together, one that might just yield a next generation of leaders for a next generation of improvement efforts.

NOTES

1. From Idea to Prototype participating campuses were Indiana University-Purdue University Indianapolis, Kent State University, Northwestern University, Stanford University, Syracuse University, Temple University, University of California-Santa Cruz, University of Georgia, University of Michigan, University of Nebraska-Lincoln, University of North Carolina at Charlotte, and University of Wisconsin-Madison. Several campuses were added in phase two of the project.

2. A special thanks to Sally Tracy at The William and Flora Hewlett Foundation and Bruce Compton at The Pew Charitable Trusts, who provided invaluable assistance in finding and retrieving archived files.

REFERENCES

American Association for Higher Education. "From Idea to Prototype: The Peer Review of Teaching." Funding proposal to The William and Flora Hewlett Foundation and The Pew Charitable Trusts. Washington, D.C.: American Association for Higher Education, Aug. 1993.

American Association for Higher Education. "From Idea to Prototype: The Peer Review of Teaching, Phase II." Funding proposal to The William and Flora Hewlett Foundation and The Pew Charitable Trusts. Washington, D.C.: American Association for Higher Education, July 1995.

Bernstein, D. J. "Representing the Intellectual Work in Teaching Through Peer-Reviewed Course Portfolios." In S. Davis and W. Buskist (eds.), *The Teaching of Psychology: Essays in Honor of Wilbert J. McKeachie and Charles L. Brewer.* Mahwah, N.J.: Erlbaum, 2001.

Boyer, E. *Scholarship Reconsidered: Priorities of the Professoriate.* Princeton, N.J.: The Carnegie Foundation for the Advancement of Teaching, 1990.

Carnegie Foundation for the Advancement of Teaching. *The Condition of the Professoriate: Attitudes and Trends, 1989.* Princeton, N.J.: The Carnegie Foundation for the Advancement of Teaching, 1989.

Collins, J. C., and Porras, J. I. *Built to Last: Successful Habits of Visionary Companies.* New York: HarperCollins, 1997.

Covington, S. *Moving a Public Policy Agenda: The Strategic Philanthropy of Conservative Foundations.* Washington, D.C.: National Committee for Responsive Philanthropy, 1997.

Diamond, R. M., and Adams, B. E. *The Disciplines Speak: Rewarding the Scholarly, Professional, and Creative Work of Faculty.* Washington, D.C.: The American Association for Higher Education, 1995.

Edgerton, R. "The Re-Examination of Faculty Priorities." *Change,* July-Aug. 1993, 25(4), 10–25.

Edgerton, R., Hutchings, P., and Quinlan, K. *The Teaching Portfolio: Capturing the Scholarship in Teaching.* Washington, D.C.: American Association for Higher Education, 1991.

Glassick, C. E., Huber, M. T., and Maeroff, G. I. *Scholarship Assessed: Evaluation of the Professoriate: A Special Report of The Carnegie Foundation for the Advancement of Teaching.* San Francisco: Jossey-Bass, 1997.

Gray, P. J., Froh, R. C., and Diamond, R. M. "Myths and Realities." *AAHE Bulletin,* Dec. 1991, 44(4), 4–5.

Hirschhorn, L., and Gilmore, T. N. "Ideas in Philanthropic Field Building: Where They Come From and How They Are Translated into Action." New York: The Foundation Center, 2004.

Huber, M. T., and Hutchings, P. *The Advancement of Learning: Building the Teaching Commons.* San Francisco: Jossey-Bass, 2005.

Hutchings, P. *Making Teaching Community Property: A Menu for Peer Collaboration and Peer Review.* Washington, D.C.: American Association for Higher Education, 1996.

Hutchings, P. "Building on Progress." *AAHE Bulletin,* Feb. 1998a, 10–12.

Hutchings, P. (ed.). *The Course Portfolio: How Faculty Can Examine Their Teaching to Advance Practice and Improve Student Learning.* Washington, D.C.: American Association for Higher Education, 1998b.

The Pew Charitable Trusts. *1993 Annual Report.* Philadelphia: The Pew Charitable Trusts, 1993.

Quinlan, K. M. "Collaboration and Cultures of Teaching in University Departments: Faculty Beliefs About Teaching and Learning in History and Engineering." Unpublished dissertation, School of Education, Stanford University, 1996.

Shulman, L. S. "Teaching as Community Property: Putting an End to Pedagogical Solitude." *Change,* Nov.-Dec. 1993, *25*(6), 6–7.

Shulman, L. S. "From Idea to Prototype: Three Exercises in the Peer Review of Teaching." In P. Hutchings (ed.), *From Idea to Prototype: The Peer Review of Teaching: A Project Workbook.* Washington, D.C.: American Association for Higher Education, 1995. Reprinted P. Hutchings (ed.), *Teaching as Community Property.* San Francisco: Jossey-Bass, 2004.

Shuman, M. H. "Why Do Progressive Foundations Give Too Little to Too Many?" *The Nation,* Jan. 12–19, 1998, *226*(2), 11–16.

The William and Flora Hewlett Foundation. *1993 Annual Report.* Menlo Park, Calif.: The William and Flora Hewlett Foundation, 1993.

Chapter Thirteen Overview

In the pages that follow, Robert Orrill reaches back more than seventy-five years to tell a fascinating and troubling story with contemporary implications. It is the tale of a foundation project gone wrong and the corrosive consequences that resulted in the wake of the failure. The case study raises large and important questions: What roles should foundations have in helping to shape important public policies? How and in what ways should foundations be held accountable for their failures? What should foundations do when their projects go awry?

From 1929 to 1934, the Carnegie Corporation of New York provided support for a National Commission on Social Studies, with a mandate to resolve how civic education should be incorporated into K–12 education. The commission was proposed by the American Historical Association; it was headed by a university professor, and its membership was composed largely of university faculty members. It was viewed by the president of the Carnegie Corporation, Frederick Keppel, as a band of higher education experts assembled to design and develop national K–12 standards for civic learning and then ensure that those standards were adopted.

In retrospect, the idea that a small group of experts from higher education could or should set national policy on civic education for K–12 students might have raised flags of caution. But Orrill explains how the commission was launched—and how it floundered from the start. In the wake of the commission's failure, as Orrill chronicles, many in higher education retreated from the public policy scene and no longer were available to help frame public policies concerning K–12 education. As a result, the country was deprived of important sources of insight and understanding.

The case study raises the basic issue whether and to what extent projects and their leaders should be independent of the foundations (and their leaders) that support them. When a foundation initiative goes wrong, what should the foundation do? Perhaps most basic, what standards of accountability should prevail? The Carnegie Corporation operated in total secrecy, and this case study vividly illustrates the dangers of that path.

Orrill is currently executive director of the National Council on Education and the Disciplines and senior adviser at the Woodrow Wilson National Fellowship Foundation. Even though the story he tells happened more than seventy years ago, the lessons of his case study bear careful reflection today.

ADDRESSING FAILURE

THE CASE OF THE COMMISSION ON SOCIAL STUDIES

Robert Orrill

WHAT KIND OF EDUCATION best sustains democratic life in a society increasingly beset by unsettling social and economic change? By the late 1920s, this question had become ensnared in a tangle of competing points of view. Some thirty years earlier, the American Historical Association (AHA) had issued an influential report that argued powerfully for a civic education centered in the study of history. The substance of this report quickly became a kind of orthodoxy when the College Board made the AHA's curricular recommendations the basis for organizing college entrance examinations. By World War I, however, the dominant position of history had come under fierce assault from a number of different sources. On one flank, it was disputed by the newly formed social science disciplines, each of which argued that it deserved a share—if not the bulk—of the time given to history in the curriculum. And from another side, prominent faculty based in schools of education (the so-called "educationists") insisted that the study of history be eliminated, or at least radically curtailed, to make way for a socially oriented education driven by attention to contemporary public issues. The result of this struggle in the schools was that a once-stable stance toward civic education had given way to what one national report called a "confusion of tongues" (Dawson, 1924, p. 254).[1] Instead of the AHA-recommended curriculum, many schools now offered an incoherent array of ill-defined courses grouped together in a loose assemblage called "the social studies."

In these unsettled conditions, from 1929 to 1934, the Carnegie Corporation of New York (hereafter "Carnegie Corporation") supported and fully funded the National Commission on Social Studies (hereafter "the commission") to address this contentious debate that had arisen about the direction of civic education in American schools. The purpose was to bring definition and order to civic education and halt the drift toward curricular anarchy in K–12 education. With its membership based solidly in elite research universities, the commission also was meant to demonstrate that higher education provided the nation with a powerful instrument for solving complex social problems.

The outcome, however, turned out to be very different from the one envisioned. Troubled from the beginning, the commission never became an effective working body, and few of its projects ever reached completion. Even worse, it staggered to a rancorous end and issued a final report that angered many and satisfied no one. For all its labors, the commission managed, by its close, only to heighten disagreement and deepen division. Five years on, then, the Carnegie Corporation somehow had to reckon with a failure long in the making.

Like many failed efforts, the commission has not been given a notable place in the annals of American philanthropy. In its own day, however, the commission was no obscure or minor affair. On the contrary, it was a high-stakes initiative that chroniclers of reform still count as "the largest, most involved, and most expensive investigation of the social studies ever made" (Andreasen, 1987, p. 8).[2] In stumbling, moreover, the commission left a lasting imprint on the history of American education. Its dissolution, in fact, marks a decisive turning point in the evolution of school-college relations, though in a direction very different from any that the Carnegie Corporation had intended. By funding this initiative, the foundation meant to back the claim that university expertise should guide the shaping of the school curriculum. The commission's failure, however, so deterred faculty in history and the social sciences that these disciplines turned away from K–12 education and began a long, still ongoing retreat from involvement in making school policy. More than a disappointment, then, the commission proved to be a near-lethal setback to the cause that the Carnegie Corporation had sought to support.

The commission was a philanthropic intervention in a matter where conflict prevailed and many voices competed to be heard. In this sense, it was an attempt to address the problem of division inherent in the increasingly pluralistic conditions of American life. Why, though, should the Carnegie Corporation support such an undertaking? What prompted the foundation to believe that it could be a positive influence in a situation where those more directly involved had not been able to resolve their differences? In short, why should the Carnegie Corporation think of disagreement and discord in a domain of public policy as the proper business of the foundation?

These are among the issues that first come to mind in turning more directly to the origins of the commission. When asked, however, such questions are not easily put to rest. Once raised, as Dennis Collins suggests, they soon lead to a search for a rationale that transcends any single case—one that speaks to the social purpose and larger aims of foundations more generally. Then we cannot avoid asking whether foundations perform a distinctive "social task" that cannot be fulfilled more effectively by some other means, and this inquiry, Collins (2004) says, takes us straight to "the debate about why foundations should exist in the first place" (p. 68). As it unfolds, this case serves as a reminder of why this debate cannot be easily settled.

The Origins of the Commission

As noted, the commission was a large undertaking with far-reaching aspirations. Not content with compromise, it sought to make a complete break with everything that had gone before and to create a new beginning for civic education in the schools. One commissioner, Charles Beard (1929), declared that he and his colleagues were engaged in nothing less than "preparing a report which ought to mark a new epoch in the intellectual history of our schools and our country" (p. 371). What prompted such an ambition? How had this visionary intent been formed? Later, many critics would say that the commission had failed because of the extravagance of its aims. If this were true, who had encumbered the project with the burden of an unattainable outcome? This question about accountability is a thread that we will follow from beginning to end in telling the story of the commission.

We find no such great expectations if we turn first to the precursors of the commission. The antecedents of the commission, in fact, were modest in scope and limited in intention. They also looked in a different direction. The starting point was a small committee appointed by the AHA in 1924 for the purpose of reporting on the status of history education in the schools. At this time, the AHA's concern was confined to determining whether history was losing ground amid the welter of courses then taught under the name "social studies." How this committee evolved and grew until it was transformed, in 1929, into the commission is a study in foundation involvement and influence.

In 1924, the AHA had nothing like a commission in mind. Uncertain about the facts, it wanted to end doubt regarding how much (or how little) the subject of history had survived the social studies tsunami that swept through the school curriculum in the years during and just after World War I. To this end, it sought foundation support to conduct a national curriculum survey designed to collect and analyze data on course offerings in the schools. Initially, then, the AHA proposed only to study and clarify a situation that had become awash in confusion. As yet, its proposal included no plan to take action based on the information gathered. Nor did the AHA suggest that it had any interest in addressing the whole of the social studies muddle. Its concern was history alone.

Why did the AHA alter its proposal? That the change began was due almost entirely to the prompting of foundations. In its search for funding, the AHA first approached the Commonwealth Fund and, later, the Rockefeller Foundation. These conversations were eventually dropped, but the AHA learned from them that any hope of funding required taking account of the foundation point of view. Indeed, in private discussions foundation staff were quite prepared to promote their own outlook—in contrast, it should be said, to how little of what they thought ever was made public. In this case, the message they delivered pointed toward what amounted to a radical reorientation of the AHA proposal. Neither foundation had any interest in a project that intended only to collect facts and which, in effect, might serve to ratify the status quo. Instead, both encouraged the AHA to adopt a reformist stance toward the problem and to seek some overall resolution of the issues under dispute. The foundations also were insistent that the project should not be dominated by an AHA bias. To gain acceptance, they said, the proposal must address the social studies debate more comprehensively and include participation from the social sciences and educationists.

Responsive to what it heard, the AHA compliantly began to turn its proposal in the direction wanted by the foundations. Its first step was to invite a few influential social scientists to join the project committee; at the same time, it modified the project by indicating that the data-collection process should prepare the way for school-based experimentation with new curricular programs. In addition, all appearances of caution were removed from the proposal, and expressions of commitment to action-oriented reform were given prominence. These revisions involved little substantive change in what the AHA had originally intended. Basically, the project still was an investigative study. What had changed, however, were the professed views of the AHA. Increasingly, these had come to resemble those held by the foundations. According to its revised proposal, the AHA now was an organization ready to respond to the call for solutions, with assurances that answers could be delivered.

Why such responsiveness? After all, the AHA could simply have dropped its proposal. Indeed, had it not said at first that the problem was much too unsettled even to be grasped without preliminary study? Why, then, conform to the reformist expectations of the foundations, when the feasibility of these aims was much in doubt? In part, it seems that the AHA acted as it did because of uneasiness that the foundations might turn the task over to a rival organization. This was no idle worry. After World War I, several foundations did, indeed, invest huge sums in establishing a professional base for the social sciences in the research universities.[3]

During these same years, moreover, both the educationists and social scientists had formed professional organizations through which they could take collective action and contest the AHA's long-held leadership in the making of school policy. In 1921, the educationists had created the National Council on the Social Studies; in 1923, Rockefeller had funded a proposal from leading social scientists to found the Social Science Research Council. Might not the foundations, therefore, elect to back the claims of these new organizations to speak for the social studies and thereby alter the balance of power among the disciplines? This was the question that now both stimulated and bothered the AHA leadership. With their almost complete freedom of action, the foundations seemingly could determine issues of authority and power among the competitors in the social studies domain. Given these stakes, the AHA could scarcely do other than heed what the foundations were saying.

After negotiations with Rockefeller and the Commonwealth Fund had lagged, the AHA approached the president of the Carnegie Corporation, Frederick Keppel, with a proposal that had been revised yet again. This time the proposal was sent to the corporation in the form of a report written by A. C. Krey—a historian of medieval studies from the University of Minnesota. In this report, the AHA pledged full cooperation with the social scientists and educationists and spoke confidently about how, with the corporation's support, a collaborative effort could resolve the issues then troubling social studies education in the schools. Perhaps deliberately, Keppel responded at first in a noncommittal way, but he agreed to consider the idea if the AHA submitted what he called full-scale "working drawings" for the project. He emphasized that, like the other foundations, the corporation's interest in the matter was dependent on an entirely new start for civic education, not in some reworking of previous AHA policies toward the school curriculum.

This prompted a second document (also written by Krey) in which the AHA attempted to satisfy Keppel's request for particulars. By this point, the modest investigative study of 1924 had been replaced by a forward-looking proposal for thoroughgoing school reform. Indeed, the list of projected outcomes in this second submission goes on and on, almost without end. In addition to constructing a new "framework" for social studies, the initiative now promised to define student performance standards, develop "objective" tests, improve textbooks, evaluate teaching methods, and support experimental programs. Moreover, it would perform these tasks for each one of the K–12 grade levels. Finally, if all this should leave anything undone, the project also would serve as a "clearing device through which . . . questions which require solutions can be shunted to the centers best qualified to furnish the answers" (Krey, 1928).

But who was the true author of this reform program? Whence came its ambition and impetus? In moving far beyond its original intentions, had the AHA not been drawn forward at the behest of the foundations? Whatever the answers to these questions may be up to this time, they are now certain after Keppel responded to the AHA's second submission. At this point, he agreed to support the project—but only if the AHA turned over leadership of the project to an independent body.

Here, in fact, is the moment when the Commission on Social Studies was born, and it is Keppel who gave it life. Instead of an AHA committee, he insisted, the initiative should be placed in the hands of a fifteen-member commission in which the membership is evenly balanced among historians, educationists, and social scientists. If this would be done, then Keppel would accept Krey as chair of the commission and the AHA as fiscal agent for the grant. He added one other precondition. Keppel wanted assurances in writing from the AHA that it would not seek to influence or intrude upon the work of the commission in any way. Compliant as always, the AHA sent Keppel a formal letter stipulating "that, though the Committee in question was formed by the American Historical Association, it is not intended to represent the particular interests of history, but a large view of the social studies as a whole" (private letter from Evarts Greene to Keppel, November 28, 1928). Thus, with a stroke of the pen, the AHA gave up ownership of a project that it had spent five years developing as it shepherded the proposal from one foundation to another.

So who owned the project, and who would be held accountable for achieving its outcomes? Not the AHA. Keppel had sought and received guarantees that the AHA would keep its hands off the project, except for ensuring that its financial affairs were kept in order. Apparently, then, Keppel believed that the commission would be self-motivated and self-organizing. But what if the initiative should falter? Who would come to its assistance or call it to account? By intervening so assertively in the beginning, had Keppel not given the Carnegie Corporation (and himself) a large share of the responsibility for setting things right? Though unasked at the outset, this question became more pressing once the commission began to lose its way.

The Faith in Experts

What, though, was the source of Keppel's faith in an independent commission? How did its establishment figure in surmounting the many objections to funding this project? After all, the establishment of the commission did little to ease Keppel's distrust of the AHA's intentions. In fact, he continued to believe to the very end that AHA domination was a grave threat to the success of the project. Even more important, there still were unanswered doubts about the feasibility of the undertaking. Many reviewers told Keppel that the proposal promised much more than could be delivered. For several, the ambitious agenda was a morass through which the commission was unlikely to find its way. One adviser wrote to Keppel that reading the proposal had brought on "steadily mounting dizziness," and, he warned, "personally, I should flee from such a project" (private letter from William S. Learned to Keppel, September 29, 1928).

Why, then, go forward with the proposal? This appears to be a question that Keppel did not believe he was obligated to answer in any direct or explicit way. So far as one can tell, in fact, transparency did not figure at all in his code of professional conduct. On the contrary, he seldom spoke openly about the Carnegie Corporation's policy or their decision making at any time. Based on extensive research in the Carnegie Corporation's archives, Ellen Lagemann (1989) reports that he made few statements for the record during his entire presidency and "rarely, if ever, explained his actions" (p. 109). Later, this absence of transparency would turn out to be important in the life of the commission. Among other questions, one that would emerge was whether the outcome of this case might have been different if Keppel had been more forthcoming (and forthright) about his own motives and point of view.

Given that there is so little documentary evidence, what, in fact, can we say about Keppel's own views? Perhaps the place to begin is to point out that funding the commission did not represent a departure for the Carnegie Corporation from long-standing policy and practice. In fact, it was illustrative of the kind of grantmaking typically undertaken during Keppel's tenure in office. As Lagemann points out, much of the corporation's financial support at this time was bestowed on projects that, in one way or another, sought to confirm the cultural authority and leadership of newly emerging professional and scientific elites.

The commission was very much an initiative of this sort. It was a venture based on the conviction that problems in the schools were best solved by competent experts drawn from the leading research universities and relevant professional organizations. One of the hallmarks of professional authority, of course, is success in solving problems when they arise in a bounded domain of competence. Acting almost as an arm of the universities, the commission was meant to be exactly this kind of demonstration in the realm of civic education.

By fostering expertise, then, the Carnegie Corporation quite rightly could understand itself as helping to provide the wherewithal needed to solve the many problems confronting American society. That the foundation served the public good, therefore, perhaps seemed self-evident to Keppel and in need of no elaborate justification. Lagemann (1989) sums up the rationale in this way:

> That expertise, defined simply as special, advanced knowledge, was necessary in a large modern society was indisputable. Clearly, therefore, in directing money to the investigations from which expertise might appear, the Corporation had performed a vital public function. (p. 254)

As Lagemann explains, however, this rationale in full was a more complicated matter. Among its advocates, expertise implied a great deal more than a command of "special, advanced knowledge" (p. 254). It also suggested that this knowledge—and the educational process through which it was attained—conferred upon experts the authority (and privilege) to govern in democratic conditions. As Robert Wiebe (1995) points out, this turn to expertise emerged from a "new political theory" that found wide acceptance within the nation's professional circles in the aftermath of World War I. Although still purportedly democratic, this theory actually had little confidence in government "of" and "by" the people. Among its proponents, tellingly, those once known as "citizens" now were called "the crowd," "the masses," or even "the human herd." From the perspective of the theory, Wiebe says, the public had "lost coherence and deteriorated into a mass of people, myopic and gullible" (p. 173).

In part, these political views were formed in reaction to war and social revolution in Europe. After the upheaval and destruction of World War I, popular movements more and more were regarded as threats to good order and stability. In such circumstances, the theory held, only trained experts were able and fit to give direction to democracies that otherwise would be beset by confusion and tumult. Therefore, they should be nurtured and recognized as what amounted to a permanent governing elite.

Constituted as a class, experts, in fact, did not so much assist democracy as substitute for it. Prior to the establishment of the commission, this point of view was argued most persuasively by Walter Lippmann in such works as *Public Opinion* (1922) and *A Preface to Morals* (1929). Later, in 1932, Lippmann figured in the life of the commission when Keppel considered asking him to come to the rescue of a faltering initiative and write the project's summative report.

What, though, set experts apart from ordinary people? How did they come to possess the qualities needed for leadership that others lacked? According to the theory, the answer was to be found in the training they received in universities dedicated to the pursuit of scientific rigor and integrity. This education formed their character and pledged them to seek the truth in circumstances where others were confused or self-interested. "The theory's advocates," Wiebe (1967) writes, "were convinced that the process of becoming an expert, by immersing oneself in the scientific method, eradicated petty passions and narrow ambitions, just as it removed faults in reasoning" (p. 161). Apart from the university, moreover, all other environments were tainted in some way. Politics was corrupt, religion was error-ridden, and business was greedy and selfish. Only the university-trained expert could see clearly and cared about what was best for all. Though seldom spelled out, these were among the underlying beliefs that informed the Carnegie Corporation in its grantmaking.

How, exactly, did experts give direction? First, by reaching agreement among themselves. A presumption of the theory was that rule by experts was a matter of collegial negotiation among elites. Once experts had arrived at a consensus about the path to take, others could be shown where and how to follow. This is how the Carnegie Corporation understood the work of the commission. The product of a major university, Keppel himself was at the forefront of those who put the new political theory into practice. In forming the commission, he simply gave instrumental expression to these emerging political convictions. For Keppel, as Lagemann says, the "natural way to proceed was through elite consensus-building" (p. 103). A body of experts drawn from the universities, then, was the one best means for finding sound and authoritative answers to the social studies problem.

There were also doubts that could not be entirely ignored. In large part, the social studies question was about what kind of civic education should be provided for the great majority of students who themselves never would enter a university. These were the great mass of future citizens who would not become experts and—if the theory were followed—should not aspire to do so. Seen in this light, the commission was an attempt by "leaders" to form an education that would tell "followers" how to be happily adjusted to their condition in life. This left the commission open to the charge that it was engaged in what amounted to an act of political indoctrination; from early on, this thought troubled many of the commissioners, impeded the work, and finally contributed to the failure to achieve consensus. Not all the experts, it turned out, were comfortable with the exalted status that the Carnegie Corporation and Keppel sought to confer upon them.

What Are "Social Studies"?

What, more specifically, was the function of the expert? According to the new political theory, it was to help society address and overcome the problem of "cultural lag" (Wiebe, 1995, p. 143). From the perspective of the leadership class, the source of this difficulty was the rush of change in modern life. This was so rapid that it outran the capacity of ordinary people to comprehend what was happening within themselves and in the world at large. In their confusion, therefore, they clung to old ideas and values that had been formed to meet conditions that no longer held. Given these circumstances, it was the task of experts to help the public reform (or "reconstruct") its thinking and thereby adapt to an altered reality. Writ large, their assignment was to give direction to a public always in peril of falling behind the times (and therefore in danger of suffering maladjustment or becoming malcontent). In the broadest sense, this was the deliverance that the Carnegie Corporation expected from the commission's final report.

Inherently, the nature of this task bestowed considerable independence upon the expert. Because no one could foresee the changes that might occur, experts had to be left free to address problems as they arose from conditions never stable and always in flux. The latitude granted them had to be sufficient to meet the contingency of events. On this score, one historian, Olivier Zunz (1998), asserts that foundation charters were left vague at this time so that experts could have the "maximum flexibility and independence" needed to adjust their actions to unanticipated challenges and shifting circumstances (pp. 32–33).

To whom, then, were experts accountable? The new political theory seems to say *only to themselves*. Apart from the review of peers, they should be left unhindered to do their work. Any encroachment on their freedom would undermine or detract from the integrity of their efforts and the outcomes they obtain. Their scientific ethic, as Wiebe (1995) puts it, separated experts "from ordinary minds; only experts were qualified to evaluate other experts" (p. 143).

When given a strict interpretation, the theory would seem to draw a definite line between the Carnegie Corporation and the commission. Once the commission was established, the foundation should not have intervened in its work. Thereafter, the commission should have been independent and represent only itself.

This, indeed, was how Keppel presented the case in the aftermath of the commission's failure. In an internal policy directive, he informed staff that discussions with trustees should stress that the foundation's relations with the commission had been governed at all times by "the doctrine of non-interference" (internal memorandum, Carnegie Corporation of New York, June 12, 1934). Disappointment that the commission had gone astray, then, did not nullify the fact that it had to be left alone to seek its own way. Thus this doctrine exempts the foundation (and Keppel) from accountability for the project's outcomes. The commission's shortcomings were its own. Even though the commission had gone wrong, Keppel could say that the foundation had held throughout to an established policy and sound practice.

Under one name or another, the doctrine of noninterference still has a place in the self-understanding of many foundations. It holds that the proper business of a foundation is to encourage initiative but to avoid prejudicing its outcomes. In this conception once a project has been funded, the foundation becomes an interested observer and awaits results. Apart from financial oversight, however, its active involvement and substantive influence has come to an end. This stance often goes hand-in-hand with a philosophy of pluralistic liberalism: the belief that all points of view deserve a fair trial and none should prevail through coercion or undue power over others. Through supporting such conditions, foundations claim that they help maintain and enliven an open society, thus justifying their autonomy and providing a rationale for their own existence in a democratic society.

In this case, however, was Keppel's concern simply that all voices in the debate be heard? Did he, in fact, approach this project with no position or bias of his own? Not entirely. At the very outset, he signaled his own leanings when he urged Krey to read William Kilpatrick's recently published *Education for a Changing Civilization* (1926). In a note to Krey, he said about Kilpatrick: "About as well as anyone with whom I have come in contact, he expresses radical ideas in a reasonable way" (private letter from Keppel to A. C. Frey, January 28, 1929). Here, then, is advocacy for a point of view and support for transformative reform. But here also is equivocation about how such change should be enacted. Keppel wanted radical results, but he suggested that they could (and should) come about without conflict and upheaval. Very probably, Krey was neither the first nor last project director to receive this kind of mixed message from a foundation.

When recommending Kilpatrick's book, what were the "radical ideas" that Keppel had in mind? In brief, they were ones just then emerging from a small group of Teachers College educationists known as "social reconstructionists." Kilpatrick was a prominent figure in the reconstructionist camp, as were two members of the commission—Jesse Newlon and George S. Counts. As disciples of John Dewey, all these like-minded educationists argued that the public schools should function actively as agencies for transforming the social order. Being more or less socialistic in their political views, they contended that the school curriculum should become the means for overturning laissez-faire individualism and replacing it with what they called a "collectivist" social ethic. To bring this about, the schools had to rid the curriculum of what Kilpatrick (1926) derided as "dead stuff"—meaning, first and foremost, that attention to the subject of history "should give way to study of [contemporary] social problems" (pp. 110–112).

With Keppel's backing, this was the platform that the reconstructionists brought to the commission. Given the right curriculum, they asserted, the schools could recast the American moral landscape. By this means, a restless people—once individualistic and sternly religious—could be made over into a sociable and happily secular society. But what was this new curriculum that could deliver such a transformative outcome?

For those who attempted to answer this question, it turned out to be a grave weakness that the quest began with a vague notion—the "social studies"—that was almost entirely empty of meaning. The term had gained impetus as a collective label for efforts in the schools to promote patriotism during World War I, but a decade later it was an idea that still eluded understanding and defied definition. So in 1929, the commission commenced without a model or recognizable image on which to base its work. Nonetheless, Beard (1929) urged educators to have faith that "there is substance, there is reality, in social studies." Still, he admitted, "The term is not entirely happy. The boundaries of the field are indefinite. The subject-matter is difficult to determine. Methods of teaching and testing are under debate. Intangibles are numerous" (p. 371).

The Commission Unravels

The commission began to stray from its task almost from the start. Unable to define *social studies,* it simply left the issue unaddressed and walked away from the problem. In consequence, therefore, much of the commission's agenda had to be either slowed or held in abeyance. Even with generous funding, little serious attention could be given to standards, tests, or any other of the project's deliverables in the absence of at least a provisional grasp of the domain in question.

This growing difficulty did not escape Keppel's attention. As the commission's work lagged, reports of trouble came to him from a number of sources. One of the most disturbing messages was sent by Robert S. Lynd, the highly respected coauthor of *Middletown* and an influential figure in both social science and philanthropic circles. Writing confidentially (private letter, February 24, 1930), Lynd told Keppel that the commission was adrift and warned him of the "serious danger of its evaporating into thin air." Regrettably, he added, several other observers shared this "troubled feeling . . . regarding the vagueness of the Krey study and the extent to which Krey really grasps what he is about." Plainly, Lynd wanted to leave no doubt in Keppel's mind about the seriousness of the situation. If the Carnegie Corporation failed to intervene, the commission would soon be lost beyond any possibility of recovery.

How did Keppel respond to these warnings? Here, clearly, is a critical moment in philanthropic decision making. What should a foundation do when one of its most important initiatives has lost direction and failed to find its way? In this case, it is telling to consider the actions that Keppel did *not* take. There is nothing in the record, for instance, to suggest that he ever spoke to Krey (directly or indirectly) about difficulties that the project had encountered. Nor did he at any time raise concerns with the commission as a whole or ever attend its meetings. And, finally, he never once indicated to the AHA that the corporation funding had been ill spent or that its continuation was in doubt. So there was nothing transparent in Keppel's approach to this emergency—no discernible step that could be counted as forthright and straightforward.

If Keppel did not consult with the commission, neither did he adhere to the doctrine of noninterference. In fact, he became very much engaged from early on in trying to save the project. Instead of taking open action, however, he sought to work through covert and indirect means. As the initiative faltered, he privately directed his efforts to avoiding stalemate and toward obtaining a strong, compelling final report from the commission. In Keppel's mind, this meant securing a document powerful and persuasive enough to have a unifying influence on public opinion. If this could be achieved, then the commission's bid for expert leadership could be vindicated, and its other shortcomings might be overlooked and the project redeemed. However, Keppel no longer expected such a result to come from a process of collegial discussion and consensus building among the commissioners. Increasingly, he believed that only a strong hand could steer the commission out of the doldrums.

In what way, then, did Keppel intervene? At one point he briefly considered inviting Walter Lippmann to write a report on behalf of the commission. Increasingly, though, he began to think of Beard, a long-time ally, as the project's one hope for salvation. On its surface, this might seem a credible idea. At the time, Beard was one of America's leading intellectuals and doubtless was the member of the commission best known to the general public. Shortly before the start of the commission, in 1927, he and his wife, Mary, had completed a general history of the United States titled *The Rise of American Civilization*—a work, as a later historian said, that "did more than any other such book of the twentieth century to define American history for the reading public" (Hofstadter, 1958, p. 299). This success, therefore, along with a sharp and assertive intellect, naturally marked Beard out for a leading role in the commission's affairs.

Perhaps even more important, though, was the long-standing relationship that existed between Keppel and Beard. Earlier, they had been colleagues at Columbia; later on, each continued to seek advice from the other after both had gone elsewhere. Once the work of the commission had commenced, these private exchanges went on much as they had earlier, with Beard often visiting Keppel in his office for confidential discussions about the project. During these closed meetings, Keppel began, almost from the beginning, to encourage Beard to take the report in hand and to supplant Krey as leader of the commission. At first, the record suggests, Beard hesitated, but Keppel kept the conversation alive and moving in the direction he wanted. After one talk, he wrote to Beard that the "members of the Commission are good fellows who won't want to present a pussy-footing report." So he told Beard, if "it looks like deadlock," and the commission must "choose a dictator," then you "ought to accept the crown if, when and as offered" (private letter from Keppel to Charles Beard, March 26, 1931).

Not one to hold back for long, Beard soon began to assert himself and, with Keppel urging him on, took more and more control of writing the commission's report. In the end, however, this did not turn out to be the blessing that Keppel expected. As Thomas Bender (1993) says, Beard was "the quintessential individualist, someone who could be contained by no institution" (p. 97). Very often, though, this meant no more than that Beard had little respect for any opinion that did not agree with his own. Indeed, after resigning in protest from Columbia in 1917, he again and again resigned from projects that he had elected to join. Each time, his complaint was that his colleagues lacked moral backbone. In his view, academics hid their social consciences under a cloak of objectivity and thereby undermined their personal commitment to reform.

Perhaps inevitably, this was a critique that Beard began to turn against his fellow commissioners and to introduce into the report. As a result, the report in many respects became an indictment of the ethical timidity of historians and social scientists. No wonder, then, that each of these disciplines found a way to disavow the report when it appeared. Keppel, however, could not have been surprised by anything that Beard wrote. He had reviewed drafts of the report up to the end and, in fact, always had encouraged Beard to express his convictions without restraint of any kind. Once when Beard suggested appeasing the historians, Keppel typically objected: "The real Guild among the Historians has never, I fear, taken the study very seriously—and I'd let them howl" (private letter from Keppel to Charles Beard, February 7, 1933). This was his consistent message. There should be no backing off a strong, forceful report.

While Keppel kept his attention on the final report, the project as a whole was coming apart and losing all coherence. In truth, as noted, it had never actually held together. Over time, several different organizational schemes were tried, but none ever brought the entire body of work under control. At first, all of the many parts of the projects were managed by an executive arm of the commission. This quickly proved unworkable, however, and responsibility for reporting on specific issues (for example, testing and pedagogy) was handed over to an array of advisory committees. Then, finally, when these committees also turned out to be unproductive, topics were parceled out to individual "investigators," who were left free to research and write their own monographs.

With its agenda dispersed in this way, the commission no longer convened on a regular basis. Late in the project, in fact, the commission did not meet a single time over a stretch of eighteen months. At this point, Beard took full advantage of the situation and drafted a final report that he was determined should stand, no matter what objections might be brought by other commission members. In the end, he got his way, but it came at a heavy price. His refusal to consider amendments meant that the report went to press against the wishes of many commission members and without the endorsement of any of the social scientists. So Beard delivered a report, but it had been done at the cost of what he later called the "bust-up" of the commission (private letter to Keppel, September 5, 1934).

In itself, this division within the commission would have been enough to sink the report. Every review emphasized that the experts had failed to agree among themselves. Even more adverse comment, however, fell on the report's call for a civic education purposely aimed at ushering in a "new age of collectivism" and ridding the nation of the prevalence of "self-ish individualism" (National Commission on the Social Studies, 1934, p. 16). For many, this message appeared to advocate radical political indoctrination rather than the education of free citizens. The most telling criticism, though, came from educators who pointed out that the report had nothing whatsoever to say about the question that the commission had promised to answer. Nowhere in the report, they said, could an educator learn anything about what was meant by "social studies," and therefore it seemed that the commission had spent five years and over a quarter of a million dollars avoiding the problem it had been funded to address.

For the Carnegie Corporation, this was an unanswerable indictment. Earlier, as mentioned, Beard himself had asked educators to have faith that the commission could show "there is substance, there is reality, in social studies." Any such substantive reality, however, turned out to be what most obviously was missing from the report. Instead of concrete curricular guidance, Beard had offered what amounted to an often sententious foray into the realm of social philosophy. As a practical matter, then, the report managed only to hand back to schools the problem of making sense of a still-murky curriculum idea for which the commission itself could form no definition, meaning, or plan of action.

Then and Now

The commission is a case of a philanthropic initiative gone very far wrong. In retrospect, then, it invites reflection about the stance that foundations take toward projects that end badly or miss their mark. What, indeed, should a foundation do when it finds that it has a failure on its hands? According to some critics, this is a question that philanthropies often suppress or shirk. This evasiveness is made possible by the autonomy that they enjoy. Because they are effectively accountable to no one, foundations can simply walk away from previous commitments and treat their disappointments as if they never happened or were of little consequence. In making this point, Joel Fleishman (2004) observes that "virtually all foundations operate with their cards held very close to the vest," and "never report publicly on their failures." Rather than openly confronting their mistakes, he asserts, they issue public statements that "are rarely self-critical" and instead are "filled with self-praise for what foundation managers regard as their successes" (p. 115).

How should foundations address and take account of their failures? Fleishman says that such projects should be regarded as badges of courage, that is, as evidence that a foundation is "pushing the envelope by experimenting with solutions to social problems that . . . entail the risk of failure" (p. 115). Many other observers join in this point of view. They worry that a philanthropy overly concerned about its accountability for results will be inclined to fund only safe, manageable projects when, in fact, it is risk taking that should be considered the surest sign of vigor and vibrancy within a foundation. This doubtless is an important consideration, but does it, in itself, settle all issues of accountability? How much, in fact, should the difficulty of a problem figure in assigning responsibility for the failure of attempts to find a solution? If it trumps most other matters, then perhaps the Carnegie Corporation (and Keppel) should be criticized very little for the commission's failings and final downfall. After all, the social studies muddle unquestionably was a messy problem rife with conflict and uncertainty.

So if there were nothing more to say, it may be that the Carnegie Corporation should be commended for taking it on and trying to find a solution. But what if a foundation comes to a problem with a bias of its own and, at many points, intervenes in an effort to have its own way? And, moreover, what if it keeps its own decision making and actions largely hidden from view as it pursues this cause? This describes the corporation's conduct in the case of the commission. Does not the weight of accountability then fall very heavily on the corporation—or on any foundation that behaves in a similar manner?

Suppose that a foundation accepts a share of the responsibility for the failure of a project. What might this entail? Should not a foundation try to learn from its mistakes and help others avoid repeating them? If done openly, this could shed light on paths to problem solving, serve the general good, and fulfill a foundation's commitment to transparency. Then foundations would deserve to be thought of as full partners in a community of inquiry and learning. This, of course, would require recognition of involvement in the work of a project instead of Keppel's resort to the doctrine of noninterference. It also might result in a foundation asking how free it should be to disengage and walk away from a problem that its efforts have worsened rather than helped.

This, in fact, was a question that arose immediately after the dissolution of the commission. At the time, several advisers told Keppel that the Carnegie Corporation should attempt to undo the harm that the project had done. Keppel rejected this advice, however, and responded that "the best thing for the Corporation to do" was to move on and "take its medicine in silence" (private letter from Keppel to William S. Learned, June 5, 1934). For the corporation, this is where the matter ended. Given its complete freedom of action, the foundation simply could begin to forget a problem that still persisted and that has long continued to plague American education. Even now, there is no answer to the question about what, if anything, is meant by "the social studies." In consequence, the center of the school curriculum—those studies that most directly prepare students for life in a democracy—has been left vacant and exposed to the often-loud assertions of many dubious claimants.

This is not to suggest that the Carnegie Corporation alone abandoned the commission or that it was entirely responsible for its faults. Like the corporation, the disciplines also turned their backs on the project and gave it no further thought. In the beginning, as mentioned, the intention was very different. When the initiative was funded, it was expected that the major disciplinary associations would endorse the commission's report and help enact its recommendations. At the end, however, no such actions were taken. Instead, the associations remained totally silent about the report and made no move whatsoever to acknowledge its existence. Moreover, it was exactly from this point that the disciplinary associations abandoned their long-standing attention to K–12 education and began what turned out to be an almost complete withdrawal from involvement in school reform. This was an especially striking development in the case of the AHA, which until this time had been at the forefront of K–12 policymaking for the better part of four decades.

Where, then, are we left? After such a long lapse, might this retreat be halted and reversed? A number of disciplines have begun to ask this question of themselves, and this is a discussion that foundations, arguably, would do well to promote and join. At stake is the intellectual depth and energy that disciplines could bring to efforts to rethink the school curriculum—strengths that now are sorely missing from a K–12 reform environment largely driven by the interests of business and government. Of course, such a move would require making a new start in asking how disciplinary expertise can best be brought to bear on issues of teaching and learning in the schools. Upon reflection, in fact, this may be the question that the travails of the commission most brings to mind.

NOTES

1. In a 2005 article in *American Historical Review,* L. Shapiro and I offer a more complete account of these developments.

2. My work on this chapter has benefited from research presented in this and three other doctoral dissertations—those by L. Vanarie (1958), H. Boozer (1960), and T. Brown (1985), along with documents from the archives of the Carnegie Corporation of New York.

3. Dorothy Ross estimates that foundations provided over $40 million in support of the social sciences and social work between 1922 and 1929. By far the largest contributor to this sum was the Laura Spellman Rockefeller Memorial, under the direction of Beardsley Ruml. See Ross, 1991 (pp. 400–404).

REFERENCES

Andreasen, B. "Reconstructing the Social Order: The American Historical Association Commission on the Social Studies." Unpublished doctoral dissertation, Department of History, Cornell University, 1987.

Beard, C. "The Trend in Social Studies." *The Historical Outlook*, 1929, *20*, 371.

Bender, T. *Intellect and the Public Life*. Baltimore: Johns Hopkins University Press, 1993.

Boozer, H. "The American Historical Association and the Schools, 1884–1956." Unpublished doctoral dissertation, Graduate Institute of Education, Washington University, 1960.

Brown, T. "The American Historical Association and the Schools: A Study of Condescension and Protection in the Twentieth Century." Unpublished doctoral dissertation, the Graduate School, State University of New York at Buffalo, 1985.

Collins, D. "The Art of Philanthropy." In H. P. Karoff (ed.), *Just Money: A Critique of Contemporary American Philanthropy*. Boston: TPI Editions, 2004.

Dawson, E. "The History Inquiry." *The Historical Outlook*, 1924, *25*, 254.

Fleishman, J. "Simply Doing Good or Doing Well." In H. P. Karoff (ed.), *Just Money: A Critique of Contemporary American Philanthropy*. Boston: TPI Editions, 2004.

Hofstadter, R. *The Progressive Historians*. Chicago: University of Chicago Press, 1958.

Kilpatrick, W. *Education for a Changing Civilization*. New York: Macmillan, 1926.

Krey, A. C. "Working Plans of an Investigation of History and Other Social Studies in the Schools," Oct. 1928. Carnegie Corporation Archive.

Lagemann, E. *The Politics of Knowledge: The Carnegie Corporation, Philanthropy, and Public Policy*. Chicago: University of Chicago Press, 1989.

Lippmann, W. *Public Opinion*. New York: Simon & Schuster, 1922.

Lippmann, W. *A Preface to Morals*. New York: Macmillan, 1929.

National Commission on the Social Studies. *Report of the Commission on the Social Studies*. New York: Carnegie Corporation of New York, 1934.

Orrill, R., and Shapiro, L. "From Bold Beginnings to an Uncertain Future: The Discipline of History and History Education." *American Historical Review*, 2005, *110*(3), 727–751.

Ross, D. *The Origins of American Social Science.* New York: Cambridge University Press, 1991.

Vanarie, L. "The National Council for the Social Studies: A Voluntary Organization for Professional Service." Unpublished doctoral dissertation, Joint Committee on Graduate Instruction, Columbia University, 1958.

Wiebe, R. *The Search for Order.* New York: Hill & Wang, 1967.

Wiebe, R. *Self Rule: A Cultural History of American Democracy.* Chicago: University of Chicago Press, 1995.

Zunz, O. *Why the American Century?* Chicago: University of Chicago Press, 1998.

PART FOUR

CROSS-CUTTING TOPICS

Chapter Fourteen Overview

Ellen Lagemann and Jennifer de Forest conclude Chapter Three with brief comments on the rise of conservative foundations and their impact on institutions of education. This chapter focuses on those foundations and addresses how they have sought to shape public policies regarding education, both directly in terms of K–12 education and indirectly by seeding major universities with conservative perspectives.

In Chapter Fourteen, Leslie Lenkowsky and James Piereson show how conservative foundations have exerted profound influences throughout American education with relatively small investments. They suggest some important lessons to be learned in terms of how to have an impact on public policies in education. The chapter also provides readers a rich narrative on which to reflect about the quintessentially American interrelationship between educational philosophy and educational practice.

EDUCATION AND THE
CONSERVATIVE FOUNDATIONS

Leslie Lenkowsky
James Piereson

ONE OF THE MOST SIGNIFICANT DEVELOPMENTS in American life over the past half-century has been the rise of conservatism from a marginal intellectual movement to its status today as the nation's most influential political doctrine. In the 1950s, conservatism barely existed at all, either as an intellectual or as a political force. In the preface to *The Liberal Imagination,* Lionel Trilling wrote in 1950 that conservatism in America was mainly an impulse rather than a coherent set of ideas; it expressed itself, as he said, in "irritable mental gestures which seek to resemble ideas" (1950, p. vii). Conservatism was thus unable to pose any genuine challenge to the tradition of liberalism that shaped the mental landscape of the nation. Yet by the 1980s, conservatism had developed a body of ideas and a network of institutions that allowed it to challenge liberalism as the governing philosophy of the nation. By the turn of the millennium, it might be said to have replaced liberalism in that role.

The rise of conservatism as a political force was accompanied by the development of a distinctive conservative philanthropy, which over the same decades traversed a similar path from the political wilderness to broad acceptance and influence. While conservative efforts in philanthropy certainly existed in the 1950s and before, they were subject to some of the same strictures that Trilling and others had leveled against conservative political thought. The challenge to conservative philanthropy in these years grew from the fact that institutional philanthropy in the United States had a liberal pedigree, originating early in the twentieth century out of the Progressive idea that social problems could be mended through expert knowledge placed in the service of government. The momentum gained by liberal reform through the Progressive and New Deal periods gave further legitimacy to liberal philanthropy to the point where philanthropy itself was identified with liberalism—or at least with reform guided by expert knowledge.

In this political setting, conservative philanthropists, much like conservative thinkers, had great difficulty developing compelling strategies or ideas that might form the basis of collaboration with influential institutions or individuals. It was only when the reform tradition began to move into new and somewhat unpopular directions in the late 1960s, and when conservative ideas began to make inroads into national politics that conservative philanthropists were able to identify strategies that would allow them to compete for influence with the liberal foundations.

Conservative philanthropy, both in general and as it relates to education, might therefore be divided roughly into two historical periods: first, the years from around 1950 to the mid-1970s, when conservative ideas and themes worked against the grain of the broader political culture, and, second, the period from the mid-1970s to the present, when conservative ideas gained influence nationally and when there emerged a correspondingly influential conservative philanthropy.

During the first period, conservative efforts in education developed out of two philosophical camps—the traditionalists and the classical liberals—who, despite some differences in approach, were often funded by the same philanthropists. In the more recent period, leading up to today, conservative philanthropy was reshaped and redefined through the influence of neoconservatism—a tendency in contemporary thought that did not exist in the 1950s. Through their association with prominent neoconservatives such as Irving Kristol, Norman Podhoretz, Michael Novak, and others, conservatively inclined foundations were able to develop their own philanthropic vision that eventually enabled them to chart an independent path to intellectual influence.

Throughout this period, the conservative philanthropies have maintained a consistent interest in the field of education. Indeed, much like the Progressives of an earlier day, conservatives in the postwar era plainly understood that education was a battleground on which competing philosophies fought for influence. The liberals and Progressives, however, operated with some clear advantages because the educational system was, more or less, a fortress they had themselves erected. Conservatives, operating as outsiders in this realm, were never in a strong position to implement their ideas, sound and thoughtful though they may have been. Yet for this very reason, the conservatives were perhaps more free to develop insightful crit-icisms of the status quo and to develop ideas for change that it was never in the interest of insiders to consider.

What, then, did the conservative philanthropies seek to accomplish in education over these many decades? What broad ideas and preoccupa-tions guided their efforts? What kinds of programs did they fund? What strategies did they follow? Where did they succeed, and where did they fail? It is possible now, looking back over a half-century of work, to offer some tentative answers to these questions.

Conservative Philanthropy, 1950–1970s

Right-of-center philanthropy in the early postwar period was shaped more by an interest in classical liberalism than in conservatism as it is widely understood today. The major individuals and organizations were the Volker Fund of Kansas City, the Earhart and Relm Foundations of Ann Arbor, the Liberty Fund and the Lilly Endowment of Indianapolis, and individual busi-ness figures such as Jasper Crane of DuPont, A. E. Hutchinson of Chrysler, Henry Weaver of General Motors, Roger Milliken of the South Carolina tex-tile family, and Anthony Fisher, a British entrepreneur who would go on to start a series of free-market think tanks in Great Britain, Canada, and the United States. These donors had but modest resources at their command. At their peak level of giving in the early 1960s, they made combined donations of perhaps $3 million to $4 million per year, as compared to the $300 mil-lion per year donated by the Ford Foundation alone during this period. Yet their giving was highly focused and guided by clear philosophical concerns.

The main intellectual influence on these philanthropists was F. A. Hayek's *The Road to Serfdom,* published in Britain in 1944 and in the United States the following year. Hayek's book was an articulate call to battle against socialism, which appeared at that time as an irresistible force that would soon overwhelm Great Britain and the other European democracies, perhaps even the United States. *The Road to Serfdom,* which was later listed in surveys as one of the most influential books of the twen-tieth century, caused a sensation when it appeared, provoking reviews by such eminent figures as John Maynard Keynes and George Orwell. No one at that time had dared to make the case against socialism with such audacious clarity and bluntness. For this reason, Hayek's book emerged as a rallying point for those on both sides of the Atlantic who had mis-givings about the advance of socialism and the welfare state.

Hayek advanced two broad propositions, the first highly pessimistic and the second somewhat hopeful. Socialism, he argued, inevitably leads to tyranny in all its forms—the paradigmatic case being Hitler's Germany, which, Hayek reminded his readers, grew out of the concept of national socialism. The effort to bring all property and economic life under the control of the state must eventually lead to efforts to control political and religious freedoms, too. The welfare state, which some saw as a compromise between socialism and market capitalism, was not, in truth, an alternative to socialism because it would have led, step-by-step, to the very same destination. The antidote to socialism, according to Hayek, was to be found in the revival of classical liberalism as it had been developed by earlier thinkers like Locke, Hume, Adam Smith, Burke, John Stuart Mill, and the authors of the American Constitution. This tradition, which had been so influential in the first part of the nineteenth century, had been eclipsed by the end of the century by socialist and welfare-statist doctrines that had won the support of intellectuals.

Hayek thus pointed to the important role of ideas in shaping political events and also to the influence of intellectuals in modern societies. Socialism, he said, had emerged as a powerful force, not because the people wanted it but because the intellectuals promoted it. It appeared, therefore, that the proponents of liberty would have to engage in a battle of ideas to convince thoughtful people that socialism, despite its utopian ideals, was in fact a recipe for tyranny. In a 1949 essay, "The Intellectuals and Socialism," Hayek set forth a long-term strategy for building a movement of thinkers that might, in time, challenge the appeal of socialism and begin to restore the forgotten tradition of classical liberalism.

Hayek's writings guided conservative philanthropy by establishing both its strategies and long-run objectives. If the ultimate objective was to restore individual liberty to its rightful place as the fundamental political ideal, then the means of doing so would have to involve the restoration of older traditions, both in philosophy and in education. Progressive theories of education (John Dewey's education for democracy, for example) were part and parcel of the contemporary movements that had eclipsed classical liberalism. Hayek's analysis thus suggested two complementary directions for philanthropic funding: one rooted in conservatism and one in classic liberalism.

In the field of K–12 education, conservative donors took the lead in funding the back-to-basics movement that took shape in the 1950s as a reaction to Progressivism in the schools. This movement was led by traditionalists, rather than by classical liberals as such; it was a loose collection of academics, intellectuals, and educators, held together by the belief that the purpose of education is intellectual training in the basic disciplines of mathematics, science, history, and languages. They attacked the Progressive nostrums of "life adjustment" and "functional education," which sought to give students guidance in such nonacademic areas as family life, use of leisure time, health, and occupational skills. The traditionalists claimed that such pursuits diverted students from the main goal of education, which was to seek genuine knowledge and understanding. They wanted to return to earlier, more classical conceptions of what children should know and jettison the various diversions from serious study that increasingly filled up the day in the modern school, as exposed by James Bryant Conant (1959) and others.

The traditionalists, moreover, vehemently denied the contention that democratic education—that is, the education of large numbers of students from many backgrounds and cultures—required the watering down of curricula and the abandonment of excellence as an objective for American schools. They asserted instead that, in keeping with the promise of equality in the Declaration of Independence, all students must be presumed capable of learning at a high level; they went further to cite Jefferson, Franklin, and other founding fathers to support their claim that a political regime based on individual liberty demanded highly educated citizens. Here was one obvious place where the concerns of the traditionalists intersected with those of the classical liberals.

Among the most articulate of the traditionalists was Arthur Bestor, professor of history at the University of Illinois and, later, at the University of Washington, who in the early 1950s, produced two notable broadsides against American education: *Educational Wastelands: The Retreat from Learning in Our Public Schools* (1953) and *The Restoration of Learning: A Program for Redeeming the Unfulfilled Promise of American Education* (1955). Bestor (1953) attacked Progressive education as "regressive education" that pointed students away from the higher achievements of civilization. "A student today needs an *education*," he wrote, "not a headful of helpful hints" (p. 64). For Bestor, a genuine education meant a liberal education—one that enlarged and disciplined the mind for intellectual purposes, irrespective of vocational or professional interests or aspirations.

Bestor was an important figure, not only because of his writings but also because he was one of the founders (and the first president) of the Council for Basic Education—a tax-exempt educational foundation established in 1955 to carry the torch for traditionalism in education. Bestor was joined in this effort by such intellectual luminaries as Clifton Fadiman, Mortimer Adler, Jacques Barzun, Mortimer Smith, and others of varied political views, united mainly by a concern for rigor and substance in American education. Yet financial support for the organization came mainly from foundations and corporations identified with a more conservative approach to public affairs. Seed funding, for example, came in the form of a six-figure dona-tion from the Volker Fund; other sustaining donations were made by the Lilly Endowment and the Relm and Earhart Foundations, as well as from corporate sources like General Electric and Milliken. This would prove to be the pattern of support over the fifty-year life of the Council (it disbanded in 2004). Liberal foundations like Ford, Rockefeller, and Carnegie expressed little interest in the Council in particular and in the traditionalist cause in general (and the Council's stalwarts, notably Barzun, criticized them in return for using their money in ways that damaged education). Neverthe-less, the Council developed into the most influential advocate for a return to basics in American education, not to be surpassed until the 1980s.

Though anti-Progressive in outlook and favoring a return to older prac-tices in education, the traditionalists were not in all cases conservatives in politics—a point that underlines the broad-mindedness of the Council's conservative funders. Bestor, for example, who grew up in the intellectual atmosphere of the Chautauqua Society, where his father served as director for three decades, was sympathetic to utopian socialism and favored uni-versal public education to enable all students to learn at the highest levels (Weltman, 2000). Similarly inclined were Adler and his associates in the Great Books movement, as well as the bulk of Harvard's faculty, which in 1946 approved a new curriculum in general education that sought to implement a vision of liberal education. For many educational thinkers, a broad education in history, politics, and philosophy was an antidote to the prejudices of religion and nationality that (they felt) animated the typ-ical American student in the 1950s and gave rise to anti-democratic politi-cal impulses, such as McCarthyism.

In the field of higher education, the conservative philanthropists of the time were able to express their convictions in the direction of both classical liberalism and traditionalism. The Volker Fund and the Relm and Earhart Foundations were especially active in promoting the study of market-oriented economics at prominent universities. The Volker Fund, for ex-ample, provided support for Hayek's appointment as professor of social and moral sciences (Adam Smith had been a professor of moral philoso-phy at Glasgow University) in the Committee on Social Thought at the University of Chicago, and also for an appointment for Hayek's mentor, Ludwig von Mises, at New York University. Volker and the other donors also provided generous support over the years for the "Chicago School" of economics, led most prominently by Milton Friedman, George Stigler, and Gary Becker. They also funded fellowships for hundreds of graduate students in economics and in the allied fields of history and government, large numbers of whom eventually secured academic teaching positions.

The same foundations subsidized the Institute for Humane Studies—a nonprofit group whose purpose was to promote an appreciation for the tradition of classical liberalism on college campuses. It was largely through the efforts of these donors that this tradition was kept alive during a period from the 1950s into the 1970s, when it was at low ebb in terms of academic and intellectual influence, and when the allure of central planning, socialism, and an expanded welfare state was at its highest. These donors thus helped to promote an important school of thought until it might be brought forward again as an alternative to collectivist approaches that began to look less attractive in the 1970s.

A somewhat different kind of critique was developed by the youthful William F. Buckley Jr.—an outspoken conservative who emerged as the best-known proponent of the traditionalist view as it applied to higher education. His first book, *God and Man at Yale*, published in 1951, took aim at his alma mater for abandoning the traditions of religion, virtue, and individual liberty upon which it was founded and for imposing in their place an educational philosophy that he described as "statist" and "atheistic." While acknowledging that professors had every right to present liberal and left-wing doctrines in their courses, he wondered why countervailing views (such as Hayek's) were not also presented to provide balance and perspective. Buckley, in tracing the advance of collectivism, echoed Hayek's diagnosis that it had succeeded by capturing the imagination of intellectuals and academics such as those on the Yale faculty.

Buckley's critique departed from those of some other traditionalists, such as Adler, Bestor, and members of Harvard's faculty, in that he called for a return to religion and moral education at Yale, while the others tended to see in liberal education a pedagogical replacement for the religious doctrines that formerly shaped the college curriculum. These two versions, the one conservative and the other liberal, thus represented the contending poles of the traditionalist argument.

In his book, Buckley urged alumni and trustees to take action to return the institution to its founding ideals—a call that generated criticism from many who saw in it an intrusion on the academic freedom of the faculty. This in some ways reinforced Buckley's point, for one of his main complaints was that the faculty had engineered a takeover of the institution from the trustees and alumni, whose responsibility it was to maintain its traditions. By invoking academic freedom, Yale's defenders implicitly acknowledged that the university's direction had been set more by the faculty than the trustees. Such a development, however, was hardly unique to Yale, for in colleges and universities across the country the faculties by the 1940s had begun wresting effective control of their institutions from meddlesome trustees. In this sense, Buckley had mainly succeeded in highlighting developments that would prove most difficult to reverse or to undo.

Yet Buckley, effective controversialist that he was, had succeeded in calling attention to the leverage over higher education that modern liberalism (or Progressivism) had managed to build over the decades. Buckley, with the assistance of Frank Chodorov, persuaded several conservative philanthropists to put up funds to institutionalize his critique of the modern academy. Thus in 1953, with the assistance of donors like the Volker Fund, Pierre Goodrich of Indianapolis, Lynde and Harry Bradley of Milwaukee, and J. Howard Pew of Pittsburgh, Buckley founded the Intercollegiate Society of Individualists (later renamed the Intercollegiate Studies Institute and known as ISI) to advance a traditionalist program at colleges and universities across the country. The ISI's programs made the positive case for liberal learning but also the negative case against those secular doctrines, from unconstrained academic freedom to Keynesian economics, which had gained control of the modern university. Neither Buckley nor the ISI succeeded in changing the course of the liberal academy, but they did raise a flag that won the support of conservative donors who would proceed in subsequent decades to underwrite other conservative causes.

The traditionalist arguments, compelling and variously textured as they were, may have won many of the debates of the time, especially in elementary and secondary education, but there is little doubt that they lost the larger war for control over the schools and the colleges. Despite endless campaigns to strengthen curricula and to raise standards in the schools, the trends in education over subsequent decades continued to move these institutions further in the direction of practicality, vocationalism, and experimentation and away from the cherished ideals of the traditionalists, whether of the liberal or conservative stripe.

Indeed, many of the Progressive nostrums that were on their way out by the 1950s were replaced in the 1960s and thereafter by newer and, in some cases, even more radical versions of the same underlying impulse. *Open classroom, experimental education, relevance, diversity,* and *multiculturalism*—these and other such terms became the catchwords of the education establishments in the last three decades of the century. These movements disparaged traditionalist formulas, albeit on somewhat novel grounds. While earlier traditionalist ideals were rejected for imposing unrealistic demands on students, they were now attacked as outdated and stale, undemocratic, or elitist. Contemporary reformers increasingly viewed the school, the college, and the graduate school as agents of change and reform and, occasionally, of revolution.

Yet for all this, traditionalism remains an enduring feature of conservative discussions of reform and renewal of American education. There is, indeed, a surprising continuity in traditionalist arguments going back to the writings of Bestor, Buckley, and others and moving forward to those of critics like Allan Bloom, E. D. Hirsch, and Diane Ravitch.

The case against fads and frills in the school curriculum is today made in much the same way as it was before, as is the case for liberal education. Conservatives today attack the leftward drift of the universities, along with the monopoly of control exercised by faculty, in ways not all that different from Buckley's indictment in *God and Man at Yale*. What is different today is that, unlike the 1950s, all these causes have gravitated to the conservative side of the political spectrum. Political liberals like Bestor and Adler who embrace the traditionalist cause in education are today few and far between and often reluctant to argue too strenuously for it. The partisan divides of the 1980s led to a drawing of sides that drove most of the remaining traditionalists out of the liberal camp. Writers like Bloom, Hirsch, and Ravitch would have been called liberals a generation ago; today they are called conservatives. Traditionalism thus endures but now as an integral part of a conservative view of education.

Conservative Philanthropy, 1970s to the Present

A second phase of conservative philanthropy took shape in the mid-1970s, largely in response to the upheavals of the 1960s, which, especially in the world of education, had left the traditionalists and the classical liberals even further from the mainstream than they were when the decade had begun.

Much as the earlier donors had looked to Hayek for intellectual guidance, the foundations involved in this newer campaign looked for intellectual direction to the neoconservatives. The editors, writers, and academics that operated under the umbrella of neoconservatism, while respectful of Hayek and the classical liberals, looked at the world from a different perspective. Many had gravitated across the political spectrum from the left, and in doing so had been influenced by figures like Trilling, Orwell, and Raymond Aron—intellectuals of Hayek's generation who focused on totalitarianism as a moral evil rather than as a threat merely to liberty. While many neoconservatives traced their intellectual lineage back to eighteenth-century liberals like Adam Smith and Edmund Burke, they emphasized more the moral dimensions in their thought and especially their conviction that virtue was an indispensable condition for liberty. Thus the neoconservatives looked beyond free markets to the political, religious, and cultural factors that were also critical to the orderly functioning of a liberal society.

The neoconservatives also brought with them a strikingly different line of argument in their attacks on post-1960s liberalism. The political world of the 1970s looked much different from the one that had so worried Hayek in 1944. Instead of leading to collectivism, as Hayek had predicted, the welfare state had produced fragmentation, disorder, group conflict, broken families, educational failure, and governmental dysfunction. The neoconservatives did not oppose the welfare state as such; rather, they opposed the antinomian philosophy they viewed as shaping it—a philosophy that disregarded traditional middle-class ideals such as work, individual responsibility, and obligations to family and community. The neoconservatives, moreover, challenged the policies and practices of the welfare state not on a priori grounds (for example, that they exceeded the legitimate powers of government) but in terms of the practical argument that they had produced undesirable and unacceptable consequences. Here the neoconservatives opened a door into the world of social science research that would prove effective in debates over education.

A seminal influence was the pathbreaking study, *Equality of Educational Opportunity*, by sociologist James Coleman. Released in 1966, its analysis showed, much to the disappointment of advocates of greater federal funding of elementary and secondary education, that increased money was not likely to have much effect in improving educational achievement, especially among students from disadvantaged groups. Far more influential were students' families and peer groups, as well as their own sense of efficacy. To neoconservatives like Kristol, Daniel Patrick Moynihan, Nathan Glazer, and James Q. Wilson, the Coleman report suggested that, measured by the results they were producing, American schools were not doing well, nor would they be improved by most of the ideas then under discussion, such as remedial programs, smaller classes, and better facilities. Instead, what would make a difference was a change in attitudes toward education by parents and young people in the direction of valuing learning and hard work and a corresponding adjustment in schools toward emphasizing academic rigor and self-discipline.

To one degree or another, perhaps a dozen or so foundations embraced this analysis and supported the neoconservative campaign. The most prominent were the Smith Richardson Foundation, The John M. Olin Foundation, the Scaife Trusts, and, beginning in 1985, the Lynde and Harry Bradley Foundation. Some of the older right-of-center foundations, especially the Earhart Foundation, also provided assistance. The assets of these foundations ranged from around $100 million (Olin, Earhart) to $500 million

(Bradley), and their combined annual expenditures at their peak did not amount to much more than $100 million per year. The conservatives were thus forced to craft an ambitious philanthropic strategy to change education, with but modest resources at their disposal.

The result was what might be called an "elite" strategy—that is, to focus the limited funds of the foundations on journals and magazines, academic programs, and research initiatives that would place their ideas in front of an elite audience of journalists, academics, professionals, and policymakers. Populist strategies such as community organizing, launching voter registration drives, and conducting advertising campaigns were deemed too expensive and cumbersome in relation to the resources available. Such strategies were also thought to be relatively ineffective in the context of the increasing "professionalization" of reform, especially in education, where expert knowledge and elite opinion had always been influential, but with the growth of educational research in the 1970s and the creation of new organizations (including, ultimately, a cabinet-level department in Washington) had become more so. Despite an on-again-off-again relationship with Al Shanker and the leadership of the emergent American Federation of Teachers, unionization also presented an obstacle to conservative efforts at the grassroots by contesting the view that American schools were in decline and dominating educational politics. But a significant body of new scholars was looking more critically at education, including many researchers not traditionally identified with conservative causes, making the elite strategy seem like a sensible approach to the new conservative foundations.

In this they were, ironically, following a formula that had earlier served the liberal foundations in good stead. Although they veered in a decidedly activist direction in the 1960s, supporting, for example, ill-founded efforts at community control of the schools in racially charged places such as the Ocean Hill–Brownsville district of New York City, the liberal philanthropies taught the conservatives that they had to build their own networks of research, litigation, and advocacy organizations if they hoped to advance their ideas on the national scene. Led most prominently by McGeorge Bundy of the Ford Foundation, the liberal foundations had helped to create a new kind of policy process in which federal courts, regulatory bodies, and blue-ribbon commissions played key roles. Such institutions, by virtue of their methods of decision making, granted unprecedented leverage to research organizations and advocacy groups. By taking such lessons to heart, a handful of modestly endowed foundations began in the mid-1970s to invest funds in a systematic way to create their own institutional networks to advance the broad concepts of limited government, federalism, free markets, educational reform, anticommunism, and national security. As a result, the various conflicts and disagreements that roiled the political process were translated into the world of philanthropy.

In conceiving and carrying out such a strategy, the leaders of the conservative foundations looked to the field of education as an obvious target of opportunity. It was plainly understood that this was an area, from kindergarten to graduate study, which was under the overwhelming influence of liberal thinking as a result of decades of Progressive-style reform. Liberals, as a consequence of their long-running dominance, now represented the educational establishment, which opened the way for conservatives to play the role of critics and to claim the mantle of reform. Conservatives could point to weaknesses and failures in the educational system, and thus call for changes in the organization of schools and for more rigorous standards in curricula, the promotion of students, and the training of teachers. Because educational policy in the K–12 area had been centralized in the states and the federal government as a result of court decisions and Great Society legislation, the conservative message could be disseminated to key decision makers at modest expense without having to take it individually to the thousands of school districts across the nation.

One direction this effort took was promoting alternatives to public schooling—an approach that came to be known as "choice in education." This was a long-standing goal of the classical liberal wing of the conservative movement. In his widely read book of the early 1960s, *Capitalism and Freedom* (1962), Milton Friedman argued for ending government control of schools, not because of concerns about what students were learning (though he might have had them), but to eliminate waste and inefficiency. Later in the decade, educational choice was embraced by left-of-center reformers, such as John Coons and Christopher Jencks, mostly as a way of redressing inequalities in school finance by allocating funds on a per-student basis rather than by schools and districts. In the early 1970s, as one of its antipoverty efforts, the federal government even underwrote an experimental school voucher program in Alum Rock, California, which produced inconclusive results.[1]

The interest of the second wave of conservative foundations developed along a different path. Not long after the publication of the Coleman report, the Council for Basic Education produced a study aimed at refuting Coleman's central finding that schools could not overcome the disadvantages of families and friends (Wilson, 1990). It did so by profiling a number of schools that seemed to be doing exactly that. Further support came from other (and more elaborate) research, including an analysis by Coleman himself that concluded that Catholic schools were having more success at educating the children of the inner-city poor than public schools did. What appeared to make the difference was that more effective schools had more rigorous academic standards, required more homework, enforced stricter discipline, had better principals and teachers, and possessed other characteristics for which educational traditionalists had long advocated.

The culmination of this research came in a book, *Politics, Markets and America's Schools* (Chubb and Moe, 1990), that was funded largely by the Olin and Bradley Foundations, but published by the Brookings Institution—a think tank with a left-leaning reputation. Its authors, John Chubb and Terry Moe, two social scientists who were not identified with conservative politics, examined the relationship between student achievement and educational governance. Their conclusion was that schools were more likely to be effective when political and bureaucratic controls were relaxed and market-like methods of accountability, such as the need to compete for students, were employed.

This study, which attracted considerable attention in elite newspapers and professional journals, came at a time when for a variety of reasons, reformers were beginning to experiment with new ways of organizing schools. In Minnesota, a former teacher and administrator, Joe Nathan, was developing the idea of "charter schools"—publicly funded but independently governed schools that would free their teaching staffs from a variety of rules and regulations (Nathan, 1996). In New York City, a district superintendent, Seymour Fliegel, was promoting the idea of "alternative" schools in East Harlem—minischools within larger ones that would embody distinctive approaches to education (Fliegel, 1993). In Wisconsin, Polly Williams, a state legislator who worked closely with the Bradley Foundation despite having supported Jesse Jackson's presidential campaigns, introduced a bill to create a voucher program that would enable the predominantly black and low-income children in Milwaukee's underperforming public schools to switch to private ones.

Chubb and Moe's research not only lent scholarly legitimacy to these efforts but also spurred a flowering of them, with support coming from conservative philanthropists that were joined, in time, with more centrist ones. Usually with the help of right-of-center think tanks and advocacy groups, new voucher programs were established or proposed in Ohio, Florida, Indiana, Pennsylvania, California, the District of Columbia, and other jurisdictions. Wealthy businessmen, such as Peter Flanigan in New York (who was also a trustee of the Olin Foundation), Patrick Rooney in Indianapolis, and John Walton in California, along with foundations such as the Bradley Foundation, created funds to increase substantially the scholarships available to the children of low-income parents who wanted to enroll them in private and religious schools. Aided by backing from moderate Democrats and, occasionally, teachers' unions, the number of charter schools grew rapidly, reaching over 3,600 in forty states by February 2006 (Center for Education Reform, National Charter School Data). Conservative foundations, including newer ones, such as the Walton Family Foundation and the Thomas B. Fordham Foundation, played key roles in providing seed money for this expansion, as did for-profit companies, which were able to establish a significant presence in the K–12 educational market as a result of the choice movement.

Nonetheless, the proportion of students in non-public schools (including charter schools) has not greatly changed since the Chubb and Moe book appeared (National Center for Education Statistics, *The Condition of Education 2005*, 2005). And professional and political opposition, as well as legal obstacles, to the use of vouchers and even to charter schools continues to be strong. But the idea of creating alternatives to public schooling, especially for low-income and minority children, is no longer a small and marginalized part of the American debate over what to do about education. Research on the merits of broadening educational choice is increasing, as are the numbers of advocacy and legal defense groups, technical assistance programs, and other elements of an organizational infrastructure for non-public schools. Most of this has been the work of conservative philanthropy.

The choice movement, however, was just one prong of the strategy that conservative foundations took toward elementary and secondary education. Just as promoting vouchers and other alternatives to public schools grew out of the classical liberal side of conservative thinking, the second approach resonated with traditionalist views about the need to restore a more rigorous curriculum in American education. As in the 1950s, many who supported such ideas were not political conservatives at all, but in the changed educational politics of the 1980s, they were able to have more of an impact.

What produced this change was a 1983 report issued by the National Commission on Excellence in Education—a commission created by the U.S. Department of Education, titled *A Nation at Risk*. "The educational foundations of our society," it warned, "are presently being eroded by a rising tide of mediocrity that threatens our very future as a Nation and a people." (p. 5) While avoiding placing blame, the report's findings and recommendations—better teaching of the "New Basics," (p. 70) "more rigorous and measurable standards," (p. 73) more school time devoted to instruction, and more teachers with "competence in an academic discipline"(p. 76)— pointed squarely toward Progressive education as the source of the problem. Even worse, perhaps, these were not the views of conservatives brought into government by the election of Ronald Reagan; rather, they came from a group consisting of distinguished college presidents, business leaders, and educators whose work was embraced and publicized by a secretary of education, Terrell H. Bell, who had himself been a former superintendent of public instruction in Utah before coming to Washington.

Although conservative foundations were not directly involved in the commission's activities, its report endorsed what their grantees had been saying for several years. Indeed, the commission's name was similar to that of one of the most influential beneficiaries of conservative philanthropy—the Educational Excellence Network. Established in 1981 by two prolific scholars—Chester E. Finn Jr., of Vanderbilt University, and Ravitch, of Columbia's Teachers College, with support from the Olin and Andrew Mellon Foundations—it was a loose network of, at most, two thousand people: scholars, practitioners, policymakers, business leaders, and parents—who were concerned about the state of the nation's schools (Finn, 1996). They shared the belief that higher standards, improved teaching, better tests, and "results-based accountability" were needed; they eventually supported the choice movement, as well, as a means of producing the organizational changes required for curricular reform.

A Nation at Risk gave these views greater legitimacy and visibility. It also paved the way for others to get involved. William J. Bennett, who had begun speaking and writing publicly on education (especially the problems faced by minorities) as executive director of the Smith Richardson Foundation–supported National Humanities Center, replaced Bell as secretary of education in 1985, bringing Finn with him as an assistant secretary, and launched a reform effort along traditionalist lines, working closely with conservative philanthropists (Finn, 1991). Not long afterwards, a University of Virginia English professor, E. D. Hirsch, wrote a surprising best-seller, *Cultural Literacy: What Every American Needs to Know* (1987), which contended that schools had placed the teaching of abstract theories ahead of concrete facts, with the result that children were becoming ignorant of important ideas in American history, literature, and other fields. With backing from conservative and middle-of-the-road grantmakers, he created the Core Knowledge Foundation to work with local schools on changing their curricula.

At conservative think tanks, Denis Doyle wrote about and assisted state officials who were trying to "take charge" of their educational systems, including Tennessee's governor Lamar Alexander (who would follow Bennett into the U.S. Department of Education). Doyle also began a series of collaborations with prominent business leaders, who saw failing schools as a threat to the nation's economy. Two of those leaders—Louis V. Gerstner Jr., head of RJR Nabisco and later the IBM Corporation, and David Kearns, chief executive officer of Xerox—would go on to launch their own organizations, aimed at raising standards and changing how schools worked.[2]

By the end of the 1980s, a solid consensus had emerged about what needed to be done to improve American education. That consensus would have at least been recognizable—and not the least bit surprising—to the traditionalists of the 1950s. Moreover, it had attracted support from some unexpected quarters, such as The Pew Charitable Trusts (which had been drifting away from the conservative camp for many years; Pew, led by program officer Robert B. Schwartz, underwrote projects to establish statewide academic standards and other reforms) and middle-of-the-road Democrats, such as Arkansas governor Bill Clinton. Conservative philanthropists continued to make grants aimed at holding schools more accountable for teaching students "the basics" and raising the level of their achievement, as well as improving teacher training. But increasingly, state governments and Washington took on the onus of doing so, most conspicuously with the passage of the No Child Left Behind Act in 2002; although their efforts may have varied considerably in quality and rigor, they reflected an insistence on fostering educational excellence that owed a great deal to the critiques of American schools, supported for over four decades by conservative foundations.

Yet if not as dominant in the practice of education as it once was, Progressivism remained well-entrenched in schools of education, which produced a steady stream of proposals for new kinds of schools and programs built on Deweyite principles—studies casting doubt on the claims of traditionalists and the choice movement, and activists eager to challenge "high-stakes testing" and other elements of the new reform consensus.

To conservative philanthropists, this was part of a much larger problem: the dominance of left-wing ideas in higher education. Following the campus upheavals of the 1960s, the trends a young William F. Buckley Jr. had decried at Yale not only continued but broadened to an extraordinarily wide range of both campuses and areas of academic life, except, to a degree, the sciences and engineering. With faculties firmly in charge of curricular affairs, trustees and administrators could do little about this, even if they had wanted to (which many did not). Furthermore, driven by a desire for the novel and unconventional, scholarly disciplines embraced radical and often controversial theories and topics of study, while prodded by interest groups and liberal foundations, colleges and universities created new degrees in fields that seemed to reflect a political as much as an academic agenda, such as women's and African American studies.

These developments did not go unchallenged by philanthropists. In 1973, in a speech to the Committee for Corporate Support of American Universities, industrialist David Packard, noting the antibusiness hostility to be found in many parts of higher education, called on philanthropists to direct their support to "those schools and departments which are strong and which also contribute in some specific way to our individual companies, or to the general welfare of our free-enterprise system."[3] Although *The New York Times* and leading university and foundation heads were critical, Packard was hardly alone in his thinking. Two years earlier, future Supreme Court Justice Lewis F. Powell Jr. voiced similar sentiments in a widely circulated memo to business leaders (confidential memorandum from Lewis F. Powell Jr. to Eugene B. Sydnor Jr., Aug. 23, 1971).[4]

And two years later, Henry Ford II, in announcing his decision to resign as a trustee of the Ford Foundation, chastised it for being insufficiently supportive of the economic system "that makes the foundation possible" (Orosz, 2002, p. 97). In a best-selling book, *A Time for Truth,* written after he had stepped down as secretary of the treasury in 1977, financier William E. Simon urged foundations and corporations to use their resources to sustain a new "counter-intelligentsia," less inclined to reject capitalism in favor of collectivism (1978, p. 229).

That was precisely what the second wave of conservative foundations tried to do. (After leaving government, Simon himself had taken the presidency of one of them—The John M. Olin Foundation.) They pursued two principal strategies: encouraging competition in ideas, both inside and outside higher education, and exposing the political biases of faculty, administrators, and scholarly disciplines. The first has had considerable influence on college and university life; the second has had less, though it has not gone unnoticed.

Not surprisingly, in view of the probusiness outlook of conservative philanthropists, economics and the law were the fields receiving attention first. With the award of the Nobel Prize in economics to Hayek in 1974 and Friedman in 1976, classical liberal economics was again coming into intellectual fashion. All the major conservative foundations established programs to identify and assist rising scholars, including Harvard's Martin Feldstein and Stanford's Michael Boskin; both eventually became top White House economic policy advisers. Research centers, such as the National Bureau of Economic Research (which Feldstein headed) and the Center for the Study of American Business at Washington University (directed by Murray Weidenbaum, who chaired President Reagan's Council of Economic Advisers), received support, not only to underwrite studies but also fellowships for graduate students.

The revival of classical liberal economics was also under way in law schools, where scholars such as Chicago's Richard Posner, Yale's Robert Bork, and Harvard's Stephen Breyer sought to apply the tools of economic analysis to a variety of regulatory and administrative issues. Others, most notably Rochester's Henry Manne, developed institutes on "law and economics" for practitioners, such as federal judges. Conservative foundations subsidized their costs, as well as provided funding for scholarly research programs. In 1982, as neo-Marxist doctrines like "critical legal studies" were gaining popularity, when a group of conservative and libertarian law school students sought to create a nationwide association to ensure that the "principles of limited government" received a "fair hearing" on campus, conservative philanthropists assisted them in starting the Federalist Society, which now includes over 5,000 students at 180 American Bar Association–accredited schools, including the twenty most highly ranked (Federalist Society for Law and Public Policy Studies, 2006).

However, economics and law were not the only academic fields that aroused the interest of the conservative foundations. In addition to criticizing them for their animus toward business, Packard had chided higher education for its Vietnam War–inspired opposition to the military, especially the expulsion of ROTC from several major campuses (Packard, 1973). Conservative foundations addressed this by funding university-based scholars and research centers that sought to revive an earlier tradition, epitomized by the young Henry Kissinger's programs at Harvard in the 1950s, of serious academic study of military strategy. Ironically, the first beneficiary was a Democrat, Samuel Huntington; he had recently returned to Harvard after serving a tour as a national security adviser to President Carter, whose administration's foreign policy was much derided by the Right. But as a result of Huntington's program and of others supported by conservative philanthropists, a new generation of civilian strategists began to emerge, many of whom have already established themselves at schools such as Princeton and Johns Hopkins or held prominent positions in government and the media.

From Adam Smith to Friedrich Hayek, proponents of classical liberal ideas have also appreciated the importance of moral philosophy; so did the conservative foundations. Of particular concern was growing opposition on many college campuses, in the name of multicultural education, to requirements to study the canonical texts of Western civilization. (At Stanford, Jesse Jackson led students in chanting, "Hey, hey, ho, ho, Western civ has got to go.") Starting early in the 1980s, they underwrote centers, led by scholars such as Allan Bloom at Chicago and Harvey Mansfield at Harvard, that aimed to encourage teaching and research about the founding principles of American democracy. These programs have provided a model for a new generation of similar organizations, often supported by conservative alumni more than foundations, that are now at over a dozen schools, with perhaps as many as fifty more being planned.

In addition to fostering competition among ideas within higher education, conservative philanthropists promoted challenges from outside by contributing substantially to building a network of think tanks, located throughout the United States, which produce books, articles, and briefing papers on a wide range of topics. All of them, to some extent (and some of them to a large extent), drew on the academic world for research talent and staff members. While not adhering to academic standards for their analyses and publications, they market their work, not just to public officials and journalists but also for use in college and university classes; some of the studies even grew out of collaborations with university-based scholars, while others drew serious responses or stimulated research designed to prove them wrong, just as more traditional academic studies might have done. None of the think tanks has gone as far as the Brookings Institution once did and offered graduate degrees, but for many conservatives with academic training but no college or university home, they provided a base, with few teaching obligations, that was increasingly acceptable as an alternative or supplementary stop (such as for a sabbatical) in an intellectual career.

In some fields, such as economics and legal studies, the results of these investments by the conservative foundations seem clear (though, arguably, in view of the ebb and flow of scholarly discourse, changes in thinking might have occurred anyway). In others, their grants may have produced fine teaching or research programs but have had a limited effect on the quality of education at a particular institution or in a relevant discipline. Nor has the tide of radical scholarship and behavior at universities and colleges that provoked conservative efforts to build a "counter-intelligentsia" noticeably subsided. Nonetheless, if still too often unnoticed and occasionally scorned, conservative ideas now coexist (and sometimes, do even better than that) in the predominantly liberal world of the academy, giving students or faculty who wish to understand them more opportunities to do so than had been the case before conservative philanthropists started championing them (Piereson, 2005).

None of this came about as a result of any significant alterations in how universities were run. Although Buckley had called on alumni and trustees to regain control of the academy, they never did and rarely tried, at least not to advance conservative goals in higher education. (In one well-publicized episode, a major university chose to return a multimillion-dollar gift from an alumnus rather than initiate a program focused on Western civilization.[5]) Liberal faculty continued to rely on academic freedom, tenure, and other aspects of institutional governance to protect their educational and political views from challenges, while using speech codes and other devices to try to restrict the expression of ideas with which they disagreed. Indeed, to conservative philanthropists, despite their successes in influencing the direction of national policies on taxes, defense, and other areas since the 1980s, institutional change in higher education seemed a tougher task and a more distant prospect than it had thirty years earlier.

That was not for lack of effort. Conservative foundations supported numerous books on the problems of universities and colleges by writers such as Bloom, Roger Kimball (1990), Dinesh d'Souza (1991), and Peter Collier and David Horowitz (1990), some of which became nationwide best-sellers. They also underwrote a network of "alternative" student newspapers that exposed violations of academic standards, politicization of the curriculum, and dangerously laissez-faire attitudes toward student conduct on campus. Public interest law firms funded by conservative philanthropists waged a campaign against admissions quotas for minorities and efforts to suppress discussion of politically incorrect topics or the use of language deemed offensive by one or another aggrieved group.

In 1985, a group of faculty members from schools in the New York City area came together to form an organization aimed at fighting for greater "democracy" in higher education, by which they meant more openness to inquiry and debate, more meritocratic standards of hiring and promotion, and heightened vigilance against the introduction of partisan and special interest viewpoints in the curriculum. With support from the conservative foundations, it evolved into the National Association of Scholars, with chapters active in forty-seven states, territories, and the District of Columbia, plus Canada. A few years later, also with funding from conservative philanthropists, the American Council of Trustees and Alumni came into being to enlist board members and annual-fund donors in the effort at reforming colleges and universities. It was led by Lynne Cheney, who, as chair of the National Endowment for the Humanities, had been highly critical of the state of American education, but also included prominent liberals on its national board, such as former Colorado governor Richard Lamm, and Martin Peretz, editor-in-chief of *The New Republic*.

After a while, these organizations could point to a number of significant accomplishments. For example, on several occasions, they were able to mobilize effective opposition to promotion and tenure actions that seemed based more on political considerations than academic ones. A series of court cases resulted in a Supreme Court ruling that racial quotas for college and university admissions should be considered temporary measures to redress past discrimination.[6] An "academic bill of rights," developed by Horowitz and an organization called Students for Academic Freedom, which sought to protect student and faculty expression of politically controversial views, received a hearing in several state legislatures. And governing boards increasingly turned to conservative groups for advice on handling campus controversies or recommendations for filling administrative vacancies, and even on occasion chose some of those suggested.

Despite swimming against the powerful tides of vocationalism, diversity, and multiculturalism that have washed over the academic enterprise in recent decades, conservative philanthropists thus made some genuine gains in higher education. Most important, they have built networks of institutions, both on and off the campus, that are now in a position to nurture conservative talent, challenge the reigning orthodoxies in the academy, and put forward alternative ideas, whether drawn from market economics, the great works of Western civilization, the ideals of the founding fathers, or variants thereof.

Conservatives, however, did not delude themselves into thinking that the American university could be transformed anytime soon into the kind of educational oasis Buckley or Bloom desired. They understood, perhaps far better than others, the strong forces pushing the academic world toward the political left and the organizational inertia of higher education. Yet they also understood that, in the world of ideas, a movement could gain disproportionate influence even while being greatly outnumbered and outspent. Such a thought has guided conservative foundations as they have worked to make sure that their ideas were at least represented in campus debates and discussions. With nearly 17 million students now attending American colleges of one kind or another, combined with the fact that these institutions educate the future leaders of the nation, they may have had little choice if they wanted conservative ideas to be anything more than historical curiosities.

Lessons of Conservative Philanthropy

Though not everything they tried succeeded, and even those efforts fell short of revolutionizing American education, the record of conservative foundations is still impressive. With far fewer dollars to spend than other grantmakers interested in education and championing proposals that often were at odds with the views of the educational establishment as well as powerful political groups, they were nonetheless able to place their ideas on the reform agenda and sometimes even shape it.

As a result of their efforts, school curricula are now more likely to be geared to rigorous academic standards than they were two decades ago. Students more frequently have to demonstrate their ability to meet these standards on regular examinations that permit comparison of performance, not only between students but also among schools, school districts, and nationally. In many places, satisfactory results on these tests are required for promotion and even for graduation. For college-bound students, the demands are even greater, including a heavy load of "core courses" in subjects such as English, science, and mathematics. While meticulous, long-term research still needs to occur, the short-term results suggest that this mixture of higher standards and regular testing is producing a narrowing of the achievement gap between white and minority students (U.S. Department of Education, 2005).

Likewise, although debate still rages, the educational choice movement can claim to have had positive effects on scholastic achievement.[7] It has also spurred a new wave of school innovation, producing widely admired models such as the Knowledge Is Power Program (KIPP) and the Core Knowledge Schools, which are based on Hirsch's work. Long-discussed ideas, such as all-day and all-year classes, extensive use of technology, new ways of preparing teachers, and single-sex schools, are now being tried in these schools, most of which did not exist as recently as 1990. In all or parts of thirty states, parents now have opportunities to pick the public schools they want their children to attend, and in five, plus the District of Columbia, they can also select private schools, including religious ones. Over forty states have charter schools laws, half of which are rated "strong" because they relax a large number of the regulations governing public schools (Center for Education Reform Fast Facts, 2006).

In contrast to the dominance of Keynesian thinking through the 1960s, most students studying economics these days will get at least some exposure to classical liberal theories and concepts in one or another form; depending on the college or university they are attending, they may get a great deal. (Political science and related disciplines have also been influenced by the renewed attention to these ideas prompted by conservative funders.) And most law school curricula will feature courses on the application of economic theories to the law, taught from liberal as well as conservative perspectives. Membership in the Federalist Society has almost become a rite of passage for students of conservative and libertarian sympathies (and by the same token, a mark against those nominated for the judiciary in the minds of Democratic opponents).

In other respects, however, today's college students encounter a world that may be even more liberal and secular than the one young Buckley did in the 1950s. Unless they were at one of the handful of schools with centers devoted to examining American political or philosophical principles, they are likely to face faculties, especially in the humanities and the social sciences, who are overwhelmingly liberal in their politics (Rothman, Lichter, and Nevitte, 2005). (How much that matters in the classroom is another matter.) On the one hand, free speech codes, "diversity" programs, "sex weeks," and a variety of politically inspired majors are well entrenched, though occasionally challenged. On the other hand, conservative faculty members, students, and trustees now have a variety of organizations to turn to for advice and aid. And increasingly, a wide range of critics is questioning aspects of the quality of higher education, ranging from grade inflation to the declining proportion of American students prepared to do graduate work in mathematics and sciences; pressure is mounting to introduce "acceptable ways to measure student progress," as *The New York Times* put it.[8]

Not all of these developments are exclusively due to the work of the conservative foundations. But their efforts played an important role in making all of them possible and, sometimes, the principal one. How they did so offers several lessons for philanthropy.

One is that in the United States, perhaps because of its antiestablishment traditions, certain advantages accrue to those who criticize the status quo and call for reform and renewal of institutions. Ironically, because American education in the twentieth century was so indebted to liberal ideas and policies, conservative foundations greatly benefited by being able to position themselves as reformers and agents of change, especially after government reports, signed by leading educators, acknowledged that significant changes were necessary. As a result, educators in elementary and secondary schools, as well as higher education, were often forced to adopt defensive or "conservative" postures in response. Change is risky, they said, or likely to make things worse rather than better.

Liberal foundations could wear the mantle of reform too, and many tried to do so. But they often lacked credibility because they were not really outsiders. For many years, for example, Lyndon Johnson's former commissioner of education, Harold Howe II, ran the Ford Foundation's education program. Retired college and university presidents frequently directed grantmaking at other large foundations, such as Carnegie, Rockefeller, and Hewlett. As a result, however carefully thought out and ingenious, their plans inevitably seemed—and usually were—an extension of the framework of liberal thinking about the proper goals and methods of schooling, an agenda that was becoming less attractive among an increasingly conservative public.

The debate over education is an object lesson as to why it is not always accurate to define *conservatism* and *liberalism* entirely in relation to their dispositions toward change and reform. One of the reasons conservative philanthropists succeeded was that they and their grantees were able to portray their opponents as more reactionary than they were.

Their identification with reform also enabled conservative philanthropists to build alliances with influential groups with whom they might disagree on other issues. Business executives, for example, did not always see eye-to-eye with conservative prescriptions for economic or foreign policy, but on the need to improve elementary and secondary education, they largely agreed; many were prepared to lend their influence and give corporate donations to promote change. More surprising was the development of working relationships with African American leaders, whose communities usually suffered most heavily from the burdens of poor public schools. Their support proved critical for conservative efforts to promote choice in education. Likewise, the growing costs of colleges and universities and the perception of bias in admissions helped make middle-class parents more receptive to criticisms of higher education, whatever their source.

Conservative ideas had always seemed somewhat out of place in the historically liberal ethos of the United States, perhaps more suited for an aristocratic than a democratic society. But as a result of their willingness to build allies among a wide range of groups (as well as with people who did not share their political views on other issues), the conservative foundations could claim that their ideas for education, rather than being the products of thinkers far removed from the concerns of ordinary citizens, had substantial popular support.

Although American education was no longer as decentralized as it once was, the large number of school districts (as well as colleges and universities), instead of presenting an obstacle to philanthropists of relatively modest means, actually worked to their advantage. Ideas for school reform that were too costly or complicated to try out in multiple sites could be supported in one place and then promoted in others, if they seemed promising. Programs that were politically controversial to initiate or sustain at Brown, Yale, or Wisconsin could be underwritten at Miami, Montana State, or UCLA, yet still influence teaching or research throughout higher education. And the openness of the educational system gave conservative philanthropists and others concerned about the failings of American schools opportunities to opt out and start their own ventures, which embodied more traditional ideas about education, such as the newer religious and independent private schools that developed during the 1990s.

Unlike liberal foundations, whose efforts frequently focused on trying to affect national policies, conservative grantmakers had little choice but to invest their resources in places where their ideas about education were likely to be received more favorably than they would have been in Washington or on many campuses. This not only led to models that could be adopted by others and to multiple routes for propagating conservative ideas, but in an era that was increasingly skeptical of ambitious government programs emanating from the nation's capital made tactical sense, too.

Still, no matter where they provided support, the conservative foundations employed a strategy directed at changing the climate of public opinion by influencing professionals, scholars, policymakers, journalists, and similar elites to think differently about education. This was an approach that had once characterized the activities of the most influential grantmakers, leading James Douglas and Aaron Wildavsky (1978) to refer to them as "the knowledgeable foundations," because so much of their work involved underwriting the production and dissemination of new ideas (pp. 10–43). And this strategy had been effectively applied to a host of issues, ranging from poverty in American cities to the threat posed by communism in the third world. But in the aftermath of criticisms from the Left that they were undemocratic; too arrogant and paternalistic; and unresponsive to the needs of women, minorities, and indigenous groups in other countries, major foundations shifted their approach toward more participatory strategies, supposedly aimed at engaging those they sought to help in shaping their grantmaking, rather than relying as much on the expertise of elites, whose claims to knowledge were, in the post-Vietnam era, looked upon more skeptically, in any event.

Perhaps because they were spared the criticisms or more likely because their efforts were influenced by people who recalled how foundations once operated, the conservative philanthropies adopted the older strategy of working with elites. To be sure, they undertook other kinds of activities too (just as the liberal foundations continued to support studies and scholars in areas they favored). But those who attribute the success of conservative donors to their willingness to concentrate their support on a small number of activist groups over a long period of time are mistaken. It was precisely because, for the most part, they did *not* do so that conservative foundations were able to exert influence in education and other policy areas disproportionate to their number and size.

Perhaps most important, it was not just how they operated but also what they stood for in education that made the difference. With remarkable consistency over fifty years, conservative donors have championed reform goals that were deeply rooted in American ideals: achieving academic excellence, expecting that all students can learn, rewarding merit, increasing opportunities for schooling, acquiring the heritage of Western civilization, especially its notions of reason and ethics, and more. They acknowledged that educational success depended on much that schools could not affect, such as the environment students encountered at home and in their neighborhoods. (Notwithstanding what conservative foundations accomplished in school reform, their most important contribution to raising the academic achievement of children in poverty may turn out to be their efforts on behalf of welfare reform, which could, in the long run, significantly improve the educational influence of families and peer groups in impoverished areas.) And although not unconcerned about educational practices such as testing and ability grouping, they focused more on the substance of education—what students should be taught—than on the processes of schooling—how students are taught.

By contrast, from the Progressive era, liberals, relying on a different interpretation of American ideals, have conceived of schools as instruments for social change: fostering greater equality, promoting civic involvement, eliminating prejudices, strengthening communities, smoothing life adjustments, and the like. In their view, other institutions also had to play a crucial role, especially government, which needed to redistribute income and other resources in ways that would enable children from less advantaged backgrounds to make the most use of opportunities for education. And while liberals had their own ideas about what ought to be taught, they gave more attention to the pedagogies of learning, such as experiential education (or service-learning), constructivism, and individualized education than the conservatives did (although the latter's insistence on "teaching the basics" was also meant as an implicit critique of the lack of substance in the Progressive methods).

The history of American education, at least throughout the twentieth century, could easily be understood as a contest between these two conceptions of what schools should do. Conservative philanthropists embraced the more traditional one and, through their support, gave it more exposure and vitality than it had enjoyed for some time. They did not win the contest, nor could they have, since it is ultimately about conflicting philosophies and visions of American education more than educational practices. On these, people will disagree profoundly, as they always have. But what the conservative philanthropists did show is that the older ideas about schooling still rang true to many Americans and that foundations willing to take a consistently principled approach to their grantmaking in education can achieve a great deal, even with slender resources.

NOTES

1. See *Private Wealth and Public Education* (Coons, Clune, and Sugarman, 1970) and "Power to the Parents? The Story of Education Vouchers" (Cohen and Farrar, 1977).

2. See *Winning the Brain Race* (Kearns and Doyle, 1987) and *Reinventing Education: Entrepreneurship in Today's Schools* (Gerstner, Semerad, Doyle, and Johnston, 1994).

3. See also "David Packard's Forgotten Legacy to Philanthropy" (Lenkowsky, 1996).

4. See also "The Legend of the Powell Memo" (Schmitt, 2005).

5. See "Don't Fund College Follies" (MacDonald, 2005).

6. *Gratz* v. *Bollinger,* 539 US 244 (2003); *Grutter* v. *Bollinger,* 539 US 306 (2003).

7. For example, see "School Vouchers: Results from Randomized Experiments" (Peterson, with Howell, Wolf, and Campbell, 2003).

8. "Proof of Learning at College" (editorial), *The New York Times,* The Week in Review. Feb. 26, 2006, p. 11. See also Bok (2005), although he rejects conservative criticisms.

REFERENCES

Bestor, A. E. *Educational Wastelands: The Retreat from Learning in Our Public Schools.* Urbana: University of Illinois Press, 1953.

Bestor, A. E. *The Restoration of Learning: A Program for Redeeming the Unfulfilled Promise of American Education.* New York: Knopf, 1955.

Bloom, A. *The Closing of the American Mind.* New York: Simon & Schuster, 1988.

Bok, D. *Our Underachieving Colleges: A Candid Look at How Much Students Learn and Why They Should Be Learning More.* Princeton, N.J.: Princeton University, 2005.

Buckley, W. F., Jr. *God and Man at Yale: The Superstitions of Academic Freedom.* Chicago: Regnery, 1951.

Center for Education Reform, Fast Facts: Charter Schools. (http://www.edreform.com/index.cfm?fuseAction=stateStats&pSectionID=15&cSectionID=44), last accessed Feb. 26, 2006.

Center for Education Reform, National Charter School Data At-A-Glance. (http://www.edreform.com/_upload/ncsw-numbers.pdf), last accessed Feb. 25, 2006.

Chubb, J. E., and Moe, T. M. *Politics, Markets, and America's Schools.* Washington, D.C.: The Brookings Institution, 1990.

Cohen, D. K., and Farrar, E. "Power to the Parents? The Story of Education Vouchers." *The Public Interest,* Summer 1977, 48, 72–97.

Coleman, J. S., and others. *Equality of Educational Opportunity.* Washington, D.C.: U.S. Department of Health, Education and Welfare, 1966.

Collier, P., and Horowitz, D. *Destructive Generation: Second Thoughts about the Sixties.* New York: Summit Books, 1990.

Conant, J. B. *The American High School Today: A First Report to Interested Citizens.* New York: McGraw-Hill, 1959.

Coons, J., Clune, W. H., and Sugarman, S. D. *Private Wealth and Public Education.* Cambridge, Mass.: Harvard University Press, 1970.

Douglas, J., and Wildavsky, A. "The Knowledgeable Foundations." In *The Future of Foundations: Some Reconsiderations.* New Rochelle, N.Y.: Change Magazine Press, 1978.

D'Souza, D. *Illiberal Education: The Politics of Race and Sex on Campus.* New York: Free Press, 1991.

Federalist Society for Law and Public Policy Studies. "Our Background" (http://www.fed-soc.org/ourbackground.htm), last accessed Feb. 25, 2006.

Finn, C. E., Jr. *We Must Take Charge: Our Schools and Our Future.* New York: Free Press, 1991.

Finn, C. E., Jr. "Farewell—and Hello Again (Finn's Last Stand)." *Network News & Views,* Dec. 1996 (http://www.edexcellence.net/institute/publication/publication.cfm?id=188), last accessed Feb. 25, 2006.

Fliegel, S. *Miracle in East Harlem.* New York: Times Books, 1993.

Friedman, M. *Capitalism and Freedom.* Chicago and London: The University of Chicago Press, 1962.

Gerstner, L. V., Jr., Semerad, R. D., Doyle, D. P., and Johnston, W. *Reinventing Education: Entrepreneurship in Today's Schools.* Boston: E. P. Dutton, 1994.

Hayek, F. A. *The Road to Serfdom.* Chicago: University of Chicago, 1944.

Hayek, F. A. "The Intellectuals and Socialism." *University of Chicago Law Review,* Vol. XVI, 1949.

Hirsch, E. D., Jr. *Cultural Literacy: What Every American Needs to Know.* Boston: Houghton Mifflin, 1987.

Kearns, D. T., and Doyle, D. P. *Winning the Brain Race.* Oakland, Calif.: ICS Press, 1987.

Kimball, R. *Tenured Radicals: How Politics Has Corrupted Our Higher Education.* New York: Harper & Row, 1990.

Lenkowsky, L. "David Packard's Forgotten Legacy to Philanthropy." *The Chronicle of Philanthropy,* Apr. 18, 1996, 43.

MacDonald, H. "Don't Fund College Follies." *City Journal,* Summer 2005 (http://www.city-journal.org/html/15_3_college_follies.html), last accessed Feb. 25, 2006.

National Center for Education Statistics. *The Condition of Education 2005.* Washington, D.C.: U.S. Department of Education, 2005.

National Commission on Excellence in Education. *A Nation at Risk: The Imperative for Educational Reform.* Washington, D.C.: U.S. Department of Education, 1983.

Nathan, J. *Charter Schools: Creating Hope and Opportunity for American Education.* San Francisco: Jossey-Bass, 1996.

New York Times Week in Review. "Proof of Learning at College," Sec. 4, Feb. 26, 2006, p. 11.

Orosz, J. J. "Henry Ford and Edsel Ford." In R. T. Grimm Jr. (ed.), *Notable American Philanthropists: Biographies of Giving and Volunteering.* Westport, Conn., and London: Greenwood Press, 2002.

Packard, D. "Corporate Support of the Private Universities." Speech to the Committee for Corporate Support of American University, Oct. 17, 1973, unpublished.

Peterson, P., with Howell, W. G., Wolf, P. J., and Campbell, D. E. "School Vouchers: Results from Randomized Experiments." In C. M. Hoxby (ed.), *The Economics of School Choice.* Chicago: University of Chicago Press, 2003, pp. 107–144.

Piereson, J. "The Left University." *The Weekly Standard,* Oct. 3, 2005, *11*(3), 20–30.

Powell, L. F., Jr. "Attack of [sic] American Free Enterprise System." Confidential memorandum to Eugene B. Sydnor Jr., Aug. 23, 1971, unpublished.

Rothman, S., Lichter, S. R., and Nevitte, N. "Politics and Professional Advancement Among College Faculty." *The Forum,* 2005, *3*(1), Article 2 (http://www.bepress.com/forum/vol3/iss1/art2), last accessed Feb. 26, 2006.

Schmitt, M. "The Legend of the Powell Memo." *The American Prospect Online Edition,* Apr. 27, 2005 (http://www.prospect.org/web/page.ww?section=root&name=ViewWeb&articleId=9606), last accessed Feb. 25, 2006.

Simon, W. E. *A Time for Truth*. New York and Chicago: Readers Digest Press and McGraw-Hill, 1978.

Trilling, L. *The Liberal Imagination*. New York: Doubleday, 1950.

U.S. Department of Education. "Nation's Report Card Shows Continued Progress—General," Oct. 2005 (http://www.ed.gov/nclb/accountability/achieve/report-card.html), last accessed Feb. 25, 2006.

Weltman, B. "Reconsidering Arthur Bestor and the Cold War in Social Education." *Theory and Research in Social Education*, 2000, 28, 11–39.

Wilson, J. Q., "Multiple Choice Test." *The New Republic*, Oct. 8, 1990.

Chapter Fifteen Overview

As an example of how a function can take many forms, operating foundations play their programmatic and diffusion roles in many guises. Their programs may involve developing ideas, doing research, awarding fellowships, undertaking program initiatives, or other ventures. Their identities may vary from free-standing entity to the sub-branch of an association to a society of the like-minded. Understandably, operating foundations do not lend themselves easily to categories.

This chapter sparkles with a passion for the place these entities occupy in the educational landscape. With their freedom to set their own agenda, however, comes the challenge (for all but an endowed few) of raising the money to pursue it. The discipline of the philanthropic marketplace keeps them honest. But once their ideas are in place and money is in the bank, operating foundations lend themselves to the development, implementation, diffusion, and improvement of educational capital in the areas they have chosen to work.

During his time as president of the Woodrow Wilson National Fellowship Foundation, Robert Weisbuch retained the reflective habits of a professor of English as he absorbed and expanded the foundation's mission. (He is now president of Drew University.) This chapter is a result of his pausing to consider what is distinctive about operating foundations and how they fit between grantmaking foundations and educational institutions.

An element of Weisbuch's writing that has special relevance for this project is his advocacy of K–12 and higher education collaborations. After noting that the more prestigious colleges and universities "have been perceived as missing in action in terms of the crises in public education," he argues the considerable virtue of collaborating in the improvement of the schools and the leadership role operating foundations can play.

15

ROBIN HOOD WITH
A DIFFERENCE

OPERATING FOUNDATIONS AND
UNIVERSITIES AND SCHOOLS

Robert Weisbuch

THE TERM *OPERATING FOUNDATION* does not get the blood pounding. In my earlier life as a professor of American literature, I actually welcomed the cocktail-party conversational opener about what I did for a living. We would be off and running on Melville or Morrison. Now when I respond to the same question by replying that I lead an operating foundation, the result is often a blank stare.

On a few occasions, the interlocutor asks innocently, "Operating foundation? Is it a medical facility?" More sensibly, "Woodrow Wilson" frequently gets confused with the other and very grand institutions named after this university and national president. But easily the most frequent misunderstanding concerns *foundation*—a noun apparently attached to a wide range of nonprofit organizations formed in the aftermath of World War II. As my conversation partner warms to the prospect of financial support, I must explain that Woodrow Wilson, like many but not all operating foundations, must seek funds, as it lacks a large endowment. Indeed, when we serve as an intermediary between a philanthropic foundation and a university or school district, we sometimes feel like Robin Hood, but with a difference: we steal from the rich, we give to the rich, and we remain poor.

Some Sorrows and Joys

This is not always the case with operating foundations—a term that is sufficiently slippery that I should indicate what I intend by it. Operating foundations, by the definition related to IRS requirements and cited by William Bowen and his colleagues (1994), "devote most (at least 85 percent) of their income to the active conduct of their programmatic activities, where 'active conduct' means direct expenditure of the funds by the organization, rather than disbursements to grantees" (p. 9). Like much about operating foundations, this is a problematic definition, for Woodrow Wilson and many other operating foundations have a subgranting property, whereby we distribute funds to individuals and institutions, but those funds originate from other, actually philanthropic, organizations.

Further, some operating foundations possess a sizeable endowment of their own, obtaining much or all of their operating funds from an endowment created by an original donor[1]—The Carnegie Foundation for the Advancement of Teaching, for instance, or the Fetzer Institute, or, more grandly, the J. Paul Getty Trust, though some, like Carnegie, may seek program grants from others. The Council on Foundations contends, on its Web site, that most operating foundations do not seek funds from the public.[2] But that contradicts practice, not only at Woodrow Wilson but also at any number of, say, museums and wildlife preserves that are also operating foundations. "Operating foundation," then, is a category in real need of subdivision. In what follows, I attend primarily to those foundations that directly expend funds rather than offer them to grantees, though I give some attention to a range of associations and centers.

This is, in part, due to a further complication in the defining of the term. Many membership organizations that are not officially foundations at all, like the American Council of Learned Societies (ACLS), the Social Sciences Research Council (SSRC), or the Association of American Colleges and Universities, seek external funds to provide programs that have a great deal to do with their institutional definition. They behave, that is, like operating foundations in much the same manner as Woodrow Wilson. For the purposes of this chapter, I discuss such grantseeking entities as if they were operating foundations, including the membership organizations mentioned earlier, while considering less often those entities that are primarily philanthropies, even as they may frequently take on an operating function.

The chief sorrow of an operating foundation largely dependent on external grants is exactly that—the lack of intrinsic funds. As a friend admonished me when I was considering whether to join Woodrow Wilson, "A foundation without a sizable endowment is like a restaurant without a kitchen. You can be nothing more than a delivery service." And this danger is exacerbated by what has been a strong trend over the last fifteen years. Grantmaking philanthropies, whether private, familial, or corporate, have tended more and more to define their own agendas, sometimes very precisely. The number of venues that open their doors and ears to proposals within a deliberately large range appears to have been much reduced. Further, some philanthropies have come to resemble operating foundations, most notably and recently The Pew Charitable Trusts.

Elsewhere in this volume, Ray Bacchetti welcomes this last trend and recommends that foundations "devote a corner of themselves to an operating foundation-like structure"—to become hybrids, as it were. I do not share this enthusiasm, for reasons that I hope are not entirely self-interested. I worry that, taken together, the movement to narrower agendas and to combining grantmaking and operating roles discourages the kind of grassroots innovation that a looser agenda on the part of a philanthropy and that innovation on the part of a more traditional operating foundation can encourage. My arguments for this anxiety—an anxiety ultimately about democratic innovation in the academy—will become plainer in considering the capabilities of operating foundations. For now, I would simply note that these trends deepen the operating foundation's worry of not being deep—that the operating foundation, reduced to a mechanism meeting the demands of external funders, will become shallow indeed.

But to sum in personal terms the negative aspect of operating foundations (and their like) that are dependent on external support, I once taught the plays of Arthur Miller; now, on some days, I can feel like Willy Loman, peddling ideas to a clientele that no longer exists. And yet on other days—on other, more frequent days—I believe an operating foundation is the finest institution in the land, and I love my life. This sense of satisfaction arises from five capacities of an operating foundation. Operating foundations can do the following:

1. Set their own agendas and then actively seek funding. This requires a choice of maintaining focus over going after every available dollar.

2. Collect and disseminate the most compelling innovations of individual schools and universities. They network and leverage fresh thought and effective practice.

3. Promulgate uncompromised academic values.

4. Listen better and gain a more accurate perspective than philan-thropies, as students and faculty may tell them more of the truth, if only because it is difficult to tell a negative truth to a direct funder.

5. Operate, true to their name—that is, put ideas into practice and transform talk into actions.

It is not a glamorous fact but an important one that operating founda-tions are free to increase their staff numbers whenever a new grant is pro-vided. They are staff-intensive and can thus do the heavy lifting that a philanthropy and certainly a government agency may well eschew.

So perhaps we do not have that kitchen, as in my friend's analogy, but a creative operating foundation can learn how to fry an egg on the side-walk. We can develop our own ideas and actively seek funding for them, discovering new sources from a next generation of wealth if the old ones have dried up. It is also the case that philanthropies and operating foun-dations often hatch the Idea Egg together, taking turns in a true col-laboration, or with the philanthropy asking honestly of the operating foundation, "We know we want to do something like this, but tell us what we mean."

In other words, this same emphasis on agenda that I find a mixed bless-ing for philanthropic foundations seems to me an unambiguous value for operating foundations. At the most, setting an agenda means saying no to some lucrative possibilities, and at the least it means being clear about what you are doing for love and what for money. The Carnegie Founda-tion for the Advancement of Teaching has its agenda-center in its very name, and Lee Shulman's period at the helm has reinforced the emphasis on instructional improvement. In contrast, the Center for Basic Educa-tion, formed a few decades ago to promulgate a traditional notion of the arts and sciences and related to a conservative social perspective, depoliti-cized itself to the point of simply cheering on the arts and sciences; the center became a randomized set of programs. It ceased utterly in 2004.

Woodrow Wilson initially had a very clear opening agenda—a famous fellowship program supporting promising students in doctoral study and helping to create the next generation of college faculty. The founders cited a worry after World War II that the best and brightest would be drawn to better-paying, higher-status professions than college teaching. After a mod-est beginning, Woodrow Wilson received very impressive Ford Founda-tion funding. When funding for that program ended over thirty years ago, once Ford determined that, if anything, all too many young people were now seeking doctoral degrees and a life in the professoriate, Woodrow Wilson came to engage a whole set of activities, each of them worthy but, taken together, something of a Rube Goldberg machine.

It has taken us years to develop the concept of the Engaged University—the notion that we link schools and universities to each other and academic expertise to social challenges, and we do this by awarding fellowships to individuals and by supporting initiatives involving whole institutions. Indeed that sentence, still too long, has itself been many months in the making; it somehow obscures our mode of operation to achieve these twin goals, which is my chief joy—that we seek good ideas and spread them. Nonetheless, by focusing on the concept of university education as publicly engaged—that is, as consciously (and perhaps more consciously than in recent academic history) committed to learning as a lever to raise the quality of life in society—we do establish a useful bounding line for our many endeavors. Such a notion, of course, may confront the objection that it undervalues learning for its own sake, or the "Truth-value" of research, but we have tried to put forward a notion of the Engaged University that does not at all see scholarship as the Evil Empire.

Even so, we came to suspect that "learning for its own sake," when taken too literally and without the notion that learning is a crucial activity for the growth of individual and collective human existence, is a notion of purity that becomes puerile. And so Woodrow Wilson committed itself to a vision of higher education aware of its social connectedness, including most obviously its relation in the overall ecology of learning to public education, or K–12, and most particularly high schools. But it also meant inquiring into its relations to other social institutions like government agencies, for-profit businesses, and cultural institutions. And it meant an awareness of the impingement of major social issues, such as equal opportunity, on the policies and conduct of colleges and universities—an awareness most recently evidenced by a Woodrow Wilson report on "Diversity and the Ph.D.," replete with data and recommendations (Woodrow Wilson National Fellowship Foundation, 2005a).

It remains to be seen whether we have the discipline to maintain the boundaries established by the notion of an engaged university and whether the concept is sufficiently defined to make those boundaries meaningful. But my point is that, without an agenda, an operating foundation really is nothing more than a mechanism—and a dull one at that.

Our significant presence, then, requires an agenda. Unlike schools and universities, our physical presence is usually trivial. We occupy reality by virtue of our self-definition, and that self-definition—that which gives the pair of hands a brain—requires ideals and ideas. The ability to enact those ideas depends on our capacity to convince disinterested others of their worth—a discipline that philanthropies may choose but operating foundations of the kind I am emphasizing must practice. This is our unique system of checks and balances: our lack of a bank balance and our need for others to sign the check restrain us usefully and require us to prove a proposed program's worth and to assess our work realistically.

The operating foundation can create its own ideas, then, but that leads to a second strength, for "our" ideas most often are not really ours. They usually come to us from a particular scholar or university program or school district that has innovated wonderfully. (My objection to the narrowed agendas of philanthropies has to do primarily with this grassroots effect. Where's a brilliant new educational practice to go if it does not fit an agenda?) As Steven Wheatly, vice president of the ACLS, argues in a letter to me, we are "both representative of and responsible to the scholarly community." The opinion of practitioners thus gets not only a voice but, in the best instance, an enactment. And this occurs not only in the creation of a program but also in its ongoing practice. ACLS fellowships, for instance, provide an opportunity for humanists to become a national community of judgment, as Wheatly writes, "that helps to reward important conceptual innovations in these disciplines while upholding enduring standards of scholarly excellence."

For all that, these practitioners, after all, come from different, often competing institutions, and this suggests another strength of the operating foundation. It can serve as a neutral site. Harvard may like a practice, but if Yale thought of it, Harvard does not want to imitate Yale's innovation, and vice versa. In all, operating foundations can franchise a great idea, and that transforms a delivery service into a giant impact machine.

It is worth staying with this notion of franchising for a moment, as it is a more complex business in education than it is in the restaurant business. The program idea rarely if ever gets replicated exactly. Each local instance is surrounded by a distinctive context, and thus the operating foundation must define the central practice with sufficient precision to retain its meaning but with enough flexibility to allow each institution to have a strong sense of ownership in the practice. If that can be achieved, and if the various sites can be brought into meaningful discussion, a powerful multiplication of worthy interpretations and additions to the central practice can occur. A network forms, lively with imitation, adaptation, and shared experience.

Operating foundations thus achieve two kinds of leveraging at once. By spreading a good idea, we help institutions avoid unnecessary duplication of effort—the reinventing of the wheel so endemic, especially at the college and university level. But also, if the idea really is a good one, institutions will supplement our funder's dollar with several of their own. Indeed, if they will not do that (or so we in the operating foundations believe), the institution does not deserve to play. Philanthropies can afford to fund the insincere, though the better ones do not; operating foundations are not even tempted.

As an example, Harvard and the Brookline School District collaborated several years ago on a highly successful program initiated by Stanley Katz and ACLS, called Teachers as Scholars, by which teachers would take research sabbaticals on a college campus. ACLS exported the idea to the University of Colorado, but eventually it did not take, in part because the organization itself had some doubts about the degree to which its mission should include precollege education. Teachers as Scholars then took the less ambitious but more flexible form of three- to five-day intensive seminars led by superb teacher-scholars at Harvard; seminars were held during the regular school year and school week, so that students would see their teachers leaving to become learners and so that districts would have to see this kind of intellectual investment in teachers as integral, not as a Saturday or summer extra.

My colleagues and I visited the program and were impressed by its direct simplicity. (Indeed, once we had become involved, an assessment of the first eight sites revealed that 93 percent of the teachers found the program "the most" or "one of the most" important events of their careers.) Woodrow Wilson gathered university and school leaders, found the means to provide some very modest start-up funds, and established a highly active network among twenty-six self-sustaining sites nationally, from Princeton to UCLA. Specifically, start-up grants of $25,000 over two years provide the impetus, after which each site becomes self-supporting through local and alumni gifts or base-budgeting from the university itself. Further, the relationships established in that simple, lovely program have developed into much more expansive school-university partnerships at many of the sites. There exists a hazier but still more important kind of leveraging as well, as the program reasserts the intellectual dignity of K–12 teachers. But even in considering only the program itself, the financial leveraging has reached an estimated ten to one, and the proportion continues to grow as the self-sustaining sites maintain themselves and grow by base budgets and local donors.

In all, operating foundations can organize a dizzyingly diverse set of educational institutions and prevent the wasteful reinvention of the wheel. And by choosing what to promulgate, operating foundations serve another vital purpose: to signify values. I mentioned this implication of values in regard to the teacher seminars, but another example might clarify the point. Woodrow Wilson administers the Newcombe Fellowships that provide funding for about thirty doctoral students in the dissertation phase of their work. The fellowship rewards work that speaks to moral and ethical issues, and this emphasis, enacted not only in the evaluation of the proposals but in the application form as well, shines a light on a specific aspect of advanced research: that it should never lose sight of human values, indeed should powerfully inform our understanding of them. In that, the program itself enacts a value. A national fellowship program of any kind lets every university president, department chair, and scholar know that there is support out there for one thing or another, and may well leverage significant internal funding. (As another example, both ACLS, through the Andrew W. Mellon Foundation, and Woodrow Wilson, through the Delmas Foundation, provide fellowships for newly tenured faculty, on the basis that they are at a crucial career stage; we have seen evidence that colleges and universities are establishing programs of their own much like this.) This is leveraging of a third kind, then, of values.

Indeed, this capacity may at times be overlooked because operating foundations have not always been very assertive in making explicit the implicit values of their fellowship programs. Too easily, a fellowship program may become a welcome but routine attribute of the academic landscape while they may need, either in their own literature and operations or in other initiatives undertaken by the operating foundation, a certain self-explanation. In other words, the world needs to be reminded of why this perennial program exists.

Sometimes, though, for all of these strengths or perhaps because these virtues are complex ones, programs do fail. When they do, operating foundations know it, whereas philanthropies that run their programs directly often learn of failure only later and sometimes never. Faculty and students tell us what is really happening, not what will move funders to continue to support them. This is not to claim that philanthropies cannot conduct their own accurate assessments (the Andrew W. Mellon Foundation was a leader in assessment long before assessment came to be emphasized); it is simply to claim that it is harder for the direct funder to do it.

More important, the operating foundation knows what is happening because the foundation helps *make* it happen. We have our ear close to the ground. An operating foundation operates. We see everything up close, whether it is the emerging intellectual trends in a set of fellowship applications or whether it is the difficult practice of creating a "third culture," combining public and higher education practices in one of the Early College High Schools that we consult for the Gates Foundation. And our capacity to serve that program began with a series of meetings (four regional and one national), in which high school and university teachers and administrative leaders spoke to each other with disconcerting frankness. Although The William and Flora Hewlett Foundation and the Carnegie Corporation of New York sponsored these meetings, there was no immediate funding at stake for the participants, and so a certain purity—sometimes the purity of rage, but useful rage—reigned. In all, if operating foundations are ourselves honest, we can become the philanthropic funder's eyes and ears.

Of course, a philanthropy may be able to become its own operating foundation, and it is here that I can locate my worry about what Bacchetti terms *hybrids*. There is surely an attraction to eliminating the middleman and going factory-direct. When this happens, however, aside from a possible loss of discipline and honest feedback, another kind of listening is easily lost; that is, a philanthropy may stop listening to voices from beyond the walls of the institution and may no longer be receptive to the best ideas from the field at large. It can seem a tyrannical giant courting a public resentment: in a phrase, *Who elected you?*

I am claiming for the grantseeking operating foundation, then, a different largeness of perspective. We get to view the educational ecosystem from every vantage, and this perspective gives us a curative capacity. That curative catholicity is vital if we are to heal the breach that has arisen between the philanthropic foundations and higher education, to which I now turn.

Universities and Foundations

That breach is summed for me in a single phrase—the Athenaeum. The Athenaeum was the most dramatic concept proposed by a committee at the University of Michigan charged with improving the undergraduate experience. We had discovered that any freshman or sophomore in a special program had a far better experience than those lost in the huge college, *regardless of program quality*. The Athenaeum was an attempt to create a special experience for every student, to guarantee each a neighborhood within the big city. A special undergraduate college would be created, and every faculty member, including those in professional schools, would spend one in six years half-time in the Athenaeum, offering small seminars. The idea was greeted with applause by the administration and the newspapers. But when it reached the faculty, we had the experience of Milton's Satan arriving back in hell from his perilous journey to the new Eden, expecting great huzzahs from the devils, who God at that moment transforms into snakes producing "a universal hiss."

For years, I attributed our failure to hubris, to ignoring too much the need to send an idea through the coils of process, going department by department, almost faculty member by faculty member, to make it a collective idea. And certainly we were too optimistic—having given the idea only a full year of vetting and testing before offering it. But now, from a distance, I am struck by the too-high degree of difficulty for an innovation. Indeed, the Athenaeum, though defeated miserably as a concept, led to a series of committees over three years that finally offered a plan whereby most first-year students would get a freshman seminar; some were taught by tenure-track professors, some not, and with colleagues in the professional schools totally absent. On the one hand, conceptual power was drained; on the other, life got a little better for first-year students. But in all too much of a process, an exquisite liquor became weak tea.

To put the issue bluntly, Why should foundations invest in already-well-resourced institutions whose democratic processes strangle change? This is an especially apt question for liberal arts colleges and graduate schools, where faculty autonomy rules. On the other hand, if change at the university is slow, it is also deep, and sometimes foundations appear not to know this. Yet that argument certainly has not succeeded with the Atlantic Philanthropies—the latest and largest philanthropic foundation to desert the good ship Higher Education. Nor has it succeeded with The Pew Charitable Trusts or the Danforth Foundation or the Rockefeller Foundation, all of which have defined themselves partly or totally away from support for university initiatives in recent years.

Though universities continue to garner increasing overall support from other sources, and though some new philanthropies (the Bill & Melinda Gates Foundation and Lumina Foundation for Education, to mention two) have made their funds available for highly defined purposes, the trend away from philanthropic support for college- and graduate-level innovation is real and decisive. It is especially calamitous for those disciplines least supported by federal agencies—that is, the arts and humanities and the humanities-oriented social disciplines.

But even more than making what is already an uneven playing field among the disciplines nearly unplayable for some, this desertion implies a widespread loss of faith in the capacity of higher education to apply its skepticism and rigor to its own habits. The foundation report card grade for colleges and universities might be considered well below a gentleman's B.

In this situation, the operating foundation can play a crucial mediating role because, by definition, it travels between the two parties to this dispute—if indeed I have characterized the reasons for a decline in philanthropic support accurately as a largely unspoken dispute. I mentioned earlier the capacity of the operating foundation to serve as a neutral site among universities that must both cooperate and compete; later I will discuss the operating foundation as a neutral site where philanthropic foundations, themselves not devoid of competitive instincts, may meet as well. In this situation, the operating foundation can play a still more active mediating role, for, by definition it travels between the two parties to this dispute. Bacchetti's essay well characterizes the potential conflict, and I have noted the conflict as well, even at one point creating a contentious debate between two parts of myself—a philanthropy aspect that I named Gatesford Pewmellon—and a faculty member, a likeably adventurous scholar dubbed Indiana Yale, for a conference on academic philanthropy at Emory University.

I will not rehearse that debate here, but it might be worth summarizing its main terms to understand better what operating foundations must confront in attempting to create collaborations between the funders and the universities. Pewmellon, as a funder confronting the slow-to-change nature of higher education, and especially the liberal arts core of four-year institutions, cites figures suggesting a move to careerism and away from the study of the basic literacies. He notes that the general culture seems to be experiencing a cultural boom, judging by the tripling of the audience for National Public Radio, strong museum attendance, the creation of mega-bookstores and cultural cable channels, at the same time as this academic bust. And he wonders, then, why universities cling to habit.

Frustrated by the intricacies—or the molasses-like quality—of faculty governance, a sense that scholarship has eclipsed a concern for teaching and for students, a perceived refusal to apply learning to social urgencies, and a faculty disdain for reasonable assessment, Pewmellon comes to an explosive conclusion: "There is poverty and hunger in the world, AIDS and overpopulation and the challenges of aging. And there is even, right next door to you, K–12, which you treat with utmost condescension as a tiny afterthought. And in each of these areas, my dollar can make a dramatic difference. But I have poured billions into your venues and see something that looks less like improvement than like arrogant isolation. Next time you want to see me, how about visiting your endowment instead, the endowment that humbles the treasury of a third-world nation for an institution with less than a small town's population."

Indiana Yale, in rebuttal, expresses the value of the academic disciplines, their capacity to push back the night of ignorance and to fire students with a love of learning as they experience their cognitive reach for a first and crucial time. He criticizes the philanthropist's own hubris in proclaiming and proscribing rather than in asking and inviting and charges that foundation types speak too much to each other than to real students and faculty. Yet even the endowments of the foundations often stemmed from advances created by university research—research that often would have escaped the reductive requirements created by the foundations and summed in the literalist word "deliverables." He wonders "by what hanging chads" the foundations were elected to set the education agenda, and he wonders as well why foundations tend only to fund change rather than to guarantee the continuation of successful practice.

Indiana Yale finally concludes, "You speak of arrogance? Man, you have cornered the market. I am just dying to see the next foundation report full of 'faculty should' and 'faculty must.' You say you want change, but you impose your idea of change without doing the homework to make change intelligent. Almost every grant opportunity is at about a 50-degree angle to what we really need. And perhaps we change gradually because so much in higher education is so fine, because K–12, giddy with change, is a mess. You seem to want universities to become more like bad high schools, to clog ourselves with every social concern, to assess ourselves into oblivion, to forget our center and live on peripheries."

At heart, I believe, this debate centers on a question about academic autonomy and civic usefulness, and it will require the universities and the foundations at their best to manage it. If the operating foundations can serve first as referee and then as coordinator, we might succeed in transforming the dispute into a collaborative effort. The very existence of an operating foundation standing at the crossroad makes a positive statement in regard to the existence of that crossroad, of values shared by higher education and the philanthropies. Making those values loudly explicit is a key part of what we do; enacting them in a university setting can make delighted collaborators of these disputants. But to achieve such collaboration, all parties need to acknowledge some home truths, and here too the operating foundation, on the way to collaboration, can serve as a friendly mediator.

We know Gatesford has a major point to make. I earned a doctoral degree without ever being asked to spend a single minute learning anything about the larger educational landscape, and no attention at all was given to how learning could contribute to the public good. Foundations—operating foundations in particular—can open the doors of faculty perception, can encourage a participatory ethic—a new notion of service—the rigorous application of expertise to social challenges. But to do that, they need to address the universities in a tone more inviting than accusatory.

At Woodrow Wilson, we tried such an approach, leaving more than usual leeway to institutions. We created an initiative, sponsored by the Atlantic Philanthropies and The Pew Charitable Trusts on the eve of their departure from the funding of higher education per se, called The Responsive Ph.D. We gathered first fourteen and then twenty diverse graduate institutions, ranging from Yale and Princeton in the East to Howard and Duke in the South to Michigan and Washington University in the Midwest to the University of Washington and Irvine in the West. We gave them pin money and asked them to engage their faculty and students in creating cross-disciplinary initiatives that would respond to four challenges:

1. How do you make learning and scholarship more adventurous? How do you encourage a crossing of habitual boundaries?

2. How can you make teaching matter more for graduate students?

3. How do we ensure a diverse doctoral cohort in all disciplines to mirror the cities and streets of America?

4. And, most of all, how do we make learning matter for the public good and create a continuing dialogue between the mentors and the consumers of Ph.D. graduates, between the faculty and those representatives of all kinds and levels of educational institutions, as well as business and government sectors?

The results were encouraging. Over forty innovative programs were created or dramatically enlarged, and the institutions are now adapting each other's best ideas—all on a total program budget of about $1 million. Yale created an alumni network to tie current students (especially but not exclusively in the humanities disciplines) to graduates who had moved beyond academia in their career pursuits. The University of Texas created cross-disciplinary courses on the application of learning and invited nonprofit organizations and even for-profits to bring to their multidisciplinary teams of students their problems and challenges. Duke University created an unusually rigorous program of assessment for each graduate department and pioneered in making the results widely available to prospective and active students. Howard University extended a program mentoring new teachers to send doctoral students to a whole range of historically black colleges and universities. Reports on these and related efforts contributed to the findings of the Woodrow Wilson report on "The Responsive Ph.D."(Woodrow Wilson National Fellowship Foundation, 2005b).

This demonstration that higher education can stretch a donated dollar as well as any cause depended, however, not only in insisting, with Gatesford

Pewmellon, that academia should be self-critical and look to the public good but by transforming his harangue into an invitation to be creative. "Require me to do something and I will balk," a faculty member at one of the institutions wrote to me. "Invite me to apply my expertise and there is little I won't do."

The program also served to illustrate another capacity of the operating foundation: to employ its name and prestige to key internal funding. Woodrow Wilson created something of a "*Good Housekeeping* seal of approval," in that the graduate schools were chosen, in part, for their record of activity, and the small sums were provided only upon application. Thus if a number of internal priorities were lined up for internal funding as if they were patrons awaiting a bus, the project's prestige allowed the graduate dean to move to the front of the line—an example of leveraging that understandably pleases funders.

Similarly, a modest program of $2,000 summer grants to doctoral students in the humanities willing to find venues for their expertise beyond the academy led a Vanderbilt philosopher to work with doctors at the university hospital on the ethics of transplant procedures and to counsel patients. It supported a Virginia historian to start a summer freedom camp on African American history for fifth-graders in Mississippi. One student worked for the NASA museum, creating biographies of the astronauts, and another employed everything she knew from cultural anthropology—storytelling, dance, autobiographical writing, art—at a home for delinquent girls who had been abused as children, to improve their sense of themselves.

Indeed, there is a definite movement in academia at present toward public scholarship. In even the most insular disciplines of the humanities, we see this movement clearly, in the form of the Chicago Humanities Festival—an annual week-long, hundred-event, sold-out cultural spectacular. Or we see it in Bard College's Clemente program, which provides poor people with experiences in reading great works and writing on them—a program whose record of breaking the cycle of poverty is eye-opening. Or we see it in the work of Jeffrey Perl and his colleagues at the journal *Common Knowledge* in challenging those disciplines that require us to view experience through the eyes of others to apply their work to relieving international conflict. As of yet, the philanthropies have been all but absent in supporting the very turn they long have demanded. Operating foundations can tap them on their shoulders.

And as for Indiana Yale, we can insist, with him, that the Truth-value of academic discovery is worthy, that scholarship is not the Evil Empire. It is indeed the subject matter of teaching, and human curiosity deserves support. Further, although some universities are wealthy, that is hardly typical, and, as we noted earlier, foundation support for carefully defined scholarly endeavors is not just about the money, but support leverages interest and further resources by spotlighting values.

Sometimes, too, such pure scholarship has the most powerful social benefit. We are familiar with examples in the sciences, but Wheatly cites the nurturing of Area Studies by his organization and by the SSRC, following World War II. Supported by foundations like Rockefeller, these efforts created "the means and the institutional space in which scholars could set the intellectual agenda for the study of world civilizations"—a protected space essential "when the study of Chinese culture, for example, was seen as an exotic excursion away from the intellectual heart of the university, which lay in Western civilization." Wheatly goes on to say that area studies may indeed have arisen without the ACLS and SSRC work, "but the initial shape and the steep slope of their growth owe much to the leadership of the scholars who worked through the two councils"(Steven Wheatly, letter to the author, 2005).

In all, we must make Gatesford Pewmellon and Indiana Yale roommates. They must learn to live together in a new residence hall where the philanthropic foundations and the college faculty can create a twenty-first-century renaissance. Such a renaissance is within our power at the cost only of foundation belligerence and faculty intransigence—a price on each side of less than nothing. I spoke earlier of the operating foundations as providing a neutral site, and this would be the most essential such site we can create. The very volume in which this essay exists, indeed, contributes to its creation.

The Schools and the Foundations

And this very chapter, in its organization, implies a division we now take so for granted that we fail to question its efficacy. We expect universities and schools to occupy separate sections of our thought, for the two largest systems of education in this country are so unlike, economically and culturally. Educational historians remind us of a time when high schools and colleges were thought of together, but we do not really believe them, not in a nation where the gap between public and higher education is arguably larger than anywhere else in the world (Judge, 1998, pp. 187ff).

I mentioned earlier the series of regional and national meetings Woodrow Wilson organized between high school and university faculty and administrators. I recall vividly the look on the faces of the university people when a high school teacher declared at the Berkeley meeting,

"Most of you came up from Los Angeles or wherever last night. No sweat. It took me three weeks of arguing to convince my principal in Oakland to let me leave half an hour early so that I would only be an hour late to this meeting."

But perhaps the most frequent complaint had to do with getting fooled by the promise of school-university partnerships. A teacher invests a great deal in one or another university outreach program (that term itself problematic and possibly arrogant), only to have it end abruptly when a principal or a department chair or a funding source departs. The impermanence, the superficiality, and the disarray, even within single universities of randomized "outreach" programs, may imply institutional nonchalance. They guarantee cynicism. What can a relatively small operating foundation do in confronting such a gigantic missed opportunity?

In fact, if we return to the five capacities of operating foundations that I listed earlier: (1) to set an agenda, (2) to take a good idea and spread it through a network, leveraging funds, (3) to promulgate new values, using its prestige to leverage funds internal to schools or universities, (4) to hear and relate how it looks from different sides, whether academics and funders or schools and colleges, and (5) to get it done, to reduce to practice an important concept—it is difficult to imagine how a more organic educational system can be created without the operating foundations.

Operating foundations that work with public education are themselves often of a fundamentally different nature from those that work with universities. Their social mission is more direct. Jobs for the Future—the excellent Cambridge-based nonprofit—has a wider purview than its name suggests. It is, for instance, the lead organization for the Gates Foundation Early College High Schools (ECHS) program of small high schools in urban neighborhoods that offer underserved students a challenging college curriculum while still in the last years of high school. But its name implies a very practical workforce orientation, and other intermediaries in the Gates effort include organizations defined by their interest in bettering conditions for students of color—the National Council of La Raza, for instance, which supports the social betterment of Americans of Hispanic origin and works with a tightly networked set of schools—or with forms of education not exclusively concerned with the liberal arts, like the Middle College Association, which creates high schools in the midst of community-college campuses.

Woodrow Wilson is an anomaly in this group for its traditional interest in higher and even graduate education and for its liberal arts orientation. But this very fact, requiring us to span, demonstrates once again a value of operating foundations: their potential reach across traditional boundaries.

Our conviction that a good educational system requires vertical integration, including the two-year colleges as well as the four-year comprehensives and the small colleges, led us to this effort. (Just so, under Robert Connor, the National Humanities Center initiated canny curricular efforts with teachers.) We had been working for two decades to engage high school teachers in the ongoing life of the disciplines, seeking teacher-leaders who now call themselves "Woodies," as tellingly distinct from our graduate school "fellows." But in working to create a third culture in actual buildings, we took a crash course in the differences between the two systems.

If inertia is higher education's challenge, a giddy trendiness is public education's problem. Higher education's surplus of skepticism is perhaps replaced by public education's gullibility, as the cure-all reform idea of the year makes its reductive, politicized, pompous, and usually not-intellectual way. Indeed, it is possible to read through volumes of school-reform literature before the notions of "content" and "disciplinary expertise" arise. But however reductive the idea is (and today's idea set involves a Gradgrindism beyond Dickens's imagination), it has the saving grace of being temporary. And this fleeting quality is complemented by the frequent replacement of key education leaders, principals, and superintendents—and even those new education experts: mayors.

The very size of public education is more challenging still, and most challenging is its nearly entropic nature. Public education has a local quality. The nature of mathematics does not change between, say, Trenton and Philadelphia, yet the shibboleth of local control may make the laws of learning mathematics widely different for students and their teachers in these two cities. An extreme alternative—a French Academy notion of standardization—seems both unlikely and intellectually unattractive. In all, then, local control, coupled with the scale of K–12, creates an enormous problem in terms of meaningful improvement. "Scaling up" is the byword in almost all discussions of public education reform, and there is often a tinge of hopelessness as people speak of it.

Yet if we return to another basic strategy for operating foundations, that is, their capacity to discover a lever, there may be a means to afford deep change. One need not be an elephant to cure an elephant's ache. One need simply (or not so simply) discover the curative serum and inject it into the correct artery. This already suggests work directed, not toward students but teachers and education leaders, not toward random schools but toward districts and model schools, with guaranteed outreach to many other schools; it even suggests curricular, school-structure, and professional-development models that can be adapted to local conditions but that have a universal efficacy. All of an operating foundation's experience with attempting to create much from little comes into play in public education.

Indeed, operating foundations actually have useful experience in confronting the extreme localism of public education. As I emphasized in the first section of this essay, operating foundations of all kinds are frequently challenged with maintaining the essentials of an innovative practice while allowing each site to refashion that practice to its circumstances. In the massive scene of public education—an ocean to higher education's sea— the hands-on requirement for operating foundations is increased by the volatility of the schools and their personnel, but that may provide stronger networking that will be useful in university-oriented programs as well.

Further, as good learning requires good educators, with expertise and enthusiasm for their subject matter, the fellowship model practiced by many operating foundations may prove apt, even as it requires a more systemic adaptation. Teach for America, for all its controversial relation to conventions of teacher training, certainly has injected a welcome new energy into the profession and recruited top students to become teachers for a short time, or longer. Woodrow Wilson's trustees have just provided some pilot funds to establish a new fellowship, modeled on our original program but applied to the level of high school rather than college teaching and with a stronger emphasis on retention. By creating three-way partnerships among the foundation, selected universities (in the pilot, Michigan, Penn, Stanford, and Texas), and urban schools in the region of each university—partnerships that provide teachers with a career rather than just a job—we hope to concentrate on terrific students who will become, and remain, extraordinary teachers. And by rewarding certain schools and the master teachers in those schools who will serve as mentors to the new fellows, we will seek to encourage new and proven lifelong teachers and lift the status of the profession. In the process, too, we can hope to heal a wound: the rift between schools of education and liberal arts colleges at the same institutions.

Could not a philanthropic foundation lead such a program? Absolutely, and indeed a new organization called Math for America is providing a very similar program in one discipline via a nonprofit supported by grants but also by a large endowment from the Simon Foundation. The Carnegie Corporation's Teachers for a New Era program, which seeks to encourage and reform teacher training at major universities, in part, by creating new alliances between the schools of education and the liberal arts colleges in those universities, is a different and laudable instance. But it is interesting that as the corporation wished to promulgate what it had determined to be good practice, it began to employ intermediaries for research, to engage staff time in site visits, and to seek external funding partners—to become, that is, more like an operating foundation per se. More usually even now, despite the trend Bacchetti describes, philanthropies have their own rigorous work to do (at best, listening to the ideas of others, evaluating many, and funding the best few) and find extensive staff work and partner-seeking a disruption. A division of labor that affords many kinds of organizational talents and capacities seems to me almost a priori wise.

But I want now to return to the problem I mentioned as mirrored in the organization of this chapter: the wide rift between the schools and the universities. That rift will prove to be both the greatest challenge and the greatest opportunity for operating foundations. The most prestigious colleges and universities have been perceived often as missing in action in terms of the crises in public education. Schools of education appear to have become bullied by their liberal arts counterparts into performing more and more research, thus leaving behind teacher training and a strong, organic connection to local schools. And in-service teachers have too often been held at arm's length, as Donald Stewart and Michael Johanek (1998) have written, by those institutions where the richest ongoing life of the disciplines gets lived.

The result can be relic knowledge and rote learning, for if teachers do not share in the discoveries and controversies of their field, it is difficult unto impossible for them to engage their students in the life of the mind. To put it more hopefully, the life of the disciplines, as experienced typically by college faculty, could mediate in the schools between a Greenwich mean of universal standards and an extreme localism—mediate or, better, raise the level of discussion by asking, What should students understand and by what sequential curriculum can such understanding be achieved? The American Diploma Project and the AAU initiative of Standards for Success are first, promising but general efforts to get at that, but it is left to the operating foundations to complete this coalescing work and to live it out in actual schools with real teachers and students. Inspired answers to this question, in fact, might reintroduce into the often grim contemporary scene the necessary missing concept for any student success: along with rigor, there must come joy. The federal government's efforts on both sides of the aisle to encourage less localism, more national standards, have too often resulted in teacher fear and student drills. There may be a different form of cohesion that the operating foundations can supply. As Indiana Yale reminded us, higher education is good at enjoying the disciplines, and that same compulsive pleasure can inform the schools. The French proverb, "One catches more flies with a spoonful of honey than twenty casks of vinegar" applies, and operating foundations can be crucial in its application.

What is at stake for the schools—and perhaps now, too, for the colleges and universities—is the liberal arts. In *Left Back,* Diane Ravitch (2000) argues that progressive educators throughout the last century have undermined the determination of the Committee of Ten—an 1892 blue-ribbon group appointed by the National Education Association and co-chaired, significantly, by Eliot and Harris, the president of Harvard and the Commissioner of Education, respectively, "that every child would benefit by receiving a liberal education of the highest quality" (p. 42). Instead, they promulgated the notion that most students were incapable of such an education and should instead be inculcated with "life-adjustment skills." There was nothing the schools could not be expected to do—except teach academic subjects to the majority of its students.

I am not convinced that Ravitch always gets the heroes and villains right, but I am convinced by her emphasis on Hutchins's insistence that "the best education for the best is the best education for all," rewritten perhaps in a less aristocratic lexicon. "The children most harmed by such practices" that neglect the liberal arts "were those who could not count on the protection of educated parents," Ravitch writes, rightly emphasizing the particular importance of the basic literacies of the arts and sciences for an ethnically diverse nation (p. 460).

We noted earlier several strengths of operating foundations, including the capacity to disseminate best practices; to create mutually educating networks of institutions while allowing for circumstantial difference; to leverage innovation, values, and funds; to assess honestly; and to translate ideas into actions that affect real students and faculty. Every one of these strengths is germane to public education. For instance, the networking we routinely achieve among universities serves as a basis for a more ambitious networking that might travel up and down the educational levels.

And again, this fording of gaps (earlier, academia and the other social sectors, or universities and philanthropies) is a capacity of operating foundations precisely because they belong entirely to neither camp. The operating foundation that conducts its operations with both schools and universities is in a thrillingly unique position. It *is* neither; it can come to understand both. It can explain to each how educational life looks from the other's vantage, but more important by far, it can move from explanation to collaborative action. There is no more literal challenge in creating such an alliance than the Early College program, where the collaboration takes place in an actual building, with faculty and administrators drawn from both public and higher education, and with student achievement—indeed, student lives—on the line as the basis for success or failure.

At a time when the removal of the liberal arts from the center of schooling appears by any number of statistics to have reached fully into higher education, a coalition among levels is all the more critical. Never have colleges and universities been less immune from whatever ills afflict the schools. More positively, there is mutual benefit available. The pedagogical sophistication of talented teachers in the schools frankly exceeds that of their college counterparts by a wide margin. If higher education does not see itself as a god carrying grace to undeserving sinners, it can benefit mightily as one term of a partnership that acknowledges difference, swaps strengths, and eventually closes the gap in status and distinction. Some universities, and indeed some schools and districts, will not see the potential for a major moment in educational history, but many more may either sense it vaguely or see it but not have the means to create it actively. And that is exactly where the operating foundation makes a crucial entrance—as an educator of educators and as a bridge over terribly troubled waters.

"Only Connect"

Intellectuals whose parents and grandparents established Harvard College condemned innocent women and men as witches in Salem Village. They did so for innumerable reasons, but one of them, as Sacvan Berkovitch (1975) has reminded us, was a horrible misapplication of a high-minded notion. America was to be the curative New Eden, the Western wild where scripture would be lived out, literally, in the details of life. In this New England, history would be rewritten and European corruption erased.[3] A rich theological literature insists on this peculiarly pragmatic utopia; thus Satan's demonic personal appearance, prophesied in scripture as the necessary prelude to Christ's second coming, was devoutly to be wished for—and fantasized into—reality.

No event more blatantly demonstrates the dangers of an American dream. The West has been a metaphor from classical times onward, both for an unspeakable bliss and a terrible chaos. It was an idea long before it was a colony or a nation for settlers from Europe. Whereas even radical Protestants in Europe and England maintained a distinction between the City of God and the City of Man, New England's City on the Hill imagined a livable paradise in the New World, and the nineteenth-century American romantics—Emerson, Thoreau, Dickinson, Whitman—recaptured after a spiritual lapse these scriptures, this time without strictures. When Emily

Dickinson writes that "paradise is of the option," when Thoreau tends beans to cultivate spirit, and when Emerson proclaims "All meaning in a potato," urging that the meanest object, viewed with spirit, discloses eternal verities—and when that same Emerson proclaims every man his own Jesus, the Puritan strain of living out vision returns in a form liberated to each individual's particular enactment—an impossibly literal dream of human fulfillment.

The organizations of civil society, in particular the philanthropies and operating foundations, are hardly free of this old American, millennial habit. Liberated from worrying about faculty protests over on-campus parking fees or student protests over an invited controversial speaker, we can urge on an uncompromised excellence. We evince, for better and worse, that American intolerance of the distance between national ideals and social realities.

There is a direct line from Emerson to Wilson to this moment. Emerson's "American Scholar" is "one who raises himself from private considerations and breathes and lives on public and illustrious thoughts. He is the world's eye. He is the world's heart." And for Wilson, both a university and a national president after all, "We are not put in this world to sit still and know; we are put into it to act. . . . The school must be of the nation."

When, for one example, we find that only 7 percent of all doctoral degrees awarded by universities in 2003 went to African Americans and Hispanic Americans, while 32 percent of the population ages twenty-five to forty is made up of these groups, we are agitated. And when we learn that nearly two-thirds of all Latino students who attend college go to two-year institutions and a very small number then proceed to the B.A. degree, we are invited to action. These figures, included in the recently completed Woodrow Wilson study of diversity and the doctorate (Woodrow Wilson National Fellowship Foundation, 2005a), are cited as a goad to action, and two of the recommended actions help to summarize what operating foundations can do: set an agenda, disseminate best practice, establish uncompromised goals, collect unbiased evidence, and act—all with a special capacity to serve as a neutral site among institutions that, seeking sometimes to be collaborative, still bear a competitive aspect.

First, the kinds of partnerships I described earlier, between schools and universities, are just the most obvious and dramatic forms of vertical integration that will be required by a strenuous social and educational effort to achieve real opportunity, equity, and excellence. The community college, the liberal arts college, the comprehensive university, and the research university all need to be linked intricately, not just "schools and universities." If the graduate faculty complains that there just are not enough Latino B.A.'s from which to recruit a doctoral class, they will be looking for snow in July. They must get into the eighth-grade classroom where students make life-altering decisions, into the community colleges, and into their own habits to make their disciplines more open, available, and germane to new Americans.

No one sector can enact these connections, and a direct philanthropic funding of coalitions has often proven balky and difficult to assess, but the operating foundation is fundamentally connective and thus has perhaps the best opportunity to serve, once again, as the neutral site, now not just for some universities but for a range of different kinds of institutions at different educational levels.

My colleagues and I wince—visibly, literally, I have witnessed it—when we are referred to by the relatively new term, *intermediary*. This word implies the realization of the operating foundation's nightmare—that it will be reduced to a mechanism carrying out a funder's will. And yet, as I emphasized in considering public education, this term can be reinterpreted most positively. It can connote instead the bridging, collaboration-building capacity of these organizations. The leader of a major philanthropy recently mentioned to me that he considered *opportunity* the new key word for academic foundations, in particular moving students, especially underserved students, from high school to college. The connective capacity of operating foundations should prove crucial to making opportunity available.

So, too, the capacity of the operating foundation to dig into detailed work. Another recommendation in the Woodrow Wilson report on diversity at the doctoral level proposes a research center and collective meeting place for all the agencies and foundations that encourage graduate education for minority students—a recommendation that arose from a startled finding that the different funders have had almost no conversation and that, with notable exceptions, assessments of the programs were few and weak. Here again, the capacities of the operating foundation to do heavy lifting and to serve as a neutral site have value.

Beyond even this crucial issue of gaining the democratic resources of the entire population as the so-called minority becomes a majority, there is, for me, a larger matter that requires participation by all kinds of institutions. The arts and sciences—the human literacies that support a democracy and that, even more fundamentally, make existence meaningful—need to travel more audaciously beyond the academy into every social sector. And here the connective role of all educational institutions, certainly including the places of learning and the philanthropies, must come into play. In the face of such a challenge, to inform every social decision by wisdom, it would be pure folly to claim any exclusive right for the grantseeking operating foundation. But as a participant most dependent and thus familiar with efforts of bridging, operating foundations certainly have a place in the effort to bring the pastoral of academic learning to the city of events. My personal sense of the future for operating foundations centers on the desirability to inform action by *best thought*—talk radio's polar opposite.

Again, this will require something of every kind of institution: for the universities and colleges, a greater sense of urgency and a renewed commitment to public purpose (in other words, a requirement to speed up and look outward); for the schools, a more meditative understanding of themselves and their possibilities and a renewed concern for the content of academic learning (in other words, a requirement to eschew fads and teach the real stuff), and for the grantmaking, philanthropic foundations, a better ear and a renewed interest in ideas from the teachers and students. And that leaves the operating foundation.

There are surely other visions for the future of operating foundations—vastly different, probably superior, certainly less pretentious. Even so, the biggest question for any operating foundation concerns its reason for existing. Why in education do we require them, and what is most largely required of them?

The answer returns us to an early point: a will to risk its very existence on commitment to an agenda and an agenda that is not afraid. There are real impediments to this boldness. Financially fragile as some operating foundations and their grantseeking like are, necessity is always a threat to an independent agenda. The recent demise of the American Association of Higher Education is another reminder of this fragility, and I would not understate it. If arrogance is the charge against philanthropy, timidity is the charge against grantseeking academic organizations; in both cases, there is a financial cause for such potential weaknesses.

Yet as I write, the grantseeking foundations appear to me more bold, more likely to set agendas, than at any time in the recent past. The American Association of Colleges and Universities has just initiated a campaign for liberal education, with extensive outreach to business and government. The Carnegie Foundation for the Advancement of Teaching, among several original efforts, is completing a stage in its own doctoral initiative that examines practice, or "stewardship," in several major disciplines by each discipline—a powerful counterpart to Wilson's Responsive Ph.D., which is organized by entire graduate schools. The American Academy of Letters and Science has pioneered data collection in the humanities—a sorely felt lack for the last quarter century. And the ACLS is investigating all digital technology in the humanities and "softer" social sciences, while the Council of Graduate Schools has initiated an attempt to investigate and rein in time-to-degree in the doctorate. With the exception of The Carnegie Foundation for the Advancement of Teaching, always a swashbuckler, these efforts constitute more adventurous efforts than are historically attributed to many of these organizations, and Woodrow Wilson has attempted to participate in this trend as well. "Only connect"—E. M. Forster's motto—has become ours.

These efforts, large and small, exemplify the adventurous spirit Franklin Roosevelt saw as the requirement of American society: "The country needs and, unless I mistake its temper, the country demands bold, persistent experimentation. It is common sense to take a method and try it. If it fails, admit it frankly and try another. But above all, try something." Or as Melville's Ishmael reminds us, "Who the devel ain't a dreamer?"

A Personal Coda

During the final weeks of developing this essay, I decided to leave Woodrow Wilson for an appointment as president of Drew University. This decision was made all the more difficult by the introspection required in writing this essay, for it led me to a renewed conviction of the import and potential of operating foundations. I had not intended to write a defense, and yet I had done just that. The depth of my enthusiasm for this kind of organization actually surprised me. I have been very lucky to be associated with Woodrow Wilson. But my decision, once made, also required me to ask if I had overlooked some of the perils of operating foundations, and I have not said anything about how it feels to work at one.

It feels scary. Operating on a thin margin, the staff at Woodrow Wilson in one particular week last month, lost a major fellowship program, gained another, received a totally unexpected bequest gift of several hundred thousand dollars, had a gift prospect balk on a pledge of almost equal value, and planned an intricate two-day conference on The Responsive Ph.D. After eight eventful years, I determined that the foundation would benefit from new energy. I also found myself homesick for campus life, especially for the kind of campus I had experienced at Wesleyan in Connecticut as an undergraduate. But most positively, I found myself thrilled by the potential of Drew, and challenged by the idea of working with faculty and administration in a particular place and over time to develop fully the life of an engaged university—for however close to the ground operating foundations are, we are not the ground itself.

Yet from our small height, we at operating foundations gain the perspective I hope to bring to my new colleagues at Drew. And while I sometimes have compared leading a foundation without a major endowment to performing on a trapeze without a net below, perhaps the sudden swoops and swerves of a rollercoaster make for a more exact analogy. Unlike that ride, this one carries the educational future as a passenger and actually may get somewhere. But moment-by-moment, experientially, the affect is apt. Frightening indeed—but, as I reminded myself in persuading my kids last summer to accompany their creaky father to Six Flags, I just love a rollercoaster.

NOTES

1. The Giving Network Web site: http//www.givingnetwork.org/ options_individualtopv5.html.

2. The Council on Foundations Web site: http://www.cof.org/index.

3. See also *Design of the Present: Essays on Time and Form in American Literature* (Lynen, 1969).

REFERENCES

Bercovitch, S. *Puritan Origins of the American Self.* New Haven and London: Yale University Press, 1975.

Bowen, W. G., Nygren, T. I., Turner, S. E., and Duffy, E. A. *The Charitable Nonprofits: An Analysis of Institutional Dynamics and Characteristics.* San Francisco: Jossey-Bass, 1994.

Judge, H. "Higher Education and the Schools." In P. Timpane, M. White, and L. S. White (eds.), *Higher Education and School Reform.* San Francisco: Jossey-Bass, 1998.

Lynen J. *Design of the Present: Essays on Time and Form in American Literature.* New Haven, Conn.: Yale University Press, 1969.

Ravitch, D. *Left Back: A Century of Failed School Reforms.* New York and London: Simon & Schuster, 2000.

Stewart, D. S., and Johanek, M. "Enhanced Academic Connections: Deweyan Waste, Ecological Pipelines, and Intellectual Vitality." In P. Timpane, M. White, and L. S. White (eds.), *Higher Education and School Reform.* San Francisco: Jossey-Bass, 1998.

Woodrow Wilson National Fellowship Foundation. "Diversity and the Ph.D.: A Review of Efforts to Broaden Race and Ethnicity in U.S. Doctoral Education." Princeton, N.J.: Woodrow Wilson National Fellowship Foundation, 2005a.

Woodrow Wilson National Fellowship Foundation. "The Responsive Ph.D.: Innovations in U.S. Doctoral Education." Princeton, N.J.: Woodrow Wilson National Fellowship Foundation, 2005b.

APPENDIX A:

GOING FOR THE GOLD IN UNDERGRADUATE EDUCATION

Russell Edgerton

Russell Edgerton is a long-time advocate for strengthening under-graduate teaching and learning. He is president emeritus of the American Association for Higher Education, program officer for education at The Pew Charitable Trusts, and a visiting scholar at The Carnegie Foundation for the Advancement of Teaching. As editors of this volume, we asked him to summarize his views for a session of The Carnegie Foundation Centennial Conference on Foundations and Education. In the pages that follow, we think he makes a provocative case for what we term building educational capital to enhance undergraduate education.

The Editors

○

○ *It is time to pay attention to the quality of undergraduate education.* America's colleges and universities are under pressure to serve more students, including ever-greater numbers of students who are neither intrinsically interested in learning nor prepared for college-level work. At the same time, fiscal constraints, market pressures, heightened competition, enrollment in multiple institutions, and other trends are undermining the traditional underpinnings for engaged learning.

The prospect of deteriorating quality is very real. At the same time, new knowledge about learning and new technologies offer an unprecedented opportunity for colleges and universities to become more effective. And a compelling reason to seize this opportunity lies in the effects of undergraduate teaching on the quality of teaching in K–12. School teachers learn how to teach from how they were taught: by faculty in the arts and sciences. What is at stake is the quality of teaching throughout the entire educational enterprise.

○ *To respond to these challenges and opportunities, higher education should set its sights on a new gold standard for college performance: deep and enduring learning for all students. To meet this standard, colleges will have to become not only more inclusive and learning-centered but also more engaging, devoted to deep learning, and evidence-driven.* The shift in focus from teaching to learning is, at bottom, a shift in who is responsible for what. Faculty have traditionally conceived their responsibility in terms of providing good teaching, by which they mean "knowing their field and professing it well." This conception leaves it up to the students to get what they can from the classroom experience. In a college that accepts responsibility, not just for teaching but learning, the faculty view good teaching as doing "whatever it takes" to cause student learning. If things go wrong, both teachers and students are responsible for trying alternative approaches.

○ *A difficulty in living up to this standard is that promising ideas and effective practices don't get to scale. And a major reason they don't is that colleges can do well (students enroll, everyone gets paid) without getting better and better at the task of teaching and learning. There is little felt need to improve.* Whether one looks at the way colleges have internally organized the process of instruction, the ground rules for training and advancement in the academic profession, the marketplace in which colleges compete for students, or the ground rules set by the policies of the states and the federal governments, the picture is the same. There are few incentives for colleges to pay close attention to teaching and learning.

Given these assumptions, improvement initiatives thus take a predictable course. Typically, faculty become enamored with a promising approach. The practice spreads. But there are only so many faculty who are willing to go against the grain. The initiative stalls for lack of support from the rest of the system.

○ *To get effective practices to scale, more effort needs to be allocated to building infrastructure and developing tools and incentives. But just spreading effective practices that leave the system unchanged won't suffice. We should focus on scaling up those practices that will permanently change the incentives and make colleges more purposeful and evidence-driven institutions that get better and better on their own.* There are many stages in the journey to scale: idea→prototype→experimentation→early replication→best practice→scale. Most of the attention and special support is focused on the early stages of the process. But it would not be necessary to push so hard if there were more pull.

○ *Initiatives that are capable of changing the system are not projects undertaken by single campuses but rather "national expeditions"—complex, multifaceted undertakings that engage a number of colleges in a purposeful effort that lasts ten to fifteen years. Strategic investing has much to do with launching and sustaining national expeditions.* The task of assembling, launching, and sustaining a national expedition in higher education requires highly proactive grantmaking. Sometimes an established institution can take the lead. For example, the Carnegie Foundation has led in the scholarship of teaching. But often it is necessary to place a big bet on a leader and invent an organization that can take the lead. The successful expeditions (Frank Newman and the creation of Campus Compact, Barbara Smith and the Washington Center for Undergraduate Education, Pat Callan and the National Center for Public Policy and Higher Education, George Kuh and the National Survey for Student Engagement) all had exceptional leaders.

○ *Stand-alone expeditions themselves are rarely sufficient to bring ideas to scale. To get to scale, initiatives from a number of sources must converge and reinforce one another.* As a result of past expeditions, many ideas, such as service learning, have turned into movements. For the movements to really take hold, support must come from within colleges, within the intellectual communities, and within the stakeholder communities. Yet the efforts of faculty to take more responsibility for student learning and the efforts of external stakeholders to hold institutions more accountable for student learning are like ships passing in the night. While the parties would probably endorse the gold standard of providing deep and enduring learning as a desirable goal, they have quite different views as to what it would take to get from here to there.

Changing the Incentives Within Colleges

Over a century ago, colleges and universities organized themselves around what John Tagg calls the "instructional paradigm." They defined their mission as providing *teaching,* and they designed an instructional process that involved taking courses and accumulating credits that meet requirements for depth and breadth of study. Although this system has many benefits, both the colleges and the students have lost sight of the ends—the student learning—that is the point of it all. Having stopped short of defining what learning they intend to bring about, colleges don't confront the consequences of succeeding or failing. Students know that once a course is completed, it is the credits, not the evidence about what learning the credits stand for, that are noted on the transcript.

It would be foolish to think that this system of courses, credits, and requirements for breadth and depth could be uprooted—or that it should be. But new processes can be introduced that refocus attention on long-term goals, as well as deep and enduring learning. Faculty can identify the qualities that characterize an ideal graduate and illuminate the pathways through the curriculum that students can take to acquire these qualities, as well as the culminating performances that represent standards of achievement. Students can be encouraged to identify the long-term learning projects they will undertake, and students can document and assemble evidence of their accomplishments in *learning portfolios*. Students can present their accomplishments to employers and other constituencies by translating their portfolios into *performance transcripts* (or passports).

○ *A priority investment: an expedition to foster state-of-the-art learning portfolios.* Learning portfolios, especially electronic versions, can enable students to generate and document evidence of their learning over time, reflect on this evidence, and represent their learning to others. The interest in learning portfolios has mushroomed into a global movement. The need now is for more examples of what portfolios at their best can be. A cluster of colleges and universities where portfolios are viewed as vehicles for documenting the attainment of general learning outcomes could be invited to form The Learning Portfolio Compact. The Compact members would receive support for working, not only on issues about the design of portfolios but on the institutional conditions essential to their quality, such as how to capture faculty time for portfolio work.

○ *A priority investment: an expedition to map pathways to civic literacy.* Apart from writing, few campuses have laid out the sequences of assignments and experiences that would enable students to progress from beginning to advanced status in a given ability, or literacy. To engage this work, faculty need to become part of communities of practice that lay out the case for the importance of a given literacy, the pathways to attaining the literacy, and examples of culminating performances that would demonstrate that the literacy has been attained.

The recent expedition in *quantitative literacy*, led by Robert Orrill under the aegis of the Woodrow Wilson Foundation, offers a model of how to proceed. The term *civic literacy* means the knowledge, skills, and values needed to be an effective citizen. A National Center on Educating for Civic Literacy could serve as a model for other centers dedicated to mapping other literacies in other arenas.

Changing the Norms of the Academic Profession

Before faculty are "faculty" they become mathematicians, engineers, and members of myriad other intellectual communities, and their views of what's worth doing are shaped by these communities. When these disciplines first came into being, prestigious scholars taught introductory courses, saw themselves at the service of their universities, and cared about education in the K–12 sector. Yet as time went on and the federal government made billions of dollars available for research, most of the disciplines retreated into a narrow research orientation.

Another development had still more damaging results. Each discipline could have spawned a subspecialty in the teaching and learning of its particular field. Instead, the academic study of teaching and learning became the province of departments of education and psychology, where the focus was on the study of teaching *in general*. Professors in the disciplines came to view teaching, not as an act of translating the concepts of their field into terms that students would understand but as a set of techniques for presenting information and managing classroom discussions—Mickey Mouse stuff, or so it seemed to them.

The Carnegie Foundation for the Advancement of Teaching has set forth an alternative vision—a vision of teaching as an intellectually interesting, scholarly activity. And it has encouraged faculty to invent ways of investigating, documenting, and displaying aspects of their teaching as "community property." The challenge now is to inject this conception of teaching into every stage of the process through which faculty become members of the academic profession: graduate school training, appointment to the faculty, promotion and tenure, and the definition of their ongoing role.

o *A priority investment: an expedition that organizes the marketplace and reinforces the "re-envisioning" process during the faculty hiring process.* A consortium of hiring and supplying universities could identify pilot fields, and these fields could develop exemplary practices for setting expectations and presenting and evaluating evidence of a candidate's qualifications in light of these expectations.

Another priority investment concerns the *promotion and tenure process:* The Carnegie Academy for the Scholarship of Teaching and Learning has inspired faculty in many fields to invent ways (such as the course portfolio) of documenting and presenting their teaching as scholarly work. But unless stakeholders such as accreditors and system offices insist that teaching should be peer reviewed, the movement will stall out.

○ *A priority investment: a National Center and Forum on the 21st Century Professoriate.* It used to be said that "the faculty are the university." But no more. We desperately need a place that can (1) systemically monitor the sea changes taking place in the faculty role and (2) engage faculty (especially young faculty) in reinventing their own profession.

Changing the Signals Coming from Stakeholders

Every major stakeholder—for example, parents, employers, accreditors, state and federal policymakers—is a potential ally in converting colleges into places where all students experience deep and enduring learning.

Here are two expeditions that, if successful, would help change the system:

○ *A priority investment: shaping a new public understanding of quality.* In many industries, competition stimulates the providers to constantly refine the quality of their products and services. But in higher education, colleges don't compete on the basis of their contributions to student learning. Rather, colleges strive for quality by acquiring resources others don't have and by investing in athletics and other means of gaining visibility. This race for prestige will always go on, but it need not be the only game in town. Efforts can be mounted that enable institutions to earn a reputation for effectiveness in contributing to student learning.

Three particular initiatives come to mind. First, *evidence of college contributions to learning could be more public.* The NSSE office, for example, could develop a template for institutions to report their NSSE scores in a format that facilitates comparisons with other institutions. Students inquiring into a particular institution could be linked to a NSSE-managed Web site, where similar evidence about twenty to thirty other institutions could be found.

Second, *there could be more occasions for recognizing high performance.* For example, a magazine such as *Atlantic Monthly* could publish the scores of the top 5 percent of performers on various NSSE benchmarks.

Third, *leaders could become more aggressive about what constitutes evidence of quality.* For example, presidents or governing boards, or both, could condition their participation in the *U.S. News & World Report* rankings on changes in the ranking methodology.

○ *A priority investment: the professionalization of regional accreditation.* Not so long ago, well-established colleges and universities viewed accreditation to be akin to a trip to the dentist. But over the past eight years, some regional accrediting agencies have reexamined the one-size-fits-all methodology of a self-study—an accreditation visit and a report—and have sharpened their focus on effectiveness. Accrediting agencies are the most promising vehicles we have for prompting and guiding the transition to more evidence-based practice. Yet accrediting agencies are still governed and financed by a philosophy that they should be just strong enough to ward off governmental intrusion but no stronger. A foundation or a consortium of foundations could create a new entity that could offer incentives and support for turning accrediting agencies into professional operations: reducing staff caseloads, training visiting teams, and building databases.

o *A final investment priority: The Learning First Forum.* This would be an agency charged with keeping the vision of a new gold standard alive. The Forum would annually convene the various expeditions and try to press the point that only by working in concert will the vision be realized.

APPENDIX B:

SELECTED DATA ON FOUNDATION GRANTS TO EDUCATIONAL INSTITUTIONS AND ON TOTAL EXPENDITURES FOR K–12 AND HIGHER EDUCATION

SETS OF NUMBERS have narratives embedded in them. The numbers that lie behind the chapters of this book sprawl across thousands of foundations. Those foundations give some $10 billion annually to several thousand colleges, universities, schools, and a substantial number of organizations that aid and support them. Estimating and extrapolating yield only approximate results. Yet if done consistently year by year, such results can reveal trends; looking at who gives and who receives can tell other stories.

The tables that follow represent a selection of consistent data and inform and amplify the chapters combining to make this book. We include them so that readers can explore their significance and think about the questions they raise. Because the Foundation Center is our principal source, this Appendix can provide a baseline against which future students of foundation-education interrelationships can secure comparably gathered numbers from the Foundation Center.

After a commentary on the data, these are the tables that follow:

- Top 100 Foundations Giving to U.S.-Based Recipients for Pre-collegiate Education, Circa 1990, 1997, and 2004. (Tables App.1–App.3)

- Top 100 U.S.-Based Recipients of Giving for Precollegiate Education, Circa 1990, 1997, and 2004. (Tables App.4–App.6)

- Top 100 Foundations Giving to U.S.-Based Recipients for Higher, Graduate, and Professional Education and Educational Institutions, Circa 1990, 1997, and 2004. (Tables App.7–App.9) o Top 100 Recipients of Grants Awarded to U.S.-Based Organizations for Higher, Graduate, and Professional Education and Educational Institutions, Circa 1990, 1997, and 2004. (Tables App.10–App.12)

o Top 100 U.S.-Based College and University Recipients of Grants Awarded by the Top 100 Funders for Higher, Graduate, and Professional Education and Educational Institutions, Circa 2004. (Table App.13)

o Estimated Total Giving to U.S.-Based Recipients for Precollegiate Education, 1990–2004. (Table App.14)

o Estimated Total Giving to U.S.-Based Recipients for Higher, Graduate, and Professional Education and Educational Institutions, 1990–2004. (Table App.15)

o Total Expenditures for Elementary/Secondary and Higher Education, 1990–2004. (Table App.16)

Commentary on the Data

The principal sources of data on foundation funding of education are the Council on Aid to Education and the Foundation Center.

The Council on Aid to Education, with co-sponsorship from the Council for Advancement and Support of Education, tracks private giving through an annual Voluntary Support for Education (VSE) survey. The survey presents data from approximately 1,000 of the nation's higher education institutions and about 250 private schools. The database includes donations of any amount from several sources, one of which is foundations. Family foundations have only recently been included; corporate foundations are excluded. VSE data are supplied directly by the institutions to the Council on Aid to Education.

The Foundation Center maintains a database that includes all foundations registered in the United States. Information is obtained from IRS Form 990-PF and other public documents. Given the size of the database (close to 68,000 grantmaking foundations, and growing), the Foundation Center derives its statistics from a sample. Compiled annually, the sample consists of all grants of $10,000 or more made by about 1,000 foundations, including over 800 of the largest 1,000 foundations in terms of total grant dollars and approximately 200 other private (independent or family, corporate, grantmaking operating) and community foundations of various sizes. Excluded from the sample are grants of under $10,000, grants made directly to individuals, grants for foundation-administered projects, and grants from one foundation to another, except when made to nongranting operating foundations or overseas foundations.

Although the Foundation Center sample is considered "suggestive of giving trends . . . but not conclusive"[1] since the early 1990s, the sample has consistently accounted for over half of total grant dollars awarded each year by the universe of grantmaking foundations and provides the most comprehensive resource available on grantmaking patterns and trends.

Because the Foundation Center's grants sample includes most of the largest U.S. foundations, it generally captures most of the largest funders for specific fields, such as education. However, the sample does not include foundations that allocate a substantial share of the annual giving for education, if their overall giving did not meet the threshold for inclusion in the sample. In addition, although the Foundation Center strives to include all of the top foundations each year, the sample will exclude top education funders if current grant data were unavailable at the time an annual sample was being compiled. Thus the absence of a particular grantmaker from the set of top education funders in a single year may reflect a decrease in that foundation's giving, or it may reflect the unavailability of its grant information. Because of the vagaries of reporting, all sample-based tables are compiled with data from more than one calendar year. The Foundation Center uses the word *circa* to indicate that a data set includes a mixture of reporting years.[2]

As the Council on Aid to Education makes clear, the VSE cannot be extrapolated from to derive national estimates, does not draw from the entire universe of foundations,[3] and does not include public schools. Accordingly, the Foundation Center's data were selected as the basis for tables in this Appendix. The sole exception is Table App.16—"Total Expenditures"—a figure derived from data compiled by the U.S. Department of Education's National Center for Education Statistics.

The precise dollar amount of foundation giving to education is unknown. The Foundation Center derives its estimates of total giving by extrapolating from the sample, adjusting for factors such as foundation size. Estimating is done only to generate totals for a sector, such as higher education. The models will not reliably estimate within-sector totals, such as giving to four-year colleges or for medical education.

The Foundation Center classifies grants according to the National Taxonomy of Exempt Entities (NTEE), which was initially designed to classify nonprofit organizations by primary purpose. In 1989, the Foundation

Center adopted an expanded NTEE coding system that allowed for additional categorizations, such as type of support, population group served, and geographic focus. "Educational Institutions and Related Activities," coded with the letter B and containing over fifty subdivisions, is one of ten major NTEE field area classifications. In that same year, the Foundation Center made changes to its sampling base, raising the minimum grant amount from $5,000 to $10,000 and significantly enlarging the size of the sample. For these reasons, pre- and post-1990 Foundation Center tables are not directly comparable.

Higher education, graduate education, and professional education tables in this Appendix include grants categorized under NTEE primary subject or recipient codes B40-B4R and B50-B5R. These codes capture all grants to U.S.-based higher-graduate-professional educational institutions, as well as grants for higher-graduate-professional education awarded to other types of institutions. The codes are consistent with standard Foundation Center usage.

Elementary and secondary education tables are also consistent with customary Foundation Center coding and include grants with NTEE primary subject codes B20–2R, B32, and B90-B95. These codes capture all grants to U.S.-based institutions for public and private elementary and secondary education and educational services, whether made to schools, school districts, colleges and universities, or intermediary agencies.

In making comparisons between sample-based tables in this Appendix and other Foundation Center data on education, please note that these tables include only giving to U.S.-based educational institutions; in contrast, standard Foundation Center tables include giving to educational institutions anywhere in the world. In addition, although the higher education tables presented here use standard Foundation Center codes, analyses performed on the data for the Foundation Center's 2003 publication *Update on Funding for Higher and Graduate Education* applied the codes only to the primary recipient organization; analyses in the annual *Foundation Giving Trends* are based only on primary grant purpose. Totals here, which include both primary-purpose and primary-recipient types, are thus higher than those reported by the Foundation Center. A final caution: for the Top 100 lists, *foundation size* is defined in terms of giving to organizations and does not reflect grants to individuals or expenditures for foundation-administered programs.

We thank Steven Lawrence and Josie Atienza for unflagging assistance in clarifying the content of Foundation Center databases and defining search strategies. Ann Kaplan at the Council on Aid to Education helped us understand the characteristics and uses of the VSE.

NOTES

1. *Foundation Giving Trends,* 2006 edition, p. 86.

2. For example, the circa 2004 sample contains grants awarded in 2004 or 2003. Although the practice is maintained, the term is omitted in reports published by the Foundation Center.

3. Exclusion of corporate foundations from the VSE is thought to account for much of the difference between its estimated total giving to higher education and that of the Foundation Center.

Table App.1. Top 100 Foundations Giving to U.S.-Based Recipients for Precollegiate Education, Circa 1990[1]

Foundation Name	State	Foundation Type	Grant Dollars	No. of Grants
1. Lilly Endowment, Inc.	IN	IN	$11,054,167	38
2. The Pew Charitable Trusts	PA	IN	7,400,000	14
3. The Annenberg Foundation	PA	IN	6,330,000	6
4. John D. and Catherine T. MacArthur Foundation	IL	IN	5,334,217	46
5. Carnegie Corporation of New York	NY	IN	4,487,890	38
6. The Ford Foundation	NY	IN	3,724,600	12
7. The Spencer Foundation	IL	IN	3,483,600	9
8. The Aaron Diamond Foundation, Inc.	NY	IN	3,210,308	70
9. The Rockefeller Foundation	NY	IN	2,980,750	27
10. Charles Stewart Mott Foundation	MI	IN	2,953,177	35
11. William R. Kenan, Jr. Charitable Trust	NC	IN	2,925,895	5
12. The William and Flora Hewlett Foundation	CA	IN	2,608,000	8
13. The Abell Foundation, Inc.	MD	IN	2,586,404	20
14. Howard Heinz Endowment	PA	IN	2,434,040	4
15. The Andrew W. Mellon Foundation	NY	IN	2,385,000	8
16. The Milken Family Foundation	CA	IN	2,185,500	14
17. DeWitt Wallace-Reader's Digest Fund, Inc.	NY	IN	2,181,242	32
18. Longwood Foundation, Inc.	DE	IN	2,168,000	10
19. The William Penn Foundation	PA	IN	2,161,204	15
20. W. K. Kellogg Foundation	MI	IN	2,086,993	15
21. The Joyce Foundation	IL	IN	2,062,318	37
22. Houston Endowment, Inc.	TX	IN	1,780,250	16

#	Foundation	State	Type	Amount	
23.	Communities Foundation of Texas, Inc.	TX	CM	1,741,652	26
24.	Lettie Pate Evans Foundation, Inc.	GA	IN	1,680,000	6
25.	T.L.L. Temple Foundation	TX	IN	1,640,252	30
26.	The F. J. O'Neill Charitable Corporation	OH	IN	1,560,000	8
27.	The Edward E. Ford Foundation	DC	IN	1,545,000	34
28.	Conrad N. Hilton Foundation	NV	IN	1,531,000	4
29.	The George Gund Foundation	OH	IN	1,475,803	22
30.	The Danforth Foundation	MO	IN	1,452,275	16
31.	ExxonMobil Foundation	TX	CS	1,417,499	19
32.	The Morris and Gwendolyn Cafritz Foundation	DC	IN	1,300,500	22
33.	The Edna McConnell Clark Foundation	NY	IN	1,292,550	10
34.	The Hearst Foundations, Inc.	NY	IN	1,275,000	47
35.	Horace W. Goldsmith Foundation	NY	IN	1,225,000	13
36.	The San Francisco Foundation	CA	CM	1,181,500	24
37.	GE Fund	CT	CS	1,177,676	16
38.	New Cycle Foundation	MA	IN	1,149,823	1
39.	Thomas and Dorothy Leavey Foundation	CA	IN	1,117,500	6
40.	The John G. and Marie Stella Kenedy Memorial Foundation	TX	IN	1,111,961	9
41.	The Bush Foundation	MN	IN	1,097,152	7
42.	James S. McDonnell Foundation	MO	IN	1,087,139	9
43.	Geraldine R. Dodge Foundation, Inc.	NJ	IN	1,079,234	22
44.	American Express Foundation	NY	CS	1,042,700	20
45.	The Emmet and Frances Tracy Fund	MI	IN	1,030,000	5
46.	James L. and Eunice West Charitable Trust	TX	IN	1,000,000	2
47.	The Needmor Fund	CO	IN	987,750	7
48.	Abell-Hanger Foundation	TX	IN	965,390	5

Table App.1. Top 100 Foundations Giving to U.S.-Based Recipients for Precollegiate Education, Circa 1990[1], *continued*

Foundation Name	State	Foundation Type	Grant Dollars	No. of Grants
49. Stuart Foundation	CA	IN	938,929	24
50. U S WEST Foundation	CO	CS	926,759	23
51. The Cleveland Foundation	OH	CM	925,935	14
52. Victoria Foundation, Inc.	NJ	IN	903,000	29
53. The Brown Foundation, Inc.	TX	IN	870,257	15
54. The Humana Foundation, Inc.	KY	CS	865,911	19
55. The Chicago Community Trust and Affiliates	IL	CM	848,796	14
56. Meyer Memorial Trust	OR	IN	833,900	5
57. The Fondren Foundation	TX	IN	825,000	4
58. IBM International Foundation	NY	CS	818,649	1
59. The UPS Foundation	GA	CS	811,421	11
60. Charles E. Culpeper Foundation, Inc.	CT	IN	806,500	35
61. Smart Family Foundation	CT	IN	794,350	4
62. The Procter & Gamble Fund	OH	CS	767,092	4
63. Altman Foundation	NY	IN	759,900	28
64. The Louis Calder Foundation	NY	IN	729,500	23
65. Turrell Fund	NJ	IN	724,550	28
66. GTE Foundation	TX	CS	711,888	8
67. Amelia Peabody Foundation	MA	IN	710,210	9
68. Oberkotter Foundation	PA	IN	710,000	3
69. Beatrice P. Delany Charitable Trust	NY	IN	700,000	15
70. Rockefeller Brothers Fund, Inc.	NY	IN	696,600	5

	State	Type	Amount	
71. Shell Oil Company Foundation	TX	CS	689,717	4
72. Capital Fund Foundation	CA	IN	671,000	8
73. Amon G. Carter Foundation	TX	IN	667,000	4
74. John & Dorothy Shea Foundation	CA	IN	657,500	6
75. The Pittsburgh Foundation	PA	CM	656,334	6
76. Scaife Family Foundation	PA	IN	650,000	2
77. The Starr Foundation	NY	IN	647,500	7
78. The Burnett Foundation	TX	IN	621,264	8
79. Jessie Ball duPont Fund	FL	IN	616,252	9
80. Dr. Scholl Foundation	IL	IN	611,700	31
81. F. M. Kirby Foundation, Inc.	NJ	IN	605,500	13
82. The Ann and Gordon Getty Foundation	CA	IN	600,000	2
83. The Cullen Foundation	TX	IN	590,000	2
84. The William Stamps Farish Fund	TX	IN	590,000	8
85. Mericos Foundation	CA	IN	585,388	4
86. Weingart Foundation	CA	IN	585,000	7
87. The McKnight Foundation	MN	IN	578,000	4
88. Z. Smith Reynolds Foundation, Inc.	NC	IN	577,000	23
89. Koret Foundation	CA	IN	569,610	8
90. L. G. Balfour Foundation	MA	IN	566,735	6
91. Target Foundation	MN	CS	561,375	18
92. The James Irvine Foundation	CA	IN	559,000	11
93. Ford Motor Company Fund	MI	CS	556,935	15
94. Charles Hayden Foundation	NY	IN	556,000	14
95. BP Amoco Foundation, Inc.	IL	CS	555,000	11
96. Joseph B. Whitehead Foundation	GA	IN	550,000	3
97. Timken Foundation of Canton	OH	IN	540,328	2

Table App.I. Top 100 Foundations Giving to U.S.-Based Recipients for Precollegiate Education, Circa 1990[1], *continued*

Foundation Name	State	Foundation Type	Grant Dollars	No. of Grants
98. The Skillman Foundation	MI	IN	537,000	3
99. The Champlin Foundations	RI	IN	536,218	12
100. Herrick Foundation	MI	IN	510,000	2
Subtotal for Top 100 Foundations			$147,164,414	1,443
Total for All Foundations			$204,761,210	3,190

Source: *The Foundation Center*

[1]Based on grants of $10,000 or more awarded by a national sample of 832 larger U.S. foundations. For community foundations, only discretionary grants are included. Grants to individuals are not included in the file.

Note: IN = Independent Foundation; CM = Community Foundation; CS = Corporate Foundation

Table App.2. Top 100 Foundations Giving to U.S.-Based Recipients for Precollegiate Education, Circa 1997[1]

Foundation Name	State	Foundation Type	Grant Dollars	No. of Grants
1. The Annenberg Foundation	PA	IN	$54,037,603	31
2. Lilly Endowment, Inc.	IN	IN	19,697,415	38
3. W. K. Kellogg Foundation	MI	IN	14,350,300	70
4. Wallace-Readers Digest Funds	NY	IN	13,821,731	40
5. The Ford Foundation	NY	IN	12,172,922	46
6. The Joyce Foundation	IL	IN	10,975,876	41
7. The Pew Charitable Trusts	PA	IN	10,380,500	16
8. The F. J. O'Neill Charitable Corporation	OH	IN	10,205,000	36
9. The David and Lucile Packard Foundation	CA	IN	9,746,998	50
10. Carnegie Corporation of New York	NY	IN	6,769,300	23
11. Connelly Foundation	PA	IN	6,445,522	89
12. The California Wellness Foundation	CA	IN	6,080,000	15
13. The Annie E. Casey Foundation	MD	IN	5,573,300	33
14. The Rockefeller Foundation	NY	IN	5,381,773	21
15. The Danforth Foundation	MO	IN	5,232,810	90
16. The Andrew W. Mellon Foundation	NY	IN	5,117,000	15
17. The Ahmanson Foundation	CA	IN	4,710,564	63
18. AT&T Foundation	NY	CS	4,629,400	62
19. John D. and Catherine T. MacArthur Foundation	IL	IN	4,530,300	23
20. Oberkotter Foundation	PA	IN	4,495,805	16
21. John S. and James L. Knight Foundation	FL	IN	4,284,767	31

Table App.2. Top 100 Foundations Giving to U.S.-Based Recipients for Precollegiate Education, Circa 1997[1], *continued*

Foundation Name	State	Foundation Type	Grant Dollars	No. of Grants
22. The Community Foundation for the National Capital Region	DC	CM	4,174,535	45
23. Walton Family Foundation, Inc.	AR	IN	4,093,108	20
24. The Lynde and Harry Bradley Foundation, Inc.	WI	IN	4,012,148	26
25. The Starr Foundation	NY	IN	3,968,600	24
26. The William and Flora Hewlett Foundation	CA	IN	3,763,000	18
27. GE Fund	CT	CS	3,585,126	56
28. J. Bulow Campbell Foundation	GA	IN	3,573,419	6
29. Charles Stewart Mott Foundation	MI	IN	3,465,500	12
30. The Abell Foundation, Inc.	MD	IN	3,436,091	27
31. The Champlin Foundations	RI	IN	3,307,920	45
32. BellSouth Foundation	GA	CS	3,288,000	32
33. James J. McCann Charitable Trust and McCann Foundation, Inc.	NY	IN	3,145,817	2
34. Ewing Marion Kauffman Foundation	MO	IN	2,877,444	33
35. The San Francisco Foundation	CA	CM	2,801,810	51
36. The Edna McConnell Clark Foundation	NY	IN	2,798,500	21
37. Victoria Foundation, Inc.	NJ	IN	2,703,923	40
38. Robert W. Woodruff Foundation, Inc.	GA	IN	2,700,000	1
39. The Milken Family Foundation	CA	IN	2,687,275	11
40. The Ford Family Foundation	OR	IN	2,658,000	22
41. Hiawatha Education Foundation	MN	IN	2,539,507	6

#	Name	State	Type	Amount	
42.	Open Society Institute	NY	OP	2,530,809	9
43.	Wayne & Gladys Valley Foundation	CA	IN	2,468,333	21
44.	Dan Murphy Foundation	CA	IN	2,457,700	17
45.	Horace W. Goldsmith Foundation	NY	IN	2,402,500	24
46.	Turrell Fund	NJ	IN	2,389,769	52
47.	The Edward E. Ford Foundation	DC	IN	2,340,000	56
48.	Geraldine R. Dodge Foundation, Inc.	NJ	IN	2,214,500	35
49.	The Boston Foundation, Inc.	MA	CM	2,172,900	49
50.	Robert R. McCormick Tribune Foundation	IL	IN	2,170,210	39
51.	The Cleveland Foundation	OH	CM	2,164,870	14
52.	Dekko Foundation, Inc.	IN	IN	2,157,157	26
53.	The Chicago Community Trust and Affiliates	IL	CM	2,147,300	25
54.	Charles Hayden Foundation	NY	IN	2,147,000	28
55.	Grable Foundation	PA	IN	2,145,297	40
56.	The Spencer Foundation	IL	IN	2,088,115	18
57.	Meyer Memorial Trust	OR	IN	2,063,900	12
58.	The George Gund Foundation	OH	IN	2,063,265	20
59.	Conrad N. Hilton Foundation	NV	IN	1,994,750	9
60.	Citigroup Foundation	NY	CS	1,971,000	52
61.	Walter S. Johnson Foundation	CA	IN	1,953,146	20
62.	Houston Endowment Inc.	TX	IN	1,875,000	18
63.	General Motors Foundation, Inc.	MI	CS	1,834,400	16
64.	The UPS Foundation	GA	CS	1,768,818	31
65.	The Charles A. Dana Foundation, Inc.	NY	IN	1,750,000	3
66.	The Freeman Foundation	NY	IN	1,738,255	11
67.	Helen Bader Foundation, Inc.	WI	IN	1,653,275	29
68.	The Louis Calder Foundation	NY	IN	1,650,000	59

Table App.2. Top 100 Foundations Giving to U.S.-Based Recipients for Precollegiate Education, Circa 1997[1], *continued*

Foundation Name	State	Foundation Type	Grant Dollars	No. of Grants
69. The Procter & Gamble Fund	OH	CS	1,629,949	15
70. The Prudential Foundation	NJ	CS	1,577,000	27
71. Presbyterian Health Foundation	OK	IN	1,575,000	3
72. The Burnett Foundation	TX	IN	1,575,000	4
73. S. H. Cowell Foundation	CA	IN	1,565,255	21
74. The Noyce Foundation	CA	IN	1,564,250	60
75. Tiger Foundation	NY	IN	1,560,000	18
76. IBM International Foundation	NY	CS	1,540,647	2
77. Peninsula Community Foundation	CA	CM	1,536,778	26
78. Gates Family Foundation	CO	IN	1,516,563	14
79. Herrick Foundation	MI	IN	1,505,278	11
80. Harold K. L. Castle Foundation	HI	IN	1,452,000	10
81. Claude Worthington Benedum Foundation	PA	IN	1,447,567	14
82. The San Diego Foundation	CA	CM	1,388,068	33
83. Communities Foundation of Texas, Inc.	TX	CM	1,384,834	37
84. Irving I. Moskowitz Foundation	CA	IN	1,364,600	7
85. The Lincy Foundation	CA	IN	1,350,000	20
86. Amelia Peabody Foundation	MA	IN	1,349,000	16
87. The William Penn Foundation	PA	IN	1,342,444	11
88. Longwood Foundation, Inc.	DE	IN	1,335,000	7
89. Weingart Foundation	CA	IN	1,328,450	40
90. Spencer T. and Ann W. Olin Foundation	MO	IN	1,312,880	4
91. Mary Stuart Rogers Foundation	CA	IN	1,305,000	5

92. J. P. Morgan Charitable Trust	NY	CS	1,247,500	33
93. Arie and Ida Crown Memorial	IL	IN	1,234,905	12
94. Meadows Foundation, Inc.	TX	IN	1,234,553	15
95. The Clark Foundation	NY	IN	1,215,000	21
96. The William G. Irwin Charity Foundation	CA	IN	1,215,000	9
97. DaimlerChrysler Corporation Fund	MI	CS	1,201,000	16
98. Texaco Foundation	NY	CS	1,167,500	17
99. The Hearst Foundation, Inc.	NY	IN	1,150,000	30
100. T.L.L. Temple Foundation	TX	IN	1,144,063	12
Subtotal for Top 100 Foundations			$384,845,962	2,650
Total for All Foundations			$554,541,289	6,763

Source: *The Foundation Center*

Table App.3. Top 100 Foundations Giving to U.S.-Based Recipients for Precollegiate Education, Circa 2004[1]

Foundation Name	State	Foundation Type	Grant Dollars	No. of Grants
1. Bill & Melinda Gates Foundation	WA	IN	$143,029,256	79
2. The Annenberg Foundation	PA	IN	48,433,466	57
3. Walton Family Foundation, Inc.	AR	IN	37,938,460	212
4. The Wallace Foundation	NY	IN	34,330,000	40
5. Carnegie Corporation of New York	NY	IN	19,161,500	32
6. Broad Foundation	CA	IN	16,595,220	50
7. The New York Community Trust	NY	CM	15,811,893	255
8. The James Irvine Foundation	CA	IN	15,212,000	36
9. Open Society Institute	NY	OP	13,650,890	13
10. The Ford Foundation	NY	IN	13,563,000	32
11. Charles Stewart Mott Foundation	MI	IN	13,477,234	49
12. The William and Flora Hewlett Foundation	CA	IN	13,066,111	30
13. John S. and James L. Knight Foundation	FL	IN	13,038,100	39
14. Oberkotter Foundation	PA	IN	11,284,207	106
15. Ewing Marion Kauffman Foundation	MO	IN	10,579,481	44
16. Avenir Foundation, Inc.	CO	IN	10,500,000	1
17. The Brown Foundation, Inc.	TX	IN	10,280,304	38
18. J. Bulow Campbell Foundation	GA	IN	9,450,000	6
19. The Joyce Foundation	IL	IN	9,313,073	31
20. Lumina Foundation for Education, Inc.	IN	IN	9,154,600	55
21. Intel Foundation	OR	CS	9,115,687	128
22. The Chicago Community Trust	IL	CM	8,923,189	39

#	Name	State	Type	Amount	
23.	The Harry and Jeanette Weinberg Foundation, Inc.	MD	IN	8,763,500	42
24.	Communities Foundation of Texas, Inc.	TX	CM	8,700,841	34
25.	The Annie E. Casey Foundation	MD	IN	8,438,414	86
26.	SBC Foundation	TX	CS	8,075,617	123
27.	W. K. Kellogg Foundation	MI	IN	8,028,879	30
28.	Verizon Foundation	NY	CS	7,983,743	152
29.	Citigroup Foundation	NY	CS	7,758,750	174
30.	Iowa West Foundation	IA	IN	7,649,917	5
31.	The MBNA Foundation	DE	CS	7,553,423	187
32.	The Virginia G. Piper Charitable Trust	AZ	IN	7,425,535	7
33.	Richard King Mellon Foundation	PA	IN	7,340,000	18
34.	The Goizueta Foundation	GA	IN	7,303,928	11
35.	The Community Foundation for the National Capital Region	DC	CM	7,203,093	105
36.	The Starr Foundation	NY	IN	7,168,000	51
37.	Thompson Foundation	MI	IN	6,938,003	33
38.	The Lynde and Harry Bradley Foundation, Inc.	WI	IN	6,744,912	43
39.	Daniels Fund	CO	IN	6,589,638	93
40.	Samis Foundation	WA	IN	6,541,080	7
41.	The Malone Family Foundation	CO	IN	6,162,626	4
42.	The David and Lucile Packard Foundation	CA	IN	6,136,667	43
43.	The William Penn Foundation	PA	IN	5,759,920	14
44.	Boettcher Foundation	CO	IN	5,728,394	12
45.	The San Francisco Foundation	CA	CM	5,599,517	132
46.	The HCA Foundation	TN	CS	5,330,040	10
47.	Robert W. Woodruff Foundation, Inc.	GA	IN	5,285,000	9
48.	Community Foundation Silicon Valley	CA	CM	5,150,566	131

Table App.3. Top 100 Foundations Giving to U.S.-Based Recipients for Precollegiate Education, Circa 2004[1], *continued*

Foundation Name	State	Foundation Type	Grant Dollars	No. of Grants
49. Peninsula Community Foundation	CA	CM	4,909,012	149
50. Boston Foundation, Inc.	MA	CM	4,905,115	112
51. The Skillman Foundation	MI	IN	4,874,000	25
52. Covenant Foundation, Inc.	TX	IN	4,806,862	5
53. Greater Kansas City Community Foundation	MO	CM	4,725,345	79
54. Cassin Educational Initiative Foundation	CA	IN	4,707,921	44
55. The Lenfest Foundation, Inc.	PA	IN	4,692,000	14
56. The Rockefeller Foundation	NY	IN	4,631,477	26
57. Community Foundation for Greater Atlanta, Inc.	GA	CM	4,631,098	56
58. The Longleaf Foundation	TN	IN	4,612,751	16
59. Community Foundation of Greater Memphis	TN	CM	4,578,902	53
60. Connelly Foundation	PA	IN	4,406,315	56
61. Charles Hayden Foundation	NY	IN	4,401,363	64
62. Stuart Foundation	CA	IN	4,323,889	21
63. Vira I. Heinz Endowment	PA	IN	4,313,000	20
64. Conrad N. Hilton Foundation	NV	IN	4,216,987	16
65. The McKnight Foundation	MN	IN	4,123,000	18
66. The Wachovia Foundation, Inc.	NC	CS	4,112,193	75
67. The Fondren Foundation	TX	IN	4,110,000	16
68. Freddie Mac Foundation	VA	CS	4,054,000	62
69. Weingart Foundation	CA	IN	3,906,725	45
70. The Cleveland Foundation	OH	CM	3,784,639	68

71. MetLife Foundation	NY	CS	3,680,000	20
72. The Denver Foundation	CO	CM	3,647,418	62
73. Comer Science & Education Foundation	IL	IN	3,634,829	5
74. The Picower Foundation	FL	IN	3,632,968	17
75. The Ahmanson Foundation	CA	IN	3,629,500	70
76. The JPMorgan Chase Foundation	NY	CS	3,599,930	87
77. Houston Endowment, Inc.	TX	IN	3,462,000	14
78. Altman Foundation	NY	IN	3,339,000	45
79. Stupski Foundation	CA	OP	3,271,076	12
80. The Louis Calder Foundation	CT	IN	3,212,834	55
81. The Columbus Foundation and Affiliated Organizations	OH	CM	3,183,801	97
82. The Michael and Susan Dell Foundation	TX	IN	3,154,349	14
83. The Danforth Foundation	MO	IN	3,125,000	3
84. The Duke Endowment	NC	IN	3,067,557	31
85. Longwood Foundation, Inc.	DE	IN	3,065,000	8
86. SC Johnson Fund, Inc.	WI	CS	3,007,100	9
87. The San Diego Foundation	CA	CM	2,981,628	68
88. The Minneapolis Foundation	MN	CM	2,975,466	43
89. The Meadows Foundation, Inc.	TX	IN	2,940,250	22
90. The Highland Street Connection	MA	IN	2,901,577	26
91. GE Foundation	CT	CS	2,816,336	46
92. The Grable Foundation	PA	IN	2,807,933	66
93. Geraldine R. Dodge Foundation, Inc.	NJ	IN	2,783,000	42
94. John D. and Catherine T. MacArthur Foundation	IL	IN	2,775,000	5
95. The Susan A. Buffett Foundation	NE	IN	2,773,148	14
96. The Richard and Helen DeVos Foundation	MI	IN	2,752,000	11
97. Foellinger Foundation, Inc.	IN	IN	2,741,370	13

Table App.3. Top 100 Foundations Giving to U.S.-Based Recipients for Precollegiate Education, Circa 2004[1], *continued*

Foundation Name	State	Foundation Type	Grant Dollars	No. of Grants
98. Turrell Fund	NJ	IN	2,685,160	63
99. Vira I. Heinz Endowment	PA	IN	2,677,000	20
100. The McKnight Foundation	MN	IN	2,670,000	13
Subtotal for Top 100 Foundations			$858,086,498	4,969
Total for All Foundations			$1,261,325,024	11,695

Source: *The Foundation Center, 2006*

[1]*Based on grants of $10,000 or more awarded by a national sample of 1,172 larger U.S. foundations. For community foundations, only discretionary grants are included. Grants to individuals are not included in the file.*

Note: IN = *Independent Foundation;* CM = *Community Foundation;* CS = *Corporate Foundation;* OP = *Operating Foundation*

Table App.4. Top 100 U.S.-Based Recipients of Giving for Precollegiate Education, Circa 1990[1]

Recipient Name	State	Grant Dollars	No. of Grants
1. Peddie School	NJ	$6,100,000	2
2. Community Leaders Allied for Superior Schools (CLASS)	IN	5,000,000	1
3. National Center on Education and the Economy	NY	3,000,000	1
4. Harvard University	MA	2,954,236	5
5. United States Basic Skills Investment Corporation	VA	2,145,000	6
6. Fund for Educational Excellence	MD	2,107,360	5
7. Perkins School for the Blind	MA	1,458,500	2
8. Developmental Studies Center	CA	1,370,500	2
9. Educational Testing Service	NJ	1,364,692	7
10. Quality Education Project	CA	1,252,000	1
11. National Board for Professional Teaching Standards	MI	1,250,000	3
12. University of Pittsburgh	PA	1,200,000	2
13. Designs for Change	IL	1,150,000	14
14. Putney School	VT	1,149,823	1
15. PATHS/PRISM	PA	1,100,000	2
16. National Board for Professional Teaching Standards	DC	1,100,000	2
17. National Association of Secondary School Principals (NASSP)	VA	1,085,717	6
18. Gilmour Academy	OH	1,070,000	3
19. Woodberry Forest School	VA	1,025,125	3
20. Diocese of Pittsburgh	PA	1,020,000	2
21. Grosse Pointe Academy	MI	1,010,000	3
22. Archdiocese of Los Angeles	CA	1,000,000	1

Table App.4. Top 100 U.S.-Based Recipients of Giving for Precollegiate Education, Circa 1990[1], *continued*

Recipient Name	State	Grant Dollars	No. of Grants
23. Yale University	CT	939,600	5
24. National Center for Family Literacy	KY	925,895	2
25. Editorial Projects in Education	MD	900,000	4
26. Midland Independent School District	TX	896,390	2
27. University of California at San Diego	CA	875,000	1
28. National Academy Foundation	NY	871,700	6
29. Central Catholic School	TX	866,000	4
30. Council for Basic Education	DC	847,000	9
31. New Visions for Public Schools	NY	835,000	8
32. Temple University	PA	828,594	4
33. Writing to Read Program	NY	818,649	1
34. Cooperating School Districts of the Saint Louis Suburban Area	MO	783,000	7
35. Indianapolis Public Schools	IN	771,728	6
36. Bryn Mawr College	PA	764,695	3
37. Pasadena Unified School District	CA	743,300	5
38. Big Shoulders Fund	IL	740,000	10
39. Teach for America	NY	740,000	10
40. McCallie School	TN	736,625	3
41. Public/Private Ventures	PA	730,000	3
42. RAND Corporation	CA	729,000	3
43. Academy for Educational Development	NY	725,692	1
44. Cushing Academy	MA	725,000	2
45. I Have A Dream Foundation	TX	716,143	2

46. Saint Edwards University	TX	713,843	1
47. American Association for the Advancement of Science	DC	700,000	1
48. Achievement Council	CA	687,000	4
49. Los Angeles Educational Partnership	CA	681,338	13
50. University of Chicago	IL	667,764	4
51. Pittsburgh Board of Public Education	PA	661,812	2
52. Saint Johns School	TX	650,257	4
53. Hill School of Fort Worth	TX	650,000	3
54. Central Institute for the Deaf	MO	645,000	3
55. Pittsburgh Public Schools	PA	614,522	5
56. Education Commission of the States	CO	602,000	5
57. Oakridge School	TX	600,000	2
58. Extra Mile Education Foundation	PA	600,000	1
59. National Congress of Parents and Teachers	IL	599,488	3
60. Public Education Association	NY	598,700	8
61. Nightingale-Bamford School	NY	595,465	7
62. Council of Chief State School Officers	DC	589,607	5
63. Houston Independent School District	TX	572,750	3
64. Fellowship Academy	CA	568,100	7
65. Episcopal High School	VA	565,600	2
66. Foxfire Fund	GA	565,000	4
67. Memorial Hall School	TX	562,500	2
68. Holderness School	NH	550,000	2
69. Positive Thinking Foundation	NY	528,776	1
70. Dalton Schools	NY	525,192	5
71. National Governors Association Center for Best Practices	DC	525,140	1

Table App.4. Top 100 U.S.-Based Recipients of Giving for Precollegiate Education, Circa 1990[1], *continued*

Recipient Name	State	Grant Dollars	No. of Grants
72. Corporate/Community Schools of America	IL	525,000	3
73. Cherokee County School District	SC	520,328	1
74. National Center for Community Education	MI	520,000	2
75. A Better Chance	MA	517,692	16
76. Indiana University Foundation	IN	511,193	2
77. Central Catholic High School	OR	504,900	1
78. Indiana State University	IN	504,415	2
79. Gould Academy	ME	500,000	1
80. Howe Military School	IN	500,000	1
81. Kinkaid School	TX	500,000	1
82. Maumee Valley Country Day School	OH	500,000	1
83. Nolan High School	TX	500,000	1
84. Tatnall School	DE	500,000	1
85. Tower Hill School	DE	500,000	1
86. Wider Opportunities for Women (WOW)	DC	500,000	1
87. Wilmington Friends School	DE	500,000	1
88. Detroit School District	MI	500,000	1
89. Waring School	MA	500,000	2
90. Hyde School	ME	500,000	1
91. Bank Street College of Education	NY	488,000	7
92. Jobs for Youth-Chicago	IL	485,000	5
93. San Francisco School Volunteers	CA	477,283	11
94. North Dakota State Board for Vocational Education	ND	477,100	1

95. Kimberton Waldorf School	PA	450,000	1
96. Waldorf School of Garden City	NY	450,000	1
97. Institute for Educational Leadership	DC	449,735	4
98. Education Alliance—Business and Community for Public Schools	WV	448,000	3
99. Exodus	GA	446,610	9
100. Aspen Educational Research Foundation	CO	437,750	4
Subtotal for Top 100 Recipients		$88,454,824	359
Total for All Recipients		$204,761,210	3,190

Source: The Foundation Center, 2006

Table App.5. Top 100 U.S.-Based Recipients of Giving for Precollegiate Education, Circa 1997[1]

Recipient Name	State	Grant Dollars	No. of Grants
1. Greater Philadelphia First Foundation	PA	$11,493,593	2
2. Bay Area School Reform Collaborative	CA	11,476,510	9
3. Brown University	RI	10,000,000	1
4. New American Schools Development Corporation	VA	7,825,000	11
5. Schools of the 21st Century Corporation	MI	7,000,000	3
6. Annenberg Rural Challenge	CO	6,365,294	1
7. Archdiocese of Indianapolis	IN	4,942,581	1
8. New Visions for Public Schools	NY	3,709,744	18
9. Public Education Network (PEN)	DC	3,216,000	9
10. Our Lady of Lourdes High School	NY	3,129,279	1
11. Chicago Annenberg Challenge	IL	2,876,000	2
12. University System of Georgia	GA	2,700,000	1
13. Galef Institute	CA	2,690,000	5
14. Yale University	CT	2,675,000	4
15. Cleveland Initiative for Education	OH	2,550,338	11
16. Partners Advancing Values in Education (PAVE)	WI	2,525,000	7
17. Community Leaders Allied for Superior Schools (CLASS)	IN	2,500,000	1
18. District of Columbia Public Schools	DC	2,492,235	15
19. Johns Hopkins University	MD	2,434,720	8
20. Big Shoulders Fund	IL	2,328,833	21
21. Southern Education Foundation	GA	2,200,000	2
22. Learning Matters	NY	2,191,000	6

#	Organization	State	Amount	
23.	Algebra Project	MA	2,110,000	3
24.	University of California at Los Angeles Foundation	CA	2,090,000	3
25.	Education Commission of the States	CO	2,051,585	5
26.	University of Chicago	IL	1,996,373	6
27.	Educational Testing Service	NJ	1,949,636	9
28.	Saint Joseph Institute for the Deaf	MO	1,930,000	5
29.	Education Trust	DC	1,900,000	1
30.	Perkins School for the Blind	MA	1,866,300	3
31.	Corporation for the Advancement of Policy Evaluation	NJ	1,815,000	6
32.	University of Pennsylvania	PA	1,804,815	5
33.	Milken Community High School of Stephen Wise Temple	CA	1,790,000	1
34.	Teachers College Columbia University	NY	1,699,818	6
35.	Boston Plan for Excellence in the Public Schools Foundation	MA	1,685,000	5
36.	National Board for Professional Teaching Standards	MI	1,670,000	6
37.	Clarke School for the Deaf	MA	1,653,000	6
38.	Sacramento City Unified School District	CA	1,650,000	1
39.	Oklahoma School of Science and Mathematics	OK	1,645,000	4
40.	Prichard Committee for Academic Excellence	KY	1,634,263	4
41.	Bank Street College of Education	NY	1,623,221	4
42.	Designs for Change	IL	1,600,000	8
43.	Reading is FUNdamental (RIF)	DC	1,596,500	24
44.	Westminster Schools	GA	1,559,169	6
45.	Puente Project	CA	1,525,000	2
46.	New York University	NY	1,518,600	13
47.	Reach and Teach USA	NY	1,510,647	1
48.	All Saints Episcopal School	TX	1,500,000	1

Recipient Name	State	Grant Dollars	No. of Grants
49. Battle Creek School District	MI	1,485,000	2
50. National Center for Family Literacy	KY	1,476,231	15
51. Harborside School	CA	1,474,670	1
52. Donors Forum of Chicago	IL	1,459,550	3
53. University of Texas	TX	1,445,000	3
54. Developmental Studies Center	CA	1,420,000	5
55. University of Michigan	MI	1,417,135	7
56. Vanderbilt University	TN	1,400,000	1
57. South Florida Annenberg Challenge	FL	1,400,000	3
58. Fremont Unified School District	CA	1,380,461	1
59. Chattanooga-Hamilton County Public Education Fund	TN	1,365,200	1
60. Philadelphia High School Academies	PA	1,350,000	4
61. School Choice Scholarships Foundation	NY	1,268,500	1
62. Roman Catholic Archbishop of Los Angeles	CA	1,255,200	1
63. University of New Mexico	NM	1,248,000	1
64. Trinity-Pawling School	NY	1,225,000	4
65. Saint Vincent Academy High School	NJ	1,216,500	7
66. YouthBuild USA	MA	1,200,000	4
67. Center for Leadership in School Reform	KY	1,190,000	5
68. Webb School of California	CA	1,150,000	2
69. Teach for America	NY	1,147,500	27
70. Covenant Foundation	NY	1,119,905	6

No.	Organization	State	Amount	
71.	Howe Military School	IN	1,100,000	2
72.	Saint Johns School	TX	1,075,000	5
73.	San Diego City Schools	CA	1,070,516	15
74.	Manhattan Institute for Policy Research	NY	1,055,000	9
75.	Classroom, Inc.	NY	1,052,500	15
76.	Urban Strategies Council	CA	1,050,000	2
77.	YMCA of Metropolitan Minneapolis	MN	1,050,000	2
78.	Chatham-Savannah Youth Futures Authority	GA	1,050,000	2
79.	Phillips Academy	MA	1,042,878	13
80.	National Foundation for the Improvement of Education	DC	1,035,000	2
81.	Greater Cleveland Roundtable	OH	1,030,790	5
82.	Cross City Campaign for Urban School Reform	IL	1,020,000	8
83.	Public Education Foundation	TN	1,017,400	4
84.	Beaumont School for Girls	OH	1,015,000	2
85.	Ursuline Academy	TX	1,010,000	2
86.	Edison Institute	MI	1,000,000	1
87.	Saint Ignatius High School	OH	1,000,000	2
88.	Middle College High School	NY	1,000,000	1
89.	Coalition of Essential Schools	RI	1,000,000	1
90.	Recruiting New Teachers	MA	1,000,000	3
91.	K C E T Associates	CA	1,000,000	1
92.	Inner-City Scholarship Fund	OH	1,000,000	1
93.	Trinity Christian School of Fairfax	VA	1,000,000	1
94.	ACHIEVE, Inc.—A Resource Center on Standards, Assessments, Accountability and Technology	MA	1,000,000	1
95.	American Friends of Ateret Cohanem	NY	987,500	1

Table App.5. Top 100 U.S.-Based Recipients of Giving for Precollegiate Education, Circa 1997[1], *continued*

Recipient Name	State	Grant Dollars	No. of Grants
96. Baltimore Curriculum Project	MD	975,000	2
97. Cotter Schools	MN	939,409	1
98. Saint Rita School for the Deaf	OH	911,833	5
99. Educators for Social Responsibility	NY	900,000	2
100. Miss Porter's School	CT	875,261	3
Subtotal for Top 100 Recipients		$204,051,993	495
Total for All Recipients		$554,541,289	6,763

Source: The Foundation Center, 2006

[1]*Based on grants of $10,000 or more awarded by a national sample of 1,016 larger U.S. foundations. For community foundations, only discretionary grants are included. Grants to individuals are not included in the file.*

Table App.6. Top 100 U.S.-Based Recipients of Giving for Precollegiate Education, Circa 2004[1]

Recipient Name	State	Grant Dollars	No. of Grants
1. Council of Chief State School Officers	DC	$33,639,666	6
2. New Visions for Public Schools	NY	33,233,333	20
3. New Leaders for New Schools	NY	13,463,751	15
4. Academy for Educational Development	DC	13,109,600	3
5. After-School Corporation	NY	10,790,000	11
6. Emma Willard School	NY	10,500,000	1
7. Jobs for the Future	MA	10,472,200	5
8. Middle College High School National Consortium	NY	9,602,735	1
9. Bay Area School Reform Collaborative	CA	8,150,000	4
10. Public Education Network (PEN)	DC	7,396,000	9
11. Urban Assembly	NY	7,100,000	2
12. Portawattamie, County of	IA	7,032,970	2
13. Saint Johns School	TX	6,941,000	5
14. Corporation for Public Broadcasting	DC	6,750,000	1
15. New York City Leadership Academy	NY	6,700,000	4
16. Accelerated School	CA	6,570,000	4
17. Teach for America	NY	6,358,600	40
18. Antioch University Seattle	WA	6,122,500	1
19. Wesleyan School	GA	6,097,750	4
20. Fund for Public Schools	NY	6,076,650	17
21. Project GRAD USA	TX	5,647,600	9
22. Thompson Educational Foundation	MI	5,500,000	2

Table App.6. Top 100 U.S.-Based Recipients of Giving for Precollegiate Education, Circa 2004[1], *continued*

Recipient Name	State	Grant Dollars	No. of Grants
23. LIFT Education	TX	5,414,572	1
24. Child-Centered Schools Initiative of Houston	TX	5,160,000	4
25. Ensworth School	TN	5,138,040	2
26. Rochester City School District	NY	5,000,000	1
27. Public Education and Business Coalition	CO	4,959,894	8
28. University of Chicago	IL	4,938,103	6
29. ACHIEVE, Inc.—A Resource Center on Standards, Assessments, Accountability and Technology	DC	4,680,931	3
30. Christian Academy of San Antonio	TX	4,585,862	1
31. Seattle Hebrew Academy	WA	4,140,395	2
32. Boston Plan for Excellence	MA	4,031,271	7
33. United Way of Southeastern Pennsylvania	PA	4,000,000	2
34. National Council of La Raza	DC	3,913,777	3
35. Institute for Research and Reform in Education	NJ	3,768,084	1
36. Perkins School for the Blind	MA	3,454,200	6
37. Saint Paul Public Schools	MN	3,410,478	6
38. Woodward Academy	GA	3,328,914	3
39. City Academy	MO	3,216,127	6
40. Partners Advancing Values in Education (PAVE)	WI	3,182,500	2
41. Seton Catholic High School	AZ	3,125,000	2
42. KIPP (Knowledge Is Power Program) Foundation	CA	3,074,553	7
43. Paul Revere Elementary School	IL	3,011,807	1

44.	Blue Ridge School	VA	3,010,000	2
45.	Families in Schools	CA	3,008,000	4
46.	Valley School of Ligonier	PA	3,000,000	1
47.	Saint Marys High School	AZ	3,000,000	1
48.	Enterprise Foundation	GA	2,994,624	1
49.	Developmental Studies Center	CA	2,986,000	6
50.	Communities in Schools	VA	2,958,500	10
51.	Kansas City, City of	KS	2,918,155	1
52.	National Center for Educational Accountability	TX	2,911,338	8
53.	Fort Worth Country Day School	TX	2,800,000	3
54.	Aspire Public Schools	CA	2,782,590	4
55.	National Academy Foundation	NY	2,753,334	12
56.	Institute of Computer Technology	CA	2,699,183	7
57.	Western Reserve Academy	OH	2,633,200	6
58.	Stanford University	CA	2,567,582	10
59.	Leadership for Quality Education	IL	2,540,000	2
60.	Johns Hopkins University	MD	2,531,950	16
61.	Clarke School for the Deaf	MA	2,462,393	15
62.	Education Development Center	MA	2,431,500	9
63.	Berkshire School	MA	2,400,500	11
64.	Urban Youth Initiative	TN	2,393,545	7
65.	Core Knowledge Foundation	VA	2,339,671	3
66.	Dalton Schools	NY	2,311,500	11
67.	University System of Georgia Foundation	GA	2,228,000	2
68.	New York City Department of Education	NY	2,190,270	3
69.	Institute for Teaching	CA	2,189,650	2
70.	Punahou School	HI	2,175,433	7

Table App.6. Top 100 U.S.-Based Recipients of Giving for Precollegiate Education, Circa 2004[1], *continued*

Recipient Name	State	Grant Dollars	No. of Grants
71. Georgia Partnership for Excellence in Education	GA	2,175,000	11
72. Rural School and Community Trust	VA	2,091,900	8
73. Lawrenceville School	NJ	2,068,158	8
74. Project Lead the Way	NY	2,060,980	2
75. University of Arkansas	AR	2,015,685	1
76. Omaha Schools Foundation	NE	2,004,912	10
77. Philadelphia School District	PA	2,004,906	6
78. Commonwealth School	MA	2,000,000	1
79. Indian Springs School	AL	2,000,000	1
80. Saint Marys High School	MA	2,000,000	1
81. Hispanic Scholarship Fund	CA	1,990,018	3
82. Saint Georges Schools Foundation	TN	1,957,206	5
83. Saint Benedicts Preparatory School	NJ	1,950,650	12
84. Advanced Placement Strategies	TX	1,943,676	6
85. Educational Testing Service	NJ	1,917,619	11
86. East Allen County Schools	IN	1,861,920	3
87. Blake School	MN	1,860,000	9
88. Carnegie Foundation for the Advancement of Teaching	CA	1,830,684	4
89. Norfolk Christian Schools	VA	1,790,000	7
90. MDRC	NY	1,775,000	6
91. Saint Andrews School of Delaware	DE	1,770,000	8
92. Abraham Joshua Heschel School	NY	1,769,000	10
93. Cathedral High School	CA	1,766,000	9

94. YMCA of Greater Long Beach	CA	1,765,000	3
95. American Institutes for Research in the Behavioral Sciences	DC	1,749,739	2
96. Eastside College Preparatory School	CA	1,745,000	23
97. Childrens Aid Society	NY	1,740,000	4
98. University of Washington Foundation	WA	1,703,876	7
99. Roman Catholic Archbishop of Los Angeles	CA	1,700,000	1
100. Center for Education Reform	DC	1,657,709	8
Subtotal for Top 100 Recipients		$440,670,419	594
Total for All Recipients		$1,261,325,024	11,695

Source: *The Foundation Center, 2006*

[1]Based on grants of $10,000 or more awarded by a national sample of 1,172 larger U.S. foundations. For community foundations, only discretionary grants are included. Grants to individuals are not included in the file.

Table App.7. Top 100 Foundations Giving to U.S.-Based Recipients for Higher, Graduate, and Professional Education and Educational Institutions, Circa 1990[1]

Foundation Name	State	Foundation Type	Grant Dollars	No. of Grants
1. Lilly Endowment, Inc.	IN	IN	$47,538,584	167
2. The Pew Charitable Trusts	PA	IN	40,669,631	158
3. John D. and Catherine T. MacArthur Foundation	IL	IN	40,552,601	110
4. The Andrew W. Mellon Foundation	NY	IN	40,244,000	152
5. Robert R. McCormick Tribune Foundation	IL	IN	39,687,500	17
6. The Robert Wood Johnson Foundation	NJ	IN	34,866,881	166
7. Lucille P. Markey Charitable Trust	FL	IN	28,100,000	9
8. The Annenberg Foundation	PA	IN	25,968,506	33
9. Houston Endowment, Inc.	TX	IN	24,042,600	74
10. W. M. Keck Foundation	CA	IN	23,100,000	49
11. W. K. Kellogg Foundation	MI	IN	21,957,408	83
12. The Kresge Foundation	MI	IN	21,724,000	46
13. The Rockefeller Foundation	NY	IN	20,578,262	185
14. The William Penn Foundation	PA	IN	17,719,672	55
15. Arnold and Mabel Beckman Foundation	CA	IN	17,191,766	8
16. The Ford Foundation	NY	IN	14,825,907	103
17. The William and Flora Hewlett Foundation	CA	IN	12,290,000	70
18. The Spencer Foundation	IL	IN	11,869,375	33
19. The David and Lucile Packard Foundation	CA	IN	11,756,798	44
20. General Motors Foundation, Inc.	MI	CS	11,426,311	129

21. Independence Foundation	PA	IN	11,000,000	19
22. Benjamin Volen Charitable Trust	IL	IN	10,461,519	1
23. The Whitaker Foundation	VA	IN	9,682,115	58
24. John M. Olin Foundation, Inc.	NY	IN	9,247,791	104
25. Ford Motor Company Fund	MI	CS	9,169,583	143
26. Alfred P. Sloan Foundation	NY	IN	8,328,154	49
27. Carnegie Corporation of New York	NY	IN	8,304,490	40
28. The Sherman Fairchild Foundation, Inc.	MD	IN	8,161,927	15
29. The J. E. and L. E. Mabee Foundation, Inc.	OK	IN	8,050,000	13
30. ExxonMobil Foundation	TX	CS	7,871,035	144
31. The Lynde and Harry Bradley Foundation, Inc.	WI	IN	7,790,585	112
32. Richard King Mellon Foundation	PA	IN	7,735,000	9
33. Weingart Foundation	CA	IN	7,337,085	29
34. McCune Foundation	PA	IN	7,310,000	10
35. The James Irvine Foundation	CA	IN	6,833,500	15
36. Stratford Foundation	MA	IN	6,778,255	14
37. Andersen Foundation	MN	IN	6,760,000	33
38. BP Amoco Foundation, Inc.	IL	CS	6,716,457	202
39. The Procter & Gamble Fund	OH	CS	6,656,907	168
40. William R. Kenan, Jr. Charitable Trust	NC	IN	6,275,000	5
41. James S. McDonnell Foundation	MO	IN	6,174,939	39
42. Lettie Pate Whitehead Foundation, Inc.	GA	IN	5,991,000	185
43. John S. and James L. Knight Foundation	FL	IN	5,802,339	32
44. The Commonwealth Fund	NY	IN	5,570,500	31
45. The Hearst Foundations, Inc.	NY	IN	5,545,000	119
46. Harcourt M. and Virginia W. Sylvester Foundation, Inc.	FL	IN	5,500,000	1

Table App.7. Top 100 Foundations Giving to U.S.-Based Recipients for Higher, Graduate, and Professional Education and Educational Institutions, Circa 1990[1], *continued*

Foundation Name	State	Foundation Type	Grant Dollars	No. of Grants
47. The Edna McConnell Clark Foundation	NY	IN	5,463,200	28
48. Mitrani Family Foundation, Inc.	PA	IN	5,375,000	14
49. Connelly Foundation	PA	IN	5,246,340	10
50. Shell Oil Company Foundation	TX	CS	5,109,698	293
51. The Aaron Diamond Foundation, Inc.	NY	IN	5,013,138	71
52. The Humana Foundation, Inc.	KY	CS	4,676,738	25
53. Horace W. Goldsmith Foundation	NY	IN	4,672,500	28
54. GE Fund	CT	CS	4,473,172	90
55. W. W. Smith Charitable Trust	PA	IN	4,415,454	69
56. The Ralph M. Parsons Foundation	CA	IN	4,386,135	14
57. Ramapo Trust	NY	IN	4,223,838	17
58. Spencer T. and Ann W. Olin Foundation	MO	IN	4,150,000	4
59. Helene Fuld Health Trust	NY	IN	4,046,313	123
60. U S WEST Foundation	CO	CS	3,982,242	92
61. The John A. Hartford Foundation, Inc.	NY	IN	3,856,160	9
62. The Fletcher Jones Foundation	CA	IN	3,842,429	20
63. Surdna Foundation, Inc.	NY	IN	3,835,415	37
64. The Arthur Vining Davis Foundations	FL	IN	3,680,000	39
65. Thomas and Dorothy Leavey Foundation	CA	IN	3,570,000	5
66. Northwest Area Foundation	MN	IN	3,432,898	18
67. Roy J. Carver Charitable Trust	IA	IN	3,371,836	7

	Name	State	Type	Amount	
68.	The Bush Foundation	MN	IN	3,330,654	27
69.	The Grainger Foundation, Inc.	IL	IN	3,188,938	2
70.	Charles Stewart Mott Foundation	MI	IN	3,188,721	41
71.	The Flagler Foundation	VA	IN	3,184,584	2
72.	The Merck Company Foundation	NJ	CS	3,145,310	113
73.	James Graham Brown Foundation, Inc.	KY	IN	3,100,000	14
74.	Charles E. Culpeper Foundation, Inc.	CT	IN	3,096,023	36
75.	Charles and Ellora Alliss Educational Foundation	MN	IN	3,054,800	20
76.	Herrick Foundation	MI	IN	3,020,000	43
77.	The Chicago Community Trust and Affiliates	IL	CM	3,008,840	18
78.	Burlington Northern Foundation	TX	CS	2,990,956	101
79.	Conrad N. Hilton Foundation	NV	IN	2,961,063	6
80.	The Kluge Foundation	MD	IN	2,900,000	2
81.	Rockwell International Corporation Trust	WI	CS	2,816,058	80
82.	Mobil Foundation, Inc.	VA	CS	2,735,250	81
83.	Beatrice P. Delany Charitable Trust	NY	IN	2,705,000	30
84.	Burroughs Wellcome Fund	NC	IN	2,690,363	22
85.	Joseph B. Whitehead Foundation	GA	IN	2,655,000	4
86.	Peter Kiewit Foundation	NE	IN	2,584,295	17
87.	The Xerox Foundation	CT	CS	2,541,258	133
88.	The George S. and Dolores Dore Eccles Foundation	UT	IN	2,535,668	19
89.	William T. Grant Foundation	NY	IN	2,523,335	19
90.	Fritz B. Burns Foundation	CA	IN	2,520,181	10
91.	The Ann and Gordon Getty Foundation	CA	IN	2,458,000	36
92.	The Wachtell, Lipton, Rosen & Katz Foundation	NY	CS	2,455,850	15
93.	DeWitt Wallace-Reader's Digest Fund, Inc.	NY	IN	2,447,185	10
94.	Booth Ferris Foundation	NY	IN	2,400,000	23
95.	G. Harold & Leila Y. Mathers Charitable Foundation	NY	IN	2,380,154	21

Table App.7. Top 100 Foundations Giving to U.S.-Based Recipients for Higher, Graduate, and Professional Education and Educational Institutions, Circa 1990[1], *continued*

Foundation Name	State	Foundation Type	Grant Dollars	No. of Grants
96. The Flinn Foundation	AZ	IN	2,378,419	8
97. The Harvey and Bernice Jones Charitable Trust	AR	IN	2,364,000	6
98. Joseph and Bessie Feinberg Foundation	IL	IN	2,340,000	4
99. Smith Richardson Foundation, Inc.	CT	IN	2,338,165	31
100. The San Francisco Foundation	CA	CM	2,332,325	20
Subtotal for Top 100 Foundations			$882,355,884	5,308
Total for All Foundations			$1,215,982,280	11,386

Source: The Foundation Center

Note: IN = Independent Foundation; CM = Community Foundation; CS = Corporate Foundation

[1]*Based on grants of $10,000 or more awarded by a national sample of 832 larger U.S. foundations. For community foundations, only discretionary grants are included. Grants to individuals are not included in the file.*

Top 100 Foundations Giving to U.S.-Based Recipients for Higher, Graduate, and Professional Education and Educational Institutions, Circa 1997[1]

Foundation Name	State	Foundation Type	Grant Dollars	No. of Grants
1. W. M. Keck Foundation	CA	IN	$99,670,000	36
2. Donald W. Reynolds Foundation	NV	IN	80,763,228	20
3. The Robert Wood Johnson Foundation	NJ	IN	79,277,979	254
4. Lilly Endowment, Inc.	IN	IN	72,624,616	182
5. The Andrew W. Mellon Foundation	NY	IN	70,799,450	207
6. Joseph B. Whitehead Foundation	GA	IN	70,447,939	1
7. The Pew Charitable Trusts	PA	IN	55,282,500	63
8. W. K. Kellogg Foundation	MI	IN	51,740,713	156
9. The Ford Foundation	NY	IN	50,355,457	264
10. F. W. Olin Foundation, Inc.	NY	IN	43,503,000	11
11. The David and Lucile Packard Foundation	CA	IN	39,678,458	153
12. The Duke Endowment	NC	IN	35,215,678	61
13. The Starr Foundation	NY	IN	31,515,550	95
14. Burroughs Wellcome Fund	NC	IN	31,420,803	95
15. The Kresge Foundation	MI	IN	29,393,333	54
16. The Whitaker Foundation	VA	IN	28,129,037	114
17. John D. and Catherine T. MacArthur Foundation	IL	IN	23,962,920	91
18. Alfred P. Sloan Foundation	NY	IN	23,618,291	117
19. The Annenberg Foundation	PA	IN	22,206,268	33
20. The Community Foundation Serving Richmond & Central Virginia	VA	CM	21,341,850	19

Table App.8. Top 100 Foundations Giving to U.S.-Based Recipients for Higher, Graduate, and Professional Education and Educational Institutions, Circa 1997[1], *continued*

Foundation Name	State	Foundation Type	Grant Dollars	No. of Grants
21. The Spencer Foundation	IL	IN	20,972,119	148
22. The Robert A. Welch Foundation	TX	IN	16,677,000	145
23. Houston Endowment, Inc.	TX	IN	16,290,871	48
24. Carnegie Corporation of New York	NY	IN	15,959,200	58
25. The San Francisco Foundation	CA	CM	15,950,794	34
26. John S. and James L. Knight Foundation	FL	IN	15,387,449	42
27. Wallace-Readers Digest Funds	NY	IN	14,790,168	53
28. The Henry Luce Foundation, Inc.	NY	IN	14,017,582	71
29. The Ahmanson Foundation	CA	IN	13,106,000	78
30. The Rockefeller Foundation	NY	IN	12,355,485	92
31. Lied Foundation Trust	NV	IN	11,993,790	15
32. The John A. Hartford Foundation, Inc.	NY	IN	11,962,396	32
33. Weingart Foundation	CA	IN	11,859,984	45
34. Andersen Foundation	MN	IN	11,475,000	49
35. The William and Flora Hewlett Foundation	CA	IN	10,580,000	71
36. The Fletcher Jones Foundation	CA	IN	10,364,071	25
37. AT&T Foundation	NY	CS	9,733,417	245
38. Robert W. Woodruff Foundation, Inc.	GA	IN	9,694,483	13
39. James S. McDonnell Foundation	MO	IN	9,618,413	95
40. The J. E. and L. E. Mabee Foundation, Inc.	OK	IN	9,450,000	12
41. Charles Stewart Mott Foundation	MI	IN	9,282,836	33

	Foundation	State	Type	Amount	
42.	The Brown Foundation, Inc.	TX	IN	8,811,100	26
43.	John M. Olin Foundation, Inc.	NY	IN	8,776,833	85
44.	Skirball Foundation	NY	IN	8,616,600	13
45.	The George S. and Dolores Dore Eccles Foundation	UT	IN	8,560,833	40
46.	Robert R. McCormick Tribune Foundation	IL	IN	8,123,650	22
47.	SBC Foundation	TX	CS	8,101,334	93
48.	The Freeman Foundation	NY	IN	8,052,896	38
49.	The Joyce Foundation	IL	IN	7,818,041	29
50.	Howard Heinz Endowment	PA	IN	7,677,600	19
51.	GE Fund	CT	CS	7,649,790	125
52.	Roy J. Carver Charitable Trust	IA	IN	7,622,891	9
53.	The Lynde and Harry Bradley Foundation, Inc.	WI	IN	7,617,608	97
54.	Ford Motor Company Fund	MI	CS	7,443,494	140
55.	General Motors Foundation, Inc.	MI	CS	7,120,693	117
56.	The James Irvine Foundation	CA	IN	7,102,500	16
57.	Evelyn and Walter Haas, Jr. Fund	CA	IN	7,051,700	10
58.	Park Foundation, Inc.	NY	IN	6,716,236	37
59.	The Harvey and Bernice Jones Charitable Trust	AR	IN	6,692,465	16
60.	J. Bulow Campbell Foundation	GA	IN	6,669,658	9
61.	Walton Family Foundation, Inc.	AR	IN	6,630,937	25
62.	The Coca-Cola Foundation, Inc.	GA	CS	6,479,966	91
63.	Ewing Marion Kauffman Foundation	MO	IN	6,392,409	135
64.	The Arthur Vining Davis Foundations	FL	IN	6,389,773	46
65.	The John W. Kluge Foundation	MD	IN	6,240,000	6
66.	The Bush Foundation	MN	IN	6,197,230	35
67.	Dow Chemical Company Foundation	MI	CS	6,153,713	113
68.	The Chicago Community Trust and Affiliates	IL	CM	6,097,275	42
69.	The Charles A. Dana Foundation, Inc.	NY	IN	6,037,500	18

Table App.8. Top 100 Foundations Giving to U.S.-Based Recipients for Higher, Graduate, and Professional Education and Educational Institutions, Circa 1997[1], *continued*

Foundation Name	State	Foundation Type	Grant Dollars	No. of Grants
70. U S WEST Foundation	CO	CS	5,993,115	80
71. F. M. Kirby Foundation, Inc.	NJ	IN	5,951,000	17
72. M. J. Murdock Charitable Trust	WA	IN	5,852,950	23
73. William Randolph Hearst Foundation	NY	IN	5,850,000	107
74. William T. Grant Foundation	NY	IN	5,826,757	24
75. Thomas and Dorothy Leavey Foundation	CA	IN	5,712,542	10
76. Christian A. Johnson Endeavor Foundation	NY	IN	5,675,971	34
77. Charles E. Culpeper Foundation, Inc.	CT	IN	5,627,577	38
78. Shell Oil Company Foundation	TX	CS	5,497,931	205
79. The Merck Company Foundation	NJ	CS	5,491,778	104
80. Research Corporation	AZ	OP	5,428,328	172
81. Mozes S. Schupf Foundation, Inc.	NY	IN	5,420,988	1
82. G. Harold & Leila Y. Mathers Charitable Foundation	NY	IN	5,416,783	26
83. Dyson Foundation	NY	IN	5,240,000	4
84. M. D. Anderson Foundation	TX	IN	5,223,000	21
85. James Graham Brown Foundation, Inc.	KY	IN	5,051,110	20
86. The Procter & Gamble Fund	OH	CS	5,012,918	127
87. Smith Richardson Foundation, Inc.	CT	IN	4,912,746	48
88. Mary Stuart Rogers Foundation	CA	IN	4,875,000	7
89. Horace W. Goldsmith Foundation	NY	IN	4,795,000	23
90. The Annie E. Casey Foundation	MD	IN	4,744,105	46

91. Foundation For The Carolinas	NC	CM	4,737,904	53
92. DaimlerChrysler Corporation Fund	MI	CS	4,719,672	126
93. John Templeton Foundation	PA	IN	4,700,122	21
94. Meyer Memorial Trust	OR	IN	4,650,000	7
95. Arnold and Mabel Beckman Foundation	CA	IN	4,645,000	5
96. The Henry J. Kaiser Family Foundation	CA	OP	4,634,056	43
97. Kansas Health Foundation	KS	IN	4,504,420	15
98. The George I. Alden Trust	MA	IN	4,501,000	86
99. The Teagle Foundation, Inc.	NY	IN	4,496,120	80
100. Tisch Foundation, Inc.	NY	IN	4,445,000	10
Subtotal for Top 100 Foundations			$1,594,945,746	6,465
Total for All Foundations			$2,276,747,029	15,557

Source: *The Foundation Center*

[1]Based on grants of $10,000 or more awarded by a national sample of 1,016 larger U.S. foundations. For community foundations, only discretionary grants are included. Grants to individuals are not included in the file.

Note: IN = Independent Foundation; CM = Community Foundation; CS = Corporate Foundation: OP = Operating Foundation

Table App.9. Top 100 Foundations Giving to U.S.-Based Recipients for Higher, Graduate, and Professional Education and Educational Institutions, Circa 2004[1]

Foundation Name	State	Foundation Type	Grant Dollars	No. of Grants
1. Lilly Endowment, Inc.	IN	IN	$291,118,184	117
2. Bill & Melinda Gates Foundation	WA	IN	107,541,682	44
3. The Robert Wood Johnson Foundation	NJ	IN	81,996,476	238
4. The Andrew W. Mellon Foundation	NY	IN	81,475,900	223
5. The Starr Foundation	NY	IN	63,119,820	81
6. Skirball Foundation	NY	IN	57,605,340	22
7. The Ford Foundation	NY	IN	56,252,526	204
8. Donald W. Reynolds Foundation	NV	IN	47,291,490	15
9. The Duke Endowment	NC	IN	46,943,122	79
10. W. M. Keck Foundation	CA	IN	44,110,000	39
11. The Freeman Foundation	NY	IN	37,894,511	161
12. The David and Lucile Packard Foundation	CA	IN	37,363,707	71
13. The Ave Maria Foundation	MI	IN	37,194,617	7
14. Alfred P. Sloan Foundation	NY	IN	36,225,791	218
15. The New York Community Trust	NY	CM	32,149,723	322
16. The William and Flora Hewlett Foundation	CA	IN	31,793,900	104
17. Lumina Foundation for Education, Inc.	IN	IN	30,956,765	101
18. The Annenberg Foundation	PA	IN	29,106,775	51
19. W. K. Kellogg Foundation	MI	IN	26,780,012	59
20. Jurodin Fund, Inc.	CT	IN	26,000,000	1

	Name	State	Amount	
21.	John D. and Catherine T. MacArthur Foundation	IL	25,876,000	IN	59
22.	Robert W. Woodruff Foundation, Inc.	GA	24,329,010	IN	15
23.	Wallace H. Coulter Foundation	FL	23,522,854	IN	6
24.	Ford Motor Company Fund	MI	23,085,644	CS	113
25.	The Robert A. Welch Foundation	TX	22,567,500	IN	181
26.	John & Cynthia Reed Foundation	NY	20,754,683	IN	6
27.	The Kresge Foundation	MI	19,225,920	IN	23
28.	Gordon and Betty Moore Foundation	CA	18,108,113	IN	15
29.	Peninsula Community Foundation	CA	16,823,567	CM	123
30.	Ewing Marion Kauffman Foundation	MO	16,070,069	IN	199
31.	The Rockefeller Foundation	NY	16,020,340	IN	80
32.	Walton Family Foundation, Inc.	AR	15,936,790	IN	26
33.	The Henry Luce Foundation, Inc.	NY	15,159,578	IN	61
34.	The California Endowment	CA	15,124,060	IN	58
35.	Carnegie Corporation of New York	NY	15,098,900	IN	70
36.	Bernard Osher Foundation	CA	15,007,028	IN	32
37.	Northwest Area Foundation	MN	14,300,587	IN	15
38.	The Annie E. Casey Foundation	MD	14,192,668	IN	121
39.	The Susan Thompson Buffett Foundation	NE	13,508,678	IN	87
40.	John S. and James L. Knight Foundation	FL	12,728,500	IN	42
41.	The Goizueta Foundation	GA	12,555,351	IN	7
42.	Houston Endowment Inc.	TX	12,257,000	IN	27
43.	Greater Kansas City Community Foundation	MO	12,246,514	CM	64
44.	Andersen Foundation	MN	12,025,000	IN	49
45.	Doris Duke Charitable Foundation	NY	11,986,440	IN	23
46.	Lamar Bruni Vergara Trust	TX	11,320,000	IN	1
47.	Pleasant T. Rowland Foundation, Inc.	WI	11,115,374	IN	8

Table App.9. Top 100 Foundations Giving to U.S.-Based Recipients for Higher, Graduate, and Professional Education and Educational Institutions, Circa 2004[1], *continued*

Foundation Name	State	Foundation Type	Grant Dollars	No. of Grants
48. The Annenberg Foundation Trust at Sunnylands	PA	IN	11,100,000	2
49. The J. E. and L. E. Mabee Foundation, Inc.	OK	IN	11,100,000	11
50. The Bank of America Charitable Foundation, Inc.	NC	CS	10,972,743	100
51. The Picower Foundation	FL	IN	10,745,000	5
52. The Cleveland Foundation	OH	CM	10,552,463	90
53. The Iris Foundation	NY	IN	10,300,000	1
54. The Merck Company Foundation	NJ	CS	10,140,899	140
55. The Virginia G. Piper Charitable Trust	AZ	IN	10,065,000	3
56. The Carson Family Charitable Trust	NY	IN	10,030,000	11
57. SBC Foundation	TX	CS	9,829,038	121
58. The Weill Family Foundation	NY	IN	9,699,000	1
59. Tisch Foundation, Inc.	NY	IN	9,659,440	10
60. The Thomas and Stacey Siebel Foundation	CA	IN	9,542,881	1
61. The Priem Family Foundation	CA	OP	9,450,000	2
62. Arnold and Mabel Beckman Foundation	CA	IN	9,446,211	103
63. Burroughs Wellcome Fund	NC	IN	9,188,351	36
64. The Columbus Foundation and Affiliated Organizations	OH	CM	9,081,617	90
65. George S. and Dolores Dore Eccles Foundation	UT	IN	8,737,333	40
66. Richard King Mellon Foundation	PA	IN	8,728,000	15
67. Bradley-Turner Foundation, Inc.	GA	IN	8,542,241	24

#	Name	State	Type	Amount	
68.	Horace W. Goldsmith Foundation	NY	IN	8,540,000	23
69.	The Procter & Gamble Fund	OH	CS	8,531,516	248
70.	Roy J. Carver Charitable Trust	IA	IN	8,404,803	35
71.	C. D. Spangler Foundation, Inc.	NC	IN	8,254,500	4
72.	The Jolley Foundation	NC	IN	8,000,000	1
73.	Verizon Foundation	NY	CS	7,628,243	250
74.	Community Foundation Silicon Valley	CA	CM	7,522,076	131
75.	The Arthur Vining Davis Foundations	FL	IN	7,437,193	42
76.	Intel Foundation	OR	CS	7,378,948	120
77.	The Richard and Helen DeVos Foundation	MI	IN	7,365,000	12
78.	Park Foundation, Inc.	NY	IN	7,315,504	41
79.	The Ahmanson Foundation	CA	IN	7,225,500	68
80.	The Packard Humanities Institute	CA	OP	7,223,497	13
81.	Jerome L. Greene Foundation, Inc.	NY	IN	7,220,000	3
82.	Lied Foundation Trust	NV	IN	7,180,000	4
83.	The Jon and Karen Huntsman Foundation	UT	IN	7,175,000	8
84.	Pritzker Foundation	IL	IN	7,150,200	11
85.	Albert and Margaret Alkek Foundation	TX	IN	7,098,900	8
86.	Wayne & Gladys Valley Foundation	CA	IN	7,086,965	12
87.	The Russell Berrie Foundation	NJ	IN	7,028,313	15
88.	Communities Foundation of Texas, Inc.	TX	CM	6,901,342	43
89.	Hall Family Foundation	MO	IN	6,775,000	6
90.	O'Donnell Foundation	TX	IN	6,750,000	6
91.	The Coca-Cola Foundation, Inc.	GA	CS	6,743,500	20
92.	The Commonwealth Fund	NY	IN	6,712,615	37
93.	James S. McDonnell Foundation	MO	IN	6,689,225	43
94.	GE Foundation	CT	CS	6,666,506	94

Table App.9. Top 100 Foundations Giving to U.S.-Based Recipients for Higher, Graduate, and Professional Education and Educational Institutions, Circa 2004[1], continued

Foundation Name	State	Foundation Type	Grant Dollars	No. of Grants
95. The San Francisco Foundation	CA	CM	6,659,928	124
96. Koret Foundation	CA	IN	6,480,046	52
97. The Joyce Foundation	IL	IN	6,412,264	39
98. The Larry L. Hillblom Foundation, Inc.	CA	IN	6,370,935	8
99. The Lemelson Foundation	NV	IN	6,329,746	48
100. M. J. Murdock Charitable Trust	WA	IN	6,282,150	44
Subtotal for Top 100 Foundations			$2,077,316,141	6,087
Total for All Foundations			$3,307,198,085	17,032

Source: *The Foundation Center, 2006*

[1]Based on grants of $10,000 or more awarded by a national sample of 1,172 larger U.S. foundations. For community foundations, only discretionary grants are included. Grants to individuals are not included in the file.

Note: IN = Independent Foundation; CM = Community Foundation; CS = Corporate Foundation; OP = Operating Foundation

Table App.10. Top 100 Recipients of Grants Awarded to U.S.-Based Organizations for Higher, Graduate, and Professional Education and Educational Institutions, Circa 1990[1]

Recipient Name	City	State	Grant Dollars	No. of Grants
1. Northwestern University	Evanston	IL	$42,847,298	85
2. Harvard University	Cambridge	MA	36,498,686	254
3. University of Pennsylvania	Philadelphia	PA	27,722,140	143
4. Stanford University	Stanford	CA	24,869,818	151
5. Columbia University	NYC	NY	18,163,972	153
6. Yale University	New Haven	CT	17,952,427	131
7. Indiana University Foundation	Bloomington	IN	17,756,221	20
8. Johns Hopkins University	Baltimore	MD	17,518,027	127
9. California Institute of Technology	Pasadena	CA	16,879,007	41
10. University of Washington	Seattle	WA	15,803,713	73
11. Brandeis University	Waltham	MA	14,825,343	35
12. Duke University	Durham	NC	14,600,829	87
13. University of North Carolina	Chapel Hill	NC	14,495,062	68
14. University of Pittsburgh	Pittsburgh	PA	13,990,267	74
15. University of Chicago	Chicago	IL	12,875,120	107
16. Massachusetts Institute of Technology	Cambridge	MA	12,751,842	89
17. New York University	NYC	NY	12,398,928	109
18. University of Southern California	Los Angeles	CA	12,260,438	73
19. Cornell University	Ithaca	NY	12,062,861	84
20. Washington University	Saint Louis	MO	11,763,567	58
21. University of Virginia	Charlottesville	VA	11,479,426	52

Table App.10. Top 100 Recipients of Grants Awarded to U.S.-Based Organizations for Higher, Graduate, and Professional Education and Educational Institutions, Circa 1990[1], *continued*

Recipient Name	City	State	Grant Dollars	No. of Grants
22. Baylor University	Waco	TX	11,381,600	12
23. University of California	Berkeley	CA	11,024,431	114
24. University of Michigan	Ann Arbor	MI	10,917,481	118
25. Carnegie-Mellon University	Pittsburgh	PA	10,515,259	62
26. Temple University	Philadelphia	PA	10,357,830	31
27. University of California	Los Angeles	CA	10,122,440	81
28. University of Rochester	Rochester	NY	9,676,975	48
29. Illinois Institute of Technology	Chicago	IL	9,665,845	25
30. University of California	San Francisco	CA	9,455,019	57
31. Rockefeller University	NYC	NY	8,913,259	34
32. University of Texas	Austin	TX	8,481,573	78
33. University of Minnesota	Minneapolis	MN	7,927,392	73
34. Emory University	Atlanta	GA	7,509,259	44
35. University of Colorado	Boulder	CO	7,264,934	29
36. University of the Arts	Philadelphia	PA	6,948,340	9
37. Vanderbilt University	Nashville	TN	6,849,725	51
38. Louisville Presbyterian Theological Seminary	Louisville	KY	6,470,563	6
39. Georgetown University		DC	6,383,380	58
40. Princeton University	Princeton	NJ	6,320,799	70
41. University of Miami	Coral Gables	FL	6,245,508	21
42. Pennsylvania State University	University Park	PA	6,020,862	51

	Institution	City	State	Amount	
43.	University of Wisconsin	Madison	WI	5,995,323	56
44.	University of Notre Dame du Lac	Notre Dame	IN	5,715,708	46
45.	Baylor College of Medicine	Houston	TX	5,619,940	21
46.	Thomas Jefferson University	Philadelphia	PA	5,558,194	11
47.	University of Illinois at Urbana-Champaign	Urbana	IL	5,467,562	53
48.	Case Western Reserve University	Cleveland	OH	5,440,029	54
49.	Mount Sinai School of Medicine	NYC	NY	5,440,000	2
50.	Tufts University	Medford	MA	4,721,614	60
51.	Berea College	Berea	KY	4,520,312	21
52.	Brown University	Providence	RI	4,295,687	51
53.	Michigan State University	East Lansing	MI	4,250,646	55
54.	Harvey Mudd College	Claremont	CA	4,216,200	12
55.	Rice University	Houston	TX	4,191,245	36
56.	Kettering University	Flint	MI	4,083,102	6
57.	Yeshiva University	NYC	NY	4,055,076	19
58.	National Academy of Education	Stanford	CA	3,950,000	2
59.	University of Houston-University Park	Houston	TX	3,887,548	33
60.	Wake Forest University	Winston-Salem	NC	3,848,715	27
61.	University of Arizona	Tucson	AZ	3,677,964	25
62.	Loyola Marymount University	Los Angeles	CA	3,600,263	7
63.	United Negro College Fund	NYC	NY	3,519,653	70
64.	University of California at San Diego	La Jolla	CA	3,461,135	22
65.	Dartmouth College	Hanover	NH	3,406,249	32
66.	University of Utah	Salt Lake City	UT	3,304,607	30
67.	University of Wisconsin Foundation	Madison	WI	3,212,403	8
68.	Flagler College	Saint Augustine	FL	3,172,584	1
69.	Howard University	Saint Augustine	DC	3,082,440	47

Table App.10. Top 100 Recipients of Grants Awarded to U.S.-Based Organizations for Higher, Graduate, and Professional Education and Educational Institutions, Circa 1990[1], continued

Recipient Name	City	State	Grant Dollars	No. of Grants
70. Colorado College	Colorado Springs	CO	2,938,495	14
71. Villanova University	Villanova	PA	2,839,645	11
72. Southern Methodist University	Dallas	TX	2,759,030	17
73. Scripps College	Claremont	CA	2,758,458	5
74. Pepperdine University	Malibu	CA	2,633,067	6
75. Wellesley College	Wellesley	MA	2,617,285	13
76. Texas Wesleyan University	Fort Worth	TX	2,601,200	7
77. Fairfield University	Fairfield	CT	2,540,500	15
78. City University of New York	NYC	NY	2,532,158	38
79. University of Iowa Foundation	Iowa City	IA	2,527,529	9
80. Occidental College	Los Angeles	CA	2,521,407	13
81. Hillsdale College	Hillsdale	MI	2,464,732	20
82. University of California	Irvine	CA	2,440,940	28
83. Allegheny College	Meadville	PA	2,439,400	10
84. Georgia Institute of Technology	Atlanta	GA	2,363,851	17
85. University of Colorado Health Sciences Center	Denver	CO	2,316,643	14
86. Texas Tech University Health Sciences Center	Lubbock	TX	2,297,985	3
87. Washington College	Chestertown	MD	2,235,000	7
88. Hispanic Association of Colleges and Universities	San Antonio	TX	2,223,723	4
89. Bowling Green State University	Bowling Green	OH	2,155,000	6
90. Purdue University	West Lafayette	IN	2,139,766	45

91. National College of Education	Evanston	IL	2,114,500	5
92. Macalester College	Saint Paul	MN	2,086,149	14
93. Boston University	Boston	MA	2,081,447	37
94. Mount Saint Marys College	Los Angeles	CA	2,060,371	10
95. Marquette University	Milwaukee	WI	2,024,225	15
96. Educational Testing Service	Princeton	NJ	2,000,000	1
97. University of Maryland	College Park	MD	1,979,764	24
98. Smith College	Northampton	MA	1,973,693	21
99. New School University	NYC	NY	1,963,825	14
100. North Carolina State University	Raleigh	NC	1,954,113	18
Subtotal for Top 100 Recipients			$746,245,566	4,354
Total for All Recipients			$1,215,982,280	11,386

Source: The Foundation Center, 2004

[1]Based on grants of $10,000 or more awarded by a national sample of 832 larger U.S. foundations. For community foundations, only discretionary grants are included. Grants to individuals are not included in the file.

Table App.II. Top 100 Recipients of Grants Awarded to U.S.-Based Organizations for Higher, Graduate, and Professional Education and Educational Institutions, Circa 1997[1]

Recipient Name	State	Grant Dollars	No. of Grants
1. Robert W. Woodruff Health Sciences Center Fund	GA	$70,447,939	1
2. Harvard University	MA	62,179,490	349
3. Columbia University	NY	52,515,900	248
4. Keck Graduate Institute of Applied Life Sciences	CA	50,000,000	1
5. Stanford University	CA	41,439,649	182
6. Duke University	NC	39,479,421	110
7. University of Chicago	IL	29,663,238	135
8. Yale University	CT	26,997,941	196
9. University of Arkansas for Medical Sciences	AR	25,753,548	6
10. University of California	CA	24,900,453	187
11. University of Michigan	MI	24,835,438	160
12. Babson College	MA	24,637,506	11
13. Brown University	RI	24,297,965	51
14. Rice University	TX	23,541,122	60
15. University of Pennsylvania	PA	23,515,176	161
16. Northwestern University	IL	22,532,676	116
17. New York University	NY	22,471,482	141
18. Johns Hopkins University	MD	20,804,623	139
19. Massachusetts Institute of Technology	MA	19,503,540	122
20. University of California at San Francisco	CA	18,490,072	62
21. California Institute of Technology	CA	17,785,506	45

22.	University of Texas at Austin	TX	17,440,354	155
23.	Cornell University	NY	16,534,458	122
24.	University of Mississippi	MS	16,500,000	1
25.	University of California at Los Angeles	CA	16,340,314	95
26.	University of Tulsa	OK	15,745,931	9
27.	University of California at Los Angeles Foundation	CA	14,269,226	44
28.	United Negro College Fund	VA	13,464,765	101
29.	University of California at Berkeley Foundation	CA	13,364,735	9
30.	Case Western Reserve University	OH	12,992,139	61
31.	Princeton University	NJ	12,666,836	85
32.	University of Washington	WA	12,430,009	82
33.	Carnegie-Mellon University	PA	11,548,653	76
34.	University of North Carolina	NC	11,389,245	80
35.	University of Utah	UT	11,278,763	48
36.	University of Pittsburgh	PA	10,763,150	93
37.	Virginia Commonwealth University School of Engineering Foundation	VA	10,470,000	1
38.	University of Wisconsin	WI	10,199,124	73
39.	Southwestern University	TX	10,164,000	13
40.	Washington University	MO	10,014,799	60
41.	Indiana University Foundation	IN	9,564,194	13
42.	University of Minnesota	MN	9,526,859	72
43.	Willamette University	OR	9,291,890	16
44.	George Washington University	DC	9,024,958	43
45.	Rockefeller University	NY	8,857,300	40
46.	University of Illinois at Chicago	IL	8,594,446	42
47.	University of California at San Diego	CA	8,440,709	45
48.	University of Denver	CO	8,267,323	13

Table App.11. Top 100 Recipients of Grants Awarded to U.S.-Based Organizations for Higher, Graduate, and Professional Education and Educational Institutions, Circa 1997[1], continued

Recipient Name	State	Grant Dollars	No. of Grants
49. Mid-South Community College	AR	8,000,000	1
50. Yeshiva University	NY	7,957,376	13
51. Louisville Presbyterian Theological Seminary	KY	7,782,965	7
52. University of Southern California	CA	7,720,906	75
53. Henderson State University	AR	7,563,323	1
54. Citizens Scholarship Foundation of America	MN	7,443,569	34
55. National Merit Scholarship Corporation	IL	6,803,446	56
56. University of Illinois at Urbana-Champaign	IL	6,796,688	65
57. Emory University	GA	6,498,098	43
58. Pennsylvania State University	PA	6,413,015	58
59. Mary Baldwin College	VA	6,403,844	6
60. University of Arizona	AZ	6,375,075	36
61. Texas A & M University	TX	6,372,769	54
62. Hebrew Union College-Jewish Institute of Religion	CA	6,336,666	13
63. University of Oklahoma Foundation	OK	6,336,270	29
64. Georgetown University	DC	6,317,056	60
65. Teachers College Columbia University	NY	6,291,291	27
66. Ouachita Baptist University	AR	6,053,300	15
67. University of Houston System	TX	6,006,052	45
68. Virginia Polytechnic Institute and State University	VA	5,981,508	30
69. Colorado College	CO	5,963,093	11
70. Michigan State University	MI	5,918,442	56

71. Dartmouth College	5,681,445	NH	57
72. University of Central Arkansas	5,648,235	AR	2
73. Boston University	5,600,887	MA	56
74. University of Virginia	5,574,425	VA	58
75. Purdue University	5,476,869	IN	62
76. University of Richmond	5,456,098	VA	12
77. Colby College	5,362,980	ME	11
78. Mount Saint Marys College	5,269,838	CA	17
79. Loyola Marymount University	5,253,002	CA	14
80. University of Notre Dame du Lac	5,217,566	IN	59
81. Ohio State University	5,075,364	OH	49
82. Purdue Research Foundation	5,055,795	IN	5
83. Brandeis University	4,890,038	MA	43
84. Ball State University	4,879,983	IN	10
85. Texas Christian University	4,879,733	TX	17
86. University of Maryland	4,813,345	MD	32
87. Vanderbilt University	4,724,683	TN	31
88. Davidson College	4,712,791	NC	19
89. University of Nevada	4,705,638	NV	16
90. Baylor College of Medicine	4,702,198	TX	22
91. University of Cincinnati	4,616,473	OH	26
92. Tufts University	4,593,653	MA	44
93. Tulane University	4,549,684	LA	28
94. University of Texas Health Science Center	4,532,539	TX	25
95. University of Georgia	4,520,316	GA	19
96. Pepperdine University	4,369,900	CA	16
97. University of Michigan	4,303,700	MI	4

Table App.11. Top 100 Recipients of Grants Awarded to U.S.-Based Organizations for Higher, Graduate, and Professional Education and Educational Institutions, Circa 1997[1], *continued*

Recipient Name	State	Grant Dollars	No. of Grants
98. San Jose State University Foundation	CA	4,256,253	11
99. Washington State University	WA	4,215,069	10
100. Lafayette College	PA	4,211,100	11
Subtotal for Top 100 Recipients		$1,279,421,217	5,496
Total for All Recipients		$2,276,747,029	15,557

Source: The Foundation Center, 2006

[1]*Based on grants of $10,000 or more awarded by a national sample of 1,016 larger U.S. foundations. For community foundations, only discretionary grants are included. Grants to individuals are not included in the file.*

Table App.12. Top 100 Recipients of Grants Awarded to U.S.-Based Organizations for Higher, Graduate, and Professional Education and Educational Institutions, Circa 2004[1]

Recipient Name	State	Grant Dollars	No. of Grants
1. Indiana University Foundation	IN	$90,599,883	20
2. Harvard University	MA	87,002,500	331
3. Johns Hopkins University	MD	80,154,326	160
4. New York University	NY	75,905,474	184
5. Columbia University	NY	66,955,798	274
6. Massachusetts Institute of Technology	MA	58,639,226	104
7. University of Pennsylvania	PA	55,675,307	163
8. Duke University	NC	55,011,599	133
9. Hebrew Union College-Jewish Institute of Religion	CA	54,948,414	28
10. Stanford University	CA	53,493,680	303
11. Purdue Research Foundation	IN	42,500,000	2
12. University of Michigan	MI	37,773,607	180
13. University of Missouri	MO	34,154,441	24
14. University of California at San Francisco	CA	29,907,525	95
15. Yale University	CT	29,324,820	156
16. Emory University	GA	29,247,487	59
17. Carnegie Mellon University	PA	29,166,885	83
18. University of Texas at Austin	TX	28,099,673	144
19. University of California at Los Angeles	CA	27,237,314	113
20. Cornell University	NY	26,523,857	116
21. Northwestern University	IL	26,295,088	109

Table App.12. Top 100 Recipients of Grants Awarded to U.S.-Based Organizations for Higher, Graduate, and Professional Education and Educational Institutions, Circa 2004[1], *continued*

Recipient Name	State	Grant Dollars	No. of Grants
22. California Institute of Technology	CA	23,411,691	40
23. University of California at Berkeley	CA	21,696,959	193
24. University of Washington	WA	21,669,939	117
25. Keck Graduate Institute of Applied Life Sciences	CA	21,260,000	7
26. University of North Carolina	NC	20,943,359	113
27. Tufts University	MA	20,343,553	60
28. University of Chicago	IL	20,044,681	100
29. University of Illinois at Urbana-Champaign	IL	19,328,391	66
30. Princeton University	NJ	18,988,920	95
31. Independent Colleges of Indiana	IN	18,922,020	4
32. University of Southern California	CA	18,492,247	102
33. Washington University	MO	17,748,077	65
34. Baylor College of Medicine	TX	17,284,960	46
35. Arizona State University	AZ	17,146,792	30
36. Ave Maria University	FL	15,560,843	1
37. Ivy Tech Foundation	IN	14,045,621	8
38. New School	NY	13,995,520	42
39. Vanderbilt University	TN	13,711,282	25
40. Bard College	NY	13,650,400	21
41. University of Missouri	MO	13,418,712	36
42. Ave Maria College	MI	13,265,500	3
43. Research Foundation of the City University of New York	NY	13,239,500	32

44. United Negro College Fund	VA	13,201,278	84
45. Westminster College	MO	13,061,675	8
46. Georgetown University	DC	13,023,342	75
47. University of Utah	UT	12,806,935	74
48. George Washington University	DC	12,280,626	49
49. Mount Sinai School of Medicine of the City University of New York	NY	12,130,475	27
50. Rice University	TX	11,916,849	61
51. University of Pittsburgh	PA	11,897,269	96
52. Dartmouth College	NH	11,564,098	59
53. Hofstra University	NY	11,482,658	14
54. Brown University	RI	11,473,790	87
55. Oregon State University	OR	11,396,905	9
56. Wells College	NY	11,345,374	8
57. Texas A & M International University	TX	11,320,000	1
58. Juilliard School	NY	11,284,500	25
59. Idaho State University	ID	11,197,646	7
60. Rensselaer Polytechnic Institute	NY	11,144,208	21
61. Robert W. Woodruff Health Sciences Center Fund	GA	11,000,004	2
62. Weill Medical College of Cornell University	NY	10,661,670	36
63. University of California at Los Angeles Foundation	CA	10,268,934	51
64. University of Nebraska Foundation	NE	10,180,741	10
65. University of California at San Francisco Foundation	CA	10,173,926	25
66. Boston University	MA	10,166,283	67
67. University of Notre Dame	IN	10,114,606	57
68. Boston College	MA	9,960,292	48
69. University of California at Santa Barbara	CA	9,789,183	35
70. Rockefeller University	NY	9,740,394	46

Table App.12. Top 100 Recipients of Grants Awarded to U.S.-Based Organizations for Higher, Graduate, and Professional Education and Educational Institutions, Circa 2004[1], *continued*

Recipient Name	State	Grant Dollars	No. of Grants
71. Case Western Reserve University	OH	9,685,896	55
72. University of California at San Diego	CA	9,612,141	64
73. Calvin College	MI	9,465,621	14
74. Temple University	PA	9,009,856	42
75. Yeshiva University	NY	8,906,038	28
76. Brandeis University	MA	8,770,721	37
77. Citadel, The	SC	8,580,800	3
78. Ave Maria School of Law	MI	8,338,828	2
79. Rutgers, The State University of New Jersey	NJ	8,274,900	40
80. University of Wisconsin	WI	7,963,915	59
81. Georgia Tech Foundation	GA	7,845,273	25
82. University of Maryland-College Park	MD	7,626,747	44
83. University of Minnesota	MN	7,616,958	58
84. Indiana University	IN	7,409,450	44
85. Southern Methodist University	TX	7,251,094	22
86. Carnegie Foundation for the Advancement of Teaching	CA	7,222,780	6
87. Columbus State University	GA	7,115,170	15
88. Michigan State University	MI	7,086,048	53
89. North Carolina State University	NC	7,084,621	28
90. University of Wisconsin Foundation	WI	7,058,765	22
91. Portland Community College	OR	6,997,047	1
92. Ball State University Foundation	IN	6,993,305	13
93. University of Rochester	NY	6,846,142	28

94. University of Texas Health Science Center	TX	6,689,481	28
95. Purdue University	IN	6,591,064	54
96. Saint Vincent College	PA	6,295,300	9
97. Antioch University Seattle	WA	6,189,000	3
98. University of Maryland-Baltimore	MD	6,138,549	13
99. John Brown University	AR	6,105,422	6
100. University of Virginia	VA	6,060,848	51
Subtotal for Top 100 Recipients		$1,938,201,312	5,936
Total for All Recipients		$3,307,198,085	17,032

Source: *The Foundation Center, 2006*

[1]Based on grants of $10,000 or more awarded by a national sample of 1,172 larger U.S. foundations. For community foundations, only discretionary grants are included. Grants to individuals are not included in the file.

Table App.13. Top 100 U.S.-Based College and University Recipients of Grants Awarded by the Top 100 Funders for Higher, Graduate, and Professional Education and Educational Institutions, Circa 2004[1]

Recipient Name	State	Grant Dollars	No. of Grants
1. Indiana University Foundation	IN	$88,187,781	10
2. Johns Hopkins University	MD	60,633,516	63
3. Harvard University	MA	57,726,457	144
4. Hebrew Union College-Jewish Institute of Religion	CA	54,157,840	18
5. New York University	NY	51,565,947	69
6. Massachusetts Institute of Technology	MA	48,587,043	57
7. Duke University	NC	45,431,997	69
8. Columbia University	NY	43,128,741	113
9. Purdue Research Foundation	IN	42,500,000	2
10. University of Pennsylvania	PA	39,443,314	64
11. Stanford University	CA	36,505,823	201
12. University of Missouri	MO	33,848,754	18
13. Carnegie Mellon University	PA	26,324,701	30
14. University of California at San Francisco	CA	23,844,645	65
15. University of California at Los Angeles	CA	23,551,208	66
16. University of Texas at Austin	TX	23,082,259	82
17. Keck Graduate Institute of Applied Life Sciences	CA	20,100,000	2
18. Emory University	GA	19,878,830	25
19. Independent Colleges of Indiana	IN	18,912,020	3
20. University of Michigan	MI	18,890,108	75
21. California Institute of Technology	CA	18,252,909	22
22. Yale University	CT	17,651,559	59

		State	Amount	
23.	Cornell University	NY	17,324,407	55
24.	University of Illinois at Urbana-Champaign	IL	16,453,594	33
25.	Arizona State University	AZ	15,675,872	11
26.	Ave Maria University	FL	15,560,843	1
27.	University of Chicago	IL	14,105,346	44
28.	University of Washington	WA	13,777,195	48
29.	Princeton University	NJ	13,469,340	46
30.	Ave Maria College	MI	13,265,500	3
31.	Tufts University	MA	13,110,315	22
32.	Westminster College	MO	13,003,638	4
33.	University of California at Berkeley	CA	12,944,945	110
34.	University of Missouri	MO	12,601,187	28
35.	Ivy Tech Foundation	IN	12,500,000	1
36.	Research Foundation of the City University of New York	NY	12,422,560	17
37.	New School	NY	12,171,600	16
38.	University of North Carolina	NC	11,948,515	52
39.	Bard College	NY	11,866,400	7
40.	Vanderbilt University	TN	11,448,364	13
41.	Wells College	NY	11,345,374	8
42.	Texas A & M International University	TX	11,320,000	1
43.	Oregon State University	OR	11,196,905	6
44.	Hofstra University	NY	11,172,075	5
45.	Idaho State University	ID	11,102,000	3
46.	George Washington University	DC	10,495,312	23
47.	Robert W. Woodruff Health Sciences Center Fund	GA	10,000,004	1
48.	Rensselaer Polytechnic Institute	NY	9,863,208	13
49.	Northwestern University	IL	9,779,328	33

Table App.13. Top 100 U.S.-Based College and University Recipients of Grants Awarded by the Top 100 Funders for Higher, Graduate, and Professional Education and Educational Institutions, Circa 2004[1], *continued*

Recipient Name	State	Grant Dollars	No. of Grants
50. Washington University	MO	9,243,110	30
51. University of Notre Dame	IN	8,879,742	26
52. Calvin College	MI	8,826,105	5
53. University of Southern California	CA	8,666,120	42
54. Ave Maria School of Law	MI	8,313,828	1
55. Citadel, The	SC	8,000,000	1
56. Boston University	MA	7,785,359	32
57. Weill Medical College of Cornell University	NY	7,628,670	14
58. United Negro College Fund	VA	7,606,770	28
59. Dartmouth College	NH	7,466,720	28
60. Rutgers, The State University of New Jersey	NJ	7,419,050	23
61. Baylor College of Medicine	TX	7,245,500	11
62. Columbus State University	GA	7,084,170	13
63. Portland Community College	OR	6,997,047	1
64. Indiana University	IN	6,684,609	21
65. University of California at San Francisco Foundation	CA	6,618,426	13
66. North Carolina State University	NC	6,530,628	22
67. Georgia Tech Foundation	GA	6,452,323	9
68. Rice University	TX	6,441,105	35
69. University of Wisconsin	WI	6,362,303	32
70. Temple University	PA	6,353,000	13
71. University of Nebraska Foundation	NE	6,228,680	4

	Institution	State	Amount	
72.	Mount Sinai School of Medicine of the City University of New York	NY	6,209,371	9
73.	University of California at San Diego	CA	6,201,021	37
74.	Antioch University Seattle	WA	6,122,500	1
75.	University of Utah	UT	5,839,523	35
76.	Brandeis University	MA	5,812,682	15
77.	University of Maryland-College Park	MD	5,719,068	30
78.	John Brown University	AR	5,594,950	2
79.	Brown University	RI	5,444,487	32
80.	University of Pittsburgh	PA	5,238,930	23
81.	University of Iowa Foundation	IA	5,140,516	11
82.	Saint Vincent College	PA	5,062,300	3
83.	Ball State University Foundation	IN	5,014,900	2
84.	University of Maryland-Baltimore	MD	4,978,549	8
85.	Case Western Reserve University	OH	4,881,343	29
86.	American Association of Community Colleges	DC	4,727,200	4
87.	Texas A & M University	TX	4,697,203	39
88.	University of Rochester	NY	4,659,097	15
89.	Clark Atlanta University	GA	4,652,500	8
90.	Boston College	MA	4,435,114	19
91.	Rockefeller University	NY	4,421,849	13
92.	University of California at Davis	CA	4,334,868	26
93.	Southern Methodist University	TX	4,311,147	6
94.	University of Rio Grande	OH	4,210,000	3
95.	University of California at Santa Barbara	CA	4,152,909	16
96.	University of San Francisco	CA	4,045,000	6
97.	University of Minnesota	MN	4,041,584	20

Table App.13. Top 100 U.S.-Based College and University Recipients of Grants Awarded by the Top 100 Funders for Higher, Graduate, and Professional Education and Educational Institutions, Circa 2004[1], *continued*

Recipient Name	State	Grant Dollars	No. of Grants
98. Davidson College	NC	3,992,533	10
99. National Action Council for Minorities in Engineering (NACME)	NY	3,982,480	8
100. Johnson C. Smith University	NC	3,969,000	9
Subtotal for Top 100 College and University Recipients		$1,456,855,168	2,704
Total for All College and University Recipients		$2,025,942,905	5,966

Source: *The Foundation Center, 2006*

[1]*Based on grants of $10,000 or more awarded by a national sample of 1,172 larger U.S. foundations. For community foundations, only discretionary grants are included. Grants to individuals are not included in the file.*

**Table App.14. Estimated Total Giving to U.S.-Based Recipients
for Precollegiate Education, 1990–2004 (dollars in thousands)**

Year	Total Giving[1]	Estimated Giving to U.S.-Based Recipients for Precollegiate Education[2]
1990	$8,676,720	$407,128
1991	9,210,565	571,055
1992	10,209,453	728,342
1993	11,113,404	753,267
1994	11,290,535	856,048
1995	12,261,612	900,615
1996	13,836,010	892,900
1997	15,985,431	1,151,207
1998	19,456,832	1,470,356
1999	23,321,482	1,685,006
2000	27,563,166	2,461,050
2001	30,502,393	2,485,557
2002	30,431,799	2,657,221
2003	30,308,835	2,775,689
2004	31,843,907	2,729,153

Source: *The Foundation Center, 2006*
[1]*Includes giving by all grantmaking U.S. foundations to U.S.-based and overseas recipients for grants, scholarships, and employee-matching gifts.*
[2]*Includes estimated giving by all grantmaking U.S. foundations to U.S.-based recipients only. However, some grants to domestic recipients may have an international focus. Estimates are based on giving by foundations in the Foundation Center's grants sample database as a proportion of total giving reported by all U.S. foundations.*
Note: *The Total Giving column refers to foundation giving for all purposes, including but not limited to precollegiate, higher, and graduate education.*

Table App.15. Estimated Total Giving to U.S.-Based Recipients
for Higher, Graduate, and Professional Education and Educational
Institutions, 1990–2004 (dollars in thousands)

Year	Total Giving[1]	Estimated Giving to U.S.-Based Recipients for Higher, Graduate, and Professional Education and Educational Institutions[2]
1990	$8,676,720	$2,173,337
1991	9,210,565	2,647,577
1992	10,209,453	2,701,625
1993	11,113,404	2,960,944
1994	11,290,535	3,122,510
1995	12,261,612	3,258,523
1996	13,836,010	3,681,159
1997	15,985,431	4,292,731
1998	19,456,832	5,017,436
1999	23,321,482	5,920,221
2000	27,563,166	6,733,402
2001	30,502,393	7,607,634
2002	30,431,799	7,451,717
2003	30,308,835	7,091,630
2004	31,843,907	7,138,396

Source: *The Foundation Center, 2006*

[1]*Includes giving by all grantmaking U.S. foundations to U.S.-based and overseas recipients for grants, scholarships, and employee-matching gifts.*

[2]*Includes estimated giving by all grantmaking U.S. foundations to U.S.-based recipients only. However, some grants to domestic recipients may have an international focus. Estimates are based on giving by foundations in the Foundation Center's grants sample database as a proportion of total giving reported by all U.S. foundations.*

Note: *The Total Giving column refers to foundation giving for all purposes, including but not limited to precollegiate, higher, and graduate education.*

Table App.16. Total Expenditures for Elementary/Secondary and Higher Education, 1990–2004 (in millions of current dollars)

School Year	All Educational Institutions	All Elementary and Secondary Schools	All Degree-Granting Colleges and Universities
1990–91	412,652	248,930	163,722
1991–92	432,987	261,255	171,732
1992–93	456,070	274,355	181,735
1993–94	477,237	287,507	189,730
1994–95	503,925	302,400	201,525
1995–96	529,596	318,246	211,350
1996–97	560,571	339,151	221,420
1997–98	594,715	361,415	233,300
1998–99	633,038	384,038	249,000
1999–2000	680,038	411,538	268,500
2000–01	734,311	442,011	292,300
2001–02	782,500	467,900	314,600
2002–03	823,100	490,900	332,100
2003–04	865,500	514,300	351,200

Source: *Compiled from* Digest of Education Statistics, 2004, *table 29, published by the National Center for Education Statistics. Data for 1995–96 forward are for four-year and two-year degree-granting institutions eligible to participate in Title IV federal financial aid programs. All data for private elementary and secondary schools are estimated. 2001–02 data for public elementary and secondary schools are preliminary, and data for colleges and universities are estimated. All 2002–03 and 2003–04 data are estimated.*

NAME INDEX

A

Adams, B. E., 307
Adler, M., 353, 354, 355, 357
Alexander, L., 363
Anderson, J. D., 236
Andreasen, B., 325
Andrews, F. E., 57
Annenberg, W. H., 62, 64, 139, 141, 142, 143, 144, 146
Arnove, R. F., 220
Aron, R., 357
Ayres, L., 51

B

Bacchetti, R., 3, 21, 37, 71, 73, 183, 249, 251, 263, 303, 306, 308, 309, 310, 312, 315, 317, 318, 319, 320, 383, 389, 391, 399
Bain, K., 26, 274
Barzun, J., 353, 354
Beard, C., 327, 336, 338, 339
Becker, G., 354
Beckham, E. F., 39, 283, 285, 289, 290
Bell, T. H., 363
Bender, T., 338
Bennett, W. J., 363
Berkovitch, S., 401
Bernstein, A. R., 220, 222
Bernstein, D. J., 316, 317
Bestor, A., 353, 354, 355
Bildner, A., 283, 286, 287, 288, 290, 291, 292, 294, 295, 296, 297, 300

Bildner, J., 283, 287, 288, 291, 292, 294, 296
Bird, R., 176
Bloom, A., 357, 367, 368, 369
Boozer, H., 342
Bork, R., 366
Boskin, M., 365
Bowen, W., 382
Boyer, E., 307
Bradley, H., 356
Bradley, L., 356
Brandt, L., 57
Brereton, J., 195
Breyer, S., 366
Brown, T., 342
Bryan, W. J., 55, 65
Buchanan, J., 190, 205
Buckley, W. F., Jr., 355, 356, 364, 367, 369, 371
Bulmer, M., 236, 238, 239
Bundy, M., 58, 60, 359
Burke, E., 357
Burkett, S. P., 197

C

Calkins, L., 78
Carmichael, L., 179
Carnegie, A., 3, 5, 6, 7, 18, 47, 49, 50, 51, 54, 55, 62–63
Carter, J., 366
Cervone, B., 64, 139, 141
Cheit, E. F., 214, 224, 225
Cheney, L., 368
Chodorov, F., 356

SUBJECT INDEX

A

Academic discipline, influence of, 216–218

Accountability of foundations: ideas and, 260–262; as source of tension, 110, 114–115; as weakness, 12

Accountability of higher education, 10, 260–262

Accountability of school districts, 114–115

Achieve, Inc., 87, 104

Alfred P. Sloan Foundation, The, 9, 244

American Association for Higher Education (AAHE), 268, 303, 306, 308–309, 310, 311–312, 313, 314–317, 318, 320, 404

American Dilemma, An (Myrdal), 58

American Historical Association (AHA), 323, 325, 327–331, 342

American Memory Project of the Library of Congress, 43

Annenberg Challenge: abiding principles of, 144–147; baton passing in, 155–157; breadth and depth of, 150–151; building capacity and, 154–155, 159; criticisms of, 141–142; defined, 141; district relations and, 151–152; evaluation of, 153–154; foundation resources given to, 17; grant awards, 148; invention vs. coherence in, 149–150; lessons of, 62, 157–160; logistics of, 64, 149; as one man's gift, 143–144; scale of, 142, 157–158; writing about, 143

Annenberg Foundation, 11, 18, 244. *See also* Annenberg Challenge

Assessment at every stage, 27–28, 81

Association of American Colleges and Universities (AAC&U), 268, 283, 288, 289, 291, 292, 294, 296, 297, 298

Atlantic Philanthropies, 4, 76, 117, 238, 244, 256, 281

B

Back-to-basics movement, 352–354

Bay Area School Reform Collaborative (BASRC), 148, 150, 153, 155–156, 174, 176–177, 178

Bilateral monopoly, 222

Bill & Melinda Gates Foundation, 11, 18, 40, 76, 111, 113, 122, 123, 126–134, 135, 136, 155, 156, 229, 244, 390. *See also* Gates Foundation's Early College High School Initiative

Board of Education, Brown v., 58

Bourdieu's social theory, 136

Bradley Foundation, The, 118, 119

Broad Foundation, 86, 104, 119, 120

Brown v. Board of Education, 58

C

Capacity to manage initiatives: case studies showing, 169–170, 172–175; external support and, 175–180; importance of, 163–164;